D1617542

V.K. Wellington Koo
and the
Emergence of Modern China

V.K. Wellington Koo

and the

Emergence of Modern China

STEPHEN G. CRAFT

THE UNIVERSITY PRESS OF KENTUCKY

Publication of this volume was made possible in part
by a grant from the National Endowment for the Humanities.

Editorial and Sales Offices: The University Press of Kentucky
663 South Limestone Street, Lexington, Kentucky 40508–4008
www.kentuckypress.com

08 07 06 05 04   5 4 3 2 1

Frontispiece: V.K. Wellington Koo, 1912 (Photo courtesy of Library of Congress)
Maps by Dick Gilbreath.

Library of Congress Cataloging-in-Publication Data

Craft, Stephen G., 1963-
    V.K. Wellington Koo and the emergence of Modern China / Stephen G. Craft.
      p. cm.
    Includes bibliographical references.
    ISBN 0-8131-2314-3 (Hardcover : alk. paper)
    1. Koo, V. K. Wellington, 1888-1985. 2. China—Foreign relations—1912-1949.
I. Title.
DS777.15.K66C73 2003
327.51'0092—dc22   2003024589

Manufactured in the United States of America.

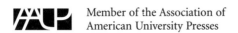

Member of the Association of
American University Presses

Dedicated to my mother,

Nancy Plymale Craft

and to the memory of my father,

James R. "Bo" Craft

CONTENTS

A Note on Chinese-English Transliteration

Throughout this work, I primarily used the *pinyin* system to romanize Chinese names, book titles, and place names. For certain Chinese individuals, such as Sun Yat-sen or Chiang Kai-shek, I used the Wade-Giles system because their names were much more familiar to the West in this form. Chinese personal names are generally written with family name first, given name last, unless an individual, such as T.V. Soong or W.W. Yen, preferred the westernized form when writing in English. I eschewed the use of pinyin to write out Koo's full name since he generally signed personal English correspondence, published articles, and treaties with V.K. Wellington Koo, and was known in the West by that name.

ABBREVIATIONS

YMCA	Young Men's Christian Association
GMD	Guomindang (Nationalist Party)
CCP	Chinese Communist Party
Comintern	Communist International
CER	Chinese Eastern Railway
ROC	Republic of China
PRC	People's Republic of China

MAPS

ACKNOWLEDGMENTS

Over the many years of researching and writing about V. K. Wellington Koo, I have accumulated numerous debts. Lloyd E. Eastman, William C. Widenor, Kai-wing Chow, Michael Hunt, Paul Schroeder, and Fu Po-shek proved indispensable in providing guidance, criticisms, suggestions, sage advice, and letters of introduction when writing the doctoral dissertation. I am also grateful to F. Garvin Davenport, Gregory Guelcher, Alan Baumler, E. Taylor Atkins, Terence Ollerhead, Chang Hui-chien, Peter Chen-main Wang, Lin Chen-chen, Lai Chiu-yueh, Chang Jui-te, Lu Fang-shang, Li Ming-yi, T'ang Chi-hua, Zhang Xianwen, and Tsai Meng-chen for their friendship and help over the years. I want to thank Patricia Tsien for permission to quote from her father's diary. Saul Kelly, Gu Liying, Li Tzu-ling, and Chien Hung-Chuan deserve appreciation for their assistance in collecting research materials. My research in Taiwan and in London was graciously supported by financial assistance provided by an Illinois-Tamkang Research Fellowship and a Pacific Cultural Foundation Research Fellowship. For nearly a decade, Bernard Crystal, of Columbia University's Rare Book and Manuscript Library did his best to assist me during my visits to peruse Koo's papers and to accommodate my requests for documents.

During the final stages of the project, the manuscript and my career benefited greatly from the support of several individuals. My colleague James Libbey, who is a model mentor for every assistant professor, graciously read the manuscript, offered his criticisms, and helped the manuscript to find a home. Although never having met either in person, Noel Pugach and Edward Ingram took it upon themselves to become mentors and assist in both reading the manuscript and providing scholarly opportunities for a fledgling career. John "zig" Zeigler and Stephen Wrinn have been an author's dream in their support of the book. I also thank Gena Henry, Nichole Lainhart, and their colleagues at the University Press of Kentucky for making the entire editorial and production process extremely smooth. Much gratitude is also owed to Nancy Parker who, as chair of the Humanities/Social Sciences department, has made time and money available to me to complete the project. Ann Cash, Sue Burkhart, Kathy Chumley, and Ed Murphey have been unstinting in acquiring sources via interlibrary loan. Donna Barbie and Terry Winemiller shared helpful advice about maps, and Dick Gilbreath provided excellent maps for the book. Glenn Dorn helped me to maintain a healthy sense of humor. Most of all, I thank my wife, Demi Wen-ling Lin, and my children, Robbie and Brittney, for their love and for assisting in ways beyond description.

Chapter 1

THE MAKING OF A CHINESE PATRIOT

THE WORLD INTO WHICH V.K. Wellington Koo was born in 1888 contrasted starkly with that of most Chinese boys, whose existence seemed rather bleak. After many years as a deputy purser with the China Merchants' Steam Navigation Company, Koo's father ran a hardware store before working as a tax collector and serving as president of the Bank of Communications. Such occupations provided the Koo family with the means to purchase a mansion in Shanghai's International Settlement, complete with a host of servants as well as property in cities outside of Shanghai.[1] Within the family compound, Koo never experienced hunger or want. Nor would his hands ever become calloused like those of peasants or his skin sunburned like the coolies, human mules, who with bitter strength carried commerce and people on their backs or pulled vessels up the Yangzi River. And for the rest of his life, the family wealth and rich wives ensured Koo of a life of comfort and ease.

Financial security, however, could not dispel the crisis of imperialism that existed in late nineteenth-century China. Years before Koo's birth, China's defeat in the Opium Wars of 1839–1842 and 1856–1860 led to the signing of "unequal treaties" with the Europeans and the United States. The Chinese viewed the treaties as a national humiliation. They weakened China's political and economic independence. For example, they robbed China of its tariff autonomy. The treaties allowed foreigners to reside in various coastal cities that became treaty ports. Foreigners enjoyed special privileges, such as extraterritoriality in which foreigners accused of crimes could only be tried in accordance with foreign, not

1

Map1. China.

Chinese, courts. The Opium Wars and the Taiping Rebellion that followed were among several crises that sapped the Qing Empire's power.[2]
Then in 1894–1895, just a few years after Koo's birth, China fought
a war with Japan over the right to politically dominate Korea and lost.
Tokyo not only exacted more indemnities and rights, but also acquired
Chinese territory. In 1898, the major Western powers demanded their
own territorial concessions in what became known as the "scramble for
concessions." In addition to its colony at Hong Kong, Britain acquired a
99-year leasehold in the Kowloon Territories across from Hong Kong
Island and a twenty-five year lease on Weihaiwei in Shandong Province.
Germany had a ninety-nine-year leasehold at Jiaozhou Bay also in
Shandong. Russia held a twenty-five year leasehold on the Liaodong Peninsula including the harbors of Lüshun (Port Arthur) and Dalian
(Dairen), and France possessed a ninety-nine-year leasehold on the port
of Guangzhou Bay (Kwangchou-wan) in Guangdong Province, across
from Hainan Island. The powers also claimed spheres of influence in
different areas in China: Britain in the Yangzi River Valley and around
Canton; Japan in southern Manchuria and Fujian and Guangdong Provinces; Russia in northern Manchuria; and France in Yunnan Province along
the border of French Indochina. In both the leaseholds and their spheres
of influence, the powers were permitted to maintain a military presence to
protect their political, economic, religious, and education interests.[3]

The increased foreign presence combined with famine in Shandong
Province led to the Boxer Uprising of 1899–1900 in which a movement
built around the martial arts sought to drive the foreigners out. The Qing
Dynasty declared war on the foreign imperialists only to be defeated by a
foreign coalition. In 1901, the powers imposed on China the Boxer Protocol, which required China to pay the foreign powers an indemnity of
$333 million with interest over thirty-nine years, to allow establishment
of a Legations Quarter in Beijing permanently defended by the powers
and to establish a Ministry of Foreign Affairs.

As a result of Western and Japanese application of political pressure and military force, the unequal treaties made China into a
semicolony. In Beijing, the powers maintained a Diplomatic Body made
up of the representatives of the eleven countries who were signatories to
the Boxer Protocol of 1901. Of those, Great Britain, Japan, Russia, Ger-

many, France, and the United States exerted the most influence. To keep the peace between them, the powers created an imperialist system in which, by way of bilateral agreements, they recognized one another's spheres in China. By laying down the limits to each country's power in China, the imperialist system maintained the status quo and, at least in theory, prevented one power from expanding at the expense of the others. In 1910, the powers established a Six-Power Consortium in order to reduce the commercial rivalry among themselves by cooperating in providing loans to China through this consortium.[4] All of these arrangements did not partition China as much as Africa had been, but the powers did carve up China into buffer zones to prevent great power conflict.

One Chinese city where imperialism laid a heavy hand was Koo's hometown of Shanghai. Growing up in Shanghai, young Koo came into daily contact with Western culture. Shanghai ultimately became the fastest growing, richest and most modern city in all of China. This eminent "Paris of the East" had the highest population of foreigners in all of the Chinese empire. Like other treaty ports, the West directly impacted the city's culture, blending together Western and Chinese notions of sovereignty. And like other treaty ports, Shanghai was a major transit point between the hinterland of China and the world outside. Unsurprisingly, the residents of Shanghai were generally more interested in that other world than they were about events in their own country. Whereas most Chinese boys rarely had the opportunity to see, much less associate with, foreigners, Koo grew up in an atmosphere in which foreigners and foreign ways dominated Shanghai life. This interesting, if not bizarre, blend of Chinese and Occidental lifestyles influenced Koo's thinking toward things non-Chinese. Chinese boys who lived in the hinterland tended to see foreigners as devils who engaged in evil magic and who sought to exploit others for great profit.[5] Koo on the other hand never viewed them as foreign devils or barbarians.

Along with the treaty port atmosphere, Koo's merchant father probably instilled in Koo a greater spirit of toleration of foreigners. During much of the nineteenth century, there were Chinese in the treaty ports known as compradores who served as middlemen between foreign and Chinese merchants. By Koo's time, gentry merchants, who interacted directly with foreign merchants and represented an important segment of the new treaty port urban elite, replaced the compradores. Koo's father was such a gentry merchant since he purchased his own civil service degree and engaged in business with foreign clients or customers. Treaty port Chinese merchants, as well as most treaty port intellectuals, tended to be progressive and cosmopolitan in the sense that they were more open to foreign ideas and more Westernized in dress and habits compared to Chinese in the hinterland.[6] Whether Koo's father was in every respect such a merchant is unknown, but the fact he allowed his sons to be educated by foreigners and that he admired the Duke of Wellington enough to make his name that of his son's suggests that Koo's father was hardly a xenophobe.

If Shanghai instilled a toleration for foreigners, its dominance by foreigners created the basis for Koo's patriotism. Chinese living in the treaty ports were ambivalent toward the Western presence. Although they engaged in cultural borrowing, treaty port Chinese retained an affinity for their culture that varied from person to person. The Westerners, who carried about them an air of cultural superiority that disparaged Chinese culture, stirred up feelings of patriotism among Shanghai's Chinese population.[7]

Besides the attacks on their culture, the manner in which the Westerners ran Shanghai under the protection of the unequal treaties guaranteed the promotion of patriotic feelings. Although Shanghai was not a colony like Hong Kong, the foreigners controlled Shanghai politically even though the Chinese population far exceeded the city's foreign population. In the section of the International Settlement where Koo lived, the Shanghai Municipal Council made the laws that governed foreign and Chinese alike. Unlike most Chinese boys that grew up accountable to only Chinese laws, Koo lived by rules and regulations made by foreigners.[8] And the manner in which the British made and enforced the laws did not endear him to this foreign system. Koo later acknowledged that he could understand his countrymen's antipathy for the British who always held themselves "aloof from Chinese society and the Chinese people" and who took measures to maintain law and order in ways that "did not seem justifiable to the Chinese."[9]

Although willing to adopt foreign ways, the treaty port urban elite were quite patriotic. In the nineteenth century, treaty port intellectuals and merchants demanded recognition of Chinese sovereignty as a result of their exposure to Western ideas and conceptions of international law. They railed against extraterritoriality, called for tariff autonomy and opposed foreign domination of China's domestic shipping. They also used their knowledge of Western law to protest foreign mistreatment and humiliation of Chinese. Treaty port merchants joined in the effort to recover China's loss of rights and urged that China's borderlands, such as Korea and Vietnam, be safeguarded against imperialist intrusion.[10]

Treaty port Chinese patriots were not nativist in the sense of seeking to throw the foreigners out. Their patriotism differed from that of some Chinese intellectuals who possessed an attitude of militant conservatism. Ideologically, militant conservatives preferred to rely solely on the cultural superiority of Confucianism in dealing with the barbarians. Xenophobic to the extent that they rejected Western technology and ideas, militant conservatives were prepared to use military force to drive the imperialists out. Such a bellicose attitude led these officials to urge war against France over Vietnam in 1884–1885 and to support a declaration of war on the imperialist powers during the Boxer Uprising only to be defeated.[11]

Treaty port intellectuals rejected that approach. Instead, treaty-port patriotism resembled that of Chinese intellectuals who Michael Hunt has described as "cosmopolitans." They realized that nineteenth-century China was too weak militarily to force the imperialists and their unequal treaties out of the country. Cosmopolitans were influenced by the ideas of Wei Yuan who, writing in the aftermath of the first Opium War, argued that China could only save itself by borrowing technology from the West, strengthening its military defenses and navy, and using diplomacy, in particular the manipulation of the powers. Cosmopolitans of the mid-nineteenth century implemented the Self-Strengthening Movement of 1862–1894. The Chinese officials behind that movement, such as Li Hongzhang, were far more accommodating in their attitude toward the foreign devils. The Self-Strengtheners believed in Chinese cultural superiority, but recognized that only by becoming a student of the mighty Western imperialists could China survive. The Self-Strengtheners relied on other stratagems, including a theory of a balance of power that was implemented by attempts to play one power off against the other. Trade, not the cannon, was seen as a preferable weapon for eliminating imperialism. Similar ideas were found among treaty port intellectuals such as Koo's father.[12]

In any case, the imperialist system in Shanghai ensured that its Chinese inhabitants, such as Koo, developed patriotic feelings. The foreign system in Shanghai adversely affected Chinese boys psychologically. They feared to look upon the Westerners that owned or occupied the best buildings and whose regulations ensured racial segregation by denying Chinese and dogs entrance into certain public parks. Koo got a taste of this foreign injustice when, at the age of nine, a British policeman fined him for riding his bicycle on the sidewalk, whereas an English boy bicycling in front of him went unpunished.[13] Koo never forgot this incident that was, for him, irrefutable evidence of the inequality between Shanghai's foreigners and Chinese inhabitants. He spent his life trying to knock down the obstacles that created the superior/inferior relations between foreigner and Chinese in order to have more equality.

Foreign Shanghai alone, however, did not instill a sense of humiliation that Koo felt over the foreign treatment of Chinese. The atmosphere of crisis in which he grew up contributed to his sense of patriotism. To learn from history textbooks of China's humiliation after the Opium Wars was enough to "lose face" over China's fate, but to come of age in a time of imperialist success against one's country had an unforgettable psychological effect on Koo. Later in life, Koo told his daughter that "The first 15 years of a child's life makes a deep impression upon him and more or less set the mould in which his future life is to be cast, as far as character, habits, taste and viewpoints are concerned."[14] The Sino-Japanese War, the "scramble," and the Boxer Uprising left Koo with a deep sense of humiliation. Indeed, at the Paris Peace Conference of 1919, Koo on several occasions referred to discussions of Japan's victory and the 'scramble for concessions' as a revival of "unpleasant memories."[15] Western imperialism and China's weaknesses tended to undermine a young Chinese's view of China's great past, and Koo devoted his career to recovering that former greatness.[16]

Koo's father shared his son's loss of face over China's inability to protect the empire from foreign encroachment. Before those series of disasters befell China, the elder Koo provided his son with a classical Chinese education in order to prepare for the civil service examination. For a time, young Koo attended local Chinese schools designed, in his words, to provide a "greater concentration on the Chinese classics and the art of writing the conventional eight-legged essays." The study of both was essential for Chinese boys aspiring to pass the civil service exams and enter into government service. Each day, the students memorized the Five Classics, which were associated with Confucius, and the Four Books, which were commentaries written by the Song dynasty scholar Zhuxi, and recited them for the teacher. Koo later acknowledged that memorizing essays helped him become "a good writer and scholar." As a child, however, he viewed such an exercise "as a waste of time and effort."[17]

In 1901, young Koo enrolled at St. John's College, an American missionary-operated school in Shanghai. For a Chinese father to allow his son to acquire a foreign education and reject the traditional Confucian education system deemed necessary to pursue a career in government suggests that Koo's father, like many other fathers, was seared by China's defeat in 1895. After the Sino-Japanese War and the Boxer Uprising, Christian schools like St. John's were extremely popular as Chinese elites looked to the West for answers to the problems plaguing China at the time.[18] The elder Koo came to the conclusion that China's distresses reflected the archaic nature of China's traditional education system. His daughter-in-law described his attitude as being that of most Chinese: "China should become a world power and not be partitioned."[19] And years before the Qing Dynasty reached the same conclusion and abolished the civil service examinations, Koo's father deemed a foreign education more beneficial for his son than a classical one.

The education Koo received at St. John's can only be described as cultural imperialism. Founded by the American Episcopal Church, St. John's College was established to replace with Western ideals the "false history, false science, false geography, false chronology, false philosophy . . . [and] false religion" that pervaded Chinese society.[20] In other words, the missionaries carried about them an air of cultural superiority; some even charged that China never invented anything but simply stumbled onto gunpowder, the magnetic compass, and the printing press. By the time Koo matriculated at St. John's, the school had moved beyond training only Christian converts to seeking to provide an education in the arts and the physical sciences to young Chinese in general. The secular Western curriculum accompanied an emphasis on instilling Christian values. The daily routine consisted of compulsory prayer time, Bible reading, and attendance at Sunday worship services. Those who failed to comply with the rules were seldom spared the rod.[21] St. John's College never converted Koo to Christianity, but he internalized the missionary/imperialist discourse that denigrated his culture's spiritual beliefs. He later claimed, "many of my superstitions were dispelled from my mind."[22]

Although the study of English was in high demand in treaty ports such as Shanghai, the school ensured that English took precedence over Chinese. In 1887, Dr. Francis Hawks Pott, an alumnus of Columbia University who was president of the institution for many years, asserted that instruction in English language and literature would broaden Chinese students' horizons and eliminate the antiforeign prejudice. By the 1890s, the majority of courses offered at St. John's, including Chinese history, were taught in English, and all official documents and announcements were written in English. Students were permitted to publish articles written in English, not Chinese, in the campus monthly *St. John's Echo* and the school yearbook, *Dragon Flag*. In fact, the *Echo* proudly claimed itself to be the "first paper published in the Orient by Chinese youths in a tongue foreign to them and only acquired after hard years of study."[23]

Although the predominance of English attracted students such as Koo who came from treaty port families, the practice sparked criticism. Students recalled that they understood more about U.S. geography or Bible stories than they did the geography and literature of their own country. Some St. John's students left the school with a better grasp of English than Chinese. Koo remembered only receiving instruction in American and British history, not Chinese, and that after seven years of study at St. John's, students only had a first-year understanding of the Chinese language. "Apparently, the aim of a missionary school," recalled Koo, "was to train Chinese not with a view to what China needed as a nation, but what the missionary movement needed."[24]

Koo's resentment was evidence of an incipient patriotism against the *kind* of Westernization, not Westernization itself, that St. John's forced on young Chinese boys. To be fair, St. John's recognized that students needed a background in Chinese language and history. The lack of interest in those areas on the part of students may not have been entirely the fault of St. John's. "Even if this be the very moment of China's partitionment," wrote one of the editors of the *St. John's Echo*, "it is regretted that Chinese do not study China's history." Chinese students had to be dispelled of the notion that reading Chinese history was not as pleasurable as Western history.[25] Likewise, students needed to grasp the importance of having a foundation in the Chinese language. In 1901, Pott made the study of Chinese mandatory, placing it on an equal par with English after the school's authorities realized that students studying Chinese were less motivated than those studying English. And in 1902, St. John's attempted to improve its Chinese program by hiring Chinese teachers, several of whom were students returned from Japan. Koo, like other students, supported this reform and new emphasis on a Chinese education, but these Chinese teachers were deemed too radical and patriotic for St. John's taste and the teachers left the school over time.[26]

St. John's viewed itself as training students to become businessmen, to contribute to their communities and to assist students in developing relations with foreigners. Fluency in English supposedly facilitated that process. In Koo's case, training in the language certainly made study abroad and his career as a diplomat much smoother. He was so fluent in English that one could forget that he was Chinese particularly when over 90 percent of his diary was written in English, not Chinese. Fluency in English also made St. John's graduates, especially the affluent students from Shanghai, feel as if they were a select group. Koo and other such notables as W.W. Yen, who was not an alumnus but a teacher there, Alfred Sze, or T.V. Soong, became known as the "St. John's clique."[27]

St. John's Americanization of Koo extended beyond language. St. John's proved to be a conduit for transmitting ideas about government and reform. From 1898 onward, two questions remained uppermost in the minds of the faculty and students of St. John's: Was China on the verge of being partitioned by the powers, and what reform measures should China implement to prevent partitioning from becoming a reality? Through their debating societies, the students took these questions

head on and divided over the issue of whether China should have a constitution and/or a republican form of government. In the context of the
Boxer Uprising, constitutionalism and republicanism were viewed as
dangerous by many because there was a belief that China was not ready
for either. Koo and his classmates generally blamed the conservatism,
superstition, and what was described as the social and educational tyr-
anny in Chinese government and society for China's ills. They were introduced to the writings of Kang Youwei and Liang Qichao, the men
behind the failed Hundred Days Reform movement of 1898, which called
for a constitutional monarchy. For students and young Chinese like Koo,
Liang Qichao represented new ideas for making China a stronger country that could resist imperialism.[28]

This did not mean that Koo and his classmates were revolutionaries. Although some believed revolution was necessary, many wanted only
political and educational reform. Koo recalled that he and his peers did
not seek to overthrow or eliminate the Qing. His educational atmosphere
did not promote revolution or radicalism. Reflecting the long-held American precept that the only good revolution was an orderly one, St. John's
frowned on radical revolution, such as the French revolution.[29] Instead,
the American institution encouraged students to seek change gradually
with Japan as a model, though the faculty opposed Japan's imperialistic
expansion into China. What St. John's hoped to produce were, as Edward Xu has written, "'practical patriots' and 'intelligent reformers' not
'hot-headed fanatics.'" Pott exemplified such thinking when he strongly
advocated "law and order," and believed the best form of democracy was
leadership of the ignorant masses by the best and wisest. He supported
the Western colonization of China, if not direct political control by the
Western powers, in order to introduce that superior Western culture to
China. However, Pott did not believe that the republican institutions of
the United States could be instantly transplanted to China. Teaching students to become gradual reformers fit many students' psychology, including Koo's, because they came from rich families who had no interest
in overturning their political and social system. Many students opposed
revolutionary change, as did Koo, and preferred a more conservative,
pragmatic approach to reform.[30]

St. John's gave young Koo an American education, and whatever misgivings about St. John's curriculum he maintained then or later, he was diligent in his studies. In 1904, his peers voted him the "brightest student."[31] St. John's also gave him the educational background necessary for study abroad. The Boxer Uprising underlined the necessity of modernization and the need for Chinese students to go abroad to learn from Japan and the West. The hope was that a new generation of young Chinese, with their modern education, would rise up to save China.[32] Between the Sino-Japanese War and the Revolution of 1911, more than 25,000 Chinese students traveled to Japan, some receiving a general education while others were trained in military schools. Japan attracted the Chinese because it was there that they could learn about the Western ideas that enabled Japan to become a great power in less than fifty years.[33] Several St. John's students hoped that China and Japan could form their own alliance.[34]

While most students went to Japan, there were young Chinese who preferred the United States. American missionaries and missionary schools in China were willing to foot the students' bills if they opted for an education in America. After 1908, over 2,000 students studied in the United States because Washington returned an $11 million surplus of the Boxer Indemnity to China for educational purposes. And there were Chinese whose patriotic opposition to Japanese imperialism in China influenced their choice of America over Japan.[35]

Young Koo's motivations for seeking an education in the United States were not monetary in nature. His motivations were ideological to the extent that he did aspire to greatness and at the same time truly desired to help his people. China's moments of crisis and despair made an impact on the young Koo who knew enough about China's great heritage and history to understand that China had fallen from a high pedestal. As a child growing up in the foreign settlement of Shanghai, he resented the imperialist system. A seed of ambition was sown within him to remove the humiliations imposed on his people during his childhood. The unequal treaties, the foreign privileges, the predominance of the foreign powers over China's political structure and institutions, and the persistent threat of the empire and later the republic dissolving away compelled Koo to make China "a free and independent country, undominated by any foreign nation; and enjoying the fundamental liberties and freedoms under the rule of law."[36] His former wife later wrote that he chose to study abroad in order to raise "China to its proper position among world powers." And he himself exhorted Chinese students in America to "make service to your mother country the aim of your studies" and to fulfill their "task to help China ascend to that position in the forefront to which she is entitled."[37] Since he had been trained in an American school, it made sense for him to travel to America. So in 1904, Koo graduated from St. John's College and headed for the United States. After spending a year at Cook Academy in Montour Falls, New York, he entered Columbia University in September 1905.[38]

As a student there from 1905 to 1912, he immersed himself into American culture. Unlike Chinese students who lacked time or confidence to participate in American social functions, Koo proved quite outgoing, made many friends, and participated in numerous extracurricular activities. Koo's involvement in so many extracurricular activities possibly stemmed from more than just an extroverted or gregarious nature. The answer may have resulted from a phenomenon that Ashis Nandy has described as the "psychology of colonialism." Although China was never formally colonized by the powers, one can say that Chinese like Koo who grew up in the treaty ports experienced a colonization of the mind. The foreigners criticized and ridiculed Chinese society and culture to such a great extent that many young Chinese internalized those criticisms. In an atmosphere of crisis in which China seemed on the verge of breakup and formal colonization, such criticisms seemed apt and led some Chinese to become cultural dependents of the West. Just as Indians viewed the British as agents of progress and "saw in turn their salvation in becoming more like the British," Koo may have felt the need to become like the Americans by participating in athletics, debating societies, and drinking parties.[39]

Study abroad was a mind-opening experience for Koo and his Chinese classmates. In its mere one-hundred-plus years of existence, the U.S.'s political and industrial development far outdistanced China. And Americans were not loath to wave that fact in the faces of Chinese students. American travelers to China returned home ambivalent about the Chinese. Whether holding the Chinese in respect or contempt, they agreed that Chinese society was, across the board, in a state of arrested development.[40] Arthur Smith, who later looked on the Chinese with greater esteem, wrote in his book *Chinese Characteristics* that the Chinese people showed a disregard for time and accuracy, a talent for misunderstanding and indirection, and an absence of public spirit, sympathy, and sincerity.[41]

Koo internalized such attacks on his culture and civilization in a rather interesting fashion and accepted the claims that his country was backward. In 1908, Koo returned to China. He traveled through the Suez Canal, Colombo, Singapore, and Hong Kong before landing in Shanghai. Shocked by the "poverty of the peoples of Asia," Koo later described his voyage "as a disheartening spectacle all along the voyage to see how poor the common people were in contrast with the prosperity and affluence of the West." When he arrived in Shanghai, the contrast between his hometown and America was "sharp" making Koo "realize how backward Shanghai was and how much needed to be done to bring the country and the people into approaching the conditions of living abroad." Although happy to see his family, the visit left Koo frustrated and with a "desire to play my part later in the modernization and rebuilding of China."[42]

The next year, Koo explained to John R. Mott of the YMCA that others like himself had "to set aside [their] former prejudice and pride and see China in her true condition." The modernity of the United States led him to despair over "the utter helplessness of his country, perhaps pouring forth a violent tirade against everything Chinese." Anger toward China's backwardness did not mean that Koo and his compatriots lost their affection for China. Their "love at heart for China" remained, Koo continued, and they were spurred to "greater activity in the service of [their] country." In comparison to Chinese who never went abroad, the students' loved their country just as much. The only difference was that the students were "only less clamorous and more careful."[43]

Living in the West clearly changed some of Koo's views about his culture, but there were limits to his cultural borrowing. America affected Koo's views of religion in general and Christianity in particular. Koo seriously considered converting to Christianity in order to "purify me of all worldly thoughts and enable me to devote the rest of my life to the work of social welfare amongst the Chinese people." The insurmountable obstacle was a promise to his mother to perform ancestral worship by praying for her "departed spirit."[44]

Although unable to embrace the Christian spirit, he became Westernized in the manner dictated by the imperialist discourse. Before leaving China, Koo cut off his queue, the symbol of subservience to the Qing Dynasty, and bought Western-style clothing as required of all students traveling to the United States. Yet, wearing Western clothes, sporting an American haircut, playing poker or golf, and smoking cigars were merely the facade of Westernization in Koo's mind. One had to adopt from the West the ideas of modernization, progress, and democratization. Koo and other students internalized American if not European imperialist discourse that China was culturally backward if not bankrupt. And he believed that Chinese students in America had the obligation to "transport to their country Western thought and Western ideals;" "see to it that . . . China does not fail to secure that form of constitutional government which will work for the greatest happiness for the greatest number of people;" and "sweep away permanently such injurious social customs as opium-smoking and foot-binding." He did add the caveat that China was "not like the potter's clay which will yield to any form that may be applied to it." Koo did not support throwing away everything Chinese, nor did he favor inundating China with everything foreign.[45]

The cultural imperialism and racism that he experienced in the United States did not transform him into an antiforeign nationalist, but a patriot who wanted to save his country. To cure the ill, he put his finger on the problem: "the weakness, inefficiency, and corruption of the Manchu dynasty." He later claimed "that China could not be strong without overthrowing this alien regime" and that "something was radically wrong with the government" since it discouraged reforms. Yet, Koo also believed that the root cause of Asia's backwardness in general and China's in particular was foreign imperialism. The places that he passed through on his trip home in 1908 "were colonies of the Western powers, either of Great Britain or France, and I felt that was probably one of the main reasons for their condition." China was no different. Koo and other Chinese like him "felt that China's troubles were due to exploitation by the Western powers."[46]

Study abroad convinced Koo and his fellow compatriots that they were, as one Chinese student at Yale put it, one of the "unique classes" in Chinese society contributing to the "nation's development." Koo believed that the torch had been passed to his generation. Chinese students like himself would become "the future leaders of China; her statesmen and diplomats; her lawyers and engineers; her teachers and professors; and her engineers and scientists of all kinds." They were given the difficult responsibility of building "a new, strong and powerful nation out of the old, tottering China, a nation which will be able to defend her own rights, whenever necessary, and ready to assist in upholding justice and peace throughout the world." And their duty was "to protect and promote the prestige of China without and to evolve a modern state within."[47]

While at Columbia, Koo made the decision to become a diplomat. Koo's choice reflected the attitude of some at the time that diplomats and diplomacy were potential saviors of the nation. Instead of using brute military force to overthrow the imperialist system, diplomacy offered more peaceful options. His desire to be a diplomat reflected some of the changes occurring in China. Early in China's long history, certain officials were selected to learn the art of diplomacy and served in a profession deemed honorable and prestigious. In time, however, diplomacy lost its allure, and few Chinese officials relished the idea of being dispatched to a far land to engage in talks with barbarians. By the nineteenth century, the Chinese bureaucracy was bereft of men who held an informed opinion of foreign affairs. Instead, cosmopolitans like Li Hongzhang surrounded themselves with a coterie of foreign affairs experts. During the Self-Strengthening Movement, Li implemented a number of foreign policy reforms including the creation of China's first foreign office in 1861 and the establishment of China's first permanent diplomatic legations abroad. The need for diplomats, especially those well-versed with the imperialists, grew.[48]

Yet, Koo also chose to become a diplomat because he wanted to help his people. He later said that he "wanted to do something in a way that would improve conditions in [China]." His goal was "to bring about reforms, especially in the conduct of foreign relations." Count Cavour, the man who worked to unify Italy in the nineteenth century and was a hero for Koo and other Chinese students, served as an example. Koo learned that Cavour "was convinced that it (the unity of Italy) could only come through diplomacy."[49] Cavour was a model for Koo whom he described as having one purpose in life: "free Italy from foreign oppression and unite all her parts into one compact State." Koo reached the conclusion that as a diplomat he could play a role in the salvation of China. At one point in his college career, he was asked by an American classmate if he wanted to be "a pink-tie diplomat or render real service to China." Koo replied, "[I am] all in earnest."[50]

His education assisted him in pursuing his career goal in several respects. As a student at Columbia University, Koo edited the campus newspaper and worked for the *New York Herald*, so he understood the power of the press and propaganda to influence public opinion. He later observed that many of the old diplomats of his early years "did not see the importance of publicity abroad." Throughout his long career, he ran propaganda machines, cultivated ties with foreign journalists, and supplied materials to those he knew could influence world opinion in China's favor. Koo was not above painting an untruthful picture of China in order to get support for whatever regimes he represented. Koo tried to use public opinion at home and abroad against the powers, though he would learn after 1919 that public opinion often set limits on what he could accomplish as a diplomat. He also believed that the diplomat was an "intelligence officer." He had to be observant and search for hidden meanings in the words used by the powers. Reading the foreign press could give insights especially into a country's public opinion and public understanding that was "reflected in the newspapers."[51]

Columbia also afforded Koo the opportunity to hone his skills as orator and debater. Koo won numerous prizes while a student. Years later, one classmate described Koo as Columbia's best orator "largely because of his successful use of the debating technique of offering his opponents polite Oriental concessions and then demolishing them with a sly and devastating thrust of logic."[52] Koo was at his best when dealing with Americans. Later, when Koo was Chinese minister to Washington, one observer noted that Koo "had as much of America in him as he had of China. It was hard to think of him as an envoy from an Eastern land." He proved an accomplished speaker in the West because of his firm grasp of English. His correspondence with Westerners was written in perfect English. One of Koo's professors once remarked that Koo wrote "English better than do most of those whose native tongue is English."[53]

As a diplomat, Koo drew heavily on his oratory and debating skills, but he also possessed a vast knowledge of international law. It was no coincidence that Koo chose to study international law as a way to raise China' status. From China's point of view, international law was of great import. During the Self-Strengthening Movement, schools for the teaching of Western languages and Western law were established to create a new generation of professional diplomats. Efforts were made as well to translate Western works on international law into Chinese. The Chinese cosmopolitans concluded that their ignorance of Western law contributed to the signing away of their political rights and power to other countries. After 1898, Liang Qichao saw international law as China's road to salvation. Since the Western powers viewed international law as one of the "standards of civilization," China needed to embrace international law if it were to achieve revision of the unequal treaties.[54]

For a young Chinese studying politics and international law, the United States provided exceptional academic opportunities. Organized in 1880, Columbia University's School of Political Science possessed a number of prominent thinkers to introduce Koo to the latest ideas in social science, law, and political science. And during Koo's Columbia years, the study of international law enjoyed its heyday in the United States. Between 1900 and 1910, Public International Law became a professional discipline in which international lawyers, academics, and private citizens, who were all interested in preventing war and promoting peace, started journals, taught courses, and wrote books on the field. Many American international lawyers saw arbitration as a method for creating a new world order, though there were some who were dissatisfied with arbitration as the sole legal tool for redressing disputes. Reflecting the domestic preoccupations of progressive reformers of the day, these legalists wanted to bring order and rational thinking based on law to international society. Most American legalists called for an international court to settle disputes between nations. They believed that public opinion, *i.e.*, the views of the great powers, would be sufficient to enforce the rules and punish offenders. But there were other ideas disseminated publicly. In 1905, the year that Koo arrived in the United States, the American Society for International Law was created to become a forum for discussing and debating the Hague Peace Conferences, world court, arbitration, disarmament, and a "league to keep the peace."[55]

One of the creators of the new society became Koo's teacher, advisor, and mentor. That individual was John Bassett Moore, who came to Columbia in 1891 to occupy the Hamilton Fish Chair of International Law and Diplomacy after serving as Assistant Secretary of State in the Grover Cleveland administration. In years to come, the study of international relations and the name of John Bassett Moore became synonymous, particularly after publication of his eight-volume *Digest of the International Law* in 1906. He was later remembered as a "true gentleman and scholar who had a social and human approach that made contact with him an inestimable privilege always remembered." Each year, he taught four courses: a history of diplomacy, a history of American diplomacy, international law, and a seminar on international law.[56]

If Koo wanted to pursue a career in diplomacy, Moore was the right man under whom to study. Many international lawyers, including Elihu Root and James B. Scott, distrusted diplomacy and diplomats, believing that international law was a business solely for men of the bar.[57] Moore did not subscribe to their point of view. By contrast, he held several famous American diplomats such as John Hay and Benjamin Franklin in high esteem and held them up for emulation. And Moore had practical experience to pass on to Koo. What Moore learned from his experience was that "diplomacy is war, war in peacetime and its weapons are different." Koo combined Moore's description of diplomacy with the ideas of the famous Chinese military strategist Sunzi who spoke of the need of understanding yourself as well as your enemy. In diplomacy, one had to "size up the opposing party and also your own strength."[58]

The "dear old professor," as Koo remembered him, also taught the young Chinese that the story of international law was one of progress. A major change in international politics was that the use of force had proved archaic and that many of the justifications for war had ceased to exist. Evidence of international law's progress was seen as well in the emergence of new rules of international behavior from congresses, such as the one at Vienna in 1815 and numerous treaties signed throughout the nineteenth century that codified new rules for conducting war and peace. The Western nations were also cooperating more than before, particularly during the Age of Imperialism, which made the great powers more interdependent, requiring more cooperation instead of conflict. If disputes arose, the powers tended to rely on arbitration. Since arbitration played such a prominent role in international politics, Moore argued for a permanent system of arbitration in order to prevent disputes from escalating into war and to prevent popular hysteria from pushing countries into war by allowing time for deliberation. To enforce decisions, Moore advised reliance on "the most efficient of all sanctions, public opinion."[59]

For Koo, international law and Moore's *Digest* were weapons to wield in diplomatic warfare. The powers imposed unequal treaties on the Chinese in part because they accused China of having a barbaric law system. Before there could be order, there had to be law. According to Moore, Japan became a member of the concert of nations because it accepted international law, showing that the "standard of international law" was a litmus test of a nation's "advancement in law, in morals, and in civilization."

Koo's embracing of law in general and international law in particular revealed his desire to help China's international relations achieve a status of civilized state. The notion of a "family of nations" was a Western construct, not a Chinese one, but Koo wanted China to become a member of the family of nations. China failed to meet such a litmus test and American international lawyers were not above looking down their noses at the Chinese. Indeed, one of Koo's American classmates remembered that when, as a student at Columbia, Koo attended the American Society of International Law conference in Washington, "the presence of a Chinese member was looked upon as a not altogether welcome novelty."[60]

Although constructs like the "family of nations" and the "standard of international law" were imperialistic discourse, Koo assumed that if China passed the litmus test, it would have a firmer basis upon which to attack the unequal treaty system. In particular, he sought elimination of extraterritoriality, which after all was premised on the powers' image of

Chinese inferiority in civilization and in law. Whether through arbitration or appealing to a league to enforce peace, Koo doggedly sought to make China a "free and independent country" by whatever diplomatic means available. If the powers could be held to their rules of international behavior, then China had less to fear with regard to its national security. Koo claimed years later that the only solution for dealing with the imperialist powers "was to stand firm on the country's rights and negotiate without yielding any important ground."[61] A strong China could avoid compromise, but not a weak one. Throughout his long career, Koo almost never negotiated from a position of strength. The result was that Koo became the master of legalistic formulas designed to save face and provide legal loopholes through which Koo could pursue a patriotic agenda.

There was no contradiction between the imperialist discourse that he internalized and his patriotism. Koo's thinking was similar to that of the eminent Chinese intellectual Hu Shi, a graduate of Cornell and a Ph.D. from Columbia University, who defined patriotism as love for one's native land, but rejected "nationalism," which he viewed as a perverse blind faith in the righteousness of one's cause. Koo could be patriotic while accepting the rules of international behavior established by the great powers. Such acceptance carried no pejorative connotations.[62]

Another aspect of Koo's thinking that carried no pejorative connotation was his belief that China could look to, if not use, the United States to secure patriotic goals. Throughout his long career, Koo used the Chinese stratagem of playing one power against others. An acquaintance remembered that in his speeches and talks given during his student years, Koo often referred to China as a 'great helpless country.'[63] Naturally, the helpless needed a helper. In this regard, one can conjure up Koo's hero, Count Cavour. Serving as both prime minister and foreign minister of Sardinia, Cavour agreed with Italian nationalists of the nineteenth century that the Austrians had to be driven out of Italy and that Italy must be reunified. From his professors at Columbia, Koo learned that Cavour "did not believe that unity could be secured without foreign aid." Cavour declared, "Whether we like it or not, our destinies depend upon France; we must be her partner in the great game which will be played sooner or later in Europe."[64]

Years of living and studying under American tutelage in Shanghai and New York reinforced the notion of a "special relationship" between the United States and China and the idea that the United States would look after China's interests. Unlike the other powers in East Asia, it was claimed that America would not exploit Beijing's weaknesses. Many Americans, including Moore, sincerely believed that America's traditional policy toward China, from the 1844 Treaty of Wangxia (the first American treaty with China) to John Hay's Open Door Notes of 1899–1900, was to ensure freedom of trade and protect the independence of China by opposing the partitioning of the Middle Kingdom.[65] Theodore Roosevelt's decision to return the surplus from America's part of the Boxer Indemnity to the Qing Dynasty so that Chinese students could afford study in the United States added another dimension to that special relationship.[66] Collaboration with a friend could only bring about benefits for China. The *Chinese Students' Monthly*, of which Koo was once an editor, declared that an alliance between the United States and China would check "the unhealthy ambitions of some Powers" and bring about "speedy reforms for China, a great market for America, and a real open door for the world." Another editorial at that time declared, "The best friend our country has is undoubtedly the United States of America. All through our intercourse with each other, friendliness and justice have been the guiding principles." Editorial cartoons in the *Monthly* reflected such sentiments. One such cartoon, presumably done by a Chinese student, portrayed sleeping China being awakened by Uncle Sam and his dogs. The dogs represented Young China and each dog wore a coat printed with the name of a particular American university. China looks up at Uncle Sam and says, "Hello, Sam! Glad you have so many barking dogs to wake me up."[67]

Long before the Chinese Communists began to use the pejorative label "running dogs of the imperialists," Chinese students viewed such images in a positive light. Like Koo, most Chinese students did not fear the United States, but instead welcomed American hegemony in the Pacific because it would bring peace to the region.[68] Cavour depended on France; whether he liked it or not, Koo depended on and manipulated the United States for almost his entire career to save China from the imperialists.

After completing the required class work for the doctorate degree,

Koo researched and wrote his dissertation, which was eventually published under the title *The Status of Aliens in China*. Koo chose this topic for several reasons. One was his experience of being fined for breaking a law of the Shanghai Municipal Council that Koo was not aware of beforehand and one that he thought largely unfair. Another was that the topic was suggested by Winifried Scott, Moore's research assistant, who advised Koo that if he wanted to be a diplomat, the topic "would put [him] in the best position to deal with China's foreign relations later—to see how China was mistreated, denied the rights to which a sovereign nation was entitled under international law."[69] Then there was, as Koo wrote, the topic's relevance to the present: "Commerce, religion, travel and other interests are drawing increasing numbers of foreigners into China, and the question of their precise status, while residing or being with her territory becomes today not only one of enhanced interest, but one of growing practical importance." Such contact naturally led to "complex problems" that could only be solved by possessing "an accurate knowledge of the rights, privileges and immunities which they [foreigners] are entitled to enjoy under laws and treaties, and of the limitations and restrictions arising from the same sources of sanction, upon such rights, privileges and immunities." Finally, Koo argued that his work filled a gap on the literature on extraterritoriality because he was not "aware of any work in existence which considers the status of aliens in China as a class, or from the Chinese point of view."[70]

The Status of Aliens in China is an important work because its conclusions say more about the author than they do about the Chinese themselves or the foreigners in China. The heart of the book examined extraterritoriality and the protection it afforded foreigners as well as its limitations. The book attacked the whole imperialist system. Koo wrote that unlike Turkey, China never had the custom of granting extraterritoriality to aliens. Instead, China early in its history granted aliens "many privileges and ample protections" and placed few restrictions on the right of aliens to travel within the empire. China eventually shifted to what Koo described as a "closed-door policy," but this was done for defensive purposes. By the 1500s, Europeans were already engaged in imperialism in Asia, and China experienced internal strife. China's rulers, "keenly apprehensive lest the strangers from the West might take advantage of

China's weaknesses and resort to schemes of occupation and conquest," placed restrictions on foreigners. The Chinese also took a more conservative stance as a result of the "bloody contests of mercantile avarice, the conspiracy and intrigue, to which the Portuguese, the Dutch and the English did not blush to resort for the purpose of excluding one another and thereby securing a monopoly of trade."[71]

China's closed-door policy increased dissatisfaction on the part of foreign merchants who, "driven by the spirit of mercantile avarice" and unwilling to submit to Chinese laws as the foreign missionaries did, wanted more privileges than the Chinese were willing to grant. The Chinese sought to maintain their "territorial sovereignty" by making imperial laws supreme. When the Chinese implemented antiopium policies in the 1830s, they operated on the assumption that China was simply "exercising a right appertaining to a sovereign and independent nation." Hence, foreigners did not enjoy the privilege of extraterritoriality until China signed, "without her consent and countenance," treaties with the Western powers beginning with that "expensive and ignoble" Opium War of 1839–1842. Koo argued that foreigners wantonly ignored and violated Chinese laws and exaggerated when they condemned China's law system as barbaric, claiming it took "life for life" in cases of involuntary manslaughter. Koo defended China, saying that the Chinese law system was not as harsh as claimed nor as barbaric as the British law system that put people to death for numerous reasons, some quite trivial.[72]

In reading Koo's description of how the unequal treaties came to be imposed on China, Koo's disdain for the British and his view of the United States as a friendly power were evident. Koo labeled British disrespect for Chinese law as "characteristic Anglo-Saxon pride and faith in the superiority of their own race and in the supremacy of their own institutions that they could not see how any of their countrymen could have committed a crime in China...." He declared that the extraterritorial system that Great Britain, not the United States, erected in China was done "without sanction of the law of nations and in defiance of the Chinese government" and that recognition of extraterritoriality "had ultimately been wrung out from the Chinese Emperor only by force of arms." True, the United States enjoyed the privilege of extraterritoriality. But the Treaty of Wangxia operated on the erroneous assumption that extraterritoriality existed previously in Europe, Asia, and Africa until it disappeared from Europe with the creation of modern nation-states that "developed a common law of nations, with its doctrines of equality and territorial sovereignty." Christian nations deemed extraterritoriality as the "rule of international law" in dealing with pagan states that had practiced extraterritoriality. China, Koo argued, was different from the Middle East and Africa in that it "had already developed into a well-organized political entity" that did not have the custom of extraterritoriality. Moreover, American merchants, unlike their British counterparts, showed no inclination to be exempted from Chinese law, though the Chinese had already decided to grant to the Americans what had been given to the British.[73]

In line with Koo's patriotism, the book attacked the unequal treaty system by looking at two particular groups that benefited from extraterritoriality—merchants and missionaries. Foreigners used past Chinese antiforeignism as an excuse for maintaining the system, but Koo declared that despite "frequent allegations that the Chinese are exclusive and antiforeign, foreigners in China enjoy very many rights and privileges which are not accorded to aliens in other countries." Koo admitted that such rights as extraterritoriality were the products of treaties forced on the Chinese by the foreigners, but he claimed "that their peaceful enjoyment of it has been made possible only by the favorable disposition toward them alike of the Government and people of China." No matter whether before or after 1842, Koo claimed that the Chinese overall maintained a "favorable disposition toward foreigners as such which led China to accord them the privilege of unrestricted intercourse with her own subjects and place them on an equal footing with the latter."[74] Although the Chinese imposed restrictions on foreigners at various times, they did so not because of any xenophobia inherent in Chinese culture. Instead, such measures were adopted "for protection against their [rights and privileges] abuse of the extraordinary immunities which they [foreigners] enjoy."

As for attacks made on Christian missionaries, Koo acknowledged their seriousness and the "disastrous consequences to China" brought about by such events. The Boxer Uprising was a prime example. However, Koo argued that the Chinese people did not attack missionaries

because of an inborn xenophobic mindset, but because of the "ignorance of the masses." And in many cases, such local incidents were exploded into international crises "whenever any of the treaty powers sought
to make political capital out of the unfortunate killing of one or two of
its venturesome missionaries."[75] Koo pointed to the fact that since the
Boxer Uprising, there were few instances of attacks made against missionaries because of efforts on both sides to maintain peaceful relations.

In making his arguments, Koo clearly imposed his own disposition
and world view on the Chinese at large. He was not antiforeign per se,
but more cosmopolitan than the average Chinese. More so than most, he
welcomed the missionary and the merchant. Both contributed to China's
social and economic progress. Koo was willing to open China's door to
foreigners, particularly to the China market. Businessmen went to China
thinking that since China had such a huge population, there was a potential market for whatever goods they possessed.[76] The China market
never fulfilled expectations and proved largely to be a myth. For much of
the twentieth century, though, many foreign and Chinese businessmen
accepted that notion as valid including Koo. Throughout his career, he
would argue that the Chinese people, since they numbered in the millions, could produce enough goods to compete with the outside world.
He would also turn that notion on its head and appeal for foreign help to
deal with many crises by waving the China market in the powers' faces.
In other words, Koo tried to lure the other powers into aiding China in
checking Japanese colonialism, for example, by pointing to how Japan
threatened the China market. And, he was willing to threaten a country's
access to the China market with boycotts as a form of economic coercion to obtain political goals.

In any case, Koo acknowledged the need to reform Chinese laws
that limited interaction between Chinese and foreigners, but asserted
that until the system of extraterritoriality was eliminated, "it is unlikely
that China will be anxious to level down the barriers which now stand in
treaties between the open ports and the interior, or to remove the restrictions, which are now found in her laws, upon the freedom of the
foreign merchant to share in the unprecedented opportunities for trading and investment throughout the country." If the foreigners wanted to

engage in trade in the great China market, extraterritoriality had to go. China only desired a quid pro quo relationship with the foreign powers: let us enforce our own laws and we can permit you your "desired freedom and free development of commerce."[77]

Koo's analysis also reflected some ideas current among American internationalists, particularly the notion that trade barriers led to war. One tenet of the American peace movement at this time was that access to markets prevented conflict between states. Some in the American peace movement referred to this concept as economic internationalism when arguing that commercial relations bound all merchants, manufacturers and laborers of all nations together "in a community of interests which has made and is evermore making powerfully for peace." In Britain, Norman Angell described the world as so financially interdependent that market downturns in one country could spread in ripple-like fashion to other countries.[78] In defense of his country, Koo claimed that China "has in recent years opened up on her own initiative, a number of new places to foreign trade and has already set herself to the task of improving her mercantile system to meet the needs of foreign commerce."[79] Cooperation between the foreigners and China promoted commerce and peace. During his years as a diplomat, Koo often used the concepts of the China market and of interdependence in order to persuade the other powers of the necessity of preventing the colonization of China on the grounds that the only outcome would be war and financial distress.

Koo had faith in the idea that China and the world could cooperate in a way that fulfilled mutual interests. Probably he was trying to dispel the Western stereotype of Chinese as barbarous and savage in the manner of Genghis Khan.[80] Koo and others often tried to convince their listeners that Chinese were lovers of peace. Koo claimed that the social unrest that affected foreign interests in recent years was more a result of a weak central government than a culturally inbred hostility.

Before Koo completed his dissertation, revolution against the Qing Dynasty broke out on October 10, 1911, and by December, Sun Yat-sen, who for years had been trying to overthrow the Qing regime by force, was made provisional president. In 1909, Sun visited Koo at Columbia and shared his political philosophy with the young man. Reflecting on the Revolution, Koo wrote that the "people of the nation have overthrown

the worn-out regime of hoary antiquity and are erecting on new foundations a strong and efficient government." With the "moral support" of
the powers, "the rise of a powerful and progressive China will surely be
hastened a hundredfold. And China in progress and power means the
Far East in permanent peace."[81] The notion of a benign China is important because it is a theme that appears often in Koo's later speeches. Although usually not very specific about the idea, Koo implied that China
would never engage in territorial expansion beyond its borders and
threaten other nations.

Koo had nearly completed his dissertation in March 1912 when he
was offered the position of English secretary to Yuan Shikai. Yuan became president of the new Republic of China after Sun Yat-sen stepped
down as president in favor of Yuan in an effort to establish unity between the north and south. Tang Shaoyi, who was premier and once a
student in the United States himself, recommended Koo to Yuan. Koo
first met Tang in 1908 when the latter was in the United States to discuss
the remission of the Boxer Indemnity surplus with President Roosevelt
and to persuade the U.S. government to invest capital in Manchuria.
Before traveling to the United States, Yuan told Tang "to look out for
bright young men with a view to recommending them for service in
China." The purpose was to fill posts throughout the bureaucracy with
individuals who had majored in political science, international law, diplomacy or the humanities.[82] In other words, the new government looked
for experts in their fields who would be loyal to the government and give
the government a veneer of legitimacy.

Personal relationships or connections (guanxi) were also vital. Two
relationships besides family were important for success in government:
a schoolmate connection and a locality connection.[83] Koo did not have
many classmates in the foreign ministry, but there were people like W.W.
Yen—who had a teacher/student relationship with Koo—and Alfred
Sze—Koo's relative—who represented the so-called St. John's faction.
And, many in the government—Tang Shaoyi, Lu Zhengxiang, W.W. Yen
and Alfred Sze to name a few—were from Shanghai. When Tang Shaoyi
arrived in the United States, Yen was the Washington Legation's Secretary and he made arrangements for young Chinese men throughout the
United States to meet with Tang. Koo impressed Tang so much that he

chose the young man to be his son-in-law and later recommended him to Yuan Shikai.[84] Before traveling to the United States, Koo's father arranged a marriage with a traditional Chinese woman in Shanghai whose father was a physician, but in 1908, Koo secured a divorce from the woman. Koo claimed he "was too modern and too imbued with western ideas" to accept an arranged marriage, especially one with someone who lacked a cosmopolitan background or education. Not long after, Koo remarked that "the influence of modern civilization" had nearly destroyed the social system of matchmaking, which he described as making "hundreds of thousands of families . . . unhappy and millions of lives of the ill-mated couples . . . miserable."[85] At any rate, Koo married Tang's daughter, May, in June 1913. May, like her siblings, had been taught English, studied Chinese history, and was encouraged to take interest in current events. Besides her strengths as a future diplomat's wife, this consummation with May Tang was viewed by some foreign observers as "politically wise," with the foreign and Chinese communities generally assuming that the main motive was that the bride's father was an influential man in Chinese politics who could prove "useful to [an] aspiring young man in the Chinese diplomatic service." In a country where personal connections were essential to success and where nearly all marriages were made on the basis of convenience, not love, (though it is apparent that Koo did love or come to love May Tang), marriages like his to May Tang were not atypical.[86]

As a young man committed to making China free in his lifetime, Koo jumped at the offer to serve a man whom he, as chairman of the Patriotic Committee of Chinese Students in the United States, asked the United States to accord diplomatic recognition.[87] The Chinese minister advised Koo to "purchase all the indispensable works on international law and diplomacy, with particular reference to China." Koo bought a set of *Foreign Relations of the United States* and Moore's *Digest of International Law*, submitted his dissertation upon his return to Columbia and arrived in China in May 1912, where he went to work for the new president of China.[88] Koo embarked on a diplomatic career that would span over forty years. He came of age in an atmosphere of crisis, and he returned to a China where the fear of partitionment pervaded the government. And unknown to Koo, his country would soon be confronted with the crisis of Japanese imperialism.

Chapter 2

CHINA AND WORLD WAR I

IN 1912, KOO WENT TO WORK for a government that was faced with numerous problems and was searching for solutions. The new government needed a constitution, diplomatic recognition, and a loan. The powers refused to grant the new government recognition and money until it proved to be stable and willing to abide by the unequal treaties. Internal stability proved more difficult to achieve. Soon after Koo went to work, Tang Shaoyi broke with Yuan Shikai when the latter refused to appoint a fellow revolutionary to take over the military governorship of Zhili Province, where Beijing was located. Although Koo tendered his resignation, he was back in Beijing working in the foreign ministry within a few weeks, much to Tang's regret. And he remained loyal to Yuan even after Sun Yat-sen's political party, now renamed the GMD, won a majority in parliament and expected one of its members to replace Yuan as president. Instead, the man was assassinated presumably at the behest of Yuan who did not believe in constitutional succession of power, particularly in his own case. The assassination led to a civil war that Yuan easily quashed. The GMD was outlawed and Sun Yat-sen spent some time in exile.[1]

Besides these internal problems, the specter of partition remained. In 1913, the Treaty Study Commission, of which Koo was a member, observed that the powers delayed recognition of Yuan's government because they had territorial ambitions and really did not want see a stable government in China. Russia sought sovereignty over Mongolia, which declared independence in 1911, and Britain pursued sovereignty over Tibet which declared independence in 1913.[2] Although a republic, men

Map 2. Shandong Province Railroads

like Koo believed that China's boundaries should be that of the old Qing Empire. At his presidential inauguration in 1912, Yuan Shikai described the Chinese republic as a unified state that included Manchuria, Mongolia, and Tibet. And foreign-educated or native, the consensus among government officials was that China could not suffer further foreign encroachment, and territories lost had to be recovered. In Koo's mind, every loss enabled an imperialist power to make inroads into the country at China's expense.[3]

Foreign affairs naturally captured most of Yuan Shikai's attention, and fortunately he possessed much experience in that arena. Born in 1859, Yuan chose a military career and oversaw much of the military modernization that took place in the final years of the Qing Dynasty. In 1907, Yuan was named head of the ministry of foreign affairs. For the next two years, he attempted to recover China's rights and at the same time tried to use U.S. investments in Manchuria to offset Japanese encroachment in the northeast. Although some Chinese elites were critical of his close association with the Western powers, Yuan saw the folly of trying to throw the foreigners out of China as the Boxers had attempted to do a few years before, and recognized the potential benefits that cooperation with friendly powers could entail.[4]

Like his subordinates, Yuan wanted to bring Mongolia and Tibet back into the ROC's control, and he wanted to eliminate the specter of partition. To assist him, Yuan Shikai filled the foreign ministry bureaucracy with Western- and Japanese-educated Chinese men. In this way, Yuan surrounded himself with men whose foreign affairs expertise and skills he could draw upon. He needed U.S.-educated men like Koo because China dealt with Western imperialist powers, in particular Britain and the United States. Koo spoke their language and was trained in Anglo-American history, diplomacy, and rules for international behavior. He better understood Anglo-American thinking and could better advise the president. Moreover, the selection of foreign-educated men to government posts, especially those with a law background like that of Koo's, showed the foreign powers that China was civilized and had a firm foundation in Western law. Finally, by appointing foreign-educated Chinese to positions of power, Yuan hoped to improve relations with particular countries. Yuan's decision to employ Japanese-educated men was calculated to provide peace and stability in Sino-Japanese relations. In the same respect, the employment of Koo and others like him was done in order to win American financial backing, and Yuan often reminded Americans that his government relied heavily on U.S.-trained specialists.[5]

Some of Yuan's Chinese protagonists faulted him at the time for gathering about him foreign-educated men that lacked the qualifications to serve in government. Fortunately for Koo, Yuan permitted these young men to obtain diplomatic experience. He met with his "brain-trust" of foreign-educated officials in order to get their input before making some major decisions, and worked closely with his subordinates, hovering in the background whenever they engaged the foreign powers. When Yuan assigned Koo to negotiate with the British minister, Yuan carefully went over their notes of conversation, marking in red or blue points to be ignored or emphasized. "In short," Koo remarked later, "President Yuan was painstaking in his handling of foreign relations and made himself responsible for what the government did." The result was a deep loyalty for a man later remembered on both sides of the Taiwan Strait as dictator and "father of the warlords." In Koo's estimation, Yuan was "a man of great ambition and determination, a born leader of men," a "man of action," and a "good administrator." He was "fairly modern, even liberal" while at the same time authoritarian, and he was "a patriot in the sense that he was most jealous of China's sovereignty in conducting foreign relations."[6]

In 1913, Koo was promoted to counselor to the foreign ministry, being responsible to the foreign minister and ultimately to Yuan Shikai. The promotion put Koo in a position to gain needed diplomatic experience and to put his book knowledge of diplomacy and international law to use. China's foreign minister for most of the 1910s was Lu Zhengxiang, a former Chinese minister to Holland and Russia who married a Belgian woman and converted to Catholicism. Lu wanted the foreign ministry to mirror that of the West and wanted diplomatic posts filled by professionals trained for or experienced in diplomacy. Koo assisted Lu in establishing a new foreign ministry. Some Qing officials were retained because of their knowledge of certain diplomatic cases between China and the powers.[7] In an effort to manipulate U.S. public opinion, Koo convinced the foreign ministry to fund the Far Eastern Information Bureau, which was originally created by the Chinese legation in Washington to counter criticisms of the new ROC. The Bureau sold news copy to newspapers in the United States including editorials that urged American businessmen to invest their money in China, or launched attacks against the unequal treaty system.[8]

During the time in which Koo experienced promotion, Yuan Shikai's position seemed more secure. The United States under Woodrow Wilson's leadership broke from the Six-Power Consortium, which he deemed imperialistic and a monopoly, and unilaterally recognized Yuan's government. The powers followed suit late that year, and the Consortium granted Yuan a Reorganization Loan. Unfortunately, the peace and stability that Yuan's government needed to solidify its hold over China was shattered the next year with the outbreak of World War I. War in Europe magnified the specter of China's destruction. Since the combatants had imperial interests in China, the threat of the European conflict becoming a world war was real. If China joined the allies by declaring war on Germany, Yuan feared that it would only arouse Japanese suspicions. Instead, he advocated a policy of neutrality. On August 6, 1914, the Chinese officially declared their territory and territorial waters off-limits to belligerent operations by the warring powers.[9]

The war in Europe gave Japan a golden opportunity to pursue imperial aspirations in China. To protect Britain's colony in Hong Kong and its concession at Weihaiwei, the British proposed that the Anglo-Japanese Alliance be invoked to defeat Germany's China naval squadron and protect British commercial shipping in Chinese waters. Japan intended to use the alliance to fill the imperial political vacuum in Asia created by the European War.[10] In mid-August, Japan demanded the surrender of the German fortress at Qingdao.

Yuan tapped Koo's skills during this national crisis. Utilizing his international law background, Koo authored the twenty-four article document announcing China's neutrality. Yuan also used Koo to approach the U.S. embassy in Beijing. Yuan recognized that the United States increasingly viewed Japan as a competitor, and tried to take advantage of U.S.-Japanese tensions. In the days before Japan's ultimatum to the Germans, Beijing requested that the United States and Japan assist China in obtaining the consent of the other powers to respect China's neutrality. The same day that China proclaimed neutrality, Koo expressed to an American diplomat the Chinese hope that the United States would offer its good offices in limiting the war theater to Europe by neutralizing the foreign concessions and proposing that the warring powers maintain the status quo in East Asia. Japan's ultimatum for a German surrender however undercut the Chinese effort.[11] Explaining that Japanese capture of Qingdao menaced China's independence, the Chinese implored Washington to approach Britain and Germany with a proposal to immediately transfer the leased Shandong territory to China in order to avert hostilities. Washington viewed such steps to be provocative and refused to take action.[12]

Neutrality and attempts to use the Americans to restrain Japan having failed, Yuan Shikai called a cabinet meeting to discuss China's next move. When Yuan solicited his opinion, Koo argued for war. Yuan rejected that option because of China's military weakness. On September 3, Yuan established a war zone around Qingdao so as to restrict Japanese military operations. This move allowed China to maintain neutrality and avoid responsibility for damages incurred by the warring powers. Once more, Yuan tried to bring the United States into the conflict. Koo interpreted the 1908 Root-Takahira Agreement, in which both the United States and Japan agreed to respect China's territorial integrity as stating that Japan needed to consult the United States before landing troops on Chinese soil. The Americans quickly disabused Koo of such notions, pointing out that Japan and the United States would only consult one another in "the case of internal disorders in China." Washington was not about to be dragged into a war to defend China's territorial integrity against Japan and Great Britain.[13]

On the day that the war zone was established, the Japanese navy landed troops on Shandong's coast. In November, the German garrison surrendered, presenting the Chinese with the specter of Japanese expansionism into Shandong Province and elsewhere. The Chinese had good reason to be fearful. In the aftermath of Qingdao's fall, some Japanese military men spoke of an "Asian Monroe Doctrine" in which Asia would be controlled by Asians, not the white man. For Koo, Japan's capture of Qingdao was another humiliation for China, and marked the beginning of an eight-year effort to resolve the Shandong Question.[14]

Having failed to prevent Japanese expansion onto Chinese soil, Koo and his compatriots were not defeatists. Using publicity to influence world opinion, he supplied material to journalists who he knew would be critical of Japan. And in an effort to manipulate the United States, Koo met with Paul Reinsch, the U.S. minister to China, on a regular basis. The young Chinese recognized that the former University of Wisconsin professor possessed a "great sympathy for the Chinese people and the Chinese cause" and was popular with Chinese in and out of the government. Little wonder since a subordinate described Reinsch as seeming "to have

accepted quite without criticism the handy popular division of the nations of the world into the predatory, the non-predatory and the altruis-
tic, *i.e.*, ourselves." Because of his feelings for China and manipulation
by men like Koo, Reinsch sent Woodrow Wilson numerous telegrams
complaining that Washington did nothing for a people who allegedly
modeled their government after that of the United States.[15]

Understanding that the United States would not act anytime soon,
the foreign ministry established a commission, of which Koo was a member, to analyze how to resolve the Shandong Question. The government
believed that China needed to attend the future peace conference sure to
be held once hostilities in Europe ceased. China had to have a seat and a
say at such a conference and not allow Qingdao's fate be determined by
others. With their knowledge of international law and diplomatic history, the Chinese outlined several strategies for making sure that neutral
China obtained a seat, and if not, made its voice heard. They feared not
only injustice, but also that the powers would obstruct China's efforts to
participate in the peace process.[16]

While in the midst of preparing for the future conference, Japan
dealt China another blow. With the shift in the balance of power in Japan's
favor, Tokyo took advantage of its hold on parts of Shandong Province
and the political vacuum in East Asia to assert its power over China. On
January 18, 1915, Japan presented China with the infamous Twenty-One
Demands. The demands required China not only to agree to allow Japan
and Germany to determine the final disposition of the former German
leasehold in Shandong, but to concede more rights in Manchuria. The
harshest demands, Group V, sought to turn China into a Japanese protectorate. Japan told Yuan that China had to accept the demands if better
relations were to exist between the two countries. If China did not agree
to the demands, Japan would back Chinese revolutionaries interested in
Yuan's overthrow.[17]

Koo and the rest of Yuan Shikai's advisors suggested stalling in negotiations and leaking the existence of the demands and details of the
negotiations in the hope that the powers would act in concert to restrain
Japan. If stalling and the leaks failed, war with Japan was preferable to
becoming a colony. War was not an option for Yuan Shikai. Years later,
Koo recalled that Yuan was not surprised by Japan's actions because the

other powers were preoccupied in Europe.[18] Yuan believed that Japan would be seen as a threat to the Open Door in China, and hoped that the United States would put pressure on the Japanese. Meanwhile, Yuan had his negotiators stall for time while waiting for favorable reactions from abroad.

Negotiations commenced and the Japanese demanded secrecy. Yuan originally picked Koo to be one of the Chinese negotiators, but the Japanese diplomats, for reasons unexplained, rejected his presence. Nevertheless, Koo played a vital role during the negotiations. Koo believed that Washington needed to be made aware of the demands as did Great Britain with its economic interests in the Yangzi River valley. He made frequent visits to the American and British legations, and leaked information to Western news agencies, much to the irritation of the Japanese.[19] And to a certain extent, the publicity worked. The Americans and the British alike initially treated the rumors of Group V as exaggerated. As knowledge of the demands slowly reached Washington, the White House grew so concerned that President Wilson issued a note on March 13 that upheld the principle of the Open Door. Unwilling to confront Japan, Wilson refused to go further. Britain issued a note of its own, but the British preferred to preserve the Anglo-Japanese Alliance rather than having a showdown with its ally at a moment when it fought for survival in Europe.[20] Even so, the notes issued by the British and Americans were effective in convincing the Japanese to drop Group V.

To everyone's surprise, though, Japan issued an ultimatum to the Beijing government to accept the amended demands, less Group V, by May 9 or face war. The United States urged both sides to continue negotiations and not resort to war. The British, on the other hand, advised the Chinese to acquiesce in order to keep the peace. Yuan's generals leaned toward war with Japan, but Yuan and the rest of his cabinet opposed conflict because China was too weak militarily to resist. He could expect no more than protests from the United States and advice from Britain. On May 25, Yuan acceded to the demands, except Group V, which were to be negotiated later.[21]

Koo wrote the Chinese reply to the Japanese ultimatum. The reply was a crucial document in that Koo looked to the future peace conference to right this wrong. In his reply to the Japanese ultimatum, Koo made it clear that China had been "constrained to comply with the full terms of the Ultimatum." This statement was critical because at the Paris Peace Conference, Koo argued time and again that China was forced by threat of arms to sign this treaty with Japan. Koo hoped to create a legal loophole by which he could argue for the return of Qingdao to China. His reply also stated that the Chinese "disclaim any desire to associate themselves with any revision" of past agreements between the powers to protect China's territorial integrity and maintain the "principle of equal opportunity for the commerce and industry of all nations in China."[22] In this respect, Koo clearly wanted to drive a wedge between Japan and the Western powers by convincing the West that Japan, not China, was a revisionist country and threatened Western order in Asia.

Realistically speaking, though, Koo's reply did not change the situation on the ground. The Japanese threat remained in place. For the Chinese people, the treaty was another national humiliation, and many blamed Yuan. Eugene Chen, editor of a local Chinese newspaper, told one foreigner that "the only man" in the "rotten" foreign ministry was V.K. Wellington Koo. From Yuan Shikai's point of view, he succeeded in avoiding war with Japan. As for the powers, the British were pleased that war had been averted, and that the Anglo-Japanese Alliance remained intact. The United States issued its reservation and refused, much to Japan's chagrin, to recognize the agreement because, in American eyes, it undermined the Open Door principles. Such statements sowed seeds of suspicion and rivalry in U.S.-Japanese relations, but not enough to lead to a break in relations.[23] Otherwise, Japan still occupied Qingdao and other areas of Shandong. The distant peace conference remained a faint hope at best. China did not have the political and military power to fight either for Shandong's liberation or to lure allies against Japan. Discovering some other approach was necessary if China was to roll back Japanese expansion.

Yuan's fear of Japan did not diminish after May, but rather was enhanced. China stood on the brink of destruction from forces within and without. The best solution in his mind was to establish a monarchy. Yuan considered a monarchy to be superior to a republic. Just months after becoming president, his U.S.-educated secretary, Admiral Cai Tinggan, told an American engineer that a "limited monarchy would be better than a Republic of China," and confidently predicted that China would have a military dictatorship. In the three years that Koo served Yuan Shikai, Yuan showed little respect for the institution of the presidency to which he swore an oath, the Provisional Constitution of 1912, or the power of China's Parliament. After the Twenty-One Demands episode, Yuan observed that since China was a republic and Japan a monarchy, there was "no meeting of the minds." Monarchy in China could improve Sino-Japanese relations. Yuan also made it known to his Chinese and foreign associates that he favored restoring the monarchy in order to unify the country and be in a position to be better able to "enforce his will" on a people who did not understand the meaning of "president."[24]

If the monarchy was to return to China, Yuan needed the support of Chinese officialdom and the foreign powers. And the man selected in August 1915 to sell Yuan's decision to the United States was V.K. Wellington Koo. Yuan held Koo in high regard. While complaining to George Morrison, an Australian political advisor, that China had few men "of character, knowledge and judgment," Yuan remarked that "of all the foreign trained students, he had met only two who had acquired knowledge and the ability to apply it," one of whom was Wellington Koo. But foremost in Yuan's mind was the fact that Koo had been a loyal servant. Despite Yuan's trashing of republicanism, Koo, who had rhetorically supported a republic over a monarchy and wore the symbols of the republic, such as a short haircut and Western clothing, said nothing nor did he resign in opposition. Then there was the fact that Koo spoke excellent English, was U.S.-educated, and knew many important people in the U.S., including Woodrow Wilson.[25]

On August 5, 1915, Koo left China for Washington, and officially became Chinese minister on October 25. His salary was $1,800 per month with an entertainment allowance of $2,400. Koo's primary task was to persuade Americans that China's first republic had no choice but to return to the monarchical form of government. Koo's mission was to lay a public relations groundwork in the United States in preparation for Yuan's assumption of the throne as well as to gauge public opinion. Whether Koo had any qualms about the monarchical movement is unclear. He may have agreed with his former professor, Frank Goodnow, who argued that China's historical and cultural heritage, as well as its present political, economic and social condition, militated against the viability of a republican form of government for China. Goodnow pointed to Portugal, Mexico and other countries as lessons in the failure of republicanism. Indeed, Koo first received his appointment as Chinese minister to Mexico, and the British minister explained that Koo's mission was to obtain "unfavourable reports of the working of Republican institutions in that country, which may prove useful in promoting the . . . re-establishment of Monarchical Government in China." Whatever Koo's thoughts about the Monarchical Movement, Koo feared a backlash against Yuan's desire to be emperor, and admitted to Paul Reinsch that Yuan himself was dubious of success.[26]

Selling the monarchical movement to the United States proved to be no easy task. The powers opposed Yuan's scheme, fearing that it would create instability in China. The U.S. State Department agreed that Yuan's ascension to the throne would lead to insurrection. President Wilson preferred a postponement, but felt that China's change in form of government was a Chinese domestic question and that to make protests was an infringement of Chinese sovereignty. Yuan agreed to delay his plans but tried to throw his lot in with the allies and declare war on Germany. He now saw that China's entrance into the war would be advantageous in many respects: China could end its unequal treaties with Germany and Austria, profit from arms sales to the allies, and have a voice at the peace conference, assuming the allies were victorious. The Western powers were supportive, but Japan nixed the proposal on the grounds that China's participation in the conflict would only undermine peace and stability in China.[27]

In the meantime, the monarchical movement was still on. Ignoring his doubts about the movement's chances, Koo used his rhetorical skills to persuade Americans to welcome the retreat from republicanism. In January 1916, Koo told the *American Academy of Political and Social Science* that his people fully supported Yuan Shikai's move to become emperor, though he failed to point out that there were now signs of opposition. He told his audience that the Chinese only wanted to "be let alone and given a free hand to work out their country's destiny, unharassed by fear of aggression from the strong, and assured of a just and equitable treatment in the hands of all." In another speech, Koo declared that China faced the same problems that confronted the infant United States of 130 years before. Just as there was disunity among the thirteen states, China consisted of twenty-two provinces including Tibet, Mongolia, and territory in Central Asia, which were roughly divided into north and south. Unifying the country "required the foresight and wisdom of a veteran statesman to . . . save the country from disintegration." Comparing Yuan Shikai to George Washington, Koo remarked that the people wanted and needed peace "to put the country in order and adjust her financial system, her national defense, her industries, her educational system, her communications, her commerce, her laws, to the requirements of modern conditions."[28]

Koo's rhetoric proved to be for naught. By spring 1916, Yuan Shikai was dead, and Koo was soon diplomatic representative to a government torn by civil war. Yuan's death ushered in what has become known as the warlord era in which military governors who competed for territory and revenue ruled China. The warlord era was marked by instability in China due to intensive fighting between warlord factions or cliques who competed for control of northern China while several weak warlords, as well as Sun Yat-sen, remained in the south. One particular objective of the northern warlords was the control of Beijing. The warlord who dominated Beijing not only received the prestige of foreign diplomatic recognition and legitimacy, but also the right to use the revenue acquired through the Maritime Customs Administration, all of which could be used to strengthen his power vis-à-vis the other warlords. In this respect, diplomats like Koo were indispensable because they had the training and skills necessary to deal with the powers on behalf of whatever warlord happened to be in power.[29]

Whatever faction that controlled Beijing found itself, by will or circumstances beyond its control, embroiled in imperialist rivalry. There was imperial competition not only in the realm of finance, but warlord regimes in the last years of the European War stood by helplessly as the powers determined China's fate by way of secret agreements. In 1916, Japan made a series of political maneuvers throughout the year to ensure its hold on Qingdao and its other interests on the continent. The Japanese were not about to break with their allies, but engaged in conversations in order to send a message to Britain that Japan's importance

in Asia should not be taken for granted. Not only were there rumors of
German-Japanese negotiations in which Germany and Japan were supposedly planning to divide China amongst themselves into spheres of
influence, but Russia and Japan agreed to recognize their respective rights
and privileges in the Far East, particularly in Manchuria and Mongolia.
Although the alliance accomplished little for Japan, particularly after the
March 1917 revolution overthrew the tsar, those Japanese officials who
supported the treaty believed the agreement increased Japan's power in
Manchuria.[30]

More obvious was Japan's financial dominance over China. The
warlord in charge was Duan Qirui, and government finances were in a
desperate state. Naturally, Beijing's desire to secure loans wherever possible led to a great deal of rivalry between the powers who wanted their
bankers to get a share of the market. Duan, however, looked to Japan.
The new government that came to power in Tokyo in October 1916 was
willing to make loans to China because it had embarked on a friendlier
policy toward China. The new leadership intended to protect its interests in Manchuria, Inner Mongolia, and Fujian, but took a different approach from that of the previous government that presented the
Twenty-One Demands. Between 1916 and 1918, Duan secured various
loans from Tokyo. Koo opposed borrowing money from Japan, believing that Japan would use China's dependency to acquire political capital
in China. He encouraged U.S. businessmen to invest in China and obtained a loan for $5 million from a Chicago bank, but it was impossible
for Koo to offset Japanese money with American money.[31]

In 1917, the international environment offered the Beijing government a window of opportunity to take steps toward improving China's
international status. In February, Germany announced the return to
unrestricted use of submarines against belligerent ships, including passenger liners. The Wilson administration severed diplomatic relations
with Germany and called on other neutral powers, including China, to
follow suit. Wilson insisted that neutrals had the right to sail on belligerent passenger liners. While Paul Reinsch tried to get Beijing to associate
itself with the United States, the Japanese, who previously opposed China's
entrance into the war, made an about-face. In January and February, the
allies secretly agreed to allow Japan to retain Qingdao after the war. Ja-

pan and its allies hoped that China would emulate the United States in breaking relations with Germany and become an ally by declaring war. The Beijing government demanded loans and a seat at the peace conference. On March 1, the allies accepted China's demands. Two days later, Beijing decided to break relations with Germany, and China's parliament made it official on March 14, 1917.[32]

Beijing however balked at declaring war. The cabinet was divided along two lines of policy: those opposed to declaring war and those in favor. Those leaning toward war included Duan Qirui who believed that the allies would eventually win the war, especially once the United States became a belligerent. Another motive involved the peace conference. These officials recognized that China had little voice, as long as it remained neutral. Opponents of war feared domestic rebellion as well as being crushed by Duan Qirui and his Japanese aid. There was a third road that simultaneously opposed joining the allies, but favored declaring war and aligning with the United States. American advisers to the Beijing government and nongovernment officials preferred this third road. V.K. Wellington Koo was also among their number.[33]

On April 2, 1917, Wilson went before Congress asking for a declaration of war against Germany in order for the United States to "make the world safe for democracy." The United States did not, however, enter the conflict as an ally, but as an "associate" in order to disassociate itself from the allies' imperialistic war aims. Wilson told Congress that the United States was fighting for not only democracy but for the "rights and liberties of small nations." On April 6, the United States officially declared war on Germany.[34]

Now that the United States was in the war and fighting for war aims that appealed to Koo, the Chinese diplomat believed that China should likewise become a participant in order to resolve the Shandong Question and raise China's international standing. However, he initially opposed joining the allies and wanted to come into the war on the side of the United States. Koo believed Japan planned to use the alliance to dominate China while Britain and France stood by. And with "Britain in Tibet, Russia in Mongolia, Japan in Shandong, Portugal in Macao," the only country that did not entertain some "dark scheme" against China was the United States. Koo argued in favor of aligning with the United

States because Washington would protect China's interests. As an ally of the Entente powers, China would sacrifice some of its rights. President Wilson declared that the United States entered the war in order to make a better world, and Koo believed that if China sided with America, it would reap many benefits. After the United States officially declared war, though, Koo concluded that Beijing had to declare war, be it as ally or associate, in order to get a seat at the peace conference.[35]

Internal Chinese disunity prevented Beijing from declaring war until August now that Sun Yat-sen established a separate government in Guangzhou. The instability in China led Washington to issue a note on June 4, much to the consternation of some of its "associates," declaring that stability in China was more important than China's entry into World War I. The allies ignored the note, and pressed for China's entrance into the war. Deeply disappointed by the civil war in China, Koo implored his government to bring about peace and unity in China. Otherwise, the powers would take further advantage of China's weakness.[36]

Tensions between Japan and the United States led both sides to talk over their differences. The rivalry between both countries as to who should lead China into World War I embittered the Japanese, who wanted U.S. recognition of Japan's paramount interests in China. Those talks resulted in the Lansing-Ishii Agreement in which the United States recognized Japan's special interests in China especially in Manchuria. In return, the Japanese agreed to adhere to the Open Door principles. A secret provision attached to the agreement committed both sides to not use World War I to make gains in China at the other's expense. The Lansing-Ishii Agreement disappointed Koo because it looked as if China was Japan's sphere just as Central and South America were spheres of the United States. When Koo expressed his government's reservations, Secretary of State Robert Lansing bluntly told Koo that the "time had passed when China could play off the United States against Japan." In response, Koo issued a memorandum to Washington that his government refused "to be bound by any agreement entered into by other nations."[37]

In 1918, Koo's government selected him to be a delegate to the Paris Peace Conference even though Germany had not yet been defeated. Preparing for the conference was not easy because there was much to distract him. In less than two years, he suffered the loss of two people very dear to him. The first was his father who passed away in the summer of 1917. Then in October 1918, May Tang unexpectedly died, one of the many thousands of victims of the flu epidemic. "Mrs. Koo was ill only one week," Koo explained to John Bassett Moore, "and her death was so sudden that even now I cannot fully convince myself that she has left me forever." He added: "She was such a devoted companion and helper to me in all my work and leisure that I now feel everything is different without her."[38]

Despite these personal losses, Koo had to get on with the business at hand. One measure of preparation taken was publicity. Koo and Thomas Millard, the American founder and editor of the English-language paper, *Millard's Review*, worked together to create an Information Bureau that would be attached to the Chinese delegation. Another man associated with the Bureau was Hollington Tong, a University of Missouri graduate who became a friend of Koo's when Tong worked on the staff of the *New York Times* and the *New York Evening Post*. Essentially, the Bureau was a propaganda organ that would attempt to win world opinion to China's cause. Koo advocated a propaganda policy in order to drive a wedge between the powers, primarily Britain and the United States, and Japan, and he continued to pursue such a policy at Paris.[39]

More importantly, Beijing wanted to revise the imperialist system. As a member of the delegation, Koo likewise thought it was time that China aired "her grievances internationally at the coming peace conference in order to win back some of her lost rights." The Chinese patriotic program first pursued the elimination of the foreign concessions. By 1917, there were ninety-two treaty ports, with sixteen having foreign settlements. Koo viewed the international concessions and settlements as antiquated and an unnecessary "infraction upon the territorial integrity of China." The leased territories "served to create a balance of power in China, but a balance of power not between China and other Governments but between different Governments who had interests in China." Koo believed that abrogation of those territories and elimination of the spheres of influence would maintain that balance of power while restoring China's political integrity. Along with the foreign concessions, extraterritoriality had to go too because it, likewise, was "a hindrance to the free and full development of China." Finally, China needed to have full control of its tariff if it was to raise the necessary revenue to govern a state whose burgeoning population drained national resources.[40]

In Koo's opinion, the foreign concessions, extraterritoriality, and lack of tariff autonomy prevented China from industrializing. China possessed no investment capital and was forced to borrow money from foreign banks on "harsh terms." The low tariff prevented development. And foreign manufacturers, who established factories in the foreign concessions, were able to prosper because they were "beyond the taxing power and regulatory power of the Chinese government." Chinese factories could not compete with the predominantly British and Japanese manufacturers in China.[41] Since this was China's program, Koo spent much of his time searching international law for precedents that would strengthen his case.

With regard to Qingdao, Koo understood the limitations of international law. The Japanese could claim Qingdao as a right of conquest. If diplomacy failed to secure the return of the territory, Koo had another option: Woodrow Wilson. As a student at Columbia, Koo met Wilson when the latter went there to present lectures on government and administration and even had the opportunity to join Wilson for dinner, where the future president plied Koo with questions "about China and the possible political development of the Chinese people." In his tenure as president, Wilson presented himself to the world as an anti-imperialist and antimilitarist. In his China policy, he had broken away from the consortium, unilaterally recognized China, and unilaterally issued denunciations of Japan. Like other educated Chinese enamored to the man, Koo held Wilson in a certain reverence.[42]

The extent to which Koo looked to Wilson for help at Paris was revealed in 1918. On January 8, Wilson put forth his famous Fourteen Points before Congress, and called for, among other things, open treaties and open diplomacy; arms reduction; and a free, open-minded, and absolutely impartial adjustment of all colonial claims in which questions of sovereignty are determined by the interests of the populations concerned. Many of the ideas laid down in the speech were not new to Wilson and had been espoused by internationalists and Wilson for some time. Events in Russia forced Wilson to restate American war aims. The previous year, Vladamir Lenin and the Bolsheviks succeeded in overthrowing the Provisional Government in Russia that came to power earlier in March and eventually got Russia out of the war with Germany. Within weeks after the Bolshevik Revolution, Leon Trotsky, the Commissar for Foreign Relations, published the treaties signed between Tsarist Russia and its allies, which proved the allies were just as imperialistic in their war aims as the Germans were. Publication of those treaties was part and parcel of Trotsky's "New Diplomacy," which opposed the old, secret diplomacy in an effort to foment revolution abroad. The Bolsheviks demanded to know to what democratic and liberal end the allies were fighting to convince Russia to stay in the war. Wilson laid down his Fourteen Points to answer this challenge as well as rally people at home and abroad behind war aims that sought to create a better world and sow dissension between Germany and Austria-Hungary by offering peace terms to both.[43]

One other aspect of Wilson's Fourteen Points that held out hope to Koo was Wilson's desire to create a league of nations to provide mutual guarantees of political independence and territorial integrity to great and small states alike. One can speculate that Koo viewed the organization as giving China prestige, a voice in world affairs, and security, especially if it was a "Wilsonian" league. In telegrams to Beijing, Koo differentiated between the Americans and the other powers by pointing to Wilson's commitment to establishing a league, the existence of which he asserted was opposed by other powers. Koo understood too that international law needed to undergo some sort of transformation so that small and weak nations coexisted with the great powers with a relative sense of peace and security. Like some internationalists, he leaned toward the "league" concept or something that could improve on international law.[44]

Overall, Wilson's Fourteen Points were a statement of Wilson's anti-imperialism. This explains why Koo later referred to the Fourteen Points as "a ray of hope for the oppressed nations in Asia." In fact, when Wilson gave the speech, he did not have Asia, Africa, or Latin America on his mind. Wilson's words were directed at Europe, where boundaries would be redrawn and new nation-states created. His anti-imperialism amounted to merely stopping the imperialism of Europeans against Europeans. Although Korean, Indian, Vietnamese and Chinese nationalists fighting colonialism or semicolonialism took his words to heart, Wilson had no intention of freeing Asians from the throes of imperialism.

This fact did not stop Wilson from assuring Koo of his support for China. Before traveling to Europe, the American president told Koo "that there would be nothing for China to fear from the discussions at this conference." Wilson admitted that it would not be easy to apply his principles to the Far East, but declared "that mere difficulty was no good reason for not applying them there." But at Paris, Wilson justified his stance to not deny Japan's claim to Qingdao, because he could not see how the Fourteen Points applied. Hence, Koo made the mistake of arguing for the return of Qingdao on the basis of Wilson's Fourteen Points. Given the circumstances of Japan's strong legal case and the collusion between Japan and the allies, Koo had little choice. Wilson offered to transcend the old rules and old diplomacy and create new rules and a new diplomacy that would give China justice. With his government powerless to drive Japan out and given his opposition to collaboration with Tokyo, Koo went to Paris hopeful that Wilson's Fourteen Points would fulfill his patriotic aspirations. He sowed the seeds of his own failure when he cabled the foreign ministry that China "could count upon American support alone" at the conference.[45]

On November 9, 1918, a civilian government forced the military leadership of Germany from power by seeking an armistice on the basis of Wilson's Fourteen Points. Two days later, an armistice was reached. The next month, Wilson announced the controversial decision of going to Paris as head of the American delegation. There was no tradition of American presidents traveling abroad to attend peace conferences, but Wilson insisted that he had to be in Paris to ensure the success of his foreign policy and the fulfillment of his Fourteen Points. Wilson's decision gave Koo a decided advantage, because the man in whom he placed so much hope would be there to assist in the struggle to recover Qingdao. At this point, no one foresaw disaster in 1919, most of all Wellington Koo. He assumed that Wilson would remain committed to his own principles and would persuade the other powers to embrace a peace based on the Fourteen Points. Egging Koo on in maintaining such illusions were members of the American delegation, who reiterated that China should trust America.[46]

After the Chinese delegation assembled in Paris, everything began to go wrong. Initially, the conference allotted China's delegates five seats only to reduce them to two on the grounds that China's contribution to WWI was minimal. Lu Zhengxiang headed the delegation followed by C.T. Wang, a Yale-educated GMD politician who sat on the delegation as representative of Sun Yat-sen's government. Although Koo was junior to Alfred Sze, Koo insisted that he be the number three man because of his close ties with Wilson and the U.S. delegation. Koo also looked down his nose at Wang because he claimed that Wang was a diplomat, not because he had acquired "at least a basic knowledge of international law and diplomatic history," but only because he could speak English and possessed an academic degree from abroad. C.T. Wang and Alfred Sze increasingly opposed Lu Zhengxiang's leadership, whereas Koo supported Lu with the result that there was much competition for leadership of the Chinese delegation.[47]

Besides the friction within the Chinese delegation, there were obstacles to China's pursuit of a patriotic agenda. One problem for the Chinese delegation was that the Asian questions arising out of the war were peripheral to the major questions to be discussed at the conference: Germany, Austria-Hungary, the Ottoman Empire, Poland, Czechoslovakia, and other issues. There was the question of what kind of league to establish, an issue on which the powers were not agreed, and what kind of covenant would govern this league. The allies were not fond of Wilson's Fourteen Points nor his league. And the conference operated in an atmosphere of fear because the Bolsheviks provided an ideological challenge and threat to Europe and Asia in calling on the peacemakers to seek a peace without territorial aggrandizement and in spreading revolution to a discontented Europe. The allies and their associates intervened in the civil war by sending forces and various aid to Russia. They hoped the White Russians would crush the Bolsheviks.[48]

More importantly, Koo's own government completely gutted his legal case. Duan Qirui needed Japanese arms and money if he were to carry out his policy of reuniting the country by force, and he signed a series of loans with Japan on September 28, 1918. They included an exchange of notes that said the Chinese government "gladly agreed" to permit Japan to station troops in Shandong to protect the Jiaoji Railway.

Although the government made extensive preparations to argue for the return of the old German leasehold, Duan told the cabinet that the Chinese delegation should limit itself to revising the unequal treaties. With regard to the Shandong Question, Duan argued that China should trust Japan, which promised to return the territory, and hinted that China should not challenge Japan's claim to Jiaozhou Bay and Qingdao until the government understood Japan's intentions. Supporting Duan's position was Cao Rulin, the Japanese-educated official who believed in Sino-Japanese cooperation and who was responsible for negotiating the loans that benefited Duan Qirui. As Lu Zhengxiang traveled to Paris, he stopped in Japan where he reached an agreement that China would support Japan's claim to Qingdao in return for Japanese support of China's patriotic program of revising the unequal treaty system. In Paris, Lu informed them of the September 28 treaty, but he could not divulge the treaty articles to them. According to George Morrison, the Chinese delegation's unofficial foreign advisor, a box containing treaties and other documents relevant to China's case turned up missing, possibly stolen.[49]

Koo had no inkling of the events that had occurred, and if he had, he would have opposed the policy because he distrusted Japan too much to consider cooperation with the Japanese. A member of the foreign ministry suggested to Koo that China not participate in the peace conference in order that "Japan may not claim to represent our interests" at the conference, but instead seek a Far Eastern conference separate from the upcoming Paris conference. Koo adamantly opposed the idea. Chinese nonparticipation at the Paris conference might be viewed as willingness to let the powers settle questions related to China "without our voice." Koo also believed that a special Far Eastern conference "may lead to international tutelage like Turkey" and, more importantly, "actualize [Japan's] hegemony in Asia." After Lu informed the delegation of recent events, Koo argued that now was the time for China to press its case for Qingdao, because the conference dealt with problems arising out of the war. Otherwise, China would not be able to reclaim her territorial sovereignty.[50]

In late January, the conference took up the issue of Germany's colonies. The Japanese delegation presented its claims to Germany's former leased territory in Shandong on the basis of right of conquest. Before

Japan could return the territory to China, Tokyo had to reach an agreement with Germany, transferring Germany's rights to Japan. Possessed with the knowledge that Lu Zhengxiang did not intend to demand the return of Qingdao, Koo took matters in his own hands. He became, in the words of George Morrison, the "most aggressive member of the Delegation." After the Japanese delegates made their claim to Germany's former concession in Shandong, the Chinese delegation asked for, and received, permission to present their case prior to the conference making a decision. Woodrow Wilson, who was "surprised and angry" at Japan's claim to inherit Germany's rights in Shandong, assured the Chinese of his desire to help and advised Koo of the necessity of putting forth China's case as succinctly as the Japanese had done. In the meantime, Lu Zhengxiang asked Beijing for permission to bring the 1918 treaty before the conference as a way of appealing to public opinion and possibly having the treaty made null and void by the conference.[51]

The following day, Koo presented China's case for recovering its territory. Unaware of the September treaty's articles, Koo argued that the 1915 treaty should not be binding since Japan forced China to sign. Then speaking for China's "400 millions," Koo referred to Shandong as the "cradle of civilisation, the birthplace of Confucius and Mencius, and a Holy Land for the Chinese." Koo added that, "China had a right to the restoration of these territories." In an exchange with Baron Makino, the Japanese delegate, Koo called for direct restitution of Qingdao on the basis of *rebus sic stantibus*, a notion in international law that treaties could be revised or eliminated because the conditions in which they were written had changed. Koo argued that China's entry into the war "had in itself put an end to the leases obtained by Germany in Chinese territory."[52]

It was the greatest speech of his career, presented in what one American described as "perfect English, and in a cool, lucid and logical argument which carried the members of the Council right along with him." One member in particular who "sympathized with the Chinese point of view" was Woodrow Wilson, who was annoyed by his fellow peacemakers. He described himself as in the minority in regard to "captured colonies," because the "majority of the delegates wanted to 'divide the swag,' and then have the League of Nations created to perpetuate their title."

Koo's speech forced the Japanese delegates to admit that Japan had a treaty with China and led Wilson to ask Japan to make the treaty public. Wilson also made promises he could not fulfill. Wilson assured the president of China, "that in all circumstances you can count upon the good will of the United States and the interests of her Government in the independence, safety, and prosperity of China." In the days following Koo's speech, euphoria and optimism abounded "that China would win her case at the Conference," but that euphoria was based largely on the assurances made by the U.S. delegation.[53]

Fortunately for Koo, the speech was well received in China, where the Beijing government only admonished the delegation against being overzealous. Koo's actions infuriated the Japanese, who thought they had reached a deal with Beijing to not contest Japan's claim to Qingdao. Koo met with Wilson and pleaded for assistance, because Japan was no doubt incensed by his presentation. And he warned Robert Lansing as well that he "greatly feared the Japanese would attempt to intimidate the Beijing Government, and persuade that Government to disown [his] representation here." Koo was right: Japan threatened military intervention and to make Shandong a permanent part of the Japanese empire.[54]

Another negative consequence of being the "man on the spot" was that the other Chinese delegates were either resentful of Koo's close relationship with the Americans or simply jealous of Koo's instant stardom. C.T. Wang and Alfred Sze were furious with Koo, who they believed was running the delegation. Sze threatened to resign if he continued to be pushed aside. Some in the Chinese delegation distrusted Koo because he relied so heavily on Wilson. In an effort to impugn Koo's character, C.T. Wang told the delegation that Koo intended to marry Cao Rulin's daughter, suggesting that Koo would represent the pro-Japanese elements in Beijing.[55] For his part, Koo believed Wilson afforded China a wonderful opportunity to resolve the Shandong Question even though the British and French warned the delegation that they had treaties with Japan. Koo did not believe Japan would simply hand Qingdao back without some kind of catch. Some have criticized Koo for not allowing Japan its claim to Qingdao in return for Japanese support of China's patriotic program. Yet the powers, least of all Japan, were not interested in treaty revision, so there was no real trade-off. One can fault Koo, though, for thinking that Wilson's popularity and prestige could overrule the interests of the allies. Through both the speech and relying on the Americans, Koo dug a hole for himself. And the Americans were the only ones around to keep the Japanese from burying him in it.[56]

For the next few weeks, the Shandong Question remained on the backburner. There was the question of what kind of league to create. Koo saw that it was in China's interest to express support for Wilson's league and use the Chinese press at home to rally Chinese public opinion behind the league. Wilson's league called for an Executive Council of five great powers and four small powers. The alternative was a league run by the great powers. Koo and the other small power representatives voiced support for Wilson's plan. Koo warned that a league based on only the great powers would "allow a gulf to grow" between the great and small because the latter would feel "they were outsiders . . . and not fully part and parcel of the League." Otherwise, the only time the small powers had any voice in the league would be when they were "either aggressive or victims of an aggressor." And if the great powers clashed while in executive session, the "Council would be deprived of the influence of world opinion and find it difficult to effect a settlement of the question." David Hunter Miller, coauthor of a plan that called for a league based on only great powers, commented that Koo "made one of the best speeches of the Commission" when he advocated small power representation. Ultimately, the small powers won their victory when a majority voted in favor of Wilson's plan.[57]

On the controversial issue of racial equality, Koo sided with the Japanese. In February, the Japanese asked for inclusion of a racial equality clause in the League of Nations Covenant. Initially, when the Japanese delegation asked the Chinese for their support, Koo was sympathetic "but felt that China had more important questions at stake and had to look out for them first." The British and Woodrow Wilson opposed the amendment, and the racial equality clause was not included in the covenant, though the Japanese delegates reserved the right to raise the issue later. In April, when they brought racial equality back to the table, a member of the Japanese delegation looked at Koo with an expression that persuaded the Chinese diplomat to stand up and support the clause. Although he felt that the many problems that revolved around the Japanese amendment would be solved in time, he declared that he was "very glad indeed to see the principle itself given recognition in the Covenant." Despite a majority vote in favor of the Japanese proposal, the British, backed by Wilson, killed the amendment.[58] Koo's support for the racial equality clause became a great controversy within the Chinese delegation later in the month when China was denied a place on the Council of Nine. Many of the Chinese delegates who agreed that it was necessary for China "to disassociate herself from Japan" blamed Koo. Alfred Sze and Eugene Chen claimed that Colonel House, Wilson's political advisor, was counting on China's support in defeating the racial clause. In return, the United States would back China's admission to the Council of Nine, but Koo did not "keep faith with America." There is no evidence that such a deal was made, and, as Morrison defended Koo in his diary, "How could [Koo] an Asiatic have done otherwise?"[59]

When the Shandong Question finally returned to the fore, the pendulum of support for China swung the other way. In the United States, numerous critics, including Senate leaders, assailed Wilson's proposed League of Nations. The allies, emboldened by Wilson's critics across the Atlantic, threatened to kill the league unless granted territorial annexations. The French and the Italians demanded the right to annex territory. When Wilson refused, the Italians walked out of the conference. They eventually returned, but a black cloud hung over the proceedings. Then it was Japan's turn. Japan needed to gain something from the conference, and since it had been denied the racial equality clause, Japan now had leverage to demand retention of Germany's former leased territory.[60]

Despite these potential setbacks, hope remained. On March 24, Wilson queried Koo as to Japan's real desire in Shandong. Koo replied that Japan not only wanted Qingdao, but also the railway in order to have a Japanese settlement in the area much like Britain's in Hong Kong. "If Japan was to have the railway and exclusive settlement in the best part of the leased territory," Koo went on, "it would mean the returning of the shadow to China, while leaving the substance to Japan." "[I]n other words," Wilson answered, "China would be getting back nearly the useless part of the leased area."[61]

Encouraged by Wilson's attitude toward the Shandong Question, Koo went to work on a memorandum that laid out China's claim to

Qingdao. Koo argued that the loss of Qingdao would *"jeopardize her po-litical independence, territorial integrity and economic welfare,"* (Wilson's emphasis) because it was *"the best harbor* on the coast of China." For this port and its railways to be controlled by a foreign power was "to place in its hands the most powerful weapons for securing trade domination and for jeopardizing the principle of equal opportunity for the commerce of all nations." Wilson's Fourteen Points negated the validity of the 1915 Sino-Japanese agreement and the secret treaties between Japan and the allies. Finally, direct restitution would have a "desirable effect" on Chinese public opinion because the Chinese people looked to the United States and the other powers for justice.[62] Koo limited his arguments to the 1915 treaty because he admitted to George Morrison that the September 1918 treaty, which he now possessed, was a "stumbling block." When Koo handed the memorandum over to Wilson, the American president, speaking "in a way that gave the Chinese face," again expressed his sympathy and spoke of the "friendship of the United States," adding that Lansing was working on a plan to solve the Shandong Question. The Chinese left Wilson's presence "uplifted."[63]

When the powers met, the Japanese rejected Wilson's proposal to make Qingdao a trusteeship of the League of Nations, and threatened to not join the League of Nations if denied their claim. Prime Minister Lloyd George of Britain tried to convince Japan to allow the former German concession to be made into a league mandate but Japan refused. Lloyd George sympathized with the Japanese position because the notion of internationalization could be applied to Britain's economic concessions in the Yangzi River valley. He also had little respect for China's war contribution. Since Britain had a secret agreement with Japan, Lloyd George intended to honor it, not wanting to undermine the Anglo-Japanese Alliance. The French followed Britain's lead and supported the Japanese claim. Wilson had no choice but to accede to Japan's wishes. The most he could achieve was Japan's promise to give political control to China while retaining economic rights.[64]

Wilson summoned Koo to his residence where he dropped the bombshell on China's hope to recover Qingdao. Wilson rejected China's claim, since Beijing had been "pleased to agree" to the September 28, 1918 agreement with Japan and in light of Wilson's view that China's

declaration of war did not cancel the 1915 agreement. Naturally disappointed, Koo pleaded for reconsideration on the grounds that the 1915
treaty "had been imposed upon China by Japan." And with Japan already in Manchuria, the Japanese presence in Shandong meant that
Beijing "would be—as it were—in a pincers." Wilson and Lloyd George
gave the Chinese two options: allow Japan to inherit Germany's rights or
accept the 1915 treaty with Japan. Koo retorted that "both alternatives
were unacceptable," but he chose the latter while still preferring direct
restitution to China. Koo warned that although his government believed
in the justice of the West, there were people in China who "believed in
Asia for the Asiatics and wanted the closest co-operation with Japan." He
feared that China "might be driven into the arms of Japan" if it did not
get justice. Annoyed by the remark, Wilson defended his action saying
there was no injustice and that the "sacredness of treaties had been one
of the motives of the war." Wilson apparently forgot or ignored that his
government refused to recognize the 1915 agreement. He conveniently
forgot his admission in private at the conference that a nation at any
time could denounce a treaty it was bound to. Wilson may have realized that to reject the 1915 agreement would allow the Chinese to demand revision of the unequal treaties that likewise were signed under
duress.[65]

Koo departed Wilson's residence downhearted. His whole strategy
of using Wilsonianism for China's advantage was in shambles. Only less
than two weeks before, Koo told a reporter that, "Our main hope is
American love of justice." Publicly, he did not fault Wilson, whom he
described as a "defender of China," but George Morrison told a member
of the American delegation that Koo and his compatriots blamed Wilson, since it was Wilson who insisted time and again that he was on
China's side and could be relied upon. Indeed, it was believed that Koo
was behind an anonymous manifesto released to the press that declared:
"China has been stabbed to the heart in the house of its friends." Despite
his anger, Koo refused to break from the Americans. He believed that
Italy's brief withdrawal from the conference made Wilson cautious toward Japan. And besides British and French support for Japan, a member of the American delegation informed Koo that Britain threatened to
not join the league if Japan did not.[66]

Koo knew that the decision, regardless of the causes behind it, was a reneging on Wilson's own principles. In light of their secret treaties, he understood why the British and French hesitated to support China, but he thought that Wilson's Fourteen Points "at least in spirit nullified those engagements." Koo acknowledged as well that the Europeans might not be inclined to give deference to the Fourteen Points. He told Colonel House if that was the case, "China's only hope lay with the United States." And the Chinese diplomat believed that "if President Wilson was disposed to insist on a just solution of this question, China would get her satisfaction." He warned House that failure to achieve a pro-Chinese solution on the Shandong Question would drive China to Japan. He added: "Such a feeling, which could not be conducive to the interests of the Occident in China, might require years to modify it when once rooted in the minds of the Chinese people."[67]

In a similar vein, Koo remarked to E.T. Williams, another American delegate, that China had taken a strong stand on the Shandong Question because it thought it could "rely on the firm support of the United States." Koo continued, "If China should again be left in the cold at the last moment," the episode "would serve to convince the Chinese people in general of the unwisdom of the Chinese policy on this question from the inception."[68] Without admitting as much, Koo's reputation was on the line. More than anyone else, he relied upon Wilson and the United States to resolve the Shandong Question in a manner favorable to China. And it was Koo who made statements to the press that gave people in China the hope that the United States would come to China's rescue and right the wrong done by Japan. If Wilson did not abide by the principles he espoused and which inspired Koo, the latter would come out looking the fool.

With those thoughts in mind, the Chinese reminded Wilson of the conflict between the secret agreements reached between Japan and its European allies and his Fourteen Points. The delegation suggested four solutions: the surrender of Germany's rights in Shandong to the powers who in turn would restore them to China; Japan's agreement to restore those rights one year after signing the Versailles Peace Treaty; China's compensation of Japan's military expenses incurred during its attack on Qingdao; China making Jiaozhou Bay a free, commercial port. The Chinese delegation also called on the powers to abrogate the 1915 treaty. Wilson refused to consider the options because he could not suffer Japan's defection from the league.[69]

Wilson's refusal left the Chinese delegation so depressed that serious thought was given to withdrawing from the conference. Otherwise, the delegates had only two choices: sign the treaty with reservations or not sign at all. Complicating the matter was the May Fourth Movement in China in which educated Chinese were, as Koo warned Wilson, venting their indignation against the powers' decision. Thousands of students gathered at Tiananmen (Gate of Heavenly Peace) and Beijing University, shouting "Return Qingdao." Soon, Chinese merchants and workers joined in. Those government officials responsible for the 1918 agreement were physically attacked. Chinese students in Paris were so outraged that members of the American delegation received death threats and there was fear that Wilson's life might be in danger. Fearful himself, Koo told Colonel House that if forced to sign the treaty by his government, "I shall not have what you in New York call a Chinaman's chance. . . . It would be my death sentence."[70] Asking Beijing for a quick decision to sign or not, Koo told the government that if China did not sign, he feared the powers' wrath for undermining the alliance. If China signed with reservations, there was no guarantee the reservations would be included in the treaty. Koo viewed the moment as not propitious to China, saying that Britain, Japan, and France all sought to expand their spheres of influence in China.[71]

While the Beijing government mulled its options, Koo approached Wilson with the idea that China be permitted to sign with reservations. Koo explained that his people were disappointed and there was a consensus that China should not sign the treaty. On the other hand, his government did not want to damage the alliance and preferred to sign with reservations. The Chinese delegation would "make a protest in order to satisfy public opinion in China" with a view toward revising the Shandong articles later.[72] Wilson opposed the reservations on the grounds that the U.S. Senate would add its own reservations to the treaty before ratification. Koo recalled later that probably Wilson felt that granting the Chinese delegation the right to enclose a reservation in the treaty would open a can of worms. Other delegations might be moved to do the same with respect to their grievances, such as the Italians who wanted and were denied territory. The powers agreed that China could not sign with reservations, and that China could protest only after the signing. Koo rejected these terms, saying that China had no choice but to withdraw from the conference and should not be held responsible for the consequences.[73]

Although the Beijing government wanted the delegates to sign the treaty, reservation or not, students, intellectuals, merchants, and urban workers, who were angered by the government's attempt to quell anti-government demonstrations, besieged the government. The warlords and politicians agreed that China should not sign, and under pressure, the government eventually ordered its delegates to abstain from signing the treaty. Years later, Koo remembered walking through the deserted streets of Paris thinking that day "must remain in the history of China as the day of sorrow." For Koo, the conference was an almost complete failure. In China, he was a national hero, but that was little comfort for a man who had put his hope in Wilson.[74]

There was a significant difference between Koo's reaction to the Versailles Treaty and that of other Chinese patriots. Koo was partly right about the impact of the powers' decision on China. Many Chinese students in America who had previously looked to the United States as China's friend became disenchanted. Instead of looking to the West, the Chinese were urged to solve their problems themselves and not rely on others. People like Mao Zedong and Chen Duxiu, future founders of the Chinese Communist Party, were thoroughly disillusioned with the West and soon looked to Soviet Russia, which won praise from Chinese organizations for renouncing the unequal treaties. Sun Yat-sen wanted another political revolution. Those leaning toward communism wanted a social revolution.[75]

Koo rejected revolution in favor of cooperation with the powers. Indeed, if the powers had agreed to allow the reservation, Koo would have signed the treaty even though the people back home decried such an action. Unfortunately, the powers brought about what Koo described as a "turning point in China's history." Years later, Koo remarked that Chinese history might have been different if Qingdao had been handed back to China.[76] Without saying so, he thought the revolutions that followed in Chinese history and the Sino-Japanese conflict of the 1930s might have been forestalled. None of those events, however, were foreseeable in 1919. At the moment, Koo would not advocate revolution, or what became known as Boxerism, in which the foreigners were kicked out of China. Either would only worsen the situation by inviting more imperialist intervention and maybe more unequal treaties. The only alternative in Koo's mind was diplomacy and collaboration with the imperialists to eliminate the unequal treaties and secure Shandong, but this approach increasingly grew untenable, as Koo now had to face Chinese nationalism.

Chapter 3

CHINESE NATIONALISM
AND TREATY REVISION, 1921–1928

IN 1920, BEIJING APPOINTED KOO to be Chinese minister to Britain. Koo found that "the contrast between London and Washington, the set-up of the diplomatic corps and diplomatic procedure as well as social customs and life in general, was quite noticeable." For their part, the British really knew little about Koo. The British minister to Washington described him as "well liked socially. . . . He is cultured, and has great charm of manner." In February 1921, when Koo presented himself to the King of England, Sir Miles Lampson wrote, "His views are distinctly progressive and he is considered a typical representative of 'Young China.'" After several months of giving speeches and getting involved in British social circles, however, an American living in London observed that the British were "inclined to look down their noses a little bit at him" especially because of the "new Mrs. Koo." The year he went to Britain, Koo married Oei Hui-Lan, recently divorced daughter of a rich "sugar-king" in Java, and the gossip in England and the United States hurt Koo's image. The British Foreign Office also did not like Koo's portrayal of China: "Since his arrival in England he has done much 'window dressing,' and loses no opportunity of misleading public opinion, in the interests of his country, as to the true state of affairs in China."[1]

The "true state of affairs" was that Koo represented a government that did not possess complete control over China's provinces. Duan Qirui's warlord clique only fully controlled eight provinces and half of

V.K. Wellington Koo, 1921 (Photo courtesy of Library of Congress)

two others, including Zhili, wherein Beijing was located. After the Paris
Peace Conference, other warlords, infuriated by Duan's close relations with
Japan and China's failure at Paris, demanded not only the renewal of peace
talks between North and South but the reduction of Duan's military. When
Duan refused, war broke out in July 1920. Eventually, a warlord coalition

defeated Duan and controlled all of northeast China and eight other provinces. The rest of China's provinces were controlled by a mixed assortment of warlords and Sun Yat-sen's Guangzhou government.[2]

Despite China's disunity, Koo and his government faced increasing pressure back home to recover Chinese territory controlled by the imperialists and to revise the unequal treaty system. Chinese hopes had been raised before the conference only to be dashed. The Chinese people wanted to see the perceived injustice done at Paris undone. They wanted Qingdao recovered, but they adamantly opposed direct negotiations between their government and Japan. The September 1918 treaties, which undermined Koo's efforts at Paris, left a bad taste for most Chinese who refused to countenance more secret deals. Under such circumstances, the League of Nations was one option. But the United States did not ratify the Versailles Treaty and never joined the league. And since the great powers dominated the league, Koo did not expect China to get a fair hearing regarding Qingdao.

The other demand made on the government regarded the unequal treaties. The unequal treaties were a great symbol of humiliation and weakness for a proud people; they were likewise a great yoke that held China down, preventing it from progressing and achieving the greatness that it enjoyed less than two hundred years before. Japan emerged as a great power, freed itself from the unequal treaties, and joined the "family of nations." If only China could break the chains of bondage, it too could follow the path pioneered by Japan. As much as any Chinese, Koo wanted to make China a free and independent country, and tried to get the powers to agree to *revise*, not eliminate, the treaties. When Chinese proposals were submitted to the Paris Peace Conference, they were ignored by the powers that possessed neither the time nor the will to revise the imperialist system. Nevertheless, China made some progress in treaty revision. In May 1921, Germany repudiated "all its special rights, interests and privileges," and forewent the Boxer Indemnity.[3] Similar treaties were signed with Hungary and Turkey.

With those gains came demands for more, and potentially there was hope that another power would agree to revise its unequal treaties with China.[4] News of the Bolshevik Revolution of 1917 and the subsequent civil war reached China, but reports on the revolution and Lenin were sketchy if not confusing. Two announcements that came out of Bolshevik Russia sparked Chinese interest. In the summer of 1919, seeing the Chinese anger toward Japan and the West and hoping to see revolution go to China, the Bolsheviks issued the first Karakhan Manifesto. In return for diplomatic relations, Bolshevik Russia promised the Chinese everything they had sought at Paris: abolition of extraterritoriality, the unequal treaties, and the Boxer Indemnity, as well as the return of Russia's territorial concessions. The Bolsheviks also agreed to return the CER, the stretch of the Trans-Siberian Railway that ran through Chinese territory, to Beijing without compensation. When this manifesto was officially communicated to Beijing in March 1920, it was well-received by Chinese radicals who were thoroughly disillusioned with the West after the Paris debacle.

The Beijing government, however, could not take full advantage of the Bolshevik offer. China was constrained by its allies, which it had joined in militarily intervening in Russia's civil war in 1918. Although Beijing pulled its forces out in early 1920, it was still obligated to act in concert with the allies, who showed no inclination to recognize the Bolshevik government. This did not prevent Beijing from engaging in talks. In August 1920, a Bolshevik mission went to Beijing seeking recognition of the new government. Talks proceeded so well that the Bolsheviks issued the Second Karakhan Manifesto in September. The Soviet government reaffirmed its previous promises, though it retracted the promise to return the CER without compensation. The powers nixed any hope of an agreement because they feared the collapse of the entire unequal treaty system if the Bolsheviks surrendered extraterritoriality. Koo knew that the United States did not want to lose the right of extraterritoriality. The U.S. State Department expressed the opinion that eliminating Russia's treaty rights would kill foreign loans and investment and might invite the powers to take over and manage Russia's rights in China. Indeed, all of the powers agreed that Russian interests should be placed under international control. Despite the de facto elimination of Russian unequal treaty rights, the powers did not intervene, though recognition of the Bolshevik government was delayed several years. Meanwhile, Bolshevik agents went to China to meet with Chinese radicals, and in 1921 the CCP was formed.[5]

These gains vis-à-vis Russia did not translate into a power nexus that could assist Beijing in preventing more great power expansion. Koo opposed alienating the powers by aligning with the Bolsheviks, and his own conservative political nature showed no inclination in buying into a communist revolution. Without any other viable option, Koo wanted to somehow further drive a wedge between Japan and the United States, if not Japan and Britain. While his government spoke with Soviet agents, Koo suggested that Beijing persuade the United States to hold bilateral discussions over how to eliminate extraterritoriality. Koo knew the United States needed time to debate the impact such a step posed for American businessmen, but the key was for China to guarantee that American businessmen would not suffer any losses. Koo's rhetoric reflected the thinking of some in the Chinese Foreign Ministry who were willing to make political and economic concessions to the United States in order to get an alliance that enabled Beijing to eliminate extraterritoriality and secure tariff revision.[6]

In November 1920, the Republicans won the presidency, and with British encouragement they considered holding a conference to discuss naval disarmament. Secretary of State Charles Evans Hughes wanted to prevent a naval arms race with Japan from becoming entangled in the Anglo-Japanese Alliance, Japanese imperialism in China, and the balance of power in Asia. He also believed that the United States would never go to war to stop Japanese imperialism against China and opposed giving China any military guarantees. The United States wanted to cooperate with Japan and Britain in perpetuating the imperialist system, though in a new guise.[7] Washington may also have been interested in finding some way to forestall a communist revolution in China that would threaten the imperialist system. Whatever the case, the United States agreed to hold a conference in Washington to discuss the Anglo-Japanese Alliance, naval arms limitation, and issues affecting China. When the Chinese were informed of the impending conference, they immediately made it clear that the Shandong Question and unequal treaty revision had to be on the table. Japan opposed raising the Shandong Question, preferring to settle the issue before the meeting commenced. The British and Americans agreed.[8]

In August 1921, the United States invited the Beijing government, as well as other states, to send representatives to Washington in November. One power not invited was the Soviet Union. The Chinese were no doubt aware of the general feeling of American ill will toward Britain and Japan, and they sought to capitalize on the situation. Koo also believed that the new Republican administration would fulfill promises made during the presidential campaign to render China justice.[9]

In early October, Beijing chose Koo, Alfred Sze, and Wang Chonghui, a Western-educated international attorney who served on China's Supreme Court, to be China's chief delegates. In regard to the Shandong Question, the government, backed or pressured by Chinese public opinion of students, merchants, intellectuals, and workers, refused to either compromise on Shandong or to negotiate directly with Japan. The previous summer, Washington tried and failed to bring the Chinese and Japanese together to discuss the Shandong Question. Just before he left London, the U.S. ambassador to Britain warned Koo to not raise Qingdao at the conference. Otherwise, it would adversely affect the conference atmosphere. In Beijing, Jacob Gould Schurman, the American minister to China, told W.W. Yen, the foreign minister, that China and Japan should settle the Shandong Question on their own, before the Washington Conference commenced.[10]

The Chinese were not interested in negotiating, but the powers pushed for China and Japan to resolve the Shandong Question outside of the conference. Koo expressed dissatisfaction with this approach because of public opinion back home. Koo's arguments were rejected by Britain's Lord Curzon with the retort that China "must give up the policy of trying to play off one European Power against the other" and allow that great power cooperation, not rivalry, was China's salvation. The British could see that the Chinese were trying to use the Anglo-Americans against Japan. Curzon advised China to allow the surplus population of Japan to expand into Manchuria, which he claimed was not Chinese territory. Expansion there was far more preferable to Japanese expansion into the heart of China via Qingdao. Koo disagreed, saying that Japan did not want a population outlet but "complete control over the economic and industrial resources of China, and reducing the latter to an ultimate position of vassalage."[11]

Besides the Shandong Question, there were the unequal treaties.

The Chinese delegation prepared a ten-point program that included a call for tariff autonomy, abolition of extraterritoriality, and respect for China's territorial integrity.[12] Koo apparently decided to go for broke at this conference believing that the United States was behind him all the way. Public opinion in America certainly favored the Chinese, but Koo did not fully appreciate the attitudes within the Harding administration. The Republicans were more interested in naval disarmament, elimination of the Anglo-Japanese Alliance and cooperation with the powers than in stealing thunder from the Bolsheviks over the treaties.[13]

Arriving in Washington, Koo remained bent on pushing his patriotic agenda. Chinese students in the United States ensured that the delegation remained on that path by demonstrating outside the conference building. Jiang Tingfu, a doctoral student at Columbia University, was in Washington, and he remembered that the debate among the students hinged on whether the abolition of the unequal treaties should be "gradual or sudden."[14] Student agitation, in some cases egged on by Sun Yat-sen's separatist government, made for a highly charged atmosphere that put the diplomats on notice to accomplish something.

On November 16, Alfred Sze presented China's ten-point agenda to the conference in which China demanded full control of its internal affairs. The enumeration of these ten points did not have nearly the effect that Koo's speech on Shandong had had nearly three years before. Some of the powers might be willing to surrender their leaseholds in China but nothing more. Britain, for example, was willing to negotiate the surrender of Weihaiwei. Some of the powers found it difficult to take Koo and company seriously considering the fact that Beijing in reality only represented a small portion of the country. And even that government was fighting to stay alive financially. Elihu Root, one of the American delegates, remarked that there was no desire on anyone's part to "interfere with the validity of treaties," but if some action was taken, it "should be confined to what all would recognise as 'China proper.'" Root's proposal found favor with everyone except Koo, who declared that his delegation could not recognize any definition of China that "did not accord to the Chinese constitution. It must include twenty-two provinces." Root retorted that it was not in the realm of the conference to decide 'what is China,' adding that he wanted "to avoid controversial topics and do something useful."[15]

Although Koo won a resolution affirming his position, his stance angered a lot of people. Koo remembered that Hughes was "sympathetic to China," but he found Root to be "of a different type; he gave me the impression that he understood Japan far more than China."[16] One British diplomat remarked that Senator Henry Cabot Lodge "was intensely annoyed by Mr. Koo's attitude and did not trouble to conceal this from Koo." Robert Lansing, an adviser to the delegation, noted that Lodge "spoke bitterly and contemptuously of [the] Chinese." Another participant commented to Lansing that Koo was "too clever, that he had changed much." Koo struck William R. Castle, an American delegate, as "a slippery man, without a trace of morals of any kind; agreeable enough to talk to, but not at all a man to be trusted and not in the same class with Sze." One journalist observed that while both Koo and Sze were Westernized, Koo "gave the impression of having been rather the more thoroughly Westernized, the more completely smartened up according to modern American standards." Sze, on the other hand, "suggested a background, a residuum of the philosophy and point of view of his race, a calm that rests upon the wisdom of centuries. For this quality, Dr. Sze seemed a little more appealing."[17] Apparently, Koo did not live up to the Occidental expectation of how a Chinese should carry himself.

The British found little to like about Koo's remarks that China be recognized as constituting twenty-two provinces. Such statements made the British suspicious that Koo might demand that independent Tibet be returned to China. London considered telling Beijing to rein in Koo. Sir Beilby Alston, the British minister at Beijing, advised otherwise. Confused newspaper reports gave Chinese readers the perception that the conference was seriously taking up tariff autonomy and the elimination of extraterritoriality. Worse, Koo's countrymen viewed him as a hero. Others in Britain's Far Eastern Department doubted whether Beijing was "able, or even willing, to prevent Mr. Koo from being petty and foolish." Beijing was likewise under pressure to accomplish something positive at the conference and reining in Koo would only anger Chinese students and intellectuals.[18]

The real reasons why people were angry with Koo were two-fold.

The powers wanted the conference to be a success, but Koo's insistence on following through with his patriotic agenda muddied the waters. One participant observed to Lansing that while "the sympathy of all was with China to begin with . . . the course of Koo and Sze, particularly Koo, is causing much discontent and weakening that sympathy."[19] Then there was Koo's refusal to be a pliant Chinese who followed the beck and call of the powers.

On November 21, Root outlined the ideas later embodied in the Nine Power Treaty in which the powers promised to protect China's territorial integrity, assist China in maintaining "an effective and stable government," give China "unembarrassed opportunity" to establish "an effective and stable government," safeguard the Open Door in China, and cease taking advantage of China by seeking "special rights or privileges." Two days later, Koo submitted more specific proposals before the Committee on Pacific and Far Eastern Questions: tariff autonomy; abolition of extraterritoriality; removal of fortifications from the Leased Territories; and elimination of foreign troops, foreign police, and the foreign postal service. The powers only promised to create a Tariff Revision Conference that would consider an increase of the tariff. Likewise, a commission would study whether or not to eliminate or modify extraterritoriality, though no power was obligated to accept the commission's findings. Koo also attacked the Leased Territories for being an 'imperium in imperio' that not only undermined China's national defense but laid the basis for conflict in Asia between the powers. Although willing to relinquish control over some Chinese territory, the powers generally were in no mood to agree with full-scale retreat.[20]

While Koo and the powers argued over treaty revision, China and Japan negotiated the Shandong Question. On December 1, the Chinese delegation caved to American and British pressure to negotiate directly outside the conference in the presence of observers from their delegations.[21] In response, the secretary general and other members of the Chinese delegation resigned, and Wang Chonghui, either out of conviction or fear of Chinese public reaction or both, threatened to resign unless Koo and Sze stopped compromising. Representatives of Sun Yatsen's government stirred up much hostility against the delegates, calling them traitors. Chinese students delayed the first meeting between the

Chinese and Japanese delegates by staging protests against direct negotiations.[22]

Over the next two months, Koo and his compatriots negotiated for
Qingdao despite threats by students to assassinate members of the delegation. And in the process they further angered the Americans and British who grew impatient with the Chinese for squabbling over details, for
goading the Japanese, and for dragging out the negotiations. The obstacle was the Jiaoji Railroad. The Japanese not only wanted the Chinese
to borrow $25 million from Japan for a railroad they never built, but
Tokyo wanted its people to hold important administrative positions over-
seeing the railroad. A deadlock ensued. Pressure from the other delegations eventually forced Koo, Sze and Wang to agree to a formula of
compromise, but they could not sell it to their own people. GMD members of the delegation came out against the compromise, and Chinese
students surrounded the house where the delegates were staying to prevent them from meeting with the Japanese. Koo and the other delegates
were able to resume negotiations, but they also continued to balk because of, or in spite of, public pressure. Koo later remarked that "in diplomacy you must not aim at achieving 100% success." However, the
students, engaging in what Koo called "People's Diplomacy," did aim at
100% success. Such an approach could "never bring success, and only
spoils the negotiations."[23]

Thereafter, negotiations went nowhere until the United States and
Britain applied pressure. They wanted the Chinese delegates to accept
the Japanese loan and a Japanese manager for the Jiaoji Railroad. All the
above were anathema to Koo. In order to save face and at the Chinese
delegation's behest, Washington informed Beijing that China could not
get any better terms from Japan, and refusal to accept those terms would
be "intolerable."[24] Such statements had their effect, and the Chinese and
Japanese delegations reached a settlement based on the compromise.

When the Washington Conference ended in February 1922, Japan
agreed to return Qingdao for a sum of money. The powers also handed
China a "Washington formula" in which the unequal treaties would be
revised once China proved itself capable of efficient self-government.
With the Nine Power Treaty, the Washington Conference created a system to prevent a great power conflict in China, which benefited China

by preventing war and further imperialist expansion. However, the powers maintained their hold on their imperialist rights in the midst of China's changing realities, including the threat of communist revolution. The powers were interested neither in following the lead of the Bolsheviks who at least rhetorically renounced the unequal treaties nor in surrendering their rights in order to win back the Chinese who were disillusioned by Paris. The so-called Washington formula was simply another excuse to not sacrifice Western rights.[25]

Most Chinese formed an opinion of the conference based on expectations. If one expected sweeping revisions of the imperialist system, then one's appraisals tended to be negative because the imperialist system remained mostly intact. If one expected only gradual change, appraisals tended to be more positive. In the words of Jiang Tingfu, "Although China did not achieve much at the Conference in relation to tariffs, concessions, or extraterritorial rights, the Washington Conference was, nevertheless, a very important stage in China's recovery of rights."[26]

Koo returned to China in 1921 after being away for six years. He faced the daunting task of establishing order and stability in China in order to secure revision of the imperialist system. To say that China was politically unstable was an understatement. From 1916 to 1928, there were twenty-four Cabinets, eight presidents, and over twenty different individuals who served as premier or provisional premier, in some cases more than once. Another war was being waged between warlords Wu Peifu and Zhang Zuolin of Manchuria. The war lasted only a few days, but the number of troops involved and casualties inflicted were higher than the previous war. Wu Peifu avoided defeat, but neither could he decisively defeat his enemies. In 1922, Wu Peifu's warlord clique roughly controlled eight of China's provinces as well as Beijing. There was little room for optimism as one of Koo's subordinates explained to John Bassett Moore: "What will befall the nation ultimately is a matter of uncertainty. As China has a plethora of difficult problems, she is in urgent need of a host of honest and energetic leaders."[27]

Upon his return, Koo found Chinese intellectuals and Western friends of China speaking increasingly of the need for "good government" in China. People like Wang Chonghui and Hu Shi drew up a manifesto calling for "good government" and a "planned government." The manifesto argued for political reform based on constitutional government and publicity to influence public opinion and government planning. Moreover, good or "able men" were needed to implement this policy. The manifesto's progressive program sought to end the North-South division, reduce the number of Chinese under arms, implement direct election of officials, and create a national financial administration.[28] Koo approved of the manifesto, and blamed the "great confusion and strife" on the "absence of a complete Constitution." China's poor financial situation was a matter of concern, but he believed the future "was brighter" if one looked ahead two years to the day when there would be financial reorganization. The latter was necessary because Koo foresaw the government collapsing in a matter of months due to "financial stringency."[29]

Throughout the summer of 1922, a series of "tea meetings" were held at Koo's home in Beijing to discuss and debate a strategy that would unify the country and open the way to revising the unequal treaties in the context of the Washington agreements. Most of the participants, such as Hu Shi, Wang Chonghui, and Lo Wen'gan, were Western educated, but also in attendance were older intellectuals, such as Liang Qichao, who presented their own views. After hearing different approaches, the group focused on the notion of federalism. The idea was not a new one. Before the 1911 Revolution, Liang Qichao, Sun Yat-sen, and others held the conviction that "national strength [could be] based on local self-government."[30] The idea revived in the 1920s. Some people pointed to the overcentralization of power in the government's hands as the principal reason for the breakdown of society and the rise of the warlords. Following the American model, proponents hoped that every province would have its own constitution and become self-governing. A central government would remain in Beijing and it would maintain a national army "in order to avoid the occupation of territory by war lords." Hu Shi faulted "the attempt to unify China by force from above." Instead of using force, good government had to exist in every province in order to establish a stable civil authority. The sources of China's disunity were not imperialism, warlordism, or capitalism, but rather the lack of strong local institutions. As he argued in his political journal, the *Endeavor*, "Internal reform is a pre-condition for resistance to imperialism." Federalism and constitutionalism would help China break out of the shackles of the unequal treaties and emerge as a free and independent country.[31]

Such ideas were more palatable to someone like Koo who not only supported federalism but could not subscribe to the view of throwing out the imperialists in order to save China. His outlook agreed to a certain extent with that of Hu Shi who, after the Washington Conference, argued that China no longer had to fear imperialist aggression and that the powers were willing to work with the government to create a stable and peaceful China. Hu refused to call them imperialists, but instead saw them as "investors." Koo opposed the imperialist system and foreign meddling in China's internal affairs, but he welcomed the foreign presence and capital as long as Chinese sovereignty was not circumscribed. And although Koo acknowledged later that his foreign policy was to eliminate the unequal treaties, he preferred gradual change. His intention was not "to adopt a policy of unilateral action with regard to the unequal treaties." Koo wanted to eliminate the unequal treaties "by an orderly method of negotiation, in the hope and expectation that the foreign powers concerned would be well disposed to cooperate with China." Koo would unilaterally denounce the unequal treaties "only after the foreign powers made it clear that they would not agree to a revision of the treaties by negotiation or that they would obstruct the achievement of China's national purpose in this direction." [32]

Such beliefs put men like Koo at odds with the fledgling CCP. After the Paris Peace Conference, the liberal Western model of development was in disrepute as was the emphasis on gradualism in political development if not foreign affairs. Before the CCP was founded, Chinese radicals blamed the warlords, corrupt government officials and politicians, and the imperialist powers for making China backward. Once the CCP was formed, it took on the issues of warlordism and imperialism. In May 1922, the CCP produced slogans that called for the overthrow of those two isms. Two months later, participants in the second party congress wrote a platform that condemned the powers, especially the United States, for their exploitation of China, particularly during the Washington Conference. And Chinese radicals rejected Hu Shi's conclusion that China had nothing to fear from the imperialists. They condemned the collaboration that took place between the powers and the warlords and the compradores such as Koo who were backed by Britain and the United States. Over the next three years, the CCP railed against the British and Americans and called for a revolution that would remove the warlords and government collaborators who served as conduits for imperialism and the disunity of China.[33]

For the moment, Koo and his compatriots were preoccupied with making good government work and could ignore the CCP, which was a minor political force. After Wu Peifu defeated the Manchurian warlord Zhang Zuolin earlier in the year, Wu set out to establish a new government in Beijing. Impressed by Wu, Koo gave his full support to the warlord because the latter's ideas were more in accord with Koo's political convictions. Although antiforeign by nature, Wu leaned toward Britain and the United States instead of Japan, making him more acceptable to Koo, who admitted that he was distrustful of Japan. At the time, Wu Peifu seemed progressive in the sense that he was supposedly honest, supported rule by law, and stressed "peaceful constitutionality." He restored the former parliament that had been dissolved in 1917 in a bid to undermine Sun Yat-sen's government in Guangzhou and bring about national unity. He also appointed Li Yuanhong to be president. Li served as president after Yuan Shikai died until being forced from the presidency in 1917. Before taking his post, Li insisted that the warlords reduce troop levels and reform the Beijing government.[34]

One other measure Li Yuanhong took in August 1922 was to bring together bright and modern-minded Chinese to form a new cabinet composed of Wang Chonghui (Ph.D. in International Law from Yale) as premier, Lo Wen'gan (Ph.D. in International Law from Oxford) as minister of finance, and Koo as minister of foreign affairs. It became known as the "Able Men" Cabinet. All were believers in the notion of government by men of intellect and proven ability. In Koo's case, he was also very popular in China. In October, *The Weekly Review*, an English-language newspaper published by American owners, asked nearly 25,000 teachers and students who they thought were the "twelve greatest living Chinese." Koo ranked third with 1,211 votes, only 114 votes behind Sun Yat-sen, who ranked first.[35]

The road to stability and order was not an easy one. Koo, who wore the hats of foreign minister and chairman of the financial discussion commission, found the government stuck with the problem of inadequate funding. Of the government's three main goals—writing a constitution, unification and financial reorganization—the latter was of greatest concern. Even before the Washington Conference commenced, the Beijing government went bankrupt. Revising the unequal treaties would prove worthless unless the government laid its hands on some hard cash. Otherwise, Koo predicted the government might collapse in six months. Some at the time, including Chinese newspapers that believed Koo's connections abroad would lead to suspension, if not cancellation, of the Boxer Indemnity payments, were confident of Koo's abilities. People felt that if he could avoid corruption in the government, there was hope yet for China's financial situation.[36]

To alleviate Beijing's financial crisis, Koo attempted to obtain a consolidation loan from the Consortium. The powers were asked to suspend the Boxer Indemnity payments and agree to loan China the money necessary to reorganize the government and put it on a firm economic basis. American and British government officials supported granting the loan believing that Beijing's stability ensured access to the China market. Japan disapproved, not wanting Wu Peifu to benefit by the money. Koo requested an ¥18 million loan to be provided over the next several months, but the Japanese again balked declaring that they refused to support any particular Chinese party or faction. Neither would they nor American and British bankers throw money down a sinkhole, in this case the sinkhole being a Beijing government that already reneged on the payment of previous loans.[37]

Another difficulty was making constitutional government work in the midst of warlord intrigue. Factional politics led to the downfall of the "Able Men" Cabinet in November. Koo remained out of the government until April 1923 when he was appointed foreign minister once more. The "Able Men" Cabinet became symbolic of future cabinets that rose and fell in succession from 1922 to 1928, and the lack of stability in Beijing became a source of embarrassment for many Chinese. The "Able Men" were indeed bright but not adept at playing Beijing politics. Koo admitted later that "it had always been my desire to bring about a revision of China's unequal treaties and I had no taste for politics or political rivalry." Although he aspired to be a leader, he did not want to curry political favor, and refused to join a political party, not doing so until 1942 when he became a member of the GMD.[38]

With the downfall of the "Able Men," the belief that constitutional government was the road to China's salvation waned. Koo later argued that without a tradition of representative government in China, warlords, politicians, and peasants did not possess an understanding of "what democracy really was or should be even though they were living under the Republic." Education was key to resolving the root cause of constitutionalism's failure. He believed that representative government had to be taught throughout the entire Chinese school system so that young Chinese grew up understanding that "whether at a private gathering, a public meeting, or in discussions in a council, freedom of speech and the right of objection should be recognized and that where honest differences of opinion exist, there is always a way of finding a workable compromise." Koo's faith in education led him to support David Yui's "Citizenship Training" movement of the 1920s. China's partial failure at the Washington Conference convinced Yui, a graduate of St. John's and Harvard and head of the Chinese YMCA, that the Chinese people needed to be awakened through a citizenship training movement. The movement promoted an understanding of political theories as well as national and international problems. Yet Koo was not overly idealistic. He recognized that it was all a matter of time and training: "Democracy cannot be born overnight."[39]

The problem facing China was that the powers were not that patient. The spirit of cooperation that supposedly flowed out of the Washington Conference between the powers and the Chinese government never materialized. A China divided by the warlords drove away potential investors. Foreign businessmen took their money to stable Japan. Meanwhile, the powers stood by passively (except for selling arms) and took no positive action to bring peace to China. The powers' agreement to allow the Chinese to solve their own problems without interference from outsiders became a legitimate reason to not implement the programs laid down at the Washington Conference. As a result of China's internal political breakdown and the conservative nature of the powers, Chinese officials, such as W.W. Yen, grew pessimistic that the Washington Conference formula would be put into action.[40]

The Lincheng Incident convinced the powers that their refusal to

revise the imperialist system was justified. In May 1923, twenty-five foreign subjects were kidnapped from a train by Chinese bandits.[41] The
majority of the captives were Americans. Negotiations between foreign
consular officers, Chinese officials, and the bandits got underway but
made little progress until the bandits were threatened with foreign military force. By June 12, all of the captives were released. The powers demanded not only compensation but indemnities as well. And there was
talk of stationing more troops in China in order to protect foreigners.

After several weeks of living in "retirement," Koo returned as foreign minister in July. In response to the powers' demands, Koo called for
patience. Even though the republican form of government was being
put to the test, Koo declared that China continued to pursue democracy
and the "ability to solve her own problems." In August, however, the powers pressed for compensation for the victims and the guarantee that the
railway police would be reorganized under foreign officers. The powers
took the position that the Lincheng Incident was similar to the Boxer
Uprising of 1900, but Koo believed that the powers' demands went "far
beyond what was justifiable in the circumstance." Before the powers could
place Chinese railways under foreign officers, the Chinese Foreign Ministry leaked the scheme to the Chinese public. Public outrage against the
reorganization plan led the foreign and Chinese press to denounce "the
project as an encroachment on China's sovereign rights."[42]

The British were furious with Koo, who not only refused to squelch
the torrent being unleashed against Britain but was believed to have ghost-
written some of the articles appearing in newspapers criticizing the British. The situation only worsened when Koo responded with his own note
declaring the Chinese government not liable for the Lincheng Incident.
Koo later recalled that he believed the Lincheng Incident to be an internal Chinese matter not subject to foreign interference and argued that
"nothing should be done which would infringe upon China's sovereignty
as an independent nation or would be contrary to or would go beyond
the principles and rules of international law in regard to the protection
of foreign nationals on the territory of China." The incident resulted,
not from an antiforeign movement such as the Boxer Uprising but from
a train robbery on a scale similar to what happened in the American
West. He admitted to Jacob Gould Schurman, the U.S. minister, that his

note "would not entirely satisfy either Chinese or foreigners but he had to take account of Chinese public opinion as [the] diplomatic body also had probably been influenced by foreign opinion in making their demands."[43]

In regard to the foreigners he was right. His note angered many in the foreign community in China. The editor of the *North-China Herald* accused Koo of trying "to treat the Lincheng outrage as if it were an isolated event, a thing indeed to be regretted, but not worse than might have happened anywhere, which the Chinese government could not have expected and for which it cannot be blamed." The editor further observed that the incident underscored the "widespread state of lawlessness" and "the disgraceful anarchy which made Lincheng possible."[44] Koo's note irritated the British intensely. They believed Koo was trying "to curry favor with the Chinese Parliament and student classes and thus consolidate his somewhat insecure political position and . . . to score a diplomatic success at the expense of His Majesty's government." If true, Koo was successful to an extent. He eventually compensated the victims while ducking the railway reorganization scheme.[45] If not responsible for leaking the railway scheme, he probably condoned the act because he opposed further loss of sovereignty.

The Lincheng Incident embarrassed Koo and government personnel who were trying to convince the powers of China's stability. Koo played down the incident because he knew that the powers would use it as an excuse to not fulfill the promises made at the Washington Conference. At one point in this episode, the powers threatened to drop recognition of Beijing if the government did not accede to their demands. Secretary of State Hughes warned Koo "that such outrages as that of Lincheng . . . should not be encouraged and that when the Chinese talk of the integrity and sovereignty of China they should maintain a Government capable of discharging its international obligations."[46]

The deleterious effects of Lincheng on Beijing's relations with the foreign powers were felt almost immediately when Koo attempted to put the Washington Conference principles into practice. In the spring of 1924, Koo sent out feelers to see if the powers were interested in holding the Commission on Extraterritoriality in the fall. In particular, he called on the United States to use its good offices, since it was the United States that had called the Washington Conference to order. Koo argued that sending the Commission to China in the near future would "encourage [the Chinese people] to get together to solve their political problems."[47] By June, though, none of the powers could agree on a date. The Lincheng Incident convinced the powers that China's disunity prevented the Beijing government from maintaining law and order and from protecting foreign nationals, and they had no reason to take up revising the imperialist system.[48] Although not dead yet, the spirit of Washington was dying.

If Lincheng proved a serious setback for a man like Koo who sought revision of the unequal treaties, it also had an important impact on the Chinese people. The Lincheng Incident contributed to the general awakening of the Chinese people in the 1920s. The Chinese were captivated by the whole incident, and as John Fitzgerald has written, "This was a tale of captivity with a difference: it was not China that was held against its will but uninvited Westerners." The foreigners were more humiliated than were the members of the Chinese government, and in their overreaction, the foreign powers further stirred up nationalism in the Chinese people who increasingly held the foreigners in contempt.[49] On the one hand, the incident rallied people to the government and Koo could use this nationalism as a weapon against the foreign powers. On the other hand, Koo found it more and more difficult to make compromises with the imperialists and to maintain law and order in China in the face of Chinese nationalism.

From 1923 on, the Beijing government found itself in increasing ideological competition with Sun Yat-sen's GMD party and the fledgling CCP. From 1918 to 1922, Sun appealed time and again to the powers, especially Japan and the United States, for assistance. The United States, which generally respected Sun in 1911, now viewed Sun as irresponsible, if not imbalanced. Japan demanded that Sun accept the 1915 Twenty-One Demands before recognizing his government, leaving Sun little choice but to refuse. Then in 1923, the Soviet Union expressed a willingness to help. The previous year, Adolph Joffe, a Soviet leader and diplomat, and Foreign Minister Koo tried to reach an agreement to pave the way to mutual diplomatic recognition. Although no communist, Koo wanted a deal in order to ensure the security of the CER and promote trade. The negotiations broke down because of a disagreement over the

CER, so Joffe went south to meet with Sun. The two men negotiated the Sun-Joffe Agreement that committed the Soviet Union to backing Sun politically, economically, and militarily. The Soviets promptly sent advisers to Guangzhou to help Sun reorganize the GMD, imbue it with a more anti-imperialistic ideology, and provide military assistance. The agreement also formed the first united front between the GMD and the CCP in an effort to present solidarity against the imperialist powers.[50]

The marriage between Sun and the Soviets led him to modify his previous views of the foreign powers. Earlier in his career, Sun cooperated with the foreign powers to accomplish his revolutionary goals. Now he called for throwing out the imperialists and the warlords who were the enemies of the nation. Sun argued that the state had to mobilize the people in order to free China from the grip of the foreign powers, and not until the people served the state would China's semicolonization end.[51] In the past, he frowned on the notion that foreign economic imperialism was inherently dangerous to China and initially welcomed foreign capital. After 1923, Sun revised publicly those earlier views and attacked imperialism for its economic, political, and military oppression of the Chinese people. In short, the imperialists became a target of Sun's revolutionary propaganda. In January 1924, the GMD Party Congress issued its own manifesto blaming the powers for China's instability and disunity. The GMD's foreign policy platform called for abrogation of the unequal treaties and offered most-favored-nation status to those countries that voluntarily gave up the treaties' unequal privileges.[52]

By 1924, Chinese students, intellectuals, merchants, and workers influenced by Marxist-Leninism and Sun Yat-sen's Three Principles of the People, began denouncing imperialism and demanded treaty revisions. And they allowed little room for compromise. This was clear in 1924 when Koo tried to recover Weihaiwei, the small port given to the British during the 1898 "scramble for concessions." The twenty-five-year lease expired in 1923. An Anglo-Chinese Commission met throughout the fall of 1922 to discuss its return to China but ended when the Chinese negotiator suggested that since the British agreed to turn over Weihaiwei, China should allow the British to use a nearby island as a summer resort for the British navy. When that concession became public knowledge, the negotiator was accused of being a traitor and was forced to resign. When Koo tried to restart negotiations in 1924, he laid down terms deemed unfavorable by the British. The British minister feared not reentering into negotiations because there was sure to be "anti-British agitation" like that during the summer over the Lincheng Incident. On the other hand, the diplomat recognized that Koo was under public pressure to secure an agreement that was "tantamount to unconditional surrender" on the part of the British. Otherwise, Koo and the government would "be accused by their political opponents of sacrificing 'sovereign rights.'" Eventually an agreement was reached that still permitted British naval facilities, but before either side could sign it, a *coup d'état* forced Koo to take sanctuary, ironically, in Weihaiwei.[53]

Another foreign policy issue influenced by the vagaries of Chinese nationalism involved normalization of relations with the Soviet Union. The Soviet initiative with Sun Yat-sen naturally affected Beijing. In 1923, Lev Karakhan, the Soviet Union's Deputy Commissar for Foreign Affairs, arrived in China. Karakhan demanded recognition of his government before negotiating a new agreement, but Beijing refused. The impasse was broken in part when Britain recognized the Soviet Union, but mostly because of agitation in Beijing. In February 1924, forty-seven Beijing University professors urged Koo to recognize the Soviet Union. The warlord Wu Peifu likewise called for resumption of negotiations.[54]

Koo and other cabinet members wanted to accord recognition. By March, Karakhan and C.T. Wang, Koo's nemesis from the Paris conference, had an agreement. In addition to reestablishing diplomatic relations, the Soviets gave up extraterritoriality, abrogated old treaties, returned the Boxer Indemnity, and agreed to withdraw from Mongolia. Yet Koo and others in the cabinet opposed the agreement for several reasons. First, the Soviets made a series of pledges to discuss numerous issues raised in the agreement at a future conference. Neither Koo nor W.W. Yen trusted Soviet pledges of good faith. The Chinese cabinet felt that the old treaties should be abolished immediately, and not at some uncertain future date. Second, the Soviets refused to annul a 1921 treaty with Outer Mongolia that recognized Mongolian independence. The cabinet wanted Soviet recognition of Mongolia as Chinese territory. When C.T. Wang initialed an agreement that did not contain a Soviet promise to cancel their treaty with Outer Mongolia, Koo, who rivaled Wang in the pursuit of glory, rejected the agreement.[55]

Chinese students had their own interpretation. The general assumption was that Koo opposed recognizing the Soviet Union because he was pro-American. Since the United States was the only major power not to recognize the Soviet Union, the students concluded that Koo wanted to follow the lead of the United States. Students, led by a CCP founder, went to the foreign ministry, carrying placards that accused Koo of betraying the country and demanded recognition of the Soviet Union.[56] Chinese students tended to accept Karakhan's version that negotiations failed because of foreign interference. Joining the students were the warlords who urged the government to continue negotiations.[57]

Along with moral pressure, an attempt was made on his life either to frighten Koo into signing an agreement or simply to eliminate him. On May 15, 1924, a package containing a bomb arrived at Koo's home. Upon being opened, the bomb exploded, injuring several in the Koo household, but not Koo himself. Who was responsible was never determined, though Koo claimed later that two Beijing University students had planted the bomb. To place the blame on prorecognition individuals is not far-fetched, and Koo himself suspected individuals with communist connections. The assassination attempt was a matter of concern for some of the powers. Basil Newton, in Britain's Far Eastern Department of the Foreign Office, expressed the fear that as a result of this attack, Beijing would be "more than ever reluctant to come to decisions, e.g. in regard to Weihaiwei, which can expose them to criticism however unreasonable."[58]

Eventually, Koo and Karakhan resumed negotiations, and the two sides signed an agreement that was not significantly different from the one reached earlier by C.T. Wang. Although Koo claimed he was "not entirely satisfied with some of the provisions," he accepted the agreement because "China with her vast interests in the re-establishment of normal relations with Russia naturally could not defer the settlement of this question longer than she could help it." At the time, recognition was deemed a limited victory because normalization was one more blow to the imperialist system that could be used as a tool against the other powers in revising the unequal treaties. Moscow, which had interests to be served, gave Beijing recognition at a time when the Soviets were supporting Sun Yat-sen, potentially breaking Sun's monopoly on relations with the Soviet Union. And normalization was an example of Beijing asserting itself in its foreign relations in the face of opposition from France, Japan, and the United States, which opposed the agreement. Since Moscow in theory gave up extraterritoriality, Koo sent an open letter to all the powers demanding they too surrender this unequal privilege.

Otherwise, recognition did Koo's government little good. The agreement allowed the Soviets to open an embassy in Beijing with an ambassador, not a minister as was the case with the other powers, from where they could carry out propaganda work. And even though Koo could potentially threaten closer Sino-Soviet cooperation, renewed relations never translated into bargaining leverage when Koo met with the other powers to renegotiate treaties. The Sino-Soviet conference was never held, the Chinese never reasserted their influence over Mongolia, joint Sino-Soviet management of the CER remained a sore point, and the supposed gains that the treaty gave the Chinese were in fact secured by Beijing since 1921 in one form or another. The treaty was pro forma.[59]

The significance of both the aborted rendition of Weihaiwei and recognition of the Soviet Union was the role of public opinion. To a certain extent, the students cowed Koo. Years later, in criticizing the Indian people for demanding independence now, Koo remarked that, "It seems Oriental people attach too much importance to . . . principles and take too academic [a] view of great problems. Is it due to their political immaturity in the face of the experienced European politicians and imperialists?" The Indian people of the 1940s reminded Koo of Chinese students and intellectuals of the 1920s in being unrealistic in demanding the impossible now. There was not always a straight path to "the attainment of a cardinal object." Koo went on, "One should be realistic and resourceful in seeking its attainment."[60]

In the months after the normalization of Sino-Russian relations, Koo's stock declined. Hints of corruption impugned his character including suggestions that the Soviets bribed Koo to sign the treaty. Then there were reports that Koo's wife bribed members of parliament in order to secure confirmation of Koo's appointment as foreign minister.[61] For the rest of his career, Koo did not win the complete trust of either his compatriots or foreigners when involved in financial matters as a result of these accusations.

Besides impugning his character, Chinese students increasingly attacked Koo for being "too friendly to America."[62] The CCP criticized the United States for its imperialist policies and essentially accused Koo and others like him of being puppets of the American capitalists.[63] By the mid-1920s, fellow travelers and noncommunists alike gradually focused their critical eye on the American presence in China and America's unexceptional China policy.[64] In 1925, a broadsheet portrayed Wu Peifu as a dog being led on a leash by Uncle Sam: the caption read 'The truth about imperialism and warlords.'[65] Charges that Koo was a pawn of the United States were unfounded. Koo admired American culture, but he was no puppet. The real issue was not that Koo was a pro-American, but that the growing support for using military force and revolution to overthrow the unequal treaty system eclipsed his gradualist approach to solving China's problems.

Politically, the situation worsened for Koo after 1924. The October 1924 coup forced Koo into "retirement" for the next year and a half. Meanwhile, antiforeign feelings among Chinese students, merchants, and laborers increased, creating tension for all the powers in China. In May 1925, Japanese police attacked striking Chinese workers, killing one. On May 30, hundreds of Chinese demonstrators marched on a British police station in Shanghai, leading British police to open fire, killing nine. The result was a spontaneous outpouring of Chinese anger against the foreign powers and the imperialist system. Nationwide strikes, boycotts, and demonstrations followed. In Beijing, students, teachers, workers including rickshaw pullers, merchants, and journalists were organized and demonstrated with anti-British and anti-Japanese placards and banners. The demonstrations were citywide. The outpouring of anger led the foreign powers to increase their military presence. Both the GMD and the CCP experienced a surge in their membership rolls, and in Beijing, both parties were able to organize because Feng Yuxiang, the Soviet-backed warlord, provided protection. Koo joined Liang Qichao, Hu Shi, Jiang Tingfu and others in condemning those striking and in the boycotting of Boxerism. They called for law and order while imploring the powers to sit down with Beijing to discuss how to handle the massacre.[66]

In response to these events, the powers agreed to hold a Special Tariff Conference in October. After the meeting convened, students held anti-imperialist demonstrations over the next several months. On March 18, 1926, warlord troops opened fire on a CCP rally at Tiananmen, killing fifty and wounding two hundred, mostly students. Then in April, a major warlord war pitting Zhang Zuolin and Wu Peifu against the Soviet-backed Feng Yuxiang broke out, making the conference seem surreal. In May 1926, after the rise and fall of several cabinets, Koo became minister of finance under the premiership of W.W. Yen. In the opinion of John V.A. MacMurray, the U.S. minister, the new Cabinet possessed "scarcely more than a color of legality." Beijing exercised little power over provinces dominated by numerous warlords, and the GMD soon expanded into the Yangzi River valley. Besides disunity, there was a lack of cooperation among the powers meeting at the conference. The British, Americans and Japanese agreed to grant tariff autonomy in 1929, but the three powers could not agree on the tariff rate in the interim. Because of the civil war, the tariff conference died for lack of interest by the powers. A Commission on Extraterritoriality met the same fate in 1926.[67]

After Zhang Zuolin asserted his control over Beijing, Koo switched allegiance from Wu Peifu to Zhang. Sir Miles Lampson, the British minister at Beijing, described this period as "the low-water mark in the history of the Chinese Government." As far as Lampson could tell, Koo, who was both premier and foreign minister, and the cabinet "seemed to have little claim to represent anyone but themselves." There was a great deal of truth in the statement. Zhang Zuolin only controlled China's northeast provinces and two other provinces. China's remaining provinces were divided among four major warlords, numerous minor warlords, and then the GMD-CCP United Front. In joining Zhang Zuolin, Koo threw his lot in with one of the most conservative and least progressive of the warlords. For example, Zhang performed Confucian rituals and aspired to become an emperor.[68]

Koo apparently found the anticommunist Zhang more appealing than the so-called Reds in the south. Early in 1925, Sun Yat-sen died of cancer in Koo's Beijing palace home when Sun went there to make peace between North and South. Chiang Kai-shek, a Japanese-educated military man and Sun's protégé, managed to wrest power and succeed Sun as leader of the GMD. His principal foreign policy goals were, in his words, those pursued by Sun Yat-sen: "to remove the restrictions imposed on China by other powers, and to attain international equality." The left-wing of the GMD party espoused a "revolutionary foreign policy" in which it would either negotiate or use pressure from the masses, such as strikes and boycotts, to abrogate the unequal treaties. Chiang represented the right-wing faction of the GMD, which took a more moderate approach to treaty revisions, but many foreigners and Chinese did not know that such a distinction existed. The GMD's alliance with the CCP and Soviet aid led some China observers to mistakenly refer to Chiang as the "Red General" though he was in fact not a communist.[69]

Zhang Zuolin, on the other hand, had no Soviet connection. Since 1925, Zhang competed for British support to defeat Feng Yuxiang. Conservative foreigners in Beijing, particularly those with British interests, preferred Zhang to Feng because the former provided order in the northern capital and put down antiforeign protests in Shanghai. GMD and CCP cadres were forced to operate in secret after Zhang arrested and killed a number of party members. Moreover, Zhang Zuolin followed a policy that was, according to Gaven McCormack, one of "gradualism in foreign affairs, respect for the treaties, recognition of foreign loan obligations, prohibition of anti-imperialist movements and of strike propaganda."[70] For Koo, Zhang's policy was more in line with his thinking. Koo was not about to sign on to social revolution and communism.

On the basis of their anticommunism, Koo and Zhang sought foreign support in order to defeat the Soviet-backed GMD-CCP alliance. The changes in China, however, led the powers to reconsider their policies. In 1926, Chiang Kai-shek launched the Northern Expedition, an attempt to unify China by force. The success of the Northern Expedition moved the British to lean toward recognizing the Guangzhou government in order to protect British interests there that were being attacked by boycotts. In April, Britain withdrew recognition of Beijing, though it did not immediately recognize Guangzhou. Later in the year, the British government announced a new policy in the famous December Memorandum, which declared that the powers had to accommodate themselves to the reality of the GMD movement in the south, that China should be permitted tariff autonomy, and that the Chinese desire to revise the unequal treaties was a legitimate one. The British, however, wanted the December Memorandum to be a joint statement made by all the powers. When Lampson met with Koo, the Chinese foreign minister asked Lampson for his credentials. The British diplomat thought Koo was acting "a little stuffy in this," and made it clear that he would reveal his credentials once London recognized a government in China. Waving the Nine Power Treaty in Lampson's face, Koo declared that China had a right to be consulted before London dispatched the December Memorandum. Koo obviously would have accepted revising the unequal treaty system but not at the expense of surrendering power to the GMD. Lampson felt that Koo might make trouble for him particularly since Koo's attitude was rather cold: "Butter would not melt in his mouth."[71]

Trouble did come, but it was not entirely Koo's fault. When Zhang Zuolin pressed for British political, military, and financial assistance in dealing with what he called the Bolsheviks of the south, Lampson refused. Zhang threatened to remove Sir Francis Aglen, the Inspector-General of China's Maritime Customs Administration, from his post. The Beijing government derived a third of its income from these customs, and they ensured a financial lifeline to whatever government controlled them. The GMD independently collected the surtaxes established at the Washington Conference, and Aglen went south in December 1926 to discuss the issue with GMD officials. Infuriated, Zhang Zuolin believed that Aglen was throwing in his lot with the GMD.[72]

In February 1927, Koo relieved Aglen on the pretext that the Briton disobeyed instructions from Beijing, causing a great stir among the international community. Koo later claimed that Aglen flirted with the GMD.[73] In fact, the GMD government warned Aglen that if he tried to collect surtaxes in GMD-controlled territory, it "would consider it an 'act of war.'" Koo, who earlier admitted the impossibility of collecting the surtaxes in the south, now demanded that Aglen carry out his duties. The powers' diplomatic representatives presented Koo with a memorandum advising him not to pursue Aglen's dismissal, warning that such an act would lead to the collapse of the customs administration with dire consequences for both Chinese and foreign interests. And they reminded Koo that he and the rest of the Chinese delegation at the Washington Conference declared that Beijing would take no actions that would prove to "disturb the present administration of the Chinese Maritime Customs." John V.A. MacMurray warned Koo that while Washington did not want to interfere in China's internal affairs, he saw dangerous consequences if Koo carried out his threat to relieve Aglen of his duties.[74]

Koo decided to take a middle ground approach. He fired Aglen, but named another foreigner to head the Customs Administration.[75] A contingent of diplomats met with Koo to discuss his actions. To no avail, Lampson "harangued [Koo] till I had exhausted my vocabulary."[76] For his part, the powers annoyed Koo by interfering in what he deemed to be an internal Chinese matter. Koo later asserted that Chinese public opinion looked upon his actions "as a legitimate assertion of China's sovereign right . . . [and] strengthened my conviction that, if China stood on her legitimate rights, her action, no matter how striking or even shocking it might appear in the Far East or Asia in general, would be fully understood abroad." To a limited degree, Koo played a role in what Robert Bickers has described as the dismantling of Britain's informal empire by laying the foundation of what would be the eventual Sinification of the maritime customs that reflected *imperium in imperio.*[77] More importantly, the issue revealed the competition between the GMD in the south and the Beijing government for public support: a competition that extended to the unequal treaty system.

Although Koo refused to unilaterally overthrow the treaty system, he recalled that "China's policy from the Paris Peace Conference on had always been to regard the revision of the unequal treaties as a national policy." In 1927 in a conversation with Lampson, Koo underscored that his top foreign policy goals were still tariff autonomy and abolition of extraterritoriality. Instead of a unilateral call for the end of the unequal treaties, Koo took a legal approach by relying on diplomacy and international law. In particular, he intended to use the principle of *rebus sic stantibus.* Koo demanded revision of the unequal treaties because "the conditions prevailing at the time when those treaties were made had changed, and the changed conditions made those treaties out of date and called for their revision in accordance with current conditions."[78]

In his competition with the GMD government for the prestige and support of the Chinese people, Koo needed to take some positive steps toward destruction of the imperialist system. Using the principle of *re-bus sic stantibus*, Koo implemented a policy of automatic termination of treaties once they expired. In December 1926, Koo oversaw abrogation of the Sino-Belgian Treaty by allowing the treaty to expire without nego-tiating its renewal. Belgium resisted Koo's maneuvering but to no avail. Koo later referred to it as "a landmark in Chinese diplomatic history because it was the first time that an unequal treaty was declared com-pletely abrogated in the face of the open and official opposition of the other party in the treaty." Koo focused his attention on Belgium because that country was incapable of flexing military or political muscle in or-der to protect its imperial rights. This move upset many in China's for-eign community because of the precedent that it set: "a precedent to prove China's determination to act in order to bring an end to the re-gime of unequal treaties from which China had suffered for a century," was how Koo put it. According to the *New York Times*, the Belgians lost extraterritoriality "at a time when the shell of a Government is grasping for anything that will enable it to seem alive and to catch popular atten-tion by a gesture of nationalism."[79]

Koo's activities of the previous months to eliminate the unequal treaties were indeed desperate measures to fulfill his patriotic goals while at the same time trying to win enough public support for his actions to undermine Chiang Kai-shek's revolution. His success with the Belgians led him to revise China's treaty with Spain. Then Koo informed the Japa-nese and the French of his intention to negotiate new treaties with those countries. Like that of the tariff conference the treaty negotiations were conducted in surreal conditions. Everyone knew that the Beijing gov-ernment was more fiction than fact, and since the GMD army moved ever closer to the northern capital, Beijing's days were numbered. Sir Miles Lampson wrote that it was "this fiction of a Government, secure in the knowledge that they could always count on the support and approval of the country as a whole when it came to baiting the foreigner and play-ing to the Nationalist gallery, which . . . abrogated the treaty rights of Belgians, and notified Japan of China's intention to revise the Japanese treaty within six months."[80]

Valid criticism aside, Koo defended his actions, telling foreign cor-respondents that "China's lack of unity could not justify delay in the

negotiation of new treaties." He added that "fears that a change in Government in China might lead to repudiation of such new treaties were
entirely groundless."[81] However, success proved elusive. Negotiations with
Japan got underway in January 1927, but broke down because the Northern Expedition caused the collapse of the Beijing government. And the
days spent at the bargaining table made it clear that Japan would not
grant tariff autonomy. Japan's attitude was similar to that of Britain's. As
Lampson explained to Koo, the British government was not about to
make a wholesale abandonment of its vested rights in China. Koo simply
would not compromise on the issue of tariff autonomy. He viewed the
tariff revenues as essential for putting the Beijing government and ultimately the entire country on a sound financial basis.[82] As for the French,
negotiations also commenced, but protests from the GMD grew too loud
to be ignored and proved unfruitful.[83]

While engaged in these negotiations, Koo turned to Washington
for assistance in revising the imperialist system. In January 1927, the
United States, following the British lead of the previous month, expressed
willingness to revise the unequal treaties with "any Government . . . or
delegates who can represent or speak for China." Washington expected
most-favored-nation treatment and would relinquish extraterritoriality
if the Chinese could guarantee protection for American citizens in Chinese courts. The next month, the U.S. House of Representatives passed
the Porter resolution, which called on the president to enter into negotiations with "accredited agents of the Government of China, authorized
to speak for the entire people of China" with a view to revise existing
treaties between China and the United States. The U.S. State Department's
January announcement, however, did not clearly delineate with whom
Washington planned to negotiate the treaties: Koo or the GMD. Secretary of State Frank Kellogg observed that neither side "could singly claim
to represent the whole of China." Washington's policy to wait and see who
would form a stable central government blindsided Koo. The American
insistence on only negotiating with a government that truly represented
China struck many Chinese as a convenient excuse for delaying talks.[84]

Chiang's Northern Expedition brought Koo's efforts to revise the
unequal treaties to a swift end in 1927. In June, Koo resigned and retired
to his villa in the Western Hills. He saw the handwriting on the wall.

Beijing soon fell to Chiang Kai-shek, and Koo knew that whatever government came to power would not undo his work but would build on it. Although an opportunist, Koo was a patriot who saw the abolition of the unequal treaties as the basis for building a modern China regardless of who was in control. In the meantime, Chiang Kai-shek turned against the CCP and the Soviet Union, and either defeated the northern armies or made political deals with some of the northern warlords. Zhang Zuolin made a deal with Chiang that permitted him to return to Manchuria while the GMD flag flew over Beijing. Chiang Kai-shek renamed the old capital Beiping, or Northern Peace, and established the new capital at Nanjing. For people like Chiang, Beijing carried a stigma, a foul odor that stank of Yuan Shikai, Duan Qirui, Wu Peifu, and Zhang Zuolin.[85]

In 1928, Koo received a rude jolt when the GMD government ordered his arrest, forcing him to flee to Great Britain's Tianjin Concession. Lampson declared that if GMD officials produced an arrest warrant, the British would execute it. Lampson had no idea why the GMD wanted to arrest Koo. He speculated that they sought revenge for the arrest of GMD students in late 1926 by Zhang Zuolin. Frank Ashton-Gwatkin of the Far Eastern Department believed the motives were more personal: "Wellington Koo, I understand, is one of the most hated of the foreign-educated 'Young China' group among his own compeers, because in his own meteoric rise to fame he let down so many of his friends." With regard to C.T. Wang, who was soon the new foreign minister, Koo was "on particularly bad terms."[86]

Koo made it to Weihaiwei and checked into a local hotel under the name of Mr. Wei. Once there, he asked for British protection. R.F. Johnston, the local British Commissioner, observed, "Although Dr. Koo is one of the Chinese statesmen who have advocated the abolition of the 'unequal treaties,' and foreign concessions, he has on several occasions shown himself very ready to avail himself of the protection which those treaties and concessions afforded to . . . embarrassed Chinese politicians to find peace and protection here under the British flag." With the GMD in control of China, Koo, not wanting to be arrested, left China and spent most of 1929 in Europe. In the fall of 1930, he returned to China to work with Zhang Xueliang, the son of Zhang Zuolin who was murdered by the Japanese military outside of Mukden. The younger Zhang asked

Chiang Kai-shek to rescind the arrest order, a move staunchly opposed by Koo's old enemies in the Nanjing government.[87]

After Chiang came to power, C.T. Wang continued the work started by Koo and other previous governments to revise the unequal treaties. Seeking to improve relations with the United States and Britain, the new government took a moderate approach to treaty revision in which Wang negotiated separately with each power but in a manner designed to be conciliatory toward the Western countries. The U.S. State Department recognized Chiang's government in July 1928 because Nanjing was the only government that promised stability for China, and the Americans believed that it was incumbent upon them to contribute to improving Sino-American relations. Along with recognition, the United States granted the new government tariff autonomy in return for mutually guaranteed most-favored-nation status. The United States, though, did not surrender its extraterritorial rights nor did it withdraw its military forces from China.

As for Britain, the new Chinese government toned down anti-British sentiment and took the initiative to win British recognition and demand revision of existing Sino-British treaties. Britain reciprocated because Chiang Kai-shek was preferable to the CCP and its Soviet friends, and there was the lingering idea that British trade with China would become immensely important in the future. The British officially granted Nanjing tariff autonomy in December 1928, opening the door to recognition. In 1930, the rendition of Weihaiwei, which was aborted in 1924 when Koo was in office, finally took place. Yet, Britain intended to carry out imperial retreat with as much grace as possible and not be thrown into a rout. The Empire still included Hong Kong and Kowloon, British forces still protected British interests, and extraterritoriality still gave British subjects an unequal position. In 1930, Japan caught up with Britain and the United States by granting China tariff autonomy, though it too was not ready to forfeit extraterritoriality.[88]

Looking back at the 1920s, Koo's patriotism differed from that of the Chinese students, merchants, teachers, and workers, many of whom were influenced by Sun Yat-sen's Three Principles as well as Marxist-Leninism. The antiforeign nationalism of the 1920s deemed the warlords to be China's domestic enemies.[89] By being in bed with the enemies of the people—that is, the warlords and the imperialists—Koo was seen as part of the problem. There was a growing belief that only a social revolution could overthrow the warlords and the imperialist powers, such as had taken place in the Soviet Union. And as these beliefs grew in intensity, Koo's diplomatic approach grew less and less attractive. Hence, Koo's approach only partially succeeded. The consummation of Koo's lifework was performed by the Nanjing government, which relied on a combination of popular support, military power, and diplomacy.

But just as World War I set the stage for the 1920s, the 1920s set the stage for a renewed crisis with Japan. The Nanjing government's announcement of 1928 declaring past treaties to be invalid and the willingness of Tokyo to grant Chiang's government tariff autonomy in 1930 brought about an improvement in Sino-Japanese relations. It alienated, however, civilian and military right-wing radicals in Japan who viewed such policies as appeasement of anti-Japanese sentiment in China. Worse, Chinese boycotts of Japanese goods and Nanjing's control of Manchuria threatened Japan's economic security in the middle of the Great Depression. Japanese militarists soon instigated a crisis that brought Koo back into China's policymaking circles.

Chapter 4

CHINA, JAPANESE IMPERIALISM, AND COLLECTIVE SECURITY, 1931–1937

IN 1929, KOO RETURNED TO CHINA to assist Zhang Xueliang, known as the Young Marshal, who controlled Manchuria but gave his allegiance to Chiang Kai-shek. At the time, Koo's career looked finished. On one or more occasions, Koo tried to get a position in the Nanjing government only to be rebuffed, particularly by his old nemesis, C.T. Wang. Koo had little choice but to remain in Manchuria as a private individual. He had purchased land in Manchuria years before and now purchased more in an effort to establish a land development enterprise. "I wanted to leave the political sphere," Koo asserted later, "and had the intention of giving up my diplomatic and political life altogether. But things do not always turn out as one would wish."[1] The event that brought him out of the wilderness and back into Chinese politics was the Manchurian Crisis of 1931.

For years, Manchuria was a sore spot in Sino-Japanese relations. Both China and Japan viewed Manchuria as both a potential source for raw materials and an outlet for growing populations. Japan in particular viewed access to China's markets and resources as vital in providing Japan with the economic security necessary to wage total war. Japan perceived Chiang Kai-shek's Northern Expedition to unify China as a threat to those vital interests because Chiang was seen as a pawn of the Soviet Union. Kwantung Army officers blew up Zhang Zuolin to create a pretext for Japanese military intervention in Manchuria to prevent the GMD flag from flying over Manchuria. The plot backfired, sparking anti-Japanese

Chinese delegation to the League of Nations, 1930s. Koo is fourth from the left. Sitting to his left is W.W. Yen. (Author's collection)

boycotts and resentment in Zhang Xueliang who used his authority in Manchuria to undermine Japan's treaty rights. While Koo stood by the Young Marshal's side, Japan returned to its previous policy of noninterference while still claiming its special position in Manchuria.

Theoretically, Japan remained committed to internationalism by virtue of its membership in the League of Nations, and of being a signatory to disarmament agreements signed at the Washington Naval Conference and the London Naval Conference of 1930, as well as the Kellogg-Briand Pact of 1928 that outlawed war. The navy and army, however, grew increasingly disgruntled with military cutbacks and cooperation with the West that circumscribed rather than enhanced Japan's position as a power in Asia. The Great Depression of 1929 reminded the Japanese army of Manchuria's place in Japanese security. And although Sino-Japanese relations were improved by Japan's granting of tariff autonomy to Chiang's government in 1930, the move alienated civilian and military right-wing radicals who viewed such policies as appeasement of Chinese nationalism. Japanese officers of the Kwantung Army in Korea decided to take action. On September 18, 1931, a section of the South

Map 3: Japanese expansion into Manchuria.

Manchurian Railway on the outskirts of the Manchurian city of Mukden exploded. The Kwantung Army immediately occupied Mukden and moved its forces deeper into Manchuria, but Chiang Kai-shek ordered Zhang Xueliang not to resist so that Chiang could focus on dealing with his internal enemies.[2]

Japanese expansion could not have come at a worst time for Chiang Kai-shek. He had only nominally unified China since the revolution of 1928 and believed that China could not deal with external threats until the country was unified.[3] There were a number of warlords who ruled independently of Nanjing and feared Chiang's growing power. Besides the warlord problem, there was the communist problem. The CCP, whom Chiang turned against in 1927, remained a threat though it was splintered ideologically and geographically. The CCP created a number of rural soviets that focused on using peasants and guerilla warfare to create revolution while the urban CCP leaders continued to look for a revolution in the cities along orthodox Marxist lines. By 1931, after a series of failed uprisings, Mao Zedong was in charge of the largest CCP soviet located in Jiangxi and Fujian Provinces.

More significant than the communist threat was the factionalism within the GMD. In May 1931, a number of Chiang Kai-shek's rivals, including various factions and militarists, formed a separate government in Guangzhou. Koo backed this government, blaming Chiang Kai-shek's "autocratic methods" for not allowing this motley group a wider participation in his government.[4] The disunity within China played right into the Kwantung Army's hands. Although both Guangzhou and Nanjing understood that the Kwantung Army could take advantage of China's inability to speak and act with one voice, the Guangzhou government pursued closer political ties with Tokyo and pushed its military forces outward from Guangzhou into neighboring provinces. While Chiang Kai-shek requested that Zhang Xueliang send some of his forces south to assist in dealing with the Guangzhou government, Chiang also advised the Young Marshal not to take any actions in Manchuria provocative of Japan.[5]

Now that China faced a new crisis with Japan, Chiang created a Special Foreign Policy Commission to determine what kind of policy to pursue in regard to Japan. Koo was appointed to that Commission as

Zhang Xueliang's representative to share his expertise on the League of Nations and diplomacy in general. One important connection that Koo had with the government was T.V. Soong, the Columbia- and Harvard-educated minister of finance. Soong was a brother-in-law to Chiang Kai-shek by virtue of the generalissimo's marriage in 1928 to his American-educated sister, Soong Meiling. The marriage was viewed as a political deal in which Chiang received needed financial banking in return for giving T.V. Soong a position in the government. Soong, and another brother-in-law, rich U.S.-educated businessman H.H. Kung, held numerous ministerial positions till the end of World War II. Both Soong and Kung also formed factions composed of Anglo-American educated Chinese. Although rivals, they tried to give Chiang's regime a veneer of democracy.[6] Koo and his wife knew both men and their families well since they all represented Shanghai's upper-class. Over the next seventeen years, Koo worked closely with T.V. Soong. The two men did not always agree on foreign policy issues, but they found common ground during the early 1930s when they found Chiang's policy toward Japan unpalatable.

The question facing China was whether or not to rely on the League of Nations. On September 21, Chiang Kai-shek informed the international body that there was a dispute, but he did not request action at that time. There were reasons to not expect much from the league. In 1929, Chiang nearly quit the international organization for good after the league responded weakly to tensions between Zhang Xueliang and the Soviet Union. The next year, when China tried to become a nonpermanent member of the League Council, there was opposition because of China's disunity and its inability, if not refusal, to pay its dues. Still, some in the government, such as T.V. Soong, wanted to rely entirely on the league. Yet, when Koo met with Chiang and the Special Foreign Policy Commission, he doubted the body's efficacy. Instead of looking to the League of Nations, he argued for direct negotiations with the Japanese, believing that refusal to negotiate played "into the hands of the Japanese strategy of facing up to the League of Nations." Although the League Council asked Japan to withdraw its forces, the League Covenant, in Koo's opinion, provided the group with "no power to enforce its decision." Recognizing the limits of its power and with Japanese opposition to the League

Council's proposal, Koo believed direct negotiations to be essential. However, he wanted Sino-Japanese negotiations to be carried out on a basis like that which took place at the Washington Conference in which a third of the power or league observers were on hand.[7]

Chiang agreed, but he wanted Japan to withdraw and accept the dispatch of neutral civil officials to the area. In a matter of days, though, Japan's answer was clear. It would neither withdraw nor allow a third party to participate in negotiations. And on October 26, Japan put before the League Council its own proposals for negotiations, including the demand for Chinese recognition of Japan's treaty rights in Manchuria. The League Council sided with China by voting against Japan's proposals and in favor of China's recommendation to negotiate after a Japanese troop withdrawal. This action reassured Koo, but he remained skeptical of the league's ability to handle the crisis. In November, the League Council proposed sending a commission to Manchuria to assess the situation. While the League Council engaged in bitter debate, the Kwantung Army expanded further in Manchuria in defiance of its own government and world opinion. Initially, Koo rejected the proposed commission "as being too vague and not providing for evacuation" of Japanese troops despite warnings from the British and American ministers that rejection could put China "at serious tactical disadvantage." A counterproposal was prepared, but Sir Miles Lampson, the British minister, cautioned Koo that China could "find herself accused of turning down compromise sponsored by the Council and see world opinion turn against her." Koo did not reject the commission out of hand. He simply thought that to not impose a deadline for Japanese evacuation was to condone "the act of wanton aggression on the part of Japan." It also gave the impression that "instead of dealing frankly with this issue," the League Council put forth the commission idea "with a view to providing the Council with a means of exit from its difficulty." Despite his qualms, Japan and China reluctantly accepted the League Commission on December 10.[8]

The powers' unwillingness to confront Japan over its expansion into China weakened the League of Nations. European newspapers generally argued against the involvement of their respective countries in the affair. Some condemned Japan, and some thought Japan was justified in its acts, considering past Chinese recalcitrance over the treaties. The British tended to sympathize with Japan, blaming the Chinese for trying to undermine Japan's position, which was based on treaties, and denounced Chinese talk of going to war as foolish. France's government likewise did not view Japan's actions with any sense of opprobrium and did not want the League of Nations to become wrecked on an issue that was not an act of war on Japan's part. More importantly, French officials worried about Germany, where right-wing conservatives controlled the Weimar Republic. For the moment, a European crisis was not imminent, but the French did not want to be preoccupied with the Sino-Japanese dispute should a crisis break out closer to home. Besides, confronting Japan could ultimately threaten French Indochina, and given French hostility toward communism and Comintern activities, France did not want to discourage the Japanese from pushing northward.[9]

If the British and French did nothing, then there were the two nonleague members, the Soviet Union or the United States. As the United States reeled from the Great Depression, Washington could not entirely sympathize with Japan's economic and demographic problems that justified Japan's expansion into Manchuria, but it hesitated to brand Japan an aggressor. Neither President Herbert Hoover nor Secretary of State Henry Stimson wanted the United States dragged into war. Japan's actions were immoral but understandable, since it needed to preserve order on the continent to protect its vital security interests against Bolshevism. Since Japanese expansion into Manchuria posed no security threat to the United States, Hoover rejected economic sanctions or military actions against Japan. As for the Soviet Union, relations between Nanjing and Moscow had not been restored, but the Soviets worried about the creation of a Japanese colony on its border and the potential for Japanese expansion into Mongolia. Moscow wanted to take action against Japan especially now that the Kwantung Army controlled the CER. But Joseph Stalin could see that no other power wanted to restrain Japan and he did not believe the Soviet Union was strong enough militarily to deter further Japanese expansion. To avoid conflict, Moscow offered to sell the CER to Manchuria's puppet government and signed a nonaggression pact with Japan.[10]

The international situation left Chiang with few options. With war against the militarily superior Japan impossible and the likelihood of outside help just as impossible, Chiang preferred to negotiate. "The Generalissimo was a realistic statesman," Koo observed later. "He felt it was necessary to negotiate with Japan. On the other hand, as a shrewd politician, he did not wish to profess openly a policy of direct negotiation." Chinese students, however, rejected that option. Displeased with the government's handling of the Manchurian crisis, they entered the foreign ministry in September, attacking and nearly killing Foreign Minister C.T. Wang, who promptly resigned. Nearly a month later, Koo accepted the appointment as Wang's replacement. Lampson believed Koo's decision to accept the post showed "considerable courage."[11] Indeed, students attempted to intimidate and bully Koo much as they had Wang because Koo favored direct negotiations. Koo's tenure as foreign minister lasted only ten stormy days. Angered with the government's policy of direct negotiations and demanding that China walk out of the League of Nations, students surrounded the foreign ministry and threatened to beat Koo, who sought protection in Chiang's Nanjing residence. Overseas, Chinese confronted and attacked Alfred Sze, forcing his resignation as China's delegate to the international body. The atmosphere was of such anger and excitement that Koo feared that peaceful resolution of the crisis might prove impossible. In the face of demands for war, Koo sought a nonmilitary solution to the crisis. He suggested creating a neutral zone in Manchuria, only to backtrack in order to avoid public disapprobation.[12] Although supported by intellectuals like Hu Shi and Jiang Tingfu, Chinese students were, in Koo's words, "hostile and inflamed against any suggestion that China and Japan negotiate directly respecting a neutral zone" in Manchuria. On December 15, thousands of Chinese high school and university students attacked the Chinese Foreign Ministry. Chiang Kai-shek announced his retirement, and Koo resigned as foreign minister.[13]

The same month that Chiang Kai-shek "retired," the Kwantung Army expanded into Manchuria, taking advantage of the disunity that remained in Nanjing and the weak response from the powers. Although ordered to resist to the last man, Zhang Xueliang put up only token resistance and then pulled out, removing all army forces from Manchuria. Meanwhile, the coalition government that replaced Chiang Kai-shek collapsed. In late January, Wang Jingwei, a longtime GMD politician, took

the reins of civilian power with Chiang Kai-shek being in charge of the
military. T.V. Soong took up the post of finance minister, and Lo Wen'gan,
the Oxford Ph.D. who served in various cabinets with Koo in the 1920s,
was made foreign minister.[14]

No sooner did this new government come to power than it was
faced with another crisis. The Sino-Japanese conflict expanded to Shanghai where the Japanese military instigated an incident, creating a pretext
to militarily intervene in Shanghai to punish China for its anti-Japanese
boycotts. Following other instigated incidents of fighting between the
Japanese and Chinese, local Japanese naval forces demanded the cessation of such boycotts, an apology, restitution, and removal of Chinese
army forces from Shanghai. When Shanghai's mayor did not answer the
ultimatum to the navy's satisfaction, Japanese marines engaged in street
fighting with Chinese forces that turned into pitched battles complete
with naval and aerial bombardment. By late February, both sides raised
the stakes with reinforcements that risked blowing the situation up into
full-scale war ultimately involving the other powers.[15]

In the midst of this crisis, Koo explained to his foreign counterparts that the Sino-Japanese conflict was not a local one but rather an
international question to be solved by a conference of all the powers
concerned. If Japan got away with this kind of expansion, not only did it
undermine the treaties, but it would "so upset the balance of power and
the relative positions between Pacific Powers that the consequences and
effect would be far-reaching." Koo wanted a conference of those nations
who had signed the Nine Power Treaty and were committed to protecting the territorial integrity of China and guaranteeing the Open Door.
As the Shanghai conflict continued, replies to Koo's queries as to the
possibility of the United States cooperating with the League of Nations
in imposing sanctions against Japan were in the negative.[16]

The powers took interest in events in China, but they did not respond in a manner satisfying to China. In January 1932, Secretary of
State Henry Stimson announced what became known as the Hoover-
Stimson Doctrine in which the United States refused to "recognize any
situation, treaty or agreement entered into between" China and Japan
that impaired U.S. treaty rights in China including the Nine Power Treaty,
which upheld the Open Door. Japan and the other powers that were

party to the Nine Power Treaty ignored Stimson's declaration until the flare-up in Shanghai. After fighting broke out in Shanghai, the British, not wanting to face Japan alone, submitted an appeal to the League of Nations that included much of the Hoover-Stimson Doctrine. The appeal, though, did not condemn Japan. Although appalled by events in Shanghai, French foreign policymakers reflected the same caution and were not very receptive to Stimson's proposal. Like the British, they did not want to give the impression of abandoning the League of Nations and lent their support to the British proposal.[17]

In March 1932, a ceasefire was finally arranged between the two contestants in Shanghai. On March 15, the League Commission of Enquiry, led by Lord Lytton, arrived in China. Koo reluctantly agreed to be the Chinese representative accompanying the various commissioners to Manchuria, soon to be renamed Manchukuo by the Japanese. This assignment involved a great deal of risk. Along with an assassination plot against Koo's life in order to embarrass Chiang's government, there were threats by the Manchurian authorities to have Koo arrested because of his former connection with Zhang Xueliang. Under this pretext, the Kwantung Army in theory provided Koo with protection, but in reality they spied on him and restricted his movements.[18]

In April and May, the commission traveled throughout Manchuria under strict surveillance by the Japanese. Policemen and secret agents watched their every move. Packages and clothing were searched. The intense surveillance led Koo to term the atmosphere "oppressive and heavy." After the commission reached Mukden, a parade was held in a square outside of the place where Koo was staying. There with the aid of binoculars, Koo watched several thousand Chinese and Japanese boys and girls preparing to receive Japanese troops with Manchukuo's national anthem playing in the background. The scene left Koo feeling "sorrowstricken." The Japanese were doing most of the singing and flag-waving while the Chinese "remained silent and immobile." The Japanese also brought in heavy equipment to mine for coal. As he stood amidst the equipment, surveying the work, Koo "was depressed to think that such [a] rich treasure storehouse was taken away from China to be utilized by others. There are probably many more elsewhere, but Ch[ina] has not tried to utilize them. What has she been doing all these years?"[19]

After Koo returned from his trip, he told Chinese journalists that China had to solve its own problems. China could not prevent further Japanese expansion merely by depending on others. As he explained to an Italian diplomat, "The responsibility of checking and forcing Japan to withdraw from Manchuria belongs primarily to China." Along with the fact that the powers provided little real assistance, his visit to Manchuria "renewed feelings of indignation at those responsible" for its loss. Koo believed in the right of self-defense, a right not exercised in 1931. Self-defense had been exercised, though, at Shanghai with Chinese forces holding off the Japanese until a truce was reached. That valiant stand by Chinese forces in Shanghai may have strengthened Koo's conviction that Manchuria could have been defended. Later in the summer, he told his government that it had to resist Japanese aggression.[20]

The problem for Koo was that his government was not listening. During the entire Shanghai Crisis, Wang Jingwei, the premier, followed a policy of "resisting while negotiating." By resistance, Wang did not mean war, and by negotiating, he did not intend to sign a treaty with the Japanese that represented a complete sellout. After the failure of the League of Nations to do anything substantive to punish Japan, Wang argued for direct negotiations with the Japanese in which conflicts between both sides would be settled on a case-by-case basis. But since China's military was too weak to take on modernized Japan, the Chinese military had to settle for passive resistance while surrendering more territory to Japan. It was this policy that moved Wang to sign the Shanghai Truce Agreement with Japan in May that led to the withdrawal of Japanese forces from the city. Many Chinese, including government officials, condemned the agreement, but an effort to impeach Wang Jingwei failed because of Chiang Kai-shek's intervention.

In June 1932, Chiang, Wang, and other high-level GMD leaders met at a conference in Lushan where Chiang laid down his policy of "first internal pacification, then external resistance." Earlier in the year, Chiang used his armies against the CCP in Jiangxi Province. Chiang wanted to destroy the CCP before taking on the Japanese even though his policy was unpopular with those Chinese who viewed Japan, not the CCP, as the real danger. He pulled out troops from Shanghai during the crisis so that he could mass 500,000 men around the Jiangxi Soviet, and there Chiang remained throughout this period. For months to come, Chiang gave speeches trying to convince his own military of the soundness of his policy. But opposition to his policy was mounted by the Guangzhou politicians and by Wang Jingwei, who believed Chiang's policy undermined his "resistance while negotiating" policy. The key to success was having the military around to provide leverage when negotiating with the Japanese, but Chiang insisted on using his best troops to fight the CCP, leaving the responsibility of resisting Japan to local forces.[21]

Koo likewise opposed Chiang Kai-shek's policy. If China put up armed resistance and the Western powers applied diplomatic pressure, Japan would back down. Sources from Japan convinced him there was opposition to the Kwantung Army's expansion into Manchuria and that Japan was on the verge of "an internal revolution or an external war." Koo wanted his government to take the fight to the Japanese so as to place such economic strains on Japan that it would quit the fight. Koo admitted that the "main difficulty with the [GMD] was that it was divided among itself." Yet, he was confident that China would finally unite in the face of the Japanese threat. And although he acknowledged that the Japanese militarists "prevented the more sober-minded statesmen and industrialists in Japan from voicing their true opinion," he told Nelson T. Johnson, the American minister to China, that if "China and [the] Powers worked together, there would be a settlement."[22] In fact, Koo's analysis was rather flawed. In May, Japanese officers assassinated the prime minister, bringing party rule and the hope of a moderate civilian solution to an end. And as time revealed, the powers were incapable of cooperating to stop Japanese expansion.

In August, Nanjing appointed Koo to be the Chinese minister to France as well as a League of Nations delegate at Geneva. That same month, Japan recognized the state of Manchukuo. Soon after his arrival in France, Koo joined the Chinese delegation to the League of Nations. Koo had not attended league sessions for over ten years, but having helped draft the League Covenant, "I was no stranger to the workings of the League or to many of the members of its delegations." China placed the Manchurian question entirely in the hands of the Geneva-based group. The previous year, China invoked the League Covenant in requiring the League Council to bring about settlement of a dispute. If a settlement could not be reached, then the League Council had to draw up a report that assessed blame and recommended avenues of resolution. A League Committee, called the Committee of Nineteen, was created to examine the Lytton Report and issue its recommendations. Koo believed the report would decide whether China's policy had been a good one or not.[23]

In October 1932, the much anticipated Lytton Report was published. Softening the language to avoid a breach with Japan, the report did not condemn the Japanese. However, it stated that Japan's use of force was unjustified and that the people living in Manchukuo did not support the government. It concluded that the Manchukuo government was Japan's puppet. On the other hand, the report was critical of Zhang Xueliang's oppressive rule and commented that instability in China was "an obstacle to friendship with Japan." The report recommended that Manchuria be placed under Chinese control but that Japanese economic interests be protected. Despite the report's attempt to be balanced and fair, the Japanese viewed it as hostile and asked for a six-month delay to examine its contents.[24]

There were aspects to the report that troubled Koo. He believed that the Lytton Commission had "misinterpreted Chinese nationalism" to be the cause of "many international disputes." He was disappointed that the commission did not see Japan's "internal political disputes" as a "real menace to international peace." And Koo was deeply disturbed by the report's criticism of the Chinese use of boycotts. In vain, he tried to convince Lytton that if Japanese forces withdrew from China, his government "would be willing to do her best to stop not only the boycott but the anti-Japanese movement" even though he really could not guarantee such an eventuality. As long as the Japanese remained, Koo defended his country's use of the boycott as a "legitimate defense against Japanese aggression." He explained to an Irish delegate at Geneva that the boycott should not be condemned because it was a "peaceful instrument of resistance and defence in the possession of militarily weak countries." Besides, "economic retaliation," such as quotas and tariffs, was widely practiced around the world without provocation. The boycott, on the other hand, was a legitimate act as described in the League Covenant.[25]

On November 21, the League Council met to discuss the Lytton

Report. Koo called on the Council to take "prompt and effective action" on China's behalf, but the Japanese, who opposed the report, openly questioned whom Koo actually represented: Chiang Kai-shek or Zhang Xueliang. Koo tried to counter arguments that China was disunited and unstable but he faced a hard sell. A number of league members were aware of the fact that Wang Jingwei now resided in Europe after a disagreement with Chiang, refusing to return to China. Meanwhile, Chiang Kai-shek remained vigilant in his efforts to destroy the CCP. The Japanese proved antagonistic by refusing to allow members of the Lytton Commission to express their views of the report and the situation in Manchuria. The commissioners were discharged from their duties. From this point on, the league, in Koo's words, betrayed a tendency to postpone the "issue on pretext [of] trying conciliation first." The council met six more times, but accomplished nothing of substance. The report was passed to the League Assembly for consideration.[26]

On December 6, the Special Assembly convened. The Japanese delegate argued that Japan had done the people of Manchuria a favor by saving them from the clutches of dictators. The small powers demanded that the League of Nations implement the report's recommendation that Manchuria be turned into an autonomous region with foreign advisers. Some even favored Japan's expulsion from the league. Much to their disappointment, the great powers threw cold water on the whole proceedings. The delegates from France, Great Britain, and Italy advocated realism and conciliation and rejected taking action against Japan. The attitude of the British and French generally was that there was no reason to condemn Japan. Sir John Simon, Britain's foreign minister, was, in Koo's words, "unfriendly to China," as Simon proceeded to quote at length the parts of the Lytton Report that were unfavorable to China. On December 9, a resolution condemning Japan for recognizing Manchukuo and rejecting Japan's self-defense argument was defeated in the League Assembly; instead, the Lytton Report and Japan's Observations on the Report were referred back to the Committee of Nineteen.[27]

When the assembly passed the buck back to the Committee of Nineteen, Simon hoped that the United States and the Soviet Union could participate in forming proposals to reach conciliation. U.S. and Soviet officials were in Geneva representing their respective countries at the

World Disarmament Conference. Although neither were members of the League of Nations, the British wanted to make the United States partially responsible for whatever solution was agreed to while seeing the Soviet Union as having a natural right to participate, given its proximity to Japan. The idea never got off the ground. Japan opposed those countries' participation on the grounds that they could not share responsibility in the league by virtue of not being members of the club. The Committee accomplished nothing and recessed for the holidays.[28]

While the league dallied, events in China took a turn for the worse. On January 3, 1933, the Kwantung Army occupied Shanhaiguan, the gateway to Rehe, a northeastern province bordering Manchuria. The army had wanted to occupy the area for some time but held off to avoid further damaging Japan's position at the League of Nations. The league's growing opposition gave the military the green light for expansion. Local Chinese forces put up resistance but were forced to retreat. The fact that the Manchus used Shanhaiguan to conquer ultimately all of China was not lost on the Chinese. While protests were made to the league, Chiang Kai-shek came under intense pressure from the Guangzhou government and the Chinese delegation at the League of Nations to break off his communist extermination campaign in Jiangxi and send troops to Rehe. Chiang refused. In February, the Chinese suffered humiliation as many of Zhang Xueliang's forces beat a fast retreat, forcing an embarrassed Young Marshal to resign. As Zhang took early retirement in Europe, Wang Jingwei returned to China where he became president of the Executive Yuan.[29]

The loss of Rehe humiliated the Chinese delegates at Geneva because they assured the league that China would defend Rehe, only to see Chinese troops withdraw without a fight. Chinese military withdrawal undermined the diplomats' efforts to convince the powers that China was serious about resisting the Japanese. As Japanese forces occupied Chinese territory, Koo grew frustrated with the League of Nations. He saw the Sino-Japanese dispute as a litmus test of "the efficacy of the League of Nations." In failing to condemn Japan, the league set a bad example for the smaller powers, which struck Koo as "seeing the Sino-Japanese dispute from the right point of view, whereas the so-called great Powers appeared to be rather short-sighted." By being short-sighted, Koo meant that the powers were destroying the league's credibility by refusing to brand Japan an aggressor and to impose sanctions. And now that Japan expanded further into China, the hope of conciliation was dead. Japan's renewed aggression "brought the nations of the world to a point where the question to consider was how to save the League of Nations from destruction." To prevent its demise, the powers needed to maintain a united front. Koo wanted "a very definite statement by the League that they stood behind the Lytton Report." He expected "the League of Nations to pronounce a moral judgement on Japan." Doing nothing did not encourage the Soviet Union and the United States to collaborate with the league.[30]

Koo was right that conciliation was dead. Although the Committee of Nineteen did not reassemble until January 16, 1933, conciliation with Japan proved impossible because some of the small powers demanded Japan's expulsion. The great powers balked at such a step. Although the Western powers (including the United States) were not united in what action to take toward Japan, they were united in what they would not do. The Western democracies would neither accord recognition to Manchukuo nor seek the expulsion of Japan from the League of Nations or impose sanctions. The Committee of Nineteen was divided between those powers still seeking conciliation and a group of small powers taking a strong anti-Japanese line. With conciliation impossible, the Committee of Nineteen passed onto the assembly its report, which reiterated the Lytton Report's recommendations to not recognize Manchukuo but also to not impose sanctions or condemn Japan. While the League of Nations debated, Japan issued an ultimatum to Nanjing to remove Chinese forces from Rehe. On February 24, forty-two of the forty-four nations in the League Assembly voted in favor of the report with Japan voting against and Siam abstaining. Afterwards, Japan walked out of the proceedings, and a month later quit the League of Nations.[31]

In the meantime, the League Assembly created and charged the Advisory Committee, composed of the Committee of Nineteen and two nonleague members, Canada and the Netherlands, with the task of settling the dispute between Japan and China. Invitations were also sent to the United States and the Soviet Union. President-elect Franklin Delano Roosevelt informed the league that he supported Stimson's nonrecognition policy and agreed to work with the league in resolving the crisis. In the Soviet Union, however, those opposed to cooperation with the league argued that the other countries would push Japan and the Soviet Union into war. Hence, the Soviet Union rejected the league invitation, though in moderate terms.[32]

With the creation of the Advisory Committee, the league members were to work in concert and not unilaterally. Koo pressed for action, especially sanctions. By isolating Japan with moral and economic pressure, Japan would capitulate. He told Lord Cecil, Britain's representative, that the younger Japanese officers would stay in power until Japan was isolated and on the verge of losing its standing among the great powers. Then, "the older people would insist on a change of policy." As far as Koo was concerned, the key "was . . . to show to Japan that the Powers" were prepared "to back up the Report with concrete measures."[33]

The big obstacle facing the Chinese delegation now was convincing the League of Nations that a state of war existed in China. League representatives time and again questioned why China had yet to break diplomatic relations with Japan. The small powers especially could not fathom China's refusal to even recall the Chinese minister to Tokyo. Tokyo could claim that no state of war existed. Koo and his compatriots at the league advised Nanjing to implement economic, financial, and diplomatic measures against Japan in order to maintain an international front. They suggested that the government implement a plan of national reconstruction "as a means of improving the China market for western goods and of enabling China to resist Japan successfully." Western trade would achieve gains in the China market if there was a boycott of Japanese goods. And the government could strengthen resistance to Japan and enlarge the opportunities for Western trade in the China market by giving the Westerners a favorable tariff.[34]

Nanjing rejected sanctions as impractical, and since the powers refused to fulfill their obligations to impose sanctions, China's diplomats were told to stop pursuing sanctions. In this respect, the government was probably right. The Western democracies, especially France, were in no mood for sanctions. Most Frenchmen cared little about events in Asia. There were developments closer to home to attract their attention. By now, the Great Depression touched France, and with rising unemployment, the coalition governments formed in these years were preoccupied with improving the economy. Moreover, Adolf Hitler was now chancellor of Germany, and after outlawing the communist party, Hitler secured passage of the Enabling Act, which made him dictator. The rise of Hitler on France's doorstep naturally pushed Japanese expansion into the recesses of most French minds.[35]

The advice of Koo and his colleagues also did not find favor back home because Chiang Kai-shek still sought an "accommodation" with Japan. Despite having many critics, Chiang's policy remained that of "first pacification, then resistance." Later in the year, Chiang told his soldiers that while Japan was a disease of the skin, the communists were a disease of the heart. Backing Chiang's policy was Wang Jingwei who became disillusioned with the League of Nations for its refusal to invoke sanctions against Japan. He concluded that China could only help itself. Wang now began to tout Li Hongzhang, negotiator of a peace treaty ending the Sino-Japanese War of 1895, as the model of compromise in dealing with Japan.

In May 1933, the Kwantung Army struck south of Shanhaiguan and was poised to attack Beijing and Tianjin. Chinese forces retreated after taking heavy casualties. Chiang feared that the fall of Beijing and Tianjin would force him to sacrifice his policy of killing communists, so he sought a truce to reduce the costs of resistance and to salvage his anticommunist strategy. On May 31, 1933, Chiang's emissary and the Kwantung Army signed the Tanggu Truce, which declared most of Hebei Province a demilitarized zone cleared of Chinese forces, and gave Japan the right to fly spotter planes over the area to ensure Chinese compliance with the truce's conditions. The Tanggu Truce saved Chiang from military disaster in the north and permitted the continuance of the "first pacification, then resistance" policy. Wang Jingwei again openly supported Chiang Kai-shek because he had no faith in China's armies and defended the truce in the face of charges that he and Chiang were traitors.[36]

News of the Tanggu Truce disappointed Koo. Years later, he held the Tanggu Truce partially responsible for undermining the work of the League of Nations in creating an arms embargo as well as determining the extent of nonrecognition of Manchukuo. Koo and his colleagues told Nanjing that the Tanggu Truce was inopportune in its effect on international public opinion. "It was felt," the men continued, "that a concrete, definite policy on the Manchurian question was necessary." No power would assist China if it "wished to pursue a passive policy and do nothing to hasten a solution of her serious question with Japan." In their opinion, such a passive policy was dangerous because it "might in fact lead to [China's] dismemberment." Possibly aware of Wang Jingwei's views of Li Hongzhang, Koo and his compatriots argued that the Sino-Japanese War opened the way for the "scramble for concessions" of 1898 because China's "willing surrender" was "interpreted by the more ambitious nations as proof of China's utter inability to maintain herself as a self-respecting, independent State." And now with increasing tensions between France and Nazi Germany, Japan would take advantage of Europe's distresses to "pounce upon China once again," as it did in 1915, and eventually go to war with the United States and the Soviet Union. Thus, China had to be prepared for world war. The memorandum went on to suggest that China join with Britain, the United States, and the Soviet Union in presenting an economic front. Internally, they advocated the creation of a united front and reconstruction.[37] China had to help itself before it could expect help from others.

There were indeed serious threats to peace in Europe. In October, Adolf Hitler, who hated the Versailles Peace Treaty, led Nazi Germany out of both the League of Nations and the Geneva Disarmament Conference. Europe's distresses gave Japan a free hand in China because it denied China outside help in the face of Japanese aggression. Wang Jingwei refused to place his hope in the West and would even declare neutrality should war break out between Japan and the West. He wanted to buy time to strengthen China internally. Chiang and Wang agreed, though, that their policy "first pacification, then resistance" should continue. Nazi Germany viewed the China market as a source of raw materials needed to build up Germany's military strength. Sino-German trade expanded after 1933, and Germany provided both military hardware and advisers were put to use by Chiang primarily against the CCP. Meanwhile, Chiang and Wang took steps to ensure they had control of their Japan policy. Government officials who represented the hard-line, anti-Japanese view within the Nanjing government were removed. From 1934 onward, anti-Japanese activities were suppressed and censorship was imposed on the media. Japanese-educated Chinese who supported Chiang's and Wang's policy generally replaced Western-educated officials in the government.[38]

Their efforts at some rapprochement with Japan were complicated by Tokyo itself. In April 1934, a Japanese foreign ministry spokesman, Eiji Amau, announced Japan's Monroe Doctrine for China in which he claimed that East Asia was Japan's special sphere and that Japan was responsible for peace in East Asia. Japan did not welcome foreign intervention into China, nor did it approve of China's efforts to seek foreign assistance. Japan was displeased with the League of Nations, Germany, France, and the United States, all of which provided loans and/or military advisers. Japan directly challenged the Open Door and the Nine Power Treaty. Koo denounced the Amau Doctrine, but his own foreign ministry issued only a mild protest. Chiang Kai-shek killed the League of Nations' financial assistance program, and Japan's opposition made it difficult for Nanjing to secure other foreign loans. Chiang and Wang's policy of "first pacification" worked to prevent a crisis from breaking out between China and Japan, but it did so at a political cost for the government.[39]

Watching these events from afar, Koo was disappointed that his advice was being ignored. "Although there has been no announcement of any change in policy," Koo wrote to a friend, "signs of the times seem to indicate that there has been a disinclination to pursue a policy of effective resistance—at any rate for the present." Koo continued: "I believe that, if this is true, it will be a costly mistake in the end; and I am continuing my efforts to make them see my point. But . . . a number of prominent Chinese in close touch with Japan have been lifting their heads and advocating a change of policy. It seems their influence is being felt more and more as time passes." Yet, Koo was not entirely despondent. He could see light at the end of the long tunnel: "That they will not succeed in the end so far as the best interests of China are concerned, I am certain." While Chiang Kai-shek's policy remained unchanged for the next year, Koo returned to China in July 1934. It was rumored that Koo might resign in protest of Nanjing's policy. He did not resign, but he was embittered with Chiang and Wang for ignoring him. Koo remained in China for another eighteen months awaiting reappointment as ambassador to France and making occasional trips to Nanjing, but he was clearly on the periphery of foreign policy making.⁴⁰

While Koo sat in China, he realized that China desperately needed an alliance to survive. The Great Depression, the rise of Hitler, Imperial decline and defeatism prevented the powers from making the League of Nations a viable deterrent both in Europe and Asia. Those factors and isolationism in the United States made the Nine Power Treaty null and void. Months before the Sino-Japanese conflict revealed the hollowness of those international covenants, Koo pushed for a broad anti-Japanese alliance. In 1936, Koo warned the British of the inevitability of war. He claimed to have seen Japanese military plans some years back that called for the "complete domination of the Asiatic continent," including Manchuria and Hong Kong. Japan also allegedly wanted to conquer Australia and obtain "naval parity with America." Only a Far Eastern pact could potentially restrain Japan. The British treated Koo's idea as simply another Chinese attempt to play one power against another.⁴¹ Neville Chamberlain, Britain's prime minister, argued that friendship with Japan was more important than that with the United States or China. Chamberlain believed that conciliation of Japan permitted Britain to concentrate on Germany, and others in the British government supported signing a non-aggression pact with Japan.⁴² Yet events in Japan suggested that Japan was out of control now that the military dominated the country's political institutions.

One glimmer of hope arrived from the United States in 1936. Chinese officials in Washington reported to Koo that Roosevelt wanted to "establish [a] regional organization for peace and hoped China might be included, but not Japan." FDR's concept fit with Koo's idea of a Far Eastern pact. Unfortunately, Roosevelt made similar statements to Maxim Litvinov, the Soviet foreign minister, in 1933 only to back off such talk, making the Soviets distrustful. Chamberlain, likewise, distrusted FDR after several similar incidents.⁴³

In March 1936, Koo returned to a Europe far different from the one he left in 1934. Hitler rearmed Germany in defiance of the Versailles Treaty. In April 1935, the Stresa Front was created between Britain, France, and Italy in which the three powers condemned German rearmament and agreed to defend the independence of Austria, Hungary, and other states in Germany's path.[44] A few months later, Benito Mussolini, Italy's Fascist dictator, stabbed France and Britain in the back when he attacked Ethiopia. The League of Nations condemned Italy's aggression. Needing Mussolini's support against Germany, the British and French opposed the use of sanctions. Public opinion in both countries expressed outrage at their governments' willingness to turn their backs on Italy's aggression. Limited sanctions were imposed but failed. By 1936, Italy conquered Ethiopia, discrediting both the West and the League of Nations. Koo, who was in Geneva, noted that there was a general "sickening atmosphere at [the] impotence and cowardice of [the] League in [the] face of [the] murder of a League member by another. Everybody felt injustice and yet no one would say it."[45]

Meanwhile, Japan sought elimination of the treaty remnants of the Washington Naval Conference. In 1936 at the London Naval Conference, Japan demanded naval parity with Britain and the United States and walked out of the conference when the answer was no. Japan's overall policy was to maintain its position on the Asian continent, resist Soviet expansion, and expand its power into Asia. The army made preparations for future war with the Soviet Union, and in November 1936 Tokyo signed the Anti-Comintern Pact with Germany in which both sides agreed that if either were attacked by the Soviet Union, the other would do nothing to help Moscow.[46]

With the situation worsening in Europe and Asia, Britain and France continued their policy of not confronting Japan. Militarily, the British were incapable of defending the home islands and protecting the empire simultaneously. In 1937, Italy's signing of the Anti-Comintern Pact left the British the task of preventing those nations from allying with Japan. As for the French, the rise of Nazi Germany, Japanese expansion in Asia, and the effects of the Great Depression bolstered by movies and books that spoke of the horrors of the next war that would far exceed those of the last one instilled much fear in the hearts of Frenchmen. By 1937, the French believed that Germany's armed forces were superior to France's, and unsurprisingly, France sought to conciliate Germany. With Britain as a weak partner, France could do nothing for Czechoslovakia and Poland should Hitler drive east.[47]

For Chiang Kai-shek, the only encouraging news emanated from the Soviet Union. In August 1935, the Comintern called for a united front against Japan. The next year, Litvinov suggested to Koo that the Soviets and Chinese discuss cooperation. Chiang leaned toward a united front because he wanted Soviet military aid and a mutual assistance pact. The Soviets, however, declined the mutual assistance pact and wanted instead a commercial treaty. With the rise of Hitler, Stalin did not want to be dragged into war with Japan. The Soviets would provide military aid but that was the limit of their intervention.[48]

In December 1936, Chiang's efforts to build a coalition were nearly destroyed by the CCP. Chiang Kai-shek flew to Xi'an to push Zhang Xueliang to attack the CCP. On December 12, Zhang kidnapped Chiang and held him prisoner, permitting the CCP leadership to meet with the generalissimo. The kidnapping shocked many inside and outside of China, including Koo. It came days after Germany and Japan signed the Anti-Comintern Pact. In Koo's mind, this agreement and other developments around the world proved the futility of Chiang's policy, which left China isolated. In Paris, Koo met with Wang Jingwei, who was recuperating there after an assassination attempt in China. Koo argued for cooperation with Britain, France, and the Soviet Union by way of "two sets of agreements" in order to "internationalize the Sino-Jap[anese] question." Koo recognized the antipathy that existed between Britain, France, and the Soviet Union, and separate agreements was his way of bridging the gap. He reasoned that Nanjing could not deal with both internal and external threats at the same time, so a united front was preferable to the suggestion that Nanjing divide its forces to deal with both. In Koo's opinion, "the J[apanese] peril was far greater" than the communist one. On December 25, the Xi'an Incident came to a close with Chiang Kai-shek's release and the creation of a Second United Front between Chiang and the CCP.[49]

Over the next several months, Koo persisted in his search for cooperation among the powers. The signing of a nonaggression pact between Britain, France, the United States, and the Soviet Union would be the first step toward the long-term goal of establishing an alliance. An alliance guaranteed peace in the Far East, because Japan would not go to war with several nations at once.[50] Koo knew though that a Pacific Pact was problematic. The French informed Koo time and again that the only "stumbling block" was Great Britain.[51] There was truth to that statement. The British Foreign Office rejected proposals that would have led to Pacific agreements, preferring to reach some kind of mutual understanding with Japan that permitted British trade with China. However, the French wanted a Pacific Pact no more than the British, because France's military weakness made it incapable of resisting Japanese expansion. And while the Soviet Union renewed a pledge to send military aid to Chiang Kai-shek, Soviet policy, like that of the other powers, was otherwise extremely cautious. The Soviets recognized there was little hope for collective security in Asia given the attitudes of the Western democracies. Moreover, Stalin purged his officer corps, weakening the Soviet Red Army at a critical moment.[52]

In the meantime, while Koo mulled over his country's fate, he maintained his weekly routine of attending meetings and exhorting the embassy staff to "develop esprit de corps." He also daily engaged in what he described as cultivating relations in that he tried to learn as much as possible of French society. Koo made it a point to meet politicians, journalists, academics, and bankers. He was present at social gatherings whenever possible, though some of the guests proved rather annoying. On one occasion, he was asked to lunch by a woman who remarked, "Japan is a big power, becoming more powerful every day. You will surely be able to swallow up China." The Madame had mistaken Koo for the Japanese ambassador.[53] Other days were far more pleasant, such as when he could take in eighteen holes of golf, a game of bridge, or a movie. It was fortunate that he did seek some leisure time, because he would have few opportunities to relax for the next eight years.

Chapter 5

SINO-JAPANESE WAR AND THE SPECTER OF SELLOUT, 1937–1941

ON JULY 7, 1937, JAPANESE AND CHINESE forces clashed at the Marco Polo Bridge near Beijing. When the Japanese Army presented demands, including Chinese withdrawal from the area and an apology for the incident, Chiang Kai-shek refused. In coming days, the Japanese government sent five divisions to China and demanded control of North China. Chiang Kai-shek agreed to be more vigilant in suppressing the activities of the communists and other anti-Japanese bodies in order to assuage the Japanese, but the Japanese demanded concessions that Chiang was not prepared to make. The generalissimo decided that he could no longer appease the Japanese by trading territory for time.[1]

News of Japanese divisions bound for China kept Koo awake all night as he sought some solution to the crisis. As both sides rushed reinforcements toward Shanghai, Koo saw that unless there was outside mediation, major war in China was certain. News from China was "depressing." Chinese forces withdrew from Beijing without a fight after the local commander defiantly declared his refusal to give up even an inch of Chinese territory. "I felt no face to see anybody," Koo wrote in his diary, "China became a joke." Although there were credible rumors that Japan was interested in reaching a settlement, Koo insisted on fighting unless Japanese forces withdrew from Beiping. The fall of Tianjin was likewise "most depressing and sickening news." When Koo learned of the bombing of civilians in Tianjin, it made his "hair stand up." On the

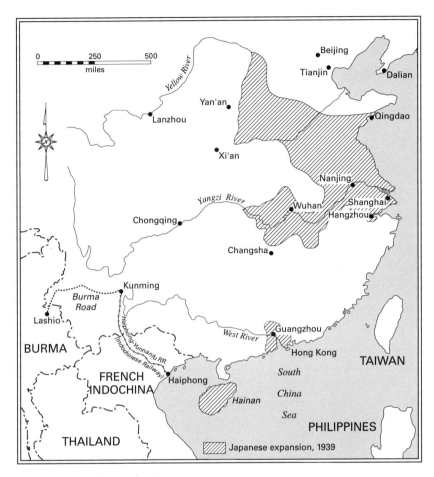

Map 4: ROC Lifelines, 1939.

day that Beijing fell, Chiang Kai-shek announced that another truce to settle differences was impossible.[2]

With the outbreak of undeclared war, Koo and other compatriots urged Chiang Kai-shek to approach Moscow to promote Sino-Soviet military cooperation with "Anglo-American-French material coopera- tion as background." Koo assumed incorrectly that the peace in Europe resulted from a equilibrium of forces. France and Britain, with the "moral sympathy and support" of the United States and with a treaty between

France and the Soviet Union in the background, gave Europe a stability that prevented aggression. Asia needed such a balance of power, and the lack of it explained why "Japan could run amuck." Since Britain, France, and the United States were anxious to avoid war at almost any cost, China and Soviet Russia could do all the fighting while the other three powers supplied material and financial aid.[3] Koo and his colleagues in Europe were not hopeful that such equilibrium of power could be formed. The Soviet Union would only act if backed by the Western democracies. The British struck Koo as not taking events in China seriously and he acknowledged that France was "impotent in the Far East."[4]

Unexpectedly, the Soviet Union did do something. In August 1937, Nanjing and Moscow signed a Treaty of Nonaggression in which both sides agreed that neither would make separate deals with Japan and the Soviets promised Chiang Kai-shek military aid. Chiang preferred an alliance that obliged the Soviets to commit their forces against the Japanese, but Moscow was unprepared for war with Japan. Over the next four years, Soviet aid in the form of advisors, aircraft and other military equipment poured into China. Depending on the type of weapon, Soviet assistance represented 80 to 100 percent of the total foreign aid given to China between 1937 and 1939. By concluding this agreement, the Soviet Union hoped to indirectly confront Japan while halting appeasement of Japan by using Chiang to pin the Japanese down in China. Unfortunately for Koo, the Soviets turned his scheme on its head. Moscow provided the military support as background, leaving China the tough task of forging an alliance with the Western democracies who already rejected a broad anti-Japanese front especially one that incorporated the Soviet Union even as background.[5]

Meanwhile, China took its complaint before the league. Although there is no evidence that either Chiang Kai-shek or Koo expected concrete actions from the League of Nations, Chiang's government demanded that the league impose military and economic sanctions against Japan. The government may have sought to win international public opinion to its side as a stratagem to lay a foundation for an anti-Japanese alliance. Although the French "advised delay," Koo believed that the league had to act to save itself. "The aggression of Japan on China was flagrant,"

Koo remarked to Yvon Delbos, the French foreign minister, "and if the League should refuse to take cognizance of it, the League would become a complete farce." The least the league could do was to brand Japan the aggressor and deal with the issue of sanctions later. In early September, Koo told league members that Japan, which was bent on domination of Asia and not expanding simply out of the need for seeking population outlets or raw materials, had to be punished.[6]

From conversations with various individuals in Geneva, Koo recognized that he was making a hard sell when calling for sanctions, because it was clear that the "League could not do much" and that the "matter hinged on Britain and France." The Soviet Union, which by now was a league member, did not fit into the equation. Although the Soviets would not take the lead to avoid worsening relations with Japan, Stalin was prepared to support the branding of Japan as an aggressor and to impose sanctions if the democracies stood unified on the issue. The democracies however believed that sanctions might provoke Japan to attack British and French interests in Asia. The British tolerated humiliation of the league should it fail to act. The French were convinced that any attempts by the league to impose sanctions would merely reveal the league's impotence, having negative repercussions for Europe where France's foreign policy was focused. Delbos told Koo point blank, "You might as well call on the moon for help as on the League of Nations." The British and French agreed that sanctions were ineffective as long as Washington was not a part of it. And if the Chinese pushed for sanctions, the United States would be forced to implement its Neutrality Acts.[7]

Although Koo agreed with his counterparts that U.S. "collaboration" was essential and that calling for sanctions was a mistake, the foreign ministry insisted that Koo push the league to impose sanctions.[8] The powers warned that American neutrality would negate whatever actions the league sought to implement, and advised Koo to take his case before the league's Far Eastern Advisory Committee, not the Assembly. The Chinese diplomat accepted this advice because he too wanted American cooperation and he thought it "useless to force things if [the] Powers were unwilling." It made sense to "work with them [rather] than against them."[9] His government insisted otherwise. On September 16, Koo asked that Japan be condemned as an aggressor and punished with an embargo of certain raw materials. At the same time, he asked the powers to provide China with the financial assistance necessary to begin an arms buildup. The powers refused.[10]

From Koo's point of view, France and Britain feared being in the position of having to apply sanctions once they did brand Japan an aggressor, and were "trying to 'pass the buck' from themselves to another." When asked to present resolutions of a general character, Koo retorted that thousands of Chinese noncombatants were being killed everyday. "Public opinion everywhere in the world was indignant," Koo argued, "and expected the League to do something." When he went before the League Advisory Committee that day, he did convince the powers to condemn Japan's bombing raids on civilians, but later when he called for creation of a sub-committee that would ask league members to do all in their power to help China, there was virtual silence. The British told Koo that creation of such a committee would delude the Chinese people into thinking that the "League intended to take stronger action than was in fact possible." Koo became even more indignant when the Advisory Committee meeting was not only postponed but Koo was asked to withdraw his resolutions.[11]

On October 1, the Advisory Committee did meet and the British representative proposed that the most effective act that the league could initiate at the moment was to call for a Nine Power Treaty conference. For Koo, the "proposal fell like a bomb, deafening all senses." On October 5, the Advisory Committee submitted to the Assembly a heavily diluted version of Koo's resolution that refused to brand Japan an aggressor and merely asked league members to do nothing that would weaken China's ability to resist. Despite Roosevelt's "Quarantine Speech" in Chicago in which FDR asserted that "The epidemic of world lawlessness" had to be quarantined, Britain and France feared that a strong resolution only invited Japanese retaliation. The League Assembly passed the resolution, an act that received Washington's blessings.[12]

The powers' decision to shift responsibility from the league to the Nine Power Treaty left Koo dissatisfied. He reminded the Advisory Committee that the "Washington Treaty cannot relieve League members of their obligations under the Covenant." The majority of the committee members, however, agreed that while they would do nothing to weaken China and did find Japan guilty of breaking treaty obligations, they could do nothing against Japan. In the words of one member, "The League was 'absolutely powerless.'"[13]

As Koo prepared to travel to Brussels where he would lead the Chinese delegation, he still sought a balance of power in Asia. To achieve such a balance, Koo knew that the Americans were essential, and he commended Roosevelt for the Quarantine Speech. He also recognized that the United States did not want to be pulled into a situation from which it could not withdraw and detected a strong pessimism among the French who felt that America would not do very much on China's behalf. And going into the conference, Koo could see that China and the powers pursued different goals. China wanted Japan declared an aggressor and material support including arms and military demonstrations by the powers. The powers preferred to simply mediate the dispute possibly with Japan in attendance. If Japan showed up, Koo feared that China would have to make concessions. If not, he feared the powers would take little action.[14]

Likewise, the Chinese Foreign Ministry seemed skeptical of success at the Brussels Conference. Whether the conference was a failure or not, the Chinese delegation was to work with the powers, get them to restrain Japan, and persuade France, Britain, and the United States to encourage Soviet Russia to use its military against Japan.[15] Although uncertain as to the American position, Koo went into the conference convinced that the "United States . . . did not like to see the Conference fail and admit defeat."[16] He could not have been more wrong.

Before the conference even began, the Americans refused to play a leadership role and later warned Koo not to make any statements that implied the United States was taking the lead. The American delegation suggested that China withdraw from the conference so that the powers could have "full liberty of discussion." China had a right to participate, but those nations who supported China entirely would be reticent in the presence of the Chinese. China was not a contractual party to the Nine Power Treaty, and Japan's actions were aggression against the powers' interests in China. There was, however, no way for China to accept such a suggestion. Koo said that the Chinese were united in their resistance of Japan and that for China to withdraw from the conference would undermine that resistance.[17]

On October 31, Koo left Paris for Brussels. His journey took him through World War I battlefields, which "led me to reflect that although the youthfulness of the trees and the relative newness of the buildings still told the story of . . . the war, the world had learned little from it. A new war was in the atmosphere everywhere." Upon arriving in Brussels, he quickly became discouraged. A couple of American journalists informed Koo of the pessimism that permeated the U.S. delegation. One delegate asked Koo what China would be willing to sacrifice in order to reach a settlement, but as Koo explained to Delbos, "China would not want peace at any price, but only peace with justice." Koo readily felt the difficult position his country was in. At a time when war was raging in China and the country was in desperate need of help, the powers' were in no mood to confront Japan. The delegations to Britain, France, and the United States repeatedly warned Koo "to pursue a policy of moderation so as not to slam the door" on the prospect of Japan's participation in one form or another.[18]

On November 3, the day the conference opened, Koo presented China's case and the facts of Japan's aggression. Although Japan rejected the conference, the powers sent a note asking Japan to accept mediation.[19] While waiting for Japan's reply, the conference utterly failed to accomplish anything. With instructions from FDR, Norman Davis told the British and French that the United States did not intend to take the lead, especially since U.S. interests in East Asia were minute. As for the French, they wanted the Americans to take the lead because they wanted to use cooperation in the Far East as a way of committing the United States to the defense of Europe. The French, like the Americans, opposed the use of sanctions and were skeptical of the viability of applying moral pressure on Japan.[20] Britain likewise wanted to secure American cooperation and not suggest any steps, such as sanctions, that would push the United States further into isolation. The overall attitude of Britain's foreign office was that British action in Asia depended upon the attitude of the United States.[21]

On November 12, Japan flatly refused to accept mediation, stating that its actions in China were a matter of self-defense. Meanwhile, the military situation in China worsened, with Japanese troops breaking through Chinese lines around Shanghai. At the same time, Germany offered to mediate direct Sino-Japanese talks. Koo continued calls for military assistance to China, but the American people would not support sanctions until they were ready to risk war or felt that such measures entailed no risks.[22] Koo did not want the conference to end "where it had begun or even before it had begun." He thought the whole conference to have been "over conciliatory toward Japan."[23] Only the Soviet Union (although not a Nine Power signatory, it was invited nevertheless) backed the Chinese at Brussels in calling for collective security in Europe and Asia.[24]

The conference ended on a sour note of failure. Meeting with the British and American delegates, Koo expressed disappointment that the powers could not provide China with more concrete assistance. Koo wanted the powers to ship arms to China and to guarantee the French protection of Indochina from Japanese attack. Such measures met with disfavor in the United States. Koo told the delegates that "Just as domestic order requires more than laws on the statute books, mere words are insufficient to restore peace and order in the face of international violence." He also told journalists that Britain acted like a friend, whereas the United States had not. An infuriated American delegate expressed displeasure with Koo's remarks, but in the same breath admitted that the United States could not provide any material assistance due to isolationism. The conference's last resolution stated that its sessions had been temporarily suspended and would meet again when it could be "advantageously resumed."[25]

The Chinese diplomat remained convinced, though, "that the United States could save the situation if it would act quickly and energetically." Otherwise, China's only alternatives were guerrilla warfare or German-Italian mediation, neither of which were, in Koo's opinion, in "the best interests of China or a constructive solution." Oversimplifying the situation, Koo blamed the failure of the Brussels Conference on the fact that the major powers that could help China were democracies. In reflecting on the attitude of the Western powers, Chen Kongbo, the Chinese ambassador to Italy, remarked that "Mussolini had told him that authoritarian States always favored positive action, whereas democratic countries always pursued a negative policy." Koo concurred with that opinion: "Democratic countries always moved slowly whereas the others could move rapidly."[26]

While the delegates at Brussels were busy burying the dead conference, the military situation proved grave. Japanese troops were driving toward Nanjing. For Chiang, the Brussels Conference was such a disappointment that he informed Nazi Germany, who previously offered its mediation services, that he was willing to meet with the Japanese military. The failure at Brussels meant no Soviet intervention, since Stalin made it clear that he would intervene only if the powers put up a united front. With the Japanese Army poised to capture Nanjing and since the powers were unwilling to take on Japan, Chiang pursued German mediation to buy time and as a tactic to frighten the powers into supporting his regime. Germany played the role of "honest broker" because it was concerned about its economic interests in China. Nazi Germany was now China's third largest trading partner, and its interests were threatened by the war. The Sino-Soviet Non-Aggression Pact also worried pro-Japanese elements in Berlin who wanted the war to end so that Japan would be a viable deterrent to Soviet expansion. The powers, as Chiang foresaw, were rather appalled that Germany might mediate cessation of the conflict, diminishing French and British prestige in East Asia. The Soviet Union increased aid to Chiang, but the United States still refused to provide any support. Koo told the Americans that German mediation was not in China's best interest. He preferred either to rely on the United States alone or to make Germany a part of a joint mediation effort as last resort.[27]

Despite the powers' concerns, nothing came of Germany's mediation efforts. Japan rejected Chiang's precondition of a truce. Then in early December, Japanese forces entered Nanjing and commenced their "rape" of the Chinese capital. Victory there led Japan to demand Chiang's recognition of Manchukuo, his cooperation in fighting communism, his acceptance of demilitarized zones, and war reparations. Although a number of the GMD government's top military and political leaders favored accepting Japan's terms, Chiang Kai-shek rejected them on the grounds that they would make China a Japanese colony. The next month, Japan announced its policy of seeking to annihilate Chiang's government.[28]

At the end of 1937, Koo recognized the powers' domestic and strategic difficulties, but, as he stated in his closing speech at Brussels, he still believed that the powers overlooked the possibility that the "violence and disorder raging in the Far East" would eventually become impossible to contain until there was another world war. In fact, Koo was surprised that the Sino-Japanese conflict had not become a wider war by now. Japanese aircraft attacked the U.S. gunboat *Panay* anchored near Nanjing, sinking it and killing several Americans. Britain, thinking that Washington was now willing to move beyond words to action against Japan, was prepared to send several battleships, the bulk of the Royal Navy, to China to prevent such outrages. Tokyo quickly apologized and paid indemnities, defusing the crisis. In Koo's mind, the *Panay* incident could have sparked a world war, "but the dark clouds blew over without breaking out into a storm."[29]

The situation for China internationally was bleak in 1938, though there were glimmers of hope. The Soviet Union pressed the CCP to give its full support to Chiang Kai-shek, who received more Soviet aid than Mao Zedong. The British provided military assistance, though they refused to loan Chiang money, fearing Japanese reprisal against vulnerable Hong Kong and potential attack by Nazi Germany in Europe or the Mediterranean. In lieu of a loan, the British built the Burma Road in order to take supplies into China. France contributed by keeping the railroad, which ran from Vietnam into China, open even though French authorities were concerned that the flow of military supplies could possibly lead France into direct conflict with Japan. The vital lifeline for Chiang Kai-shek remained open despite French threats to close it. Much of the Soviet aid passed over that railway. The French decision to keep the railway open proved crucial in coming months when Japan closed off the Hong Kong-Guangzhou-Hangzhou routes that filtered 75 percent of foreign aid into China. However, the French populace grew weary of China's attempts to involve the West deeper in the war. In January, the French press began criticizing the Chinese for trying to drag the United States and France into war with Japan.[30]

The Chinese expected more of the powers, though. Koo demanded that the league implement sanctions in order to show the world that the league had vitality. Koo also wanted the league to be an example to the United States in order to break the "vicious circle" in which the U.S. expected the league to take the lead whereas the League expected Washington to take the lead.[31] The league passed a watered-down resolution that simply stated that league members "for whom the situation is of special interest" should consult "other similarly interested powers" on what steps to take to bring about a "just settlement of the conflict in the Far East." Chiang rejected the resolution as "unacceptable," and Koo himself thought "it would be better to have no resolution at all if this was the best that could be obtained." He blamed the French for preventing the British from taking strong action "saying in effect that if the British were involved in the Far East what would happen to poor France all by herself in the Mediterranean?" At the next league meeting, Koo "spoke and dwelt upon the need of living up to obligations of membership and thereby strengthening the League." He told the league representatives that they had to preserve the "principle of collective security." Aggression unchecked in China could harm the peace in Europe.[32]

Unfortunately for Koo, Adolf Hitler peacefully annexed Austria in March. Then he turned his eye toward the Sudetanland, the German-dominated areas of Czechoslovakia. In May 1938, while Hitler ordered his generals to prepare for war against Czechoslovakia scheduled for October, he announced that Germany was withdrawing its advisers from China, cutting off aid to Chiang's government, and giving diplomatic recognition to Manchukuo. Hitler hoped the Japanese could tie down the powers in the Pacific while he expanded into Czechoslovakia. Japan had already established a pro-Japanese Reformed Government in Nanjing to oversee central China, now that Chiang made Chongqing his wartime capital. Hitler believed that Japan would ultimately win in China and expand further into Asia, and decided that leaning entirely toward Japan paid greater dividends over the long term.[33]

Chiang Kai-shek tried to lift up the morale of his people by assuring them that Japan did not have the resources to conquer China, and that eventually the United States and the European powers would enter into the Sino-Japanese conflict. But on top of China's huge battlefield casualties and the loss of major cities came bad news from Europe. In

September, a conference was held in Munich between Neville Chamberlain; Edouard Daladier, the French prime minister; Benito Mussolini; and Hitler, and it was there that Hitler got what he wanted: The Sudetanland would go to Germany on October 1, and a four-power agreement neutralized Czechoslovakia, canceling its alliances with France and the Soviet Union. Munich demoralized many within the Chinese government including Wang Jingwei who did not believe the Western powers would intervene on China's behalf. The Western democracies seemed on the verge of defeat in Europe while standing aside as Japan gobbled up China. Only the Soviet Union aided China and Wang saw this as a plot to drive China to communism. Wang wanted Chiang Kai-shek to reopen peace talks with the Japanese and sacrifice whatever was necessary to achieve peace.[34]

Back in Europe, Neville Chamberlain pronounced Munich a success and believed that he and Hitler had come to an agreement on future peace in Europe. Daladier held no such illusions; he expected Nazi Germany to expand beyond the Sudetanland and believed world war had only been postponed. From the United States came a message of congratulations from FDR for Chamberlain. Most Americans joined Britons and Frenchmen in celebrating Munich. One power clearly not satisfied with Munich was the Soviet Union, which had not been invited. Chamberlain's policy of appeasing Hitler meant that the West bought peace so that Hitler could drive east against what the democracies deemed to be Germany's natural enemy. Little wonder the Soviets now decried the League of Nations and collective security to be dead.[35]

Joining the Soviets in the chorus was Wellington Koo. Koo wanted the league to be a credible deterrent to aggression, and recognized that what the league did or did not do in Asia had an effect on events in Europe. There was also speculation that invoking sanctions, deemed by some as embarrassing to both the league and the Chinese, was to be the Chinese bargaining chip for getting Britain and France to provide China with concrete assistance as well as satisfying "a growing anti-League sentiment in Government circles in China." Whatever the case, Koo's government pressed for sanctions even though Koo warned that such a demand was "highly inadvisable." Indeed, the powers would not relent and asked Koo to postpone discussion of the Sino-Japanese dispute once Europe was confronted with the Czechoslovakian crisis.[36] Koo pressed for sanctions against Japan. In animated and acrimonious conversations, Koo stated that he refrained from invoking sanctions the year before and last May in return for "nicely-worded" league resolutions that promised action. A year later, "The resolutions remained nothing but empty words." Japan continued its aggression and "China felt completely disappointed."[37]

After Munich, Koo sent his government his analysis of the international situation. The fact that Britain and France stood by while Hitler moved into Austria and Czechoslovakia had ramifications for both Europe and the Far East. France ignored its treaties with Czechoslovakia, with the result that the weak, small states of Europe were fearful. Koo described Neville Chamberlain as an old man who ignored "obligations under international law or the principle of international morality." Koo blamed Chamberlain's desire to create another Concert of Europe, in which Germany and Britain would "dominate and control the weaker and the smaller powers," for undermining the league and believed that Chamberlain wanted to do everything possible not to offend Japan in order to protect Britain's Far Eastern interests. British and French appeasement of Hitler angered the Soviets to such extent that Stalin refused to take serious measures against Japan without having the backing of all the democracies. The only way to win Stalin's support was to enlist the cooperation of Washington.[38]

Long before the Munich Conference, though, Koo observed that the "doctrine of collective security, which was firmly held as the only sound basis of an organized peace, is considered unfeasible and discredited . . . it is perhaps no longer the fashion to talk much about the League of Nations." A few days after Munich, Koo told a Chinese audience that there was "no use to rely upon [the] West[ern] powers" after their failure to act against Hitler. Self-help was China's hope by depending on "space, time and number." The next year, attending league meetings became an even more unpleasant experience for Koo: "perhaps it was because I knew there could be no practical result from [the] effort and hard work. The League has been so weakened that any attempt to obtain concrete results is futile."[39]

Soon after Munich, Tokyo announced in November the establishment of a "New Order" in Asia that called for Japan and China to cooperate in providing stability in East Asia by defending against communism and creating a new East Asian culture. This New Order rejected the old one established at the Washington Conference that was based on the Open Door principles.[40] The next month, China's internal political situation grew more complicated. After Chiang Kai-shek turned down a Japanese peace offer, Wang Jingwei secretly slipped out of China to Hanoi and eventually headed a puppet regime established by the Japanese in Nanjing. Wang preferred Japanese domination to communism. In coming months, Koo received reports of war-weary and pessimistic government officials in Chongqing who wanted peace with Japan. In 1938, one of Wang's subordinates went to Tokyo to propose an end to hostilities, and in return, Manchuria would become Japan's concession. Later in the year, one of H.H. Kung's subordinates proposed an anticommunist pact with Japan and Manchukuo, hence giving recognition of Japan's puppet state.[41] Wang Jingwei's belief that the Western democracies would do nothing for China and that the war was leading to the communization of China still held true. The CCP enlarged its sphere of influence beyond Japanese lines in the north as resistance against the Japanese proved successful.[42]

The three democracies responded to Japan's New Order by reaffirming the Open Door. Koo interpreted the protests as evidence of a "hardening of the American attitude vis-à-vis Japan" and increased cooperation between the democracies. Koo read too much into the joint protest. None of the powers sought to apply sanctions against Japan and preferred assistance to China to retaliation against Japan. Although France permitted foreign military supplies to flow through Indochina, it refused to provide military aid. And while Roosevelt viewed economic aid to Chiang as a way of tying down Japanese armies in China and preventing further Japanese expansion, he refused to provide military support that could potentially drag the United States into war with Japan.[43] Even after FDR alluded to the dangerous threat to the democracies created by the indifference toward international lawlessness and charged that the democracies of the world could not ignore acts of aggression, Washington refused to lead those democracies by imposing sanctions.[44]

As Japan occupied Hainan Island and moved into the Spratly Islands and as Hitler gobbled up what remained of Czechoslovakia, Chiang pressed for an alliance, fearing that war in Europe would spur Japanese expansion. The Chinese leader suggested, among other things, that his government supply Chinese ground forces that would be supported by British and French naval and air power. The Chinese believed that the powers were interested in an alliance with China because they had to defend political, economic, and security interests in China threatened by Japanese expansion, especially Britain, which controlled 60 percent of all Western investments in China. Koo consistently described Japan as a nation bent on "the conquest of China, subjugation of Asia and finally domination of the world." Colonization of China made it "impossible to safeguard legitimate western rights and interests and that respect for China's sovereignty and maintenance of the open door." Hence, Koo called for broad cooperation to protect the powers' interests on the basis of the Open Door. China would defend British and French interests in the Far East while those two powers battled it out with Germany and Italy in Europe. The Western democracies rejected the plan fearing it would provoke Japan.[45]

The importance of the Open Door to China also proved a hard sell because the European powers worried more about Hitler, who now targeted Poland while Italian forces attacked Albania. Britain made security guarantees to Eastern Europe but Chamberlain's anticommunism and French fear of the Soviet Union proved insurmountable in forming an antifascist alliance.[46] Likewise, Stalin favored an alliance against Japan that threatened the Soviet Union's Far Eastern border, but the British and French rejected the idea, fearing that a mutual assistance pact directed at Japan would drive Tokyo even closer to Germany and Italy. Their policy seemed justified when Germany and Italy, not Japan, signed the Pact of Steel in May 1939.[47]

Then that summer, Japanese forces blockaded the British and French Concessions at Tianjin after the assassination of a Chinese-puppet official. The British agreed not to interfere with Japanese control in those parts of China occupied by the Japanese Army. The French likewise preferred to avoid angering the Japanese, especially if the United States refused to participate in joint action.[48] The British press at home and in China railed against the agreement as being a "Far Eastern Munich." The

British compromise infuriated Chiang Kai-shek, and the foreign ministry ordered Koo and his compatriots to express their "suppressed resentment" of the agreement. When Koo complained to journalists about Britain's "apparent disposition to accommodate aggression in the Far East," the British Foreign Office was not amused.[49]

That same summer, Roosevelt announced abrogation of the 1911 American-Japanese commercial treaty that prevented the United States from imposing trade sanctions. This step warned trade-dependent Japan that its vital link to the United States could be cut off once the treaty expired after January 26, 1940.[50] The measure seemed to reveal to Koo that the United States was willing to get tough with Japan. Chiang Kai-shek welcomed this particular American action since he was angry with the British for their appeasement of Japan over Tianjin, fearing that the same thing could happen in Shanghai where the foreign settlements remained intact. When the United States officially abrogated the treaty in January 1940, Chiang asked Roosevelt to place economic sanctions on Japan. Washington, however, would not impose sanctions for another six months after the commercial treaty expired because of its cautious policy toward Japan.[51]

The effort to build a five-power alliance was seemingly dashed on August 22, 1939, when the Soviet Union signed a nonaggression pact with Germany. With Hitler's Germany on the verge of conquering Poland, Stalin could not wait any longer on the West to conclude an alliance. He abandoned collective security and made a deal that he hoped would keep the Soviet Union out of war. Like Chamberlain, Stalin made the mistake of thinking he could indefinitely appease Hitler. The Nazi-Soviet Pact did permit Stalin to send aid to Chiang Kai-shek without being drawn directly into the Sino-Japanese War and prevented a German-Italian-Japan combination directed at the Soviet Union. Still, the Nazi-Soviet Pact shocked Chiang Kai-shek. The chance of putting together a combination of powers against Japan seemed lost.[52]

Koo found that the Nazi-Soviet Pact infuriated the French who told him that the Soviets were either promoting war in western Europe for their own narrow interests, or doing everything possible to avoid being dragged into a war in Europe. Koo told his government that the Nazi-

Soviet Pact weakened the Anti-Comintern coalition while permitting the Soviets to put pressure on Japan now that Stalin averted potential conflict with Germany. But if China was to build a broad anti-Japan coalition, there was the problem that France and Britain promoted war between the Soviet Union and Japan in order to secure their Far East interests. Nevertheless, China needed military support from the Soviets and the western powers, and Koo hoped that the Nazi-Soviet Pact would enable Moscow to provide more aid to China. Koo did worry that Japan would either try to build closer ties with Germany, Italy, and the Soviet Union or would seek better relations with Britain and France. He urged Chiang to seek closer military cooperation with the Soviet Union. If Moscow insisted on maintaining a defensive posture vis-à-vis Japan, Koo wanted to persuade the Soviets to back China in order to give the appearance of a broad united front against Japan.[53]

The ramifications of the Nazi-Soviet Pact were more negative for China than Koo perceived. The British believed that the potential for war in Asia had been reduced and that they were in a position to improve relations with Japan, which brooded over Germany's actions. The French, likewise, saw the Nazi-Soviet Pact as an opportunity for Anglo-French mediation of the Asian conflict at China's expense. Koo felt uneasy that the Western democracies were trying to find some way to prevent Asia from getting in the way of dealing with European issues. Koo's uneasiness was "aggravated" when the French suggested that China reach a negotiated settlement with Japan with a view to bringing Japan in on the side of Britain and France. France would act as mediator or possibly join the United States to bring about a settlement if the latter would not worry about China's fate.[54]

Just at that moment, the international situation took a dramatic shift. On September 1, Nazi Germany invaded Poland. On September 3, Britain and France declared war on Germany. "These are momentous days in history," Koo noted in his diary, "the beginning of a war which may alter the face of the world and civilization itself." Koo told the French that now was the moment for cooperation between the democracies and the Soviet Union in Asia. Moscow had a free hand in Europe, and it, with Western support, could bring enough pressure to bear on Japan to bring about peace in Asia for the next twenty-five years. Koo warned that any attempt by Britain and France to reach a rapprochement with Japan would be seen as a sign of weakness and only encourage further aggression. With Japan bogged down in China, the powers could, with a firm attitude, work with Japan to broker an arrangement that everyone could live with. The French, however, expected the Soviet Union to become involved in the destruction of Poland and not just stand on the side like a spectator.[55] The French were right. The Soviets eventually invaded Poland with their own forces. On September 28, Warsaw surrendered, and soon, the Soviet Union and Nazi Germany partitioned Poland among themselves .

Misperceiving relations between Moscow and Berlin, Koo observed that the Soviets were switching to the German side "with dangerous possibilities of reaction" in the Far East. He worried that the war would have a negative effect on British and French policy toward the Far East and believed that that the Soviet Union's policy was to have Germany, Britain, and France "fight" until all sides were exhausted, and "then she (the Soviet Union) could dictate." Meanwhile, Moscow was "determined to avoid war but continue to 'make hay.'" Koo warned the foreign ministry that the Soviet Union and the United States might try to conciliate "Japan in order to devote attention to Europe." The Chinese diplomat still entertained the hope that the Soviet Union, Britain, France, and the United States would cooperate. Even if the four parties were unable to sign an agreement, they could cooperate by "utilizing the strategic position of the U.S.S.R. in the north in fact" and by having the democracies speak to Japan. In fact, Koo's analysis of the situation was wrong. The Soviets entered into the Nazi-Soviet Pact both to avoid Japanese attack and to forestall an anti-Soviet alliance including a Nazi-Japanese one. The Soviet Union was still committed to aiding Chiang Kai-shek, though in a manner that prevented Moscow from being dragged into war. When Koo convinced Chiang to pursue an alliance with Britain and France in order to halt their appeasement, the Soviet Union came out in opposition to such an alignment.[56]

Worse, the Soviets threatened to cut back military aid to Chiang's government. After the fall of Poland, the Soviet Union demanded that Finland sign a nonaggression pact that permitted Soviet forces to have at least one base in Finland. Negotiations broke down and Stalin ordered the invasion of Finland on November 30. At the outset of the Winter War, Finland appealed to the League of Nations. A proposal calling for expulsion of the Soviet Union was introduced. Not wanting to alienate both sides by outright support or opposition to the resolution, China, represented by Koo, abstained while the league voted to kick the Soviet Union out of the organization. Moscow viewed China's abstention as support for the British and French and cut off aid to Chiang's government. Viewing Moscow's anger over his abstention at the league as a pretext, Chiang believed that in fact, the Soviets were working to reduce tensions with Japan.[57]

Besides the Soviet Union, the other obstacle to an alliance was the democracies. In a year and a half's time, Koo had watched Czechoslovakia, Albania, and now Poland disappear as a result of fascist expansion and the West's appeasement. "In meeting crises, democracies are clumsy and slow to act," Koo wrote in his diary, "whereas dictators count upon surprise attack and rapid crushing of victims." In his opinion, there was quite a contrast between his people and the West. Morale in China remained high, or so he claimed, on the basis of renewed Chinese counter-offensives. "The great Western democratic Powers, on the other hand," Koo observed, "had seemed to be yielding to one demand after another from Germany, which made it conspicuously evident that the country was threatening them with superior strength." The result of that "lack of resistance" on the part of the democracies was now a war with Germany.[58]

Back in China, Chiang still pursued an anti-Japan alliance even though many of his own people thought that the war with Japan could not go on once there was a European conflict. Yet in those early days of the war there was much talk and rumor of Anglo-Japanese and Franco-Japanese talks. Even though the democracies refused to recognize Wang Jingwei's puppet regime, loaned Chiang money, and kept Indochina and Burma open, Chiang feared the revival of the Anglo-Japanese alliance.[59] The U.S. State Department assured Chiang that a new Anglo-Japanese alliance was not in the making but rejected Chiang's suggestion that the United States create an anti-Japan coalition. Still anxious, Chiang wanted the United States to use its influence to prevent British, French, and Soviet appeasement of Japan, especially in the face of the conflict in Europe.[60]

Chiang's persistence in bringing about an anti-Japan bloc was dealt another blow in early 1940 when the phony war was replaced by a real one. Nazi Germany mounted offensives against the Low Countries, Norway, and France. By June, France was defeated. While Germany occupied part of France, the new government of Vichy maintained control over France's colonies abroad including Indochina. France's defeat made its Asian colony vulnerable to Japanese expansion. Japan demanded that France close the Indochina border. Throughout the summer of 1940, Koo remained in France, working with French officials in a vain attempt to keep Indochina open as a transit point. Koo found the French to be "powerless" in the face of Japanese pressure, and there were reports that Germany warned Vichy not to "provoke" Japan. In September, the Vichy government signed an agreement with Japan, under threat of war, that allowed Japanese forces to enter Indochina proper, closing off that vital lifeline. The British also agreed to close the Burma Road in July 1940 for three months in return for a Japanese promise to pursue peace. The British hoped that there could be an Anglo-American effort to settle the Sino-Japanese War.[61]

The closing of the Burma Road refueled Chiang's fear that China might be sacrificed because of the European war. To assuage those concerns, Roosevelt reiterated that no matter what happened in Europe, the United States would provide economic assistance.[62] Still, Chiang Kai-shek could not count on the United States to go to war anytime soon. A majority of Americans opposed going to war, and the Roosevelt administration sought to avoid war. Chiang tried to win U.S. support by informing it of a note received from Nazi Germany advising Chiang to reach a compromise with Japan since German-dominated Europe could no longer help him. Chiang pressed the United States and Britain for an alliance in order to not only prevent Japanese hegemony in the Pacific, but also the rise of communism in Asia. If there was a triple alliance, Chiang claimed he would uphold their interests in Asia and oppose Japan's Greater East Asia Co-Prosperity Sphere in return for money and military aid. And if Britain and America went to war with Japan, he would throw all his armies against Japan. The State Department rejected Chiang's proposal, saying that it would not be very effective.[63]

With the defeat of France, Hitler turned on Britain, now under the leadership of Winston Churchill. While the Battle of Britain raged, leadership in the Pacific shifted to the United States where the threat increased. In September 1940, Germany, Italy, and Japan signed the Tripartite Pact or what became known as the Axis Alliance. The parties agreed to support one another in creating new orders in Europe and Asia, and to assist each other if attacked by a power not presently engaged in either spheres, meaning the United States. Chiang Kai-shek welcomed the alliance. It linked the European conflict with the one in Asia, and, in his opinion, made war between Japan and the United States inevitable. Koo did not entirely agree. He believed the Axis Alliance guaranteed U.S. participation in the European conflict as well, and the problem for China was which theater would the U.S. prefer to assist first: Europe or Asia. Although Koo deemed the Asian conflict more important than the European one, he concluded that the U.S. would assist Britain first.[64]

In the end, Koo's analysis proved to be closer to the truth. FDR imposed sanctions prohibiting the sell of steel and scrap iron to Japan, but the president refused to impose an oil embargo against Japan for fear Japan would search for oil in the Dutch East Indies. At a time when FDR's military advisers agreed that the United States was not prepared for war, Washington sought to avoid exposing European imperial interests and America's colony in the Philippines to Japanese expansion. Koo even wondered if Washington would seek to mediate the Sino-Japanese dispute before taking "positive action" against Japan. After being reassured by his old friend, Hu Shi, who now was Chinese ambassador to Washington, that the U.S. did not intend to mediate the Asian conflict, Koo hoped that the United States would "liquidate" the Japanese menace now and lay the basis for a "durable peace" in the Pacific. Otherwise, he feared the United States would have to fight alone in both Asia and Europe.[65] After Roosevelt won his third term in office, he declared that America would be the "arsenal of democracy." He came up with the idea of Lend-Lease in which the United States would loan Britain the weapons to defeat Germany and Italy. China also benefited from Lend-Lease, as $26 million worth of aid went over the now reopened Burma Road. And China received a $100 million loan from America and a loan of £10 million from Great Britain.[66]

Despite these steps to aid China, a seed that created dissension in the future United Nations alliance was sowed in early 1941. Roosevelt dispatched his economic adviser, Lauchlin Currie, to Chongqing. In their talks, Currie impressed on Chiang the need to pursue democracy and to cooperate with the CCP. Throughout 1939 and 1940, there were numerous armed clashes between Chiang's forces and the CCP culminating in the New Fourth Army incident of January 1941 in which GMD troops killed thousands of CCP troops. The incident came at a bad time. The Soviet Union had just agreed to turn on the spigot only to have the New Fourth Army incident occur. The Soviets persuaded the CCP to maintain the united front while the U.S. applied pressure on Chiang Kai-shek to cooperate so that the Chinese continued to tie Japan down in China.[67]

There were other moves by the powers that were not entirely auspicious for Chiang Kai-shek. In April, Japan and the Soviet Union signed a Pact of Neutrality in which both sides agreed to not attack one another should either be at war with another power. The Soviet Union agreed as well to recognize Manchukuo. Although Stalin was unaware that Hitler already had his generals planning the invasion of the Soviet Union, tension in Soviet-German relations were sufficient to make a deal with the Japanese to avoid a two-front war. Chiang condemned the Neutrality Pact, which not only threatened his military lifeline to the Soviet Union but clearly rendered futile Chiang's four-year attempt to get the Soviet Union directly involved in war with Japan. And if Stalin could make a deal with Japan, so could the Western democracies.[68]

Then in June 1941, Hitler invaded the Soviet Union. For Chiang Kai-shek, the invasion meant a decrease in aid from that country because Stalin could not afford to provoke Japan at this moment of crisis. In July, Japan occupied southern Indochina, presenting a clear threat to both British interests in Asia and the oil-rich Dutch East Indies. The occupation of southern Indochina prompted the United States to join with Britain, Australia, New Zealand, and Holland in imposing an oil embargo on Japan. FDR also announced that China would be on an equal footing in an entente consisting of Britain, the United States, Australia, and Holland. The entente though did not go far enough for Chiang, who wanted an alliance that provided him with the political, military, and economic assistance to fight the Japanese and the CCP. The British and FDR refused to enter into such an alliance, seeing it as inciting war rather than relaxing tensions.[69]

In 1941, Chiang Kai-shek appointed Koo to be Chinese ambassador to London. For several weeks, London contemplated whether to accept him or not. Some in the British Foreign Office intensely disliked him, describing him as one of Britain's "bitterest enemies" from the 1920s. They distrusted him because of alleged financial improprieties on his part and opposed his appointment because he was not close enough to Chiang. The foreign office recalled that in 1938, Koo had been appointed ambassador to Moscow, though he allegedly declined that position. The foreign office thought otherwise and could not see any reason "why we should accept a man who . . . was turned down by the Soviet government on the same grounds as we ourselves opposed, namely that he was not close enough to the Generalissimo." The foreign office tried to persuade Chiang to appoint someone else, but the generalissimo pressed for Koo's appointment and the foreign office finally relented.[70]

Immediately, Koo set out to win British political and economic support for China's cause, but not as much assistance was forthcoming as the Chinese would have liked. In light of recent events, the Chinese increasingly feared a sellout and complained that Britain only supported China out of concern for its own interests and not for China's sake. One member of the foreign office admitted that Britain and the United States "bolster up China's resistance for our own ends" and further argued: "China's best guarantee against our 'selling out' to Japan is that it is as much in our own interests as in hers that she should continue to resist Japan." However, given the Nazi threat, "we cannot be expected to undertake lightly any further commitments which might embroil us with Japan." But many agreed with Sir John Brenan, who argued that Britain had been so cautious in its attitude toward Japan "that the Chinese are not unjustified in suspecting that we are deliberately keeping the way open for a deal with Japan at China's expense. So far our only declared Far Eastern policy has been sympathy for China coupled with the desire to improve our relations with Japan." Even if Britain could not provide more concrete assistance, it could at least bolster Chinese morale by making "an unequivocal public declaration of support" because the collapse of Chiang's resistance would "be a very serious blow" to Britain's world position. Although many in the British government agreed that China had to be kept in the war, British policy remained cautious in order to avert hostilities with Japan.[71]

This explained why the British rejected efforts by Koo to more greatly involve Britain in the Asian conflict. Over the summer of 1941, Britain and the Soviet Union signed an alliance that focused on the defeat of Nazi Germany. Koo wanted to know if Britain would come to the Soviet Union's assistance in the case of Japanese attack. The British responded in the negative and were annoyed that Koo even asked the question. Upon reading the notes of the conversation, Foreign Minister Anthony Eden wrote, "I do not like Dr. Koo nor trust him, and see no reason why we should answer his question."[72]

In July, after Japan moved into southern Indochina, Koo worried that the Japanese would attack the Burma Road. He wanted British air support to protect his government's last lifeline to the world. Eden refused to consider the request. Such a step would be an act of war against Japan on Britain's part. Britain did decide to freeze Japanese assets and abrogate commercial treaties with Japan. However, they were hesitant to inform Koo of these actions. They feared that the Chinese would leak the news creating the impression that Britain and China were acting in concert, and they initially feared that informing the Chinese of their measures "might have given an opening to the Chinese at an awkward moment for us for their persistent proposal for an alliance."[73] Despite all that the British were trying to do to aid China, Koo pressed for more. Reminding the British that they were doing themselves a favor by keeping his government in the war, he still asked for air support against the Japanese should they move against the Burma Road. Indeed, Chiang wanted an international air force established in China in which a British volunteer group could fly alongside the American volunteer group that had been established. Britain turned down the international air force scheme, but agreed to divert aircraft purchased from the United States to China.[74]

The British were clearly doing what they could to keep China in the war without being dragged into war in Asia. Caution dominated their policy toward China. In August, when a member of Parliament asked if

Britain was prepared to recognize Chiang's government as an ally against aggression, the British Foreign Office wanted the question withdrawn: "Anything we may say must be either unnecessarily provocative to Japan or disappointing to the Chinese." Brenan himself commented that "a declaration of alliance with China would entail the opening of hostilities with Japan, a development which we and the United States wish to postpone for as long as we can."[75] There was a good reason to be cautious. Britain stood on the verge of extinction at the hands of Nazi Germany.

In China, though, Chiang believed he was not treated as an equal. In August 1941, Roosevelt and Churchill held their Arcadia Conference. There they laid down the basis for the Atlantic Charter, which established that Britain and the United States would wage war on the principles that there be no territorial aggrandizement and no territorial changes anywhere without: the free consent of the peoples involved; respect for self-determination and the restoration of self-government in those areas dominated by Germany; equal access to raw materials and markets; and a postwar organization for security to replace the League of Nations. Koo complained to Eden that Chiang Kai-shek was "greatly disappointed that at the close of the conference no gesture had been made to China comparable with that which had been made with Russia." And Chiang felt that since his people "had been bearing a heavy burden almost alone for many years," their voice should be heard. He wanted the United States and Britain to firmly announce to Japan that the West not only viewed Japanese expansion into Southeast Asia as a threat, but would be equally concerned if Japan attacked the Burma Road. Eden argued that the less said about Asia publicly during the conference the better. However, Eden commented that Roosevelt would probably make a statement about Japanese aggression in the future and Britain and Holland would follow the U.S.' lead. Koo's persistent queries with regard to conversations between Roosevelt and Churchill irritated the British, but some in the foreign office knew they had to indulge Koo while London stalled on Chinese questions regarding aid and an alliance.[76]

Chiang was not satisfied with that explanation. At a dinner party, Madame Chiang harangued her American guests with the charge "that

China after 4 years fighting against aggression was ignored at the Roosevelt-Churchill meeting, express[ing] the opinion that the democracies were following the policy of appeasement toward Japan and indicated that this provoked Chinese resentment." Lauchlin Currie likewise conveyed to Washington Chiang's belief "that the democracies regard her [China] as inferior and of not being worthy of being considered an ally."[77]

Making matters worse, there was no public statement warning Japan against aggression after the Arcadia Conference. Instead, Churchill announced in late August that Japan and the United States were about to sit down for talks in Washington. Initially, Chiang had nothing to worry about. The United States insisted that Japanese forces withdraw from China, a point Tokyo could not yield. Except for the northern provinces and Hainan Island, Japan proposed to withdraw all troops from China within two years, evacuate all Japanese forces from French Indochina immediately, and promised to not attack the United States if Washington went to war with Germany. The U.S. rejected this proposal because Japanese forces would remain in China. Japan then gave the Americans a second proposal: In exchange for limited renewal of trade, including a quantity of oil, and a lifting of the embargo, the Japanese would withdraw their forces from the southern half of Indochina and promise not to advance into Southeast Asia. Again, Washington turned down the proposal.

Roosevelt gave assurances to Chiang that the talks were "exploratory," seeking a general settlement on the basis of U.S. principles, and that aid would continue to China as long as Chiang resisted. Nevertheless, Chiang and his wife tensely watched those negotiations, fearing a sellout. In his diary, the generalissimo noted that some people felt that the attitude of Britain and the United States toward China was not sincere and often betrayed China. Koo met with Richard Law, British Under-Secretary of State, who declared that it was "inconceivable that the United States should have any idea of selling China down the river." Still, Koo had the impression that Britain wanted the United States to make a deal with Japan in order to concentrate on Europe. Koo's mind was so absorbed with the war in the Pacific that in the course of talking with Law and listening to the latter remark that "events in Europe would prove to be decisive in the Pacific as well as in Europe," Koo "seemed surprised at the idea that there was a war in Europe." Koo then blurted out an acknowledgement that there was a war in Europe, but he still concentrated on the Pacific. "I tried as much as I could to bring his mind back to the Russian front," Law wrote after their meeting, "and he tried with equal zest to bring my mind back to the Pacific."[78]

For the next couple of months, Koo and his people bided their time and waited out the talks in Washington. The British were anxious that Koo say nothing that would create problems between Britain and Japan. When Koo prepared to give a speech over the British Broadcasting Service on October 10 to celebrate the Revolution of 1911, the foreign office was divided over what he should say. Some feared he would discuss the notion of an alliance between China, Britain, Holland and the United States and "inflame an already tense situation." Brenan disagreed, saying that efforts to restrict Koo "would only increase Chinese suspicions of our insincerity."[79]

Although Koo assured his government that the United States would do nothing to undermine the Nine Power Treaty, the fear of betrayal became acute. In November, Roosevelt entertained the idea of presenting a *modus vivendi* of his own to Japan: a ninety-day truce in Asia in which China and Japan would sit down and come to terms while Japan withdrew from southern Indochina, with Washington lifting the oil embargo. In a state of tremendous agitation, Chiang Kai-shek vented his anger with Washington on Owen Lattimore, his political adviser, who observed that Chiang Kai-shek's "reliance on America is the foundation of whole national policy and this would be destroyed by any loosening of economic pressure or unfreezing on our part while leaving Japan entrenched in China." According to Lattimore, Chiang felt that after four years of war with Japan, China "has not won a single ally and the nation feels politically isolated." Chiang wanted Roosevelt to either suggest to Britain and Russia to form an alliance with China or invite China to join the U.S., Britain, and other Pacific powers in a defensive alliance. In Chiang's opinion, either proposal would "safeguard China's equal footing among antiaggression peoples and remove the stigma of discrimination."[80]

In the meantime, the Chinese worked to undermine U.S.-Japanese negotiations. The Chinese embassy in London leaked the *modus vivendi* to the press. Meanwhile, Churchill commented that the collapse of China would threaten the democracies' interests in Asia at a time when the Nazis stood outside Moscow. Soviet surrender to the Germans or Japan's striking north against the Soviet Union would send the Germans back West toward Britain. The British and Chinese backlash convinced FDR to drop the *modus vivendi* and to demand complete Japanese withdrawal from China, even though Japanese forces were on the move in Southeast Asia, and Moscow and North Africa seemed within grasp of the Nazis.[81]

Despite his concerns about Japanese movements in and near China, Koo told the American Press Association in late 1941 that the Japanese, who were negotiating with the Americans, were only interested in convincing Washington to lift the oil embargo implemented over the summer. He described Japan as having an "ambition [that was] unbounded and unalterable," but Japan would not declare war now. Instead, Japan would strengthen itself while the European war exhausted the West. Although many people believed war with Japan was only a matter of weeks away, Koo disagreed. He argued that Japan "was bluffing and would continue to do so till the last second, in hope of frightening the U.S.A. and extracting concessions." He expected Japan to strike Russia, only attacking into Southeast Asia, when Great Britain and the United States were preoccupied in Europe. Thus, Japan's attack Pearl Harbor on December 7 left Koo "somewhat stunned." He agreed with others that "it was the best thing for China," but he had not expected this Japanese move. A Japan bogged down in China was unlikely to want to wage war against the West as well. He deemed such a gamble foolish because it would bring Japan to "total ruin."[82]

Japan's attack on Pearl Harbor proved advantageous for China. The United States immediately declared itself to be in a state of war with Japan. Koo told his government that should the United States declare war on Germany and Japan, the GMD government should follow suit. On December 9, Hitler declared war on the United States. That same day, China declared war on Japan, Germany, and Italy.[83] There was very little Chiang Kai-shek could do to help his allies fight Germany and Italy, but he could, in theory, assist Britain and the United States in fighting Japan. The broad coalition that Koo and his government had sought for so many years to create finally came about. What Koo did not realize was that keeping an alliance intact was nearly as difficult if not more difficult than building one. Over the next four years, relations between Chiang's government and his allies were strained by differing war aims. Looking to the postwar period, Koo did everything in his power to keep the alliance intact and to manage the crises that occurred within the alliance.

Chapter 6

SINO-BRITISH TENSIONS, 1941–1944

ON JANUARY 1, 1942, WASHINGTON TRUMPETED the United Nations Declaration in which the signatories agreed to devote all resources to the defeat of the Axis powers. The signatories were listed in alphabetical order, but the names United States, Britain, the USSR, and China headed the list, signifying that these four nations were great powers. For the first time in China's history, China was, in William Kirby's words, "an 'ally' in the modern military-diplomatic sense of the term."[1] The man responsible for China's rise as a "great power" was Franklin D. Roosevelt. With the failure of the league during the 1920s and 1930s, Roosevelt subscribed to a great power notion of collective security in which Britain and the United States would maintain the peace. Once the war got underway, FDR expanded his concept to include China and the Soviet Union in a grouping that he referred to as the Four Policemen.[2] Koo, whose life goal had been to recover China's sovereignty, hoped that China would become a great power and welcomed the declaration.

Yet only three of the policemen were engaged in war with Japan. The Soviet Union remained neutral. Although united in their desire to defeat Japan, strains in relations between Chiang and his allies, Britain and the United States, were inevitable because the allies' war aims varied. For Chiang Kai-shek, the United Nations' alliance opened the door to eliminating the last remnants of the unequal treaty system, recovering territory lost to the imperialists since the Opium War, raising China's international standing, and securing loans and supplies to strengthen his government by uniting the country by force. Chiang also planned to use the prestige that the alliance gave him to work for the independence of other countries suffering from colonialism. Chiang subscribed to Pan-Asianist ideas long articulated by numerous Chinese, including Sun Yat-sen. In laying out his Principle of Nationalism, Sun spoke of the need for China to attain its historical position as leader of Asia. Only then could China fulfill its responsibility to "Rescue the weak, save the fallen" and oppose the great powers. Carrying on Sun's ideas, Chiang Kai-shek declared in 1942 before a Chinese audience that included Koo that he wanted "to see freedom restored to the small and weak countries in Asia and the world." The generalissimo observed that Japan's claim to be an Asian leader was simply a quaint way of saying domination or hegemony. On the other hand, China had "a duty to work for freedom and equality of all nations in Asia and the world." Chiang would not use force to liberate the oppressed peoples. China would be a benign example for the weak and small nations who would "look to China as their natural leader and her civilization as a great heritage."[3]

In 1943, Chiang's ideas were elaborated upon in the book *China's Destiny* in which he declared that China had been a leader of Asia for thousands of years. And there was "no historical evidence of economic exploitation or of political domination of the peoples of Asia when China was strong and prosperous; nor was there any imperialism or colonialism." The wars that China fought in 5,000 years of history were "'righteous wars' for self-defense." In contrast, the Europeans were imperialists, and Chiang blamed imperialism as the cause of war in general. "Therefore, I believe that the end of the Second World War must also mark the end of imperialism. Only then can the permanent peace of the world be firmly assured. . . . If China cannot be free and independent, the other nations of Asia will each fall under the iron heel of the enemy, and world peace cannot have a solid foundation."[4]

Besides making China a leader of Asia, Chiang intended to use the alliance to eliminate his communist foes. Chiang believed that China had already paid its dues after several years of war with Japan while the rest of the allies avoided conflict with Japan at almost any price. Unless provided massive amounts of aid or unless his interests were threatened, Chiang remained content in pinning down Japanese forces on the Chinese continent while the allies carried the burden of defeating Japan. After Pearl Harbor, Chiang never launched a major offensive against the Japanese. Chiang placed his best troops opposite those of the communist forces, and in 1942 he launched offensive operations against them while maintaining a defensive posture vis-à-vis Japan.[5]

Chiang was able to attack his old foe without fear of retribution from the Soviet Union because no aid flowed from Moscow to Chongqing. Nazi forces were still deep in Soviet territory, and Stalin remained committed to his Neutrality Pact with Japan to avoid giving Japan an excuse to attack his rear flank. Chiang pushed for Soviet entry into the war possibly because he hoped to see the Soviet Union weakened, thus permitting Chinese expansion, and probably because he wanted the Soviets to carry the burden of fighting Japan.[6] But since Chiang could not count on the Soviet Union for any form of assistance, this meant that the British and Americans were crucial in keeping his regime alive.

Nevertheless, relations between Chiang Kai-shek and his democratic allies were tense. One issue that placed the two countries at odds was war strategy. In the days after Pearl Harbor, Chiang called on Britain and the U.S. to join China in developing a strategy for defeating Japan, with China's wartime capital of Chongqing as the center for coordinating Pacific operations. Chiang envisioned Chinese ground troops working with British and American naval and air units. His assumption was that Japan would be defeated first and Germany later. By making the Pacific theater more important than that of Europe, he could end the war quickly; reduce the number of Chinese casualties, since they would be backed by massive firepower; and acquire more war material and more of a political voice needed to shape postwar Asia. To Chiang's chagrin, the British and American position was that a "Germany first" strategy was preferable.[7] Roosevelt and others in Washington deemed Britain's survival far more crucial to U.S. security than was the survival of China. At the same time, the Americans did not want to see China knocked out of the war, thus freeing tens of thousands of Japanese soldiers to go to other areas of the Pacific. To assuage Chiang's pride, the allies made him Supreme Commander of the China Theater, which included responsibility for Thailand and Indochina. By the end of 1942, Roosevelt told Chiang Kai-shek that China would be one of the Four Policemen after Japan was defeated. Together, the two countries would maintain law and order in Asia.

The British viewed China in different terms. Churchill went along with Roosevelt's fiction that China was a great power, but the British prime minister feared that Chiang, who was described as a fascist dictator, would become Franklin Roosevelt's partner in liquidating Britain's Empire. And despite Western press reports of China's victories, the British saw that all was quiet on the front between Japanese and Chinese forces flying the GMD flag. The British did not trust the Chinese, believing that their codes were compromised or that information was being leaked across enemy lines to the Japanese.[8]

As a result of such attitudes, the British managed to reopen some old Chinese sores. Although Chiang Kai-shek was in theory the commander in chief of the China-Burma-India Theater, Britain struck Koo as feeling that it was "primarily up to her, rather than China, to hold the line against Japan in this part of the world." China was not high on any list of priorities. Chiang wanted more troops, supplies, and money. The Chinese felt snubbed by London's refusal to provide any kind of military assistance even though the British were barely able to supply their own forces, much less try to aid both the Soviet Union and China. The Chinese press in Chongqing railed against the "Germany first" strategy, but Koo found that most people in British society supported their government's policy. Chiang Kai-shek thought his Anglo-American allies' war strategy wrongheaded. He wanted to end the war with Japan as quickly as possible so that he could go about the work of reconstruction and eliminate his domestic enemies. A prolonged war was not to Chiang's advantage, especially since China had already been at war since 1937. Chiang failed to appreciate that Germany would launch another offensive against the Soviet Union within a few months.[9] A Soviet defeat would potentially lead to the collapse of the British and possibly to a Japanese push for India.

In addition to differences over strategy, many Chinese were furious with the British over the loss of Hong Kong to Japanese forces in December. The Chinese offered to help defend Hong Kong and Burma in the summer of 1941, but the British turned down the offer, believing it provocative of Japan. Also, Britain could not fulfill Chiang's request to equip 100,000 Chinese soldiers. The Chinese believed that the British underestimated the Japanese and failed to take the losses of territory seriously, whereas "to China they were vital." When Japanese forces invaded Burma, Chiang offered two armies. The British again said no, preferring to fight the Japanese with only British troops out of fear of Chinese territorial ambitions. For Chiang, the security of Burma was necessary since the Burma Road remained one of his lifelines. The British, however, believed Japan unable to launch an attack. But on January 20, 1942, two Japanese divisions pushed into Burma, and Japan took Rangoon without a fight. The British handling of the Burma campaign convinced Chiang that the British wanted to weaken China while protecting their own interests.[10]

British defeats in Hong Kong, Singapore, and Burma impacted the Chinese in two respects early in 1942. On the one hand, the Chinese were depressed by Japan's sweeping victories in Southeast Asia, the "Germany first" strategy, British refusal to treat China as an equal, and British unwillingness to give India independence. "Chinese are down in the dumps. More so indeed than I have even known them," noted Sir A. Clark Kerr, British ambassador to Chongqing. "Our stock is low and is in danger of falling still lower." On the other hand, the Chinese now viewed themselves as superior and the British as inferior. The Chinese, according to Sir H. Seymour who replaced Kerr, now believed that the war brought about the "disappearance ... of European and American domination in Far Eastern affairs and that the new China may hope to take her place as leader of Asia." Chinese victories over the Japanese in 1938 and 1939 and British defeats in 1941 and 1942 gave the Chinese a "feeling of superiority ... making the Chinese intolerant of foreign and particularly British advice." Worse, Chiang's armies did no fighting anywhere with the Japanese despite promises from Chiang that he would attack on all fronts against Japan if Britain and the United States came into the war. The British press repeated Chinese propaganda that spoke of GMD victories even though they were not fighting. The result was what Brenan of the foreign office described as the "building up [of] a picture of Chinese vigour and efficiency compared with British defeats and incompetence which is going to make it difficult for us to take a different line later if it should become necessary to do so."[11]

The British Foreign Office felt compelled to bring the critical press reports emanating from Chongqing to Koo's attention. Koo acknowledged that he knew of such reports and "frankly admitted that they worried him." However, Koo claimed that "a series of events had helped to create the present by no means happy situation" in Sino-British relations. In particular, Koo pointed to Britain's initial refusal to grant Chiang's government another loan. The previous January, Chiang asked for a £100 million loan from Britain, an amount that Anthony Eden considered rather extravagant. The British offered £50 million, but Koo informed Eden of Chongqing's unhappiness with the conditions attached to the money, particularly since the United States did not attach any to its own loan. Chiang instructed Koo to convey to London that since the loan was a "symbol of economic collaboration between democrat[ic] countries there should be no conditions what[so]ever nor security nor stipulation as to allocation of proceeds."[12] Koo asked for a revision of the loan's terms that would permit China to use the money after the war, but the British refused, insisting that the money was only for wartime use and not postwar reconstruction aid. The foreign office believed that Koo was acting on his own initiative in pressing for a revision of the loan's conditions, because he would soon be traveling to Chongqing and wanted to point to his success in revising the agreement. Eden argued that Chiang did not care about the conditions of the loan, because he only wanted it to be "a picture on the wall which he could display to his people and did not care much whether he could use it or not."[13] Nevertheless, the Chinese refused to borrow money on British terms. Chiang Kai-shek told Koo that Britain's terms caused China to lose face, and Koo was convinced that the breakdown in negotiations would have an adverse effect on Sino-British relations.[14]

The breakdown in loan negotiations did strain relations, but not as much as Chiang's attempt to be the leader of Asia. For sometime, the GMD government espoused the notion of freeing India from British colonialism for India's and Asia's sake. In August 1941, Chiang declared that once China was free, he would immediately work for the independence of India and Korea. In February 1942, Chiang and his wife paid a visit to India. Initially, London looked favorably on the visit in order to better Sino-British relations.[15] In no time, the British regretted the decision after Chiang Kai-shek evoked support for Indian independence and sought to meet Mahatma Gandhi. Chiang told the Viceroy of India that he did not want "to interfere in Britain's internal affairs," but that "China still hopes . . . to help India become free." In Chiang Kai-shek's mind, India had to be "free now and independent after the war" if the allies were to have India's support against Japan. The British, however, did not want Chiang to meet Gandhi. "It would I am sure be a great mistake," wrote Winston Churchill, "for him [Chiang] to travel many hundreds of miles across India to parley with Gandhi about whether the British Empire in India should come to an end or not."[16] Chiang feared that the loss of India to Japan would seal his fate since the allies supplied China through India. He hoped that Gandhi would not look to Japan as a savior and called on the Indian people to unite with China in resisting Japanese aggression.[17]

After his visit to India, Chiang wanted Koo to assess British public opinion. And if Churchill raised the subject, he wanted Koo to point out that if Britain voluntarily gave the Indian people political rights, India would no longer look upon the empire with disgust.[18]

On the basis of newspaper editorials and comments made in Parliament, Koo reported that though some in Britain agreed that London needed to reassess its policy toward India, there was opposition to permitting the Indians a role in the war.[19] The majority opinion in Parliament was that Britain lacked the military supplies needed to arm the Indians and that only the British colonial army could defend India. Years later, Koo remembered that British officials argued that if Britain withdrew from India, there would be "twenty years of anarchy and disorder." When Koo asked why India could not rule itself after two hundred years of contact with the Occident, the reply was that "occidental influence only penetrated the top strata of Indian society." Koo also found the British Foreign Office quite upset with Chiang Kai-shek over his statements regarding Indian independence. They accused China of suffering from "persecution" and an "inferiority complex." Koo met with Winston Churchill and found him "a little peeved and sullen." Churchill blurted out that "the British were not decadent or defeatist as was said of them in" Chongqing and then returned to his normal, genial mood.[20]

Pressure from Britain's allies, though, pushed London to send a mission led by Sir Stafford Cripps to India in March 1942. Cripps did not bring a promise of independence, but instead declared that India would be granted Dominion status after the war. Gandhi rejected the proposal not only because the British promise had to await the conclusion of the war, but because he believed that such a plan would lead to India's breakup, not unification. Gandhi launched his "Quit India" movement as a way of forcing Britain out of India while telling followers to put up peaceful resistance should the Japanese, in fact, begin to occupy Indian territory. Churchill told Roosevelt that the Indian National Congress could not speak for the Indian people. The top leaders including Gandhi were arrested, sparking widespread demonstrations and riots that led to many deaths and the arrests of thousands. Toward the end of June, the British ambassador explained to Chiang that his country could not permit the Indians independence now because Britain could not fight Japan and maintain order in India at the same time. Chiang retorted that he was not interested in fomenting chaos in India but only had the war effort in mind. Chiang explained to Koo that while he did not want to harm Sino-British relations over a British domestic question, he had to give his support to Indian independence given the history of Western intrusion into his own country.[21]

Disappointed by his British ally, Chiang appealed to Roosevelt to use his own influence to bring about Anglo-Indian cooperation and persuade the British to grant India independence now. Instead, Churchill rejected Roosevelt's mediation of the Indian question, and British officials told Koo that China should not interfere in Great Britain's personal affairs. When the Americans and British decided to grant India independence after, not during, the war, Chiang told Koo that the decision undermined the UN Alliance's underlying principles. In the future, the allies "would have no credibility with the world." Naturally Koo supported his government's policy with regard to India given his own anti-imperialism. He believed that the allies had to come up with a platform that could challenge Japan's claim of seeking an "Asia for the Asiatics." At the same time, he did not want his government to say things that would damage Sino-British relations.[22]

Wanting to repair the damage to Sino-British relations and aware of how anxious the British government was that Koo return to China for a visit to meet their own qualms about him, Koo returned to China in 1942. He even became a member of the GMD, possibly to assuage fears abroad that he was not close enough to the generalissimo.[23] In any case, Koo voiced support for an American-British-Chinese alliance after the war, because such an alliance would buy time for "world reconstruction" as well as reconstruction in China. Otherwise, Britain might drift toward Japan in the postwar period. T.V. Soong, the foreign minister, frowned on the idea of an ABC alliance, arguing that it "would destroy China's influence in Asia over the weak and small countries." Koo reminded Soong that Britain would still be a major political and military power after the war, and that it was "wise to keep her from flirting" with Japan. Japan might even join the Soviet Union against the Anglo-American group. If China only cooperated with the United States, holding aloof from Britain could be reason enough for the latter to cooperate with Japan. In other words, Koo still feared a new version of the Anglo-Japanese alliance. Friction between Britain and China would defeat the purpose of an anti-Japan alliance, and if "forced to choose between the two," the United States "would certainly choose" Britain. Finally, an ABC alliance would "confirm China's position as a major power in the world." He made essentially the same argument to Chiang Kai-shek, saying that such an alliance would give China a ten to fifteen year reprieve to "build up our strength—stronger in fact means more weight to our voice." Koo shared his ideas with many GMD leaders, but came to the conclusion that opinion was "so divided it was too early to push the idea of a Sino-British alliance, especially as feeling amongst the leaders was very strong and misunderstandings ran deep."[24]

Koo, as is typical with most diplomats, was simply the man caught in the middle trying to placate both sides in order to reduce tensions. Chiang Kai-shek, who felt very bitter about the British, was a difficult man to mollify. One of Chiang Kai-shek's nationalistic objectives was to eliminate extraterritoriality, one of the primary goals of the GMD's revolutionary diplomacy. Chiang demanded that his Anglo-American allies renounce extraterritoriality, moving China one step closer toward granting China equality in international affairs. In a conference held at Chiang's residence, Koo could not but notice the "general tendency to discriminate against Great Britain." Such sentiment placed Koo in a difficult position, because the British Foreign Office warned him that it wanted negotiations to be carried out on a basis of equality and sought more recognition of the important role Britain played in the Pacific War, as well as economic concessions. The British noted that the Chinese were more arrogant in their attitude toward Britain because of the latter's military defeats, and there was a desire to "abandon extraterritoriality with as good as grace as possible."[25]

While Koo remained in China, Chiang's government sat down with representatives from the United States and Great Britain to negotiate new bilateral treaties. Sino-American negotiations went fairly well. In October 1942, the United States agreed to abrogate its extraterritorial rights, and on January 10, 1943, the new treaty was signed. Sino-British negotiations did not go so smoothly. First, there was the problem of Tibet, which remained independent and possessed ties with Great Britain. Koo thought it "impolitic" to raise Tibet in connection with the present treaty; it was a question that could wait. Many in the British government suspected that Chiang would engage in Chinese imperialism by asserting control over Tibet. Press statements by Chiang and T.V. Soong suggested to the British "that the more chauvinist elements in the [GMD] are making their voice increasingly heard and their ambitions are certainly directed towards extending Chinese influence among the countries adjacent to China." There was also evidence that Chiang was trying to build supply routes through Tibet for the purpose of conquering it. The generalissimo, however, told Koo that Britain "must stop [its] intrigues [in Tibet] to stir up ill feeling against China: otherwise [there would be] no improvement in relations." Chiang claimed that the British were preventing China from extending its influence into Tibet, but he concurred with Koo's view and felt that not raising Tibet was a way of showing Chinese magnanimity toward Britain.[26]

Another issue affecting the treaty negotiations was India. Koo sought a formula that "would satisfy the . . . Asiatic people and yet meet the needs and views of the British and other colonial empires in Asia." On the other hand, Chiang Kai-shek still pursued his policy of leading Asian nations to freedom. Chiang thought Britain's policy toward India to be "unwise but understandable." However, if Gandhi died in prison, he would become a martyr and Great Britain would be all the more hated and despised. Having said that, Chiang ignored India as both sides negotiated.[27]

On the issue of Kowloon, the mainland territory facing Hong Kong Island, Chiang was not so magnanimous. Every Chinese patriot wanted to recover territory and sovereignty lost to the powers in the nineteenth century. Koo assured Britons that China had no territorial ambitions with regard to Hong Kong. Koo claimed later that Britons from all walks of life were interested in returning Hong Kong after the war was won. In reality, the British Foreign Office believed that the Chinese people expected Hong Kong to revert to China after the war. One official admitted that a united and strong postwar China made the British recovery of Hong Kong impossible.[28]

During talks, Chiang threatened to forego the whole Sino-British treaty unless Britain agreed to hand Kowloon back. The Americans also pressed the British to tie Kowloon with the treaty. Britain decided to dig in its heels and not relent on Kowloon. At a minimum, Koo believed that Britain should declare its intention to return Kowloon but took the position that it was a territorial question to be postponed till after the war. Raising such questions now only created dissension in the alliance, and China needed Britain when dealing with Soviet Russia in the postwar years. Chiang approved Koo's formula only to have the British negotiators turn it down. Koo feared a breakdown in negotiations and ultimately a breakdown in the United Nations' front, but Chiang Kaishek softened his position, saying that the treaty benefited China. However, when the British brought their proposed text regarding Kowloon back to the table, it was worse than the first formula. Chiang concluded there were only two options: "refuse to sign" or say nothing about Kowloon and take it by force after the war.

Koo, who feared not signing would show a serious rift in the UN Alliance, suggested signing but with a reservation on Kowloon.[29] Despite his misgivings, Chiang, persuaded by Koo, eventually gave in and the treaty was signed and China reserved the right to raise the Kowloon question at a later date. However, Chiang made it clear to the British that China was signing "in consideration of the solidarity of the United Nations," and "that the people were naturally dissatisfied with the Br[itish] refusal to discuss the K[owloon] question." On January 11, 1943, Britain signed the new treaty, giving up its extraterritorial rights, but the British attitude toward Kowloon hardened and proved more resistant to Roosevelt's suggestion that Britain surrender the territory as a gesture of goodwill. Publicly, Chiang declared that the new treaty put China "on an equal footing with Great Britain and the United States."[30] Privately, he initially thought the treaty "was a defeat." Koo never had any doubts about the treaty's significance. He thought the treaty "was really an epoch-making event—the biggest treaty in a century." He later argued that trade with Britain would increase after the war just as trade with Germany increased after World War I once the new Sino-German Treaty had abolished extraterritoriality.[31]

Some scholars have argued that China was no longer treated as a second-class power after the Sino-British Treaty became official, but that view is clearly mistaken. Though tensions over Hong Kong were reduced, relations with Britain in general did not improve with the signing of the treaty. Chiang wrote later in the year that Britain's refusal to give up Hong Kong was a "stain on cordial relations between China and England." Nor was the foreign office amused when Chiang heaped praise on Roosevelt and the United States for signing the new treaty while only giving Britain a brief note of appreciation. The difference in tone between the two announcements left some with the "impression that the Chinese feel gratitude to the Americans for a favour conferred but only a sense of justice in our case."[32]

In the remaining weeks that Koo resided in China, he could see the great impasse that existed in Sino-British relations from the Chinese point of view. Although there were government officials who agreed with Koo's idea of pursuing an ABC alliance and working for better relations, there were many who were quite embittered. And although people like President Lin Sen remarked to Koo that the "Chinese people never cherished any ambition for aggression against other countries," many in the government wanted to extend China's influence beyond its borders, suggesting a desire to break up the British and French colonies in Southeast and South Asia. There was a belief that China should not only recover Hong Kong and Kowloon after the war but should participate in any postwar discussions over Burma and Malaya. Some even reminisced of days past when northern Vietnam was a province of China, assuming that China would control north Vietnam.[33]

Naturally, such thinking instilled a fear that China would be irredentist in the postwar period. Many Britons believed that after the war, China would occupy all of Britain's concessions in China as well as Burma and Malaya, where there were large Chinese populations. Koo learned from a high-level U.S. government official that Britain pressed the United States to concentrate on Europe, in part because "China after victory would become imperialistic and be unmanageable." Indeed, some in the British Foreign Office were convinced that China would prove more dangerous than Japan after World War II. Koo thought this was typical British propaganda, but he recognized that his own people were partially to blame. In 1942, Lauchlin Currie, FDR's representative, informed Chiang that the American people were troubled by Chiang's Pan-Asianist speeches and questioned whether China in the postwar period would develop into a militaristic or imperialistic nation. China now spoke in a "high tone" to both Washington and London "and the people have been unwisely arrogant." Koo believed that the downside to all the positive press that China received in the late 1930s and early 1940s led Chinese government leaders "to think they were real heroes" and to become overconfident "in estimating their position of influence in international politics," laying the seeds of "so many misunderstandings and so many causes of friction."[34]

Koo agreed with his friends that Chiang Kai-shek's claim that China would take no action "but only assumes more responsibility in Asia is unwise because it carries an implied desire to be the leader of Asia."[35] Koo sympathized with the "Asiatic colonial people," but believed that "by emphasizing the need of equality in treating the people of Asia regardless of colour, China appeared to have an inferiority complex as if she was asking for recognition of her own status by the other United Nations." He preferred a formula based on the Atlantic Charter to meet the needs of both Asians and the colonial empires.[36]

Before leaving China, Koo sat down with Chiang Kai-shek to discuss Sino-British relations. Koo argued that Britain would seek closer cooperation with China in the postwar period because of its fear of the Soviet Union and would probably form an anticommunist alliance with the United States. He expected Britain to cooperate with China just as Britain cooperated with Japan against Russia in the post-1895 period. Chiang's decidedly anticommunist government could be counted on to join Britain in facing up to the Soviet Union. Moreover, since China possessed a large population, Britain would not want to see the China market monopolized by the United States, especially when China would remain one of, if not the largest, market for British goods. Koo expressed hope that his government would be prepared to deal with the questions of Hong Kong, Burma, Singapore, Malaya, Thailand, and North Vietnam in the postwar period. Koo expected no further colonial expansion from Britain in order to maintain what empire it had left. He wanted to settle the outstanding problems between China and Britain so both could work with the United States in establishing an ABC alliance that would place China on equal footing with the powers.

After listening to Koo's argument, Chiang expressed views that were negative. Chiang felt that a Sino-British alliance would make the Soviet Union suspicious and would tie China's hands in dealing not only with Moscow but Tokyo. If Britain proposed an alliance, Chiang preferred the ABC alliance, but if the United States refused then Chiang would consider making a pact with the British. Chiang was skeptical, however, that the United States would form an alliance, given America's tradition of avoiding such agreements in peacetime. Chiang described "English diplomacy" as "shrewd and cunning," and could make a good presentation when discussing forming alliances, but he felt that the British would "adhere stubbornly to their traditional policies." Chiang had not forgiven Churchill for commenting that China's communist problem was "similar to Britain's Indian problem." Chiang remarked that this was "intolerable and a gross discourtesy" given that the communist problem was an internal Chinese concern and not the same as "the problem of the liberation and independence of India." If Britain stopped interfering in Tibet, then China would be quiet about India. As for Hong Kong and Taiwan, FDR assured Chiang that those territories would revert back to China with the former becoming a free port. As for Singapore, Burma, and Malaya, Chiang claimed his policy was simply to insure that the Chinese people there received treatment equal with British nationals. FDR also informed Chiang that the British were adamantly opposed to other countries advising Britain on what to do with its possessions.[37]

In March 1943, Koo traveled to the United States to meet with Madame Chiang, who had already been there for some time. In an effort to improve Sino-British relations, Koo pressed the Madame to visit Great Britain. Koo feared that if she did not go to Britain after visiting Washington, this would lead to "much speculation and misunderstanding in Great Britain" and permit China's "enemies to sow the seeds of discord among the allies." Not helping Koo's efforts was Winston Churchill who publicly described Britain's postwar responsibilities and referred to the future peace organization that would be represented by Britain, the United States, and Soviet Russia. To the displeasure of the Chinese, they were left out. His statement that Britain would have to "rescue" China incensed them even more. Koo thought these statements "distasteful and slighting" and "typical of Churchill the imperialist and the realist." When Koo tried to convince T.V. Soong of the need for his sister to visit Great Britain, Soong remarked that Churchill's speech "made it all the more inadvisable. Too much like condescension in the face of a slap at China." Koo disagreed, saying that to reject an invitation would have "deplorable" consequences for Sino-British relations.[38]

In vain, Koo employed the same arguments that he made in China to convince Madame Chiang to visit Great Britain. Koo returned to his concern, shared by many in the Chongqing government, about having "a victorious Russia . . . north of China, free from worries from Germany and Japan, a big compact mass of power and strength, and with a vengeful Japan eager to alienate China from her friends, our postwar position in the world would not be too happy and even dangerous if we could not keep [Britain's] goodwill and friendship." He further argued that China needed the help of the U.S. and Britain in stabilizing China's "international position as one of the great powers" and to buy time to carry out reconstruction. Koo's argument was a reiteration of the ABC alliance if Russia refused to join, an alliance that would give China time to rebuild itself.[39]

Koo never succeeded in persuading Madame Chiang to travel to Britain. The tour of America took a toll physically and emotionally, and Chiang Kai-shek and Roosevelt both believed that she should return to

China. Yet the Madame could not forgive the British for past discrimination. And Koo, to a certain extent, could understand the Madame's
attitude toward the British. Britain made few friends in China by being
one of the imperialist powers, and many Chinese believed that their
country's troubles all led back to the "colonialism and political domination" by powers like Britain. "As a Chinese," Koo commented later, "I
could understand the reaction of my countrymen both in government
and in public circles."[40]

Koo was obviously willing to moderate his antipathy for other powers in the interest of the UN alliance, which served as a tool to facilitate
patriotic aspirations. As a result of the alliance, the powers finally treated
China, at least theoretically, as an equal. Extraterritoriality, one of the
last vestiges of the unequal treaties, was eliminated. Furthermore, the
alliance ensured the return of Chinese territory lost to Japanese imperialism. Before leaving the United States, Koo met with Franklin D.
Roosevelt, who promised that not only would Japan be disarmed but
Okinawa and Taiwan would be returned to China. FDR even declared
that the Caroline and the Marshall Islands would be held by the United
States until China developed a navy, at which time China could take possession. And China and the U.S. would administer Indochina, pending
complete independence, since "the native people there after a century of
French administration are (worse) no better off today than they were
then."[41] Naturally, China would acquire Manchuria, and the former foreign concessions in places like Shanghai and Tianjin would come under
full Chinese control.

Despite his dislike of British policies, Koo tried to be more of a
statesmen and less of an anti-imperialist in order to reduce tensions in
Sino-British, and ultimately Sino-Western, relations. He took a farsighted
view in that he looked to the postwar years when China needed the help
of other powers in rebuilding and protecting China. And yet there was
no getting around the fact that relations between China and its allies,
particularly Britain, fell to a great low by the time Koo returned to London. The "growing gulf in the feelings and relations" between both sides
absorbed all of Koo's thoughts, and he felt disappointed that he had
worked to no avail to improve them despite the slight improvement that
was taking place when he left Chongqing. "I am the more disappointed,"

Koo wrote in his diary, "that so many incidents should have arisen in the past two months to darken them again. The more deplorable because they were all incidents which a little common sense or tolerance would have been able to avoid. They were so unnecessary."[42] Over the next few months, though, Koo saw an improvement in British attitude as he observed many expressions of British goodwill toward China in which he was invited to present many speeches and had the opportunity to meet with many government leaders.

While Koo set out to do the necessary publicity work to improve relations, a surprising event occurred that seemed to repair some of the damage. In December 1943, Koo learned that Chiang Kai-shek and the Madame had traveled to Cairo to meet Churchill and Roosevelt. FDR initially envisioned a four-power conference, but Stalin refused to leave the Soviet Union, ostensibly because of the war effort. Chiang went to Cairo prepared to discuss a number of issues including the future international political organization or United Nations, the independence of Korea, and the recovery of Taiwan and Manchuria. He tactfully refused to raise Hong Kong and Tibet directly with Churchill and avoided discussion of India. The Cairo Declaration did declare that Manchuria, Taiwan, and the Pescadores would be restored to the ROC. The powers also agreed that "Korea shall become free and independent." Hence, Chiang secured commitments to support the most important aspects of his agenda. Roosevelt also explained to Chiang that since the Soviet Union would eventually intervene against Japan, taking Soviet forces into Manchuria, that Chiang should permit the Soviet Union access to a warm-water port in Manchuria and use of the railways there that connected with the ports. Chiang agreed to consider Roosevelt's proposal if the arrangements did not infringe on Chinese sovereignty. Roosevelt and Churchill also agreed to commit their forces to a landing in southern Burma. Koo heard that Chiang and Churchill did not hit it off at first but that the atmosphere slowly improved. The downside to the Cairo Conference, however, was that it justified British claims that China could not play the role of a great power.[43]

In the days after the conference, a torrent of criticism appeared in both the British and American presses. In March 1944, Britain's *Economist* ran an article that defined a great power as "a country capable of waging active and autonomous war against another great power." Using that definition, the article asserted that China's inclusion as a great power was "based on considerations other than Great Power status." "China is not a Great Power, and will not be a Great Power for many decades to come, even if the internal coherence and the economic development of the country, in the post-liberation years, are all that is now hoped." The article went on, "There would be dangers if the present inclusion of China in the Big Four were to lead to China being classified as a Great Power and reliance being placed on a strength that does not exist." No wonder that the article struck Koo and his compatriots as being "especially unfavorable to China."[44]

What disturbed Koo most was that at a time when the Chinese press had greatly toned down its criticism of Britain, the press in America and in Britain and its dominions increasingly attacked China for its totalitarianism, corruption, and fascism. Up until this point, images of China during the war years were generally favorable, but now, gradually, Americans learned the truth about the conditions in GMD-China and Chiang's willingness to fight the communists more than the Japanese.[45] Meanwhile, people in the British Foreign Office and the Ministry of Information called the Chinese "arrogant" so-and-sos who had "not been doing much fighting and could not do much." The general feeling, as explained to Koo, was that China would either break up after the war, and/or become extremely nationalistic or imperialistic. Koo blamed the communists and Whitehall for the propaganda and believed that focusing on China's shortcomings without taking into consideration its hardships was unjustified especially since it was an ally. He faulted the allies for not accepting China as the fourth great power.[46]

The powers now demanded that Chiang's government become more democratic. Although he assured Britons that China would become a democracy, Koo recognized that China was not yet prepared for such a development. One day while taking a walk, "the thought came to mind that the idea of democracy based upon the theory 'All men are born equal' is open to question. Human beings are no more equal to one another than animals." Koo saw a difference between, say, "a pure breed dog and a mongrel." "It seems law and order are designed by superior and wise men to protect not only people in general but primarily themselves first because in trials of physical strength or brute force, the least orderly or most violent would always have the advantage over the refined, cultured people." Koo was an elitist, though he did believe that "equality of opportunity should be guaranteed to all in a true democracy." He did not say how the government would fulfill the latter, but he showed signs as well that he rejected America as a model for Chinese political development. Instead, he concluded that Britain's "way of life was more suitable to China than the American way."[47]

In comparing Great Britain, the United States, and China, Koo noticed that there were great social differences that contributed to the rise of democracy in the first two. "Thinking over the highly developed political and social systems in G.B. and U.S.A.," Koo wrote in his diary, "it occurs to me that democracy is certainly the highest form of government but it is the most difficult, requiring a high average level of public and individual intelligence and morality to make it succeed. It primarily depends upon the development of a patriotic spirit." China went unmentioned in this analysis, but presumably his country did not have what it took to be the democracy that its Anglo-Saxon allies expected it to be. Indeed, before the war ended, Koo commented that China's new laws "were too advanced for the Ch[inese] people" and instead of being "based upon the experiences and models of the Occident where the average man's intelligence is very high" they should be made "in accordance with Ch[inese] established customs and practices." And he believed that one reason for the bad press was that Americans traveled to China which struck them as "behind the Western nations especially U.S.A." and that there was "so little progress in China after[ward that] for years they had heard glowing reports" about the idealistic, hard working and fighting Chinese.[48]

Koo conceded that "In a democracy, leaders came forth more easily in a time of crisis as well as in times of peace. The Government's task is thus made easier, unlike in a country of totalitarian and authoritarian or personal government where the leader shoulders the most and worries the most and still achieves less than in a democratic country."[49] On the other hand, democracies could be badly run, as he thought France had been in 1940. After Pearl Harbor, he believed "the democracies were poor nations to make war, always getting caught because of slowness in preparing and of want of vigilance." Flaws aside, the "respect for law in the Anglo-Saxon countries" impressed Koo deeply, and he admired this aspect of democratic government.[50] And he believed that where a Parliament or Congress checked governmental power, one found less corruption or unpopular policies.

Despite the admiration, he remained convinced that China was not a democratic nation because it lacked the social basis common to the Western democracies. China could have developed into a democracy earlier if Great Britain had not nipped such a movement in the bud. In 1945, Koo participated in the jubilee anniversary of the death of General Charles Gordon. A British official asked Koo to attend since the dead soldier was also known as Chinese Gordon, a name he received after supposedly putting down the nineteenth century Taiping Rebellion. For that reason, Koo almost refused to go because he believed Gordon had, in fact, quelled a "democratic and revolutionary movement for the freedom of the Chinese people, at least at its beginning."[51]

China at the moment could not become a democracy, but after the war ended, Koo felt that China could move in that direction. China was not a great power much less a democracy, though he did not acknowledge this fact in public. However, when Churchill once again spoke of the three great powers, not four, Koo admitted that "China is of course backward in many respects. The most acute of them is the shortage of trained and experienced men, with the consequence that she has to draft half-baked, inexperienced men into the service for important responsibilities. . . . It is at once ineffective and wasteful, yet probably the common experience of nations trying to catch up with others."[52] China needed peace to catch up. For example, if China was to be a competitor in the world market, the Chinese people needed "more goods and capital and skills . . . and know [that in order for] trade to grow and develop, [the market] must be made lucrative," and there would be no "cooperation from abroad unless it is profitable to those giving it." He assured British industrialists, though, that in the postwar period, his government would unify the country and pursue liberal trade policies.[53]

Koo's first years as China's ambassador to London were truly difficult ones. Koo looked to the postwar years when China needed not only peace to reconstruct itself after years of war. To ensure national security and maintain China's place as one of the Four Policemen, his government also needed to keep Britain and the United States as allies. The petty arguments and jealousies did not endear Britain to China and vice-versa. If his government lost Britain as an ally after the war, there was still the United States, but events of 1944 and 1945 would undermine American images of China and Koo's vision of postwar cooperation.

Chapter 7

SINO-AMERICAN TENSIONS, 1944–1945

WHILE KOO SAT IN LONDON fretting over the state of British-Chinese relations, Sino-American relations experienced their own tensions. By the end of 1943, government officials in Washington realized that Chiang Kai-shek's potential contribution to the war effort against Japan was minimal. In February 1942, Gen. Joseph Stilwell arrived in China to make the Chinese army more combat effective. Commander of all American forces in the China-Burma-India Theater, Stilwell controlled the Lend-Lease supplies going to China and was FDR's military representative to the generalissimo. Almost immediately, Stilwell and Chiang were at odds over strategy: Stilwell wanted to retake Burma while Chiang did not. Chiang feared that another Chinese defeat in Burma would lead Japan to take out bases in Kunming that were vital for the Hump supply route over the Himalayas. Chiang preferred to remain on the defensive. Stilwell and other Americans grew impatient with Chiang's dallying, and press reports of Chiang's dictatorship gradually captured the attention of Washington. By the time of the Cairo Conference, Roosevelt wanted to find a new leader in China should Chiang's government collapse.[1]

At the end of 1943, decisions made by three of the UN allies did not bode well for Chiang Kai-shek. In November 1943, after the Cairo Conference, Roosevelt met with Churchill and Stalin in Teheran and raised the issue of the Soviet Union and the Far East. Stalin declared that

United Nations General Assembly, San Francisco, California, 1945. In front of window, L to R, Henri Bonnet, The Earl of Halifax, Edward R. Stettinius, A.A. Gromyko, and V.K. Wellington Koo. Photo courtesy Library of Congress.

the Soviet Union would come into the war against Japan three months after the defeat of Nazi Germany, but Stalin wanted a warm-water port somewhere in the Pacific. FDR offered, and Stalin accepted, the Port of Dalian in Manchuria. And with the potential Soviet entry into the war, the operation to land Anglo-American forces into southern Burma was cancelled now that China was not needed to defeat Japan. In January, FDR rejected Chiang's request for a $1 billion loan. At Cairo, FDR advised Chiang to implement some of Stilwell's suggested reforms including combining Chiang's army units with that of communist ones and even forming a GMD-CCP coalition government. Chiang agreed to do so if he had assurances from the Soviet Union to not lay its hands on Manchuria. After Cairo, Chiang was quite disappointed, particularly as the Americans showed increasing interest in his enemies, the CCP. Chiang blamed the change in American opinion and accusations that he was not taking the war to Japan on communist propaganda.[2]

In the spring of 1944, Sino-American relations hit an all-time low. In April, Japan launched the "Ichigo Offensive." Thirty-four Chinese divisions disappeared under the weight of the Japanese assault. In May and June, the Japanese advanced farther, easily capturing cities as Chinese forces withdrew without firing a shot. By August 8, Japanese forces were in a position to overrun the Fourteenth Air Force's bases. The illusions entertained about Chiang Kai-shek were now gone. The offensive revealed the corruption, factionalism, and incompetence that lay behind Chiang's government. It also showed Chiang's true colors as he refused to use his best troops to support the provincial forces while hoarding his American supplies. The Ichigo Offensive also undermined political support for Chiang within China as liberals lost faith and as anti-Chiang movements gained momentum in the provinces. The tremendous casualties suffered at the hands of the Japanese meant that Chiang's powerbase had been dealt a mortal blow from which Chiang would not recover.[3]

It was in this atmosphere of Japanese success on the ground that the Dumbarton Oaks Conference was held to discuss the creation of a United Nations. In August 1944, the Chinese Foreign Ministry ordered Koo to Washington to attend the conference and assist the Chinese delegation with the construction of a new postwar organization for keeping the peace.[4] Koo's experiences with the league led him to pursue a more improved method of collective security. Less than a month after the creation of the UN Alliance, he wrote "While international law by its nature is apt to remain static until modified, the needs of the international community are bound to be dynamic." He called for radical measures, such as "an international police force to enforce peace and . . . an equity court to adjudicate differences."[5]

Koo's thinking paralleled Roosevelt's Four Policemen approach in that he supported the creation of regional organizations that would be part of an international organization, making it a truly global one. Koo argued that there had to be "a regional group of freedom-loving countries to co-operate in the safeguarding of peace and security . . . [that] functions as a part, and within the framework, of a general international organization endowed with the necessary power of preventing war and enforcing peace in the world and prescribing for observance everywhere the uniform rule of law and the same standard of conduct."[6] As the war progressed, Koo received encouraging and discouraging signs of the powers' attitude toward the future international organization. On the one hand, in 1943 FDR shared with Koo his desire to not have a European council, but a world council in which "peace would be planned this time on a world basis," giving Koo hope that a new world could be built. The next year, however, in a meeting of the War Crimes Commission, representatives for Britain, Australia, India, and Holland gave the impression that they would establish a separate regional organization for maintaining the peace in the Pacific *without* China.[7]

When he arrived in the United States, Koo found that he was head of a delegation that really had no official plan for how this international organization should be constructed. Five draft plans were drawn up in China, but as was explained to Koo immediately after his arrival, a list of "Essential Points" were drawn up to raise at the conference.[8] Along with the points was a list of attitudes approved by Chiang Kai-shek. In his *China's Destiny*, Chiang laid out the argument that imperialism had to be vanquished and that China needed to be rehabilitated and independent in order to be the linchpin of peace and stability in Asia. For that to be achieved, the future international organization had to embrace the principles of self-determination and equality. Failure to abide by those principles killed the League of Nations, and he opposed the appearance of notions like World Powers and Spheres of Influence in the UN charter.[9] The delegation was told that the stronger and more powerful the future security organization, the better. Chiang wanted his delegation to enjoy a position at the conference equal to the other three powers, but if they disagreed on any issues, the delegation was to pay close attention to the American point of view. Failing that, the Chinese delegation was to decide whether there was an opportunity to put forth its own principles. However, the delegation was to not take too strong a stand, to try to get along with the Soviets, and to work to make the conference a success.[10]

The Chinese delegates did not get a seat at the meetings held between the other three great powers because the Soviet Union refused to meet with the Chinese as they had when Churchill, Roosevelt, and Stalin met at Teheran earlier in the year. Although Stalin preferred to maintain Soviet neutrality in the Pacific War in order to avoid conflict with Japan until the European war was over, he, like Churchill, scoffed at the idea of China as a great power then or in the postwar world. Instead, the decision was made to break up the conference into two sessions with the Chinese participating in the second one with the Americans and British.[11] One reason why the Chinese hurriedly drew up their "Essential Points" was so that the three powers would know China's views while hammering out an agreement. Koo told the Americans that his government never intended for the conference to be divided, and there were proposals made by both the Soviets and British that he found troublesome and in need of discussion. In particular, the Soviets wanted a member who was engaged in a conflict to still have the right to vote in the Security Council.[12]

Although the delegates did not want to antagonize their allies, particularly the Americans, the Chinese felt angry over their treatment by the other powers. Before the Dumbarton Oaks Conference commenced, Churchill made another speech referring to only three great powers and stressing the need to elevate France to major power status. After Koo arrived in the U.S., the Chinese leaked details of the future world organization to James Reston of the *New York Times*, possibly to express displeasure over the Soviet refusal to include China in the talks. The leak of China's "Essential Points" annoyed Koo because they "embodied some radical proposals." He believed that China should do nothing to alienate the United States and Britain during the conference, but instead work with them to make the conference successful.[13]

Whatever notions Koo entertained about close relations with the allies, the Chinese found themselves increasingly isolated. The Quebec Conference of 1944 excluded China, even though one purpose of the meeting was to discuss a strategy to defeat Japan. Another conference was to be held with the Soviet Union at Yalta with a view to getting the latter into the war against Japan, with China again having no say in the discussions. Koo and his compatriots could see that Roosevelt and Churchill wanted to end the war with Japan without spilling much American and British blood. "The Russian card appears to them much more valuable than the Ch[inese] ally who is now in such [an] unfavourable plight," Koo noted in his diary. And the British could see that press reports of corruption and Chiang's dictatorship took their toll on China's image. The British Ambassador to Washington noted "Surprisingly little mention, for instance, has been made of China in connexion with the talks at Dumbarton Oaks. The slump in general Chinese stock is an accomplished fact and appears to be increasing."[14]

Worse, the CCP received good press coverage. From July through October, while the Ichigo Offensive was still underway, American and British journalists wrote glowing articles about Mao's government and its mobilization of the peasants to fight guerilla warfare against the Japanese. Displeased with the favorable press reports coming out of Yan'an, Koo felt the real facts would show that such press reports were hollow, but he opposed "washing dirty linen" in public, particularly since the allies deemed victory over Japan as of secondary importance. He likewise opposed using Thomas Dewey, the Republican presidential candidate in 1944, to put pressure on the administration, calling such a move "dangerous" and more likely to antagonize Roosevelt.[15]

The Chinese diplomat no longer hoped for a future four-power alliance. Instead, he believed that the four could agree to "enforce peace treaties with Japan and Germany," and in this way, Britain and the United States could assist China "against [the] possible danger from [the] U.S.S.R." Meanwhile, Koo avoided antagonizing the Soviets and refused to state publicly that China was worried about its neighbor in the north. Besides, Roosevelt warned the Chinese to get along with the Soviets because the United States could not be of much help at the moment should conflict break out between the two sides.[16]

While waiting for the powers to complete their work, Koo spoke with various Americans about the Chinese proposals. In his opinion, they were not rigid, but Stanley Hornbeck, a longtime acquaintance of Koo's who worked in the U.S. State Department, thought that of all the plans, the Chinese proposals were the most elaborate. In his opinion, they would be voted down because the Soviets wanted to build a simple house devoted to the minimum requirements of security, whereas the Chinese proposals "represented the ideal maximum." The Americans and British stood somewhere between those extremes.[17]

Along similar lines, James Reston warned Koo that it was "unwise for China to insist on the point that we maintain each other's political independence and territorial integrity." The U.S. delegation worried about that point and the idea of an international police force, because there was much American opposition to this principle and it might jeopardize passage in the Senate. Reston added, "It is like the return of the ghosts of 1919." More disturbing was news from Reston that the Soviets insisted on the unanimous vote among the permanent members, but there was no mention of a provision should the permanent members disagree or should one of them become a party to a dispute. The Chinese believed that the permanent members could not vote should they be involved in a dispute, and Koo told the British that the notion was a "generally accepted principle."[18] Koo met with Franklin Roosevelt, who remarked that the Soviets were saying "that in a case in which she was involved she wanted to be both a defendant and a member of the jury." Koo told FDR that "the question was of great importance because it touched the foundation of the new organization." Stalin also wanted all of the Soviet Republics admitted into this new international organization. Roosevelt suggested to Koo that all of China's provinces be included. At first, Koo thought the president was joking, but FDR went on to say that he wanted to see China become a great power to keep the peace in Asia while Roosevelt kept his eyes on Europe.[19]

On the eve of China's participation in the conference, the delegation met to discuss strategy. Looking at the Chinese proposals, Koo must have learned from his mistakes at the Paris and Washington Conferences. He wanted to avoid creating a "dispute" with the delegates from the United States and Britain, so he argued that the delegation needed "flexibility and latitude" and that China should present "a more realistic and practical list of proposals." Koo knew that the "Essential Points" had been drawn up with Chongqing's approval, but there were a number of issues he preferred to avoid discussing. When Koo was in China, some Chinese officials wanted to raise the idea of the principle of equality of the races. Koo wanted to press for the same principle but not in a manner that jeopardized "cordial relations with Americans." Now Koo advised against raising the issue of racial equality entirely, recalling the experience of the Japanese at the Paris Peace Conference. H.H. Kung, who headed up the delegation, admitted that raising the issue might be desirable, but there was the fact that the United States "had its own negro problem." And since China already had attained equality, to raise the issue suggested that China had not. Koo agreed.

Koo observed as well that the British and Americans disagreed on the "roles to be played by the Assembly and the Council." He preferred the American Plan, which stressed "the importance of the Council." In his opinion, the Security Council should be given a "more important role in order to ensure executive efficiency." He added that "in matter of form the small nations should be given an equal status in the World Organisation, but in the interest of effective action, importance should be attached to the Council." Koo supported the idea of an international police force, but believed that "any hard and fast formula for a strong armed force would meet with a great deal of opposition from the British and Americans and would finally result in no force at all." Hu Shi argued that great powers involved in a dispute "should not be allowed to vote in the Council." Koo commented that the American Plan was unclear on that point, and believed that the "World Organisation should on the one hand aim at the preservation of peace and on the other try not to lose the sympathy of the small nations." Some members of the Chinese delegation favored the internationalization of air forces, but Koo believed that the proposal would be turned down by the other three powers. He himself opposed the idea because China had little in the way of an air force and as a result would have little voice as to its use. He also came out against the idea of enumerating acts that constituted aggression.[20]

After weeks of waiting and receiving profuse apologies from the Americans for the delay, the Chinese part in the conference began on September 29. Edward R. Stettinius Jr., the head of the American delegation, impressed upon Koo the need to wrap up the second session by October 9 because the document had to be published before the Soviet delegation left for home. Chinese amendments would not be included in the conference document itself. Stettinius also wanted to hurry the Chinese session along, because he felt the Chinese did not understand how to make an effective international organization. The American delegates thought the Chinese placed too much faith in international law and emphasized social and economic concerns while placing far less emphasis on security.[21] Koo, who in August assured the Americans that his delegation would be more accommodating than Chongqing, was left with little choice but to go along with the Americans and accept the fact that his delegation would play no meaningful role.

Meanwhile, the situation on the battlefield in China worsened. The Japanese army threatened American airfields in Guangxi Province. Stilwell informed Washington that unless given command immediately and unless some of Chiang's old political rivals were placed in high positions of power, the United States might as well pull out of China. In July and August, FDR implored Chiang to appoint Stilwell commander of all Chinese armies including that of the CCP and that Stilwell should have the final authority as to how Lend-Lease supplies were dispersed. For a nationalistic soldier like Chiang Kai-shek, FDR's request was an extreme humiliation. The generalissimo refused to allow his armies to be combined with that of the CCP's, and played down the Japanese threat.[22] Unfazed, Roosevelt begged Chiang to put Stilwell in command before it was "too late to avert a military catastrophe tragic both to China and to our allied plans for the early overthrow of Japan." FDR reminded H.H. Kung that China was one of the four great powers because of the United States. If there was civil war, Roosevelt predicted Britain and the Soviet Union would "seize the opportunity" to take advantage of China.[23]

Roosevelt then threatened to cut off aid to China if Stilwell was not placed in command. Chiang agreed to FDR's demand but asserted that the American commander had to be someone other than Stilwell. Privately, he believed that Roosevelt was treating China like a U.S. satellite. Germany and the Soviet Union had never made such demands of him in the past, and reorganizing Chinese armies in a manner that created military efficiency undermined his powerbase. Of China's 300 divisions, only thirty were loyal to Chiang; the rest were loyal to residual warlord commanders who distrusted Chiang, especially when he withheld Lend-Lease supplies from their units or kept his armies in reserve while they had to fight off Japanese offensives. H.H. Kung wanted to take a militant attitude by blaming Britain and the United States for the losses in the Pacific and Southeast Asia, putting China in a tight spot in the first place. Naturally, Koo opposed such talk because a war of words would prove more detrimental than beneficial for China, but Kung refused to keep silent and believed that the American attitude was like salt in a wound.[24]

This strain in allied relations occurred before the Chinese played their part in the Dumbarton Oaks Conference. Koo deplored "the menace of friction bet[ween] the leaders" of America and China. He agreed with those who said that China's military leaders were "too ticklish about sovereign rights in dealing with [the] U.S.A., which we regard as our best friend and ally and which after all has no political or imperialistic ambitions in China." Koo wanted Chiang "to take a far-sighted statesmanlike view for China's sake, and, if necessary, accept the demands." Since the U.S. was China's "best friend," and had "no ambition in China," the generalissimo needed America to win the war. China was a great power because of the United States, but China would lose its position should it refuse to fight in the last months of the war. Britain's attitude toward the United States was one of "deference and tolerance," and this likewise "was the U.S. attitude toward the USSR in the interest of early victory." Koo's remark was a reference to U.S. attempts to dismantle the British Empire while averting its eyes from Soviet moves into Eastern Europe. Since it was wartime, China needed to show the same toleration toward the allies. Kung refused to send a cable to the generalissimo that took such a position, saying that it would turn Chiang into a nominal head with Stilwell exercising full power.[25]

So Koo sent a cable that laid out his thinking. He explained to Chiang that the Americans simply wanted to win the war as quickly as possible, and since that was China's primary goal, China needed American friendship now and after the war. Koo suggested patience and tolerance of the Americans in order to save the country.[26] Others already made similar statements to Chiang Kai-shek, and though he appeared "agreeable," he remained concerned about his own prestige and the idea that the CCP would be just as well-equipped as his own army. Chiang wanted Roosevelt to guarantee that the CCP would not rebel and overthrow his government, but FDR refused to give the generalissimo such an insurance policy. Chiang told Roosevelt that the "Chinese people could stand being treated as slaves for the duration in order to get aid," but Chiang himself "would not tolerate being treated as a thief," referring to Stilwell taking control of Lend-Lease supplies. He declared that he would fight "Allied imperialism." Chiang suspected that communists had infiltrated FDR's government and that Roosevelt had made a deal with Stalin that conceded north China as a sphere of Soviet influence.[27] Chiang soon sent a message to FDR demanding Stilwell's recall.

While FDR pondered his next move, the Chinese-American-British sessions began at Dumbarton Oaks. Koo had found the wait trying, "but China's present position is such that we have to be patient." However, the Chinese delegation was embroiled in controversy. Although Koo initially convinced the delegation to back away from what he deemed to be the radical ideas contained in China's Essential Points, the delegates grew uncomfortable with their standing at the conference and the future UN. The delegation reached a consensus that the delegates have their "say without insisting on it." H.H. Kung feared that without an international air force, the UN "could not be relied on" because the "teeth were not strong enough." Another third world war seemed inevitable. Koo agreed with one his colleagues who expressed fear that China was in "danger of getting a zero" out of the conference and that China needed to insist on some of its points in order to make a contribution and not disappoint the people back home. The problem for Koo was knowing which points the delegation could "insist upon with a reasonable hope of success."[28]

Just as the Chinese prepared to sit down with the Americans and British, some delegates wanted justice and a definition of aggression inserted in the charter, or otherwise the UN would be of "no use to China who is likely to be 'aggressed.'" Koo leaned toward those who said "peace is the necessary condition for ministering justice." But when a conference of the technical delegates was called, it quickly became, in Koo's words, "political." Some in the delegation, particularly those with a military background, declared that if the principles of justice, a guarantee of political independence and territorial integrity, a definition of aggression, and an international police force and air force were not included in the UN charter, the UN "would be a useless organization." Other delegates came out in favor of the document that was drawn up by the other three big powers, saying that the UN would be more effective in keeping the peace than the League of Nations. The other side, however, suggested that if those principles could not be included, China might withdraw from the conference. Kung disagreed, pointing to the tensions in Sino-American relations because of the Stilwell affair, and noting that it was better to not insist on anything. Koo argued that the whole purpose of this meeting with the British and American delegations was not to permit China an opportunity to suggest revisions to the UN charter, but rather to maintain China's position as one of the four great powers. For that reason, China had to work to make the conference a success.[29]

After the Chinese sat down with their American and British counterparts, they went over the document from the first session. Koo and his compatriots were troubled by the principle of unanimity in voting, that is, the right of a permanent member and only the permanent members to exercise a veto at any time. Moreover, the Soviets wanted a party to a dispute to have the right to vote as well. Koo regarded "the question of voting in the Council . . . to be the root of the whole question of an organization."[30] If the UN operated by that principle, the small powers would have little voice, as Koo's counterparts acknowledged. Indeed, the Americans and British surprised Koo by leaning toward the Soviets. A member of the American delegation told Koo that once a big power went to war in defense of its interests, "it would not matter much if it was allowed to vote against action directed against itself." Some U.S. senators even voiced the concern that under the original American plan, the U.S. would be "obliged to go to war when it did not wish to." The Chinese position was similar to the original Anglo-American formula. According to Koo, China wanted such an international organization in order to end the "policy of force" or "gunboat policy" practiced by the great powers against Africa and Asia. Personally, he did not want to see "China shunted aside" and the Security Council making decisions "to the disregard of China."[31] Yet, the three powers were not about to reopen a major debate that took place during the first session, so the Chinese dropped the subject.

Following the discussion of other matters, the Chinese presented their own views of how to strengthen the UN, which, Koo declared, needed to be guided by certain principles. The Americans thought the

Chinese principles "extremely idealistic," but as Robert Hilderbrand has written, the principles reflected the Chinese "desire to create an organization with teeth in it." Yet Koo would not insist that those teeth be inserted in the UN charter. He wanted to show that his government was cooperating and hoped to reduce some of the tensions in Sino-American relations. Koo wanted the conference to be success and he wanted to protect China's position as a great power. In a cable to Chiang Kai-shek, he argued that if the powers perceived China as an obstructionist, China's international position would suffer.[32]

Laying out seven particular points, Koo expressed the Chinese view that the future international organization be guided by international law so that the organization did "not degenerate into an instrument of power politics." To assure the small powers, Koo called for a provision concerning respect for the political independence and territorial integrity of member states. He wanted the term "aggression" to be defined more explicitly so as to "facilitate swift action by the Council, inspire confidence, restrain potential aggressors and enable world opinion to recognize an aggressor immediately." Along with expressing support for an international air force, the Chinese favored creation of an international court with "compulsory jurisdiction . . . over justiciable disputes." The British supported the Chinese on the point, but the Soviets were opposed and the Americans were reluctant because of the U.S. Constitution.[33] Finally, Koo called for more cultural cooperation as a way of preventing war. The Chinese believed that creation of an international cultural office could encourage friendship and peace movements and reduce tensions between nations.[34]

After discussing these points with his counterparts, Koo eventually cut his seven points down to three. All sides agreed upon the principles of justice and the development and revision of international law, but the other points were tabled. Koo wanted the three points published along with the Dumbarton Oaks document in order to give the Chinese session equal status with that of the Soviets, but the Americans and British refused, saying that doing so would only further complicate matters with the Soviets. Koo acceded to their wishes that the Chinese proposals be published after the Soviets approved them.[35]

At the end of the conference, Koo gave a speech before the Chinese delegation assessing the results. The purpose of the conference, as far as China was concerned, was to maintain China's position as a great power and "cooperate" with Britain and the United States. The hope was that an international organization more effective than the League of Nations in ensuring the "independence and integrity" of all nations would be created. There was also a desire to retain the "sympathy of the Small powers," to whom Koo wanted to give more of a voice instead of having the organization rest solely on the tune called by the great powers. Koo found aspects of the conference to be mixed in quality. Some were inadequate, others practical, and still others were idealistic. Yet he deemed the Dumbarton Oaks Conference to be generally satisfactory. The new Security Council "would be more powerful and effective than the Council of the League of Nations." It would be in constant session, available to meet with twenty-four hours' notice. The future United Nations could impose sanctions, have a security force, allow for *rebus sic stantibus* in which old treaties could be revised, and do all "in accordance with the principles of international law and justice." Koo played up China's contribution as being "valuable" and claimed later that it was at Dumbarton Oaks that China finally achieved the status as a fourth great power. He had to acknowledge, though, that the majority of the work was done by the three powers, with China simply giving a stamp of approval.[36]

Some American internationalists condemned the document that came out of this conference saying the future United Nations would be dominated by the great powers. In most circumstances Koo might have agreed because he had not quite reconciled himself to the Rooseveltian internationalist viewpoint that excluded the concerns of the small powers, but this was the best that could be achieved under the circumstances. He took solace in his belief that China had given a "moral tone to the plan by basing the new organization in deciding disputes upon justice and law."[37]

In the last days of the Dumbarton conference, Sino-American relations took a turn for the worse. On October 5, FDR agreed that Chiang could remain supreme commander of Chinese forces, but the president wanted Stilwell to retain his command in Burma. And the Roosevelt administration agreed to pay China $25 million of a $500 million loan in gold. This loan delighted Kung, but Koo suspected that "the concession was due to the desire to calm China down" now that Roosevelt ran for reelection to an unprecedented fourth term of office.[38] Chiang Kai-shek, however, viewed Roosevelt's note as so "tactless" that Chiang "exploded and changed his mind." Chiang refused to be cowed by "high-handed pressure."[39] Stilwell's continued presence would only further damage Sino-American relations. Chiang reminded Roosevelt that it was only recently that China had discarded the unequal treaties, and on the battlefield, China had to protect its "sovereignty." Roosevelt yielded and Stilwell was recalled on October 18. The CBI Theater was also divided into the China Theater and the Burma-India Theater. Stilwell's replacement, Gen. Albert Wedemeyer, did not command Chinese forces.[40]

Stilwell's recall left a bad taste in the Americans' mouths. For a brief moment, FDR considered Mao Zedong and the CCP as a viable option in China. Over the summer, the Dixie Mission, a group of American military and technical experts, proceeded to Yan'an. For the next several months, reports to Washington spoke of the night-and-day contrast between life in Yan'an and that of Chongqing. Absent was the corruption and factionalism, and present were a democracy, nationalism, fighting spirit, and an élan unheard of under Chiang's regime. The Americans also believed that Mao Zedong wanted to work with the United States. Mao propagandized the Americans by removing American illusions about Chiang Kai-shek and creating new ones: that the CCP shared more in common politically with the United States than with the GMD. Mao hoped to win military, economic, and political aid from the United States, because the Nazi invasion of the Soviet Union led to a decrease in Soviet aid to the CCP. Meanwhile, Chiang launched an offensive against the CCP with 500,000 troops in what became known as the "Third Anti-Communist High Tide." The Soviets had no leverage, but the United States did tell Chiang to reduce hostilities with the CCP.[41]

The day that Chiang rejected retaining Stilwell, Koo met with Harry Hopkins, FDR's chief aide, who raised the issue of China and the bad military situation there. Hopkins observed that "China was also not doing her best" and warned that American interest in China would wane if China did not play a prominent role in the defeat of Japan. Hopkins added that unlike Britain and the Soviet Union, Roosevelt wanted China to be a great power. Koo interjected that the American press and the CCP were exaggerating the situation. The communist problem was serious, but Koo thought that "the real remedy . . . lay in the adoption of constitutional government under which the Communist party would be recognized as a political party enjoying equal rights with other political parties, including the [GMD]." And Chiang Kai-shek "should be safeguarded" because the CCP would "hesitate to overthrow" the generalissimo, supposedly because they had no comparable leader.[42]

Privately, Koo felt differently. In a memo written that same month, Koo asserted that the CCP wanted its own military and administration while coexisting with the GMD. "Their clamor for democracy is but a political slogan," Koo continued, "to win sympathy abroad for their party." On the other hand, the concerns of the Americans were on his mind. Chiang declared that he would "not yield on a question involving sovereignty and the future of China," and that China would fight alone as it did in the early years of the war so that "she would be freer to do what . . . she saw fit." Koo thought this was the "stubborn view of an angered leader." Everyone knew that China was in a very bad way with the exception of Chiang Kai-shek, who, according to Koo, "was kept in the dark as to the real situation because his subordinates would not tell him the facts."[43] Koo saw that only the U.S. supported the notion of China as a great power, and now even China's closest supporter had legitimate doubts about China's ability to play an effective role in keeping the postwar peace.

Koo's view of the United States as a power that would not undermine Chinese sovereignty underlay his willingness to accept Stilwell's leadership of Chinese forces. Unlike Chiang Kai-shek, who believed that Stilwell or Roosevelt would ultimately undercut his own leadership in numerous ways, Koo viewed America as a true friend in the harsh world of international politics. The diplomat looked at the long term when China needed a friend in the fluid postwar period. That faith in the United States, however, was about to undergo a severe test.

Before returning to Britain, Koo met with several American officials who raised the issue of the Soviet Union and the Far East. When he met with Hopkins, FDR's aide mentioned the potential Soviet threat in East Asia. Previously, Koo spoke of renewed Soviet irredentism after the war, but now he completely reversed himself by saying "he did not think Russia would pursue a policy of territorial expansion in the Far East." He admitted, though, that Moscow wanted access to the Pacific, and that Japan's defeat "would remove an obstacle to the building of Russian naval strength in the Far East."[44]

A few days later, Admiral William Leahy, a member of the Joint Chiefs of Staff, expressed to Koo his opinion that China's fighting ability in October diminished in comparison to previous years. Although China's air force had improved, the same could not be said for the land forces. Leahy believed the Soviet Union needed to enter the war against Japan, but the Soviets expected to receive a warm-water port in the Far East in return for declaring war on Japan. He added that neither London nor Washington opposed such a price. Koo responded that such a move would negatively affect the peace in East Asia and his people would be "suspicious." In years past, the Sino-Japanese War of 1894–1895 and the Russo-Japanese War turned the Liaodong Peninsula into a battleground. China recognized Korean autonomy, and viewed giving the Soviet Union a warm-water port as "dangerous." Leahy continued to insist, however, that the only way to get the Soviet Union into the war was by granting it a port in the Far East.[45]

In a not-so-subtle manner, Leahy made Koo aware of what occurred at Teheran the previous year and what would happen at Yalta in coming months. The Americans were inclined in November 1944 to enlist Soviet aid, especially as the war effort in China worsened. The week that Stilwell was fired, Japanese forces restarted the Ichigo Offensive and overran air bases without resistance even though Chiang claimed that his forces could hold out for two months. It looked as if the Japanese would drive on to Chongqing, causing panic and confusion there. While Chinese and allied troops were being funneled into the area, the Japanese halted their advance with their objectives reached, but the damage was done. Chiang's government obviously was in no position to play a role in defeating Japan.[46]

The United States also lost its ties to the CCP, and Mao's hopes to win assistance from Washington were dashed. In 1944, FDR sent Gen.

Patrick Hurley, former secretary of war under Herbert Hoover, to China as his personal emissary. In November, Hurley, now U.S. ambassador to China, visited Yan'an after Chiang Kai-shek expressed willingness to negotiate with the CCP. Hurley signed an agreement with Mao that promised American military aid and political assistance by bringing together a GMD-CCP coalition government. However, when Hurley returned to Chongqing, Chiang demanded that the CCP surrender its military in return for political representation, so Hurley declared that the United States would only provide political, economic, and military assistance to Chiang Kai-shek. Nevertheless, Mao did not stop pursuing assistance from the United States, and Washington did not rule out working with the CCP. In December, U.S. forces in China were already working on contingency plans to pull out of the China theater should Chiang's regime collapse. It was clear that Soviet intervention against Japan was necessary and that the two latent superpowers had to prevent the Chinese civil war from dragging them into a great power conflict.[47]

In February 1945, Stalin, Roosevelt, and Churchill met at Yalta. Roosevelt not only wanted to get the Soviet Union into the Pacific War but sought cooperation with Stalin to avoid conflict over China and protect global U.S. interests. Stalin could now focus on Asia because he no longer had to fear fighting a two-front war. Allied armies were in Germany, and Hitler's Third Reich stood on the verge of defeat. Stalin wanted to prevent Japan from rising from the ashes like a phoenix and threatening Soviet interests, but he also feared a Sino-American alliance directed at the Soviet Union. The Soviet leader concluded in October 1944 that only Soviet intervention into the Pacific War could accomplish those objectives. It would guarantee the flow of Lend-Lease supplies and other American aid, prevent Japan and the United States from reaching a negotiated peace, and expand Soviet influence into northeast Asia. Before the Yalta Conference commenced, Stalin restated his price to come into the war. He wanted the lease of two warm-water ports in Southern Manchuria, Lüshun and Dalian, as well as the CER. Stalin made one other demand: The allies had to accept Soviet domination of Outer Mongolia.

After some negotiating, Stalin agreed to internationalize Dalian but still demanded a lease of Lüshun. Stalin agreed that Chiang Kai-shek should remain the leader of China even if a GMD-CCP coalition government was formed, and he suggested that a treaty could be signed between Moscow and Chongqing in April. Although Chiang would not learn the terms of the agreement until June, he received bits and pieces of information in the interim.[48]

Koo returned to China in March 1945 to discuss the Dumbarton Oaks Conference and the upcoming San Francisco Conference with the generalissimo. Koo met immediately with T.V. Soong, who was still foreign minister, and argued that it was time to put the communist problem to rest before the Soviet Union declared war on Japan and became embroiled in the China question to Chongqing's detriment. Soong demurred. He and Chiang felt that the Soviet Union would enter the Asian conflict anyway, but thought that Soong should at least travel to Moscow and reach some kind of agreement.[49]

A few days later, over dinner with the generalissimo, Koo discussed a wide range of topics that concerned the postwar period. When the topic turned toward the Soviet Union, Chiang expressed the opinion that the Soviet Union understood the Chinese better than any other power and that Stalin knew that the Chinese people "would not stand for either communism or disunity, and if the U.S.S.R. tried to divide China into two countries, it knows the Ch[inese] people would oppose it and the U.S.S.R. does not want to antagonize the whole Ch[inese] nation."[50] The two men also discussed a cable from Roosevelt stating that as a "democratic gesture," China should appoint representatives of the CCP to the Chinese delegation planning to attend the upcoming San Francisco Conference. When Chiang learned the gist of Roosevelt's message, he became "irritated and agitated." Chiang remarked that "conditions in China were different from other countries," and he believed that "Com[munist] delegates . . . [would] make trouble."

When queried as to why Roosevelt would send such a message, Koo gave several possibilities. Some nations were already complaining about the great powers having permanent seats, and since Roosevelt "sponsored China's position as a Great Power," he was "anxious about China's status in the Conf[erence] and likes to see her repres[ented] there as strongly as possible." Roosevelt might be concerned, too, that if the

"question of unity of China is not solved now, it may become an international question and thereby become more complicated and difficult to
settle." Finally, communist propaganda could very well be influencing
Roosevelt. When Koo suggested that it was "advisable not to close the
door to his [Roosevelt's] suggestion," Chiang "asked why it should not
be closed, implying that it should." The CCP "all along refused to accept orders from the Central Government," Chiang emphasized, "and
that there would be difficulty rather than help from their inclusion in
the delegation." Despite his ire being raised by FDR's demand, Chiang
acquiesced.[51]

On March 18, Chiang Kai-shek called for Koo to discuss another
cable from FDR. As before, Roosevelt urged Chiang to settle the CCP
problem. Then he revealed Stalin's desires: In order to enter the Pacific
War, Moscow wanted joint control of the CER and a lease for Lüshun
where the Soviets could have a warm-water port. Koo did not believe
that Roosevelt had agreed to any of the points, but given the heavy losses
in the Pacific campaign, FDR wanted to get the Soviets into the war with
Japan to bring about victory. Chiang could not understand why the
Americans did not see the disadvantage to the United States of giving
Lüshun to the Soviet Union. Koo agreed, but believed that Washington
wanted to end the war with Japan and get Soviet cooperation in establishing the United Nations. He suggested that Washington be made aware
of those disadvantages before agreeing to Stalin's demands. Koo remained
concerned however about Lüshun. He learned soon after that Chiang
Kai-shek had suggested to Roosevelt at the Cairo Conference that China
and America could use Lüshun jointly. Fearing another "scramble for
concessions," Koo warned T.V. Soong that China had to walk cautiously.
If China gave the Soviets a port, the other powers would line up wanting
their own port.[52]

When Koo left China for the United States at the end of the month,
he could see that the atmosphere on the eve of the San Francisco Conference was not favorable. The great powers were still arguing over how
many votes each power would have in the UN. More troubling, though,
was the rise and fall of China's status as a great power in less than four
years. Fault lay, or so said Koo, in the fact that Chongqing "did not always
understand the American, British or Russian psychology and much of

the friction which had arisen from time to time in our relations with them was due to this lack of understanding." The perception persisted that China did nothing to expedite the defeat of Japan, whereas the other powers were being bled white on the battlefield. While the other great powers made progress in the war, China "lagged way behind and we do not seem to realize it." By not pressing the fight against the Japanese, the GMD government paid a heavy political price internationally. "The result," Koo continued, "is that we are now practically left on the side even in the consideration of the war in the Pacific, as if we are of no consequence."[53]

While in the middle of contemplating China's international position, Koo received the stunning news of Roosevelt's death. He called Roosevelt a "firm and steadfast friend of China," a "great war leader and an idealistic statesman repres[enting] the hopes and aspirations of the liberty-loving peoples of the world." He wondered now about the possible effects on Sino-American relations. President Harry Truman, as with many Americans, was an unknown, but the reports that he and T.V. Soong received suggested that Truman "would be firm with Soviet Russia."[54]

Before Roosevelt died, the Chinese remained officially uninformed that the Soviet Union had been granted permission to lease Lüshun. The Americans only gave hints. While Truman studied the details of the Yalta agreement, T.V. Soong learned that Stalin did not want Manchuria but only wanted to recover the Soviet Union's original lease rights to Lüshun and the CER.[55] Chiang Kai-shek's position was that leasing any port would "revive [the] 'sphere of influence' policy of other powers and would be opposed by the Chinese people." As far as Koo was concerned, he believed that public opinion in China and the world had to be prepared "for a showdown." The world needed to be informed that Manchuria was Chinese, not Soviet, territory. A "policy of leased territories and spheres of influence would only be sowing the seeds of future conflict in the F[ar] E[ast] and the Pacific."[56] He told Admiral Leahy that "the international complications and crises in the Far East in the last 50 years had been due principally to the attempt to control Manchuria." Reversing his stance of the previous October, Koo asserted that there had to be a better solution, such as giving the Soviet Union a warm-water port in Korea "which would be a reasonable contribution for Korea to make to the cause of international security in the Pacific" as long as the port was part of a "general plan of security for the western Pacific and Far Eastern Asia."[57]

In the meantime, as more details of the Yalta agreement leaked to Chongqing, Chiang instructed Koo and Wang Shijie, soon-to-be foreign minister and Chiang Kai-shek's confidant, to analyze how China should respond. Koo explained that in the days before Roosevelt died, the American president concluded that China possessed insufficient power to defeat the Japanese. Moreover, Americans were unwilling to see more young American boys sacrificed, so Roosevelt had to get the Soviet Union into the war against Japan. Koo surmised that since the Soviets knew that this kind of territorial expansion did not fit the tenor of the times, Stalin wanted the agreement to remain secret. In his opinion, the Soviets would be "isolated" at the upcoming San Francisco Conference. Koo suggested that the delegation cooperate with the Soviets so that the Russians would not make any demands over Manchuria. Wang Shijie, on the other hand, believed that the Soviet Union entertained territorial ambitions both in Europe and the Far East. In regard to the latter, he thought the Soviets wanted to return to the position they had in Manchuria before the Russo-Japanese War.[58] Neither Koo nor Wang, however, had any particular policy to offer.

Chiang already knew what his policy would be. With Roosevelt, the great leader but communist appeaser, gone, he would make no concessions to the CCP rebels even though his closest advisers supported making a political deal with the communists before entering into negotiations with Stalin. He hoped that the United States would continue to back him despite his intransigence toward the CCP. And because of the growing tensions between Washington and Moscow over the failure to grant Poland free elections and over the future of postwar Germany, Chiang hoped that the Soviets would be more willing to make a deal more favorable to Chiang to keep peace in Asia while they were preoccupied by tensions in Europe.[59]

As Chiang Kai-shek maintained a tough line with the CCP, Koo took the responsibility to "counteract the insidious campaign going on to make the Am[erican] people believe that the Soviet [Union] had a legitimate interest in Manchuria and to justify her covetous eyes on it." And he advised T.V. Soong, now that both men were in San Francisco, to not make a visit to Moscow if Stalin refused to compromise over Manchuria. China needed to consider whether it was worth the price to ask the Soviet Union to enter the war against Japan. Soong was impressed by the argument but went to Moscow anyway.[60]

On April 25, 1945, the San Francisco Conference convened with a view to completing the work done at Dumbarton Oaks. Koo described the atmosphere as "anything but favorable" because of the voting procedure for the Security Council. The Chinese delegation went into the conference committed to establishing a different one. While he was in China, Koo learned that China would object to the American solution to voting in the Security Council. If the American position was adopted, it was meaningless for China to join the new security organization. In fact, Koo wrote in his diary that maybe it was "better for China to stay out of the ranks of the great powers, because then we could say what we wanted."[61] Eventually, though, the Chinese did accept the Yalta Formula for voting in the Security Council in which a great power could exercise a veto. Koo described the final vote as ending the great battle between the great powers and the small powers, and as "almost always happens, the big powers in the end carried their mutual will." Chongqing allegedly accepted the Yalta Formula because "in order to make the new international organization succeed, it would be necessary to preserve the unity of purpose and spirit of cooperation between the Great Powers, without which the machinery of the Security Council would break down." Although not ideal, it was a "practical compromise." "Perhaps after working together and acquiring the habit of cooperation between the Great Powers in the first years after the war," Koo told a foreign diplomat, "there might be an opportunity to revise it when suspicion and distrust would have dissipated and understanding and confidence consolidated."[62]

Going into the conference, China's other major proposals included an amendment that would better enforce the rulings of the International Court of Justice should any party refuse to abide by the Court's decisions. In fact, the Chinese considered this provision to be "necessary and very important," and wanted the Security Council to take action in such instances. The delegates representing the other three powers refused to accept this provision, simply stating that the amendment was undesirable. Only the Soviet delegate gave an explanation: The Security Council would, like the Court, have the power to issue "decisions binding upon the parties." The opposition forced the Chinese to reserve their position.[63]

Hence, throughout the conference, Koo simply followed the tune called by the other delegations. Besides going along with the Yalta Formula for voting, Koo backed the United States proposal that under the trusteeship system, there be strategic areas that would come under the control of the Security Council, meaning the big powers. The small powers rejected this proposal because the trusteeships were created to allow territories to "evolve toward self-determination and independence." Placing those territories under the control of the Security Council smacked of colonialism and was the League Mandate system all over again. In a 1943 conversation between FDR and Koo, the two men agreed that the League Mandate system had led to colonialism, with Koo adding that his government preferred "liberation and independence." Two years later, a meeting of the Chinese delegation viewed the trusteeship question as "very important for our country's future destiny," and as a "struggle" between Britain and the United States "for world power or at least a building up of strength as world powers."[64] "Reluctantly," Koo went along because of American insistence. The Chinese did get a proposal adopted that allowed the United Nations to eventually take over the administration of these trust territories. And true to his concern for small powers, Koo suggested that they have an opportunity to review the work of the conference as well as the "question of unanimity of the permanent members."[65]

Otherwise, Koo's contributions to the conference were limited to modifying the language of the Charter and putting forth rules of procedure. When his opinion was sought on the location of the new UN, Koo replied, "Geneva invoked many unhappy memories of the League which had disappointed the hopes of the Chinese people and the world," adding that since "we are setting up a new world . . . it should start in the new world." At least at this moment, Koo entertained the hope that the new postwar organization could work more effectively than the League of Nations.[66]

China's inability to be a leader in the creation of the UN was obvious. In fact, an Australian delegate complained that China was no longer the spokesman for the smaller powers, a charge Koo vociferously denied. After the war though, the Chinese were criticized by a member of the U.S. Department for not taking the lead at Dumbarton Oaks and San Francisco: "instead of striking out boldly and taking the initiative in matters about which they may have had strong opinions, they have assumed a quite secondary role, acting as conciliator and never as leader on major issues, and as far as voting is concerned, almost without exception following the lead of the United States." China disappointed its friends by showing up at Dumbarton Oaks with a "bold and imaginative plan" that would have placed greater responsibility on the great powers and have given greater authority to the small powers. In the end, China acquiesced to the other powers "even though their own plans called for a stronger organization." Likewise, the pattern continued at San Francisco in which the Chinese were willing to sacrifice some sovereignty for collective security only to retreat to commenting on procedures.[67] These criticisms, though, were too harsh given China's weak position in 1945. China could not afford to alienate the other powers and had to cooperate.

By the end of 1945, Koo believed four things had to occur in order for the peace to be safeguarded in an atomic age: control of all weapons of mass destruction; an international force with "all the newest weapons" and the ability to manufacture them at the disposal of the UN Security Council; prohibition of the manufacture and use of weapons of mass destruction; and the abolition of the veto power by permanent members of UN Security Council. Two years later, he revealed his displeasure with certain aspects of the creation, particularly the veto issue. Koo wanted the UN to succeed because "[t]here is really no sound or effective alternative. We know into what plight the old system of the balance of power and rival alliances has led the world."[68] He preferred an organization that prevented power politics, but peace depended on whether the other three powers cooperated, especially the Soviets, who held the key in the Pacific. Quoting President Truman, Koo hoped that the Soviet Union and the other powers "would use their immense power 'to serve and not to dominate.' If the powers renounced expansionism or domination, the peace of the future would be safe. Otherwise, security is a relative thing and the greater the zone of security [sought], the greater will be the need for further territory to defend it."[69]

While Koo was busy in San Francisco, T.V. Soong met with Stalin to negotiate a treaty. Now officially aware of the promises made to Stalin at Yalta, Chiang initially did not want to enter into negotiations with the Soviets as long as they wanted to "lease" the ports in Manchuria, but by late June he gave the green light for talks.[70] When informed that Soong would be traveling to Moscow, Koo opposed the trip saying that if China was "not prepared to yield—which we should not—it would be useless to make a visit without working out a plan of action." Koo preferred that his government temporize and wait until the war with Japan ended to see how the international situation developed.[71] Nevertheless, Soong went to Moscow and held the first round of talks. Stalin demanded that Chiang Kai-shek recognize the independence of Outer Mongolia, but Chiang wanted Stalin to cut off support to the CCP. Stalin was amenable if he got a thirty-year treaty over Manchuria, Soviet-control of Lüshun, and Soviet ownership of the railways.

Negotiations were interrupted by Stalin's trip to Potsdam. A second round of Sino-Soviet negotiations commenced on August 7, the day after the United States dropped an atomic bomb on Hiroshima. While the negotiations continued, the Soviet Union declared war on Japan on August 8 and rushed troops into Manchuria. The United States now told Stalin that the Chinese should not have to make concessions beyond the Yalta Agreement, but Stalin insisted that Roosevelt gave him a sphere of influence over ports in Manchuria. Because of Soviet entry into the war, Wang Shijie believed that an agreement had to be signed. The next day, a second atomic bomb exploded over Nagasaki and Japan surrendered days later.

On August 14, the Sino-Soviet Treaty of Friendship was signed. The Chinese and Soviets agreed to an alliance to prevent a resurgence of Japanese aggression. The CER and Southern Manchurian Railway were united into one Chinese Changchun Railway that would be jointly owned for thirty years, at which time it would return to sole Chinese ownership. Both countries would use Lüshun's naval facilities, and the Soviets agreed to respect Chinese sovereignty in Manchuria. The Chinese agreed to recognize the independence of Outer Mongolia, though a clear boundary was not established in order to expedite the signing of the treaty. Stalin gave assurances that he supported the unification of China under the leadership of Chiang Kai-shek. One issue that went unresolved was "war trophies" by which was meant ownership of Japanese investments in Manchuria, but otherwise Chiang paid the price to win Soviet support for his government and not the CCP.[72]

Once Koo had an understanding of the treaty's contents, he pointed to "missed opportunities and unnecessary concessions." For example, Koo thought the boundary in Outer Mongolia should have been stated in the treaty. Otherwise, "the absence of definition leaves it open to encroachment from year to year by Outer Mongolia. . . . As one who has struggled for more than four decades" for a "policy of recovering lost territory and restoring China's sovereignty and independence," Koo commented later, "I am naturally very disappointed with the Chinese stand taken at Moscow."[73]

The treaty did little to improve China's position vis-à-vis the Soviet Union, and the anger vented against the treaty by Chinese public opinion affected China's relations with other countries. There were reports that the GMD army planned to retake Hong Kong and that Soong, who was still head of the Executive Yuan, would raise the Hong Kong question at the upcoming Foreign Ministers' meeting. Koo advised Chiang and Soong to negotiate directly using Washington's good offices and warned that the British were "very sensitive to our apparently torturous way of using U.S. influence to force a settlement." The British would not give up their colony and the United States made it clear that Hong Kong's status as a colony would remain unchanged. After Japan surrendered, Chiang and Soong both demanded that Japanese forces in Hong Kong surrender to GMD troops, but the United States preferred that the British have the honor of retaking Hong Kong. The only explanation for Chongqing's policy toward Hong Kong that Koo could come up with was that Chiang Kai-shek was using Hong Kong "to offset possible reaction of Ch[inese] people to the Sino-Russian treaty and agreements at Moscow." Since Churchill's government was voted out of power during the summer, the British warned the Chinese "not do anything to embarrass or weaken the position of the new Government in London which wants first of all to strengthen its position vis-à-vis the nation and the world." For his part, while involved with the creation of the United Nations, Koo instructed the diplomatic and military personnel in London "not to get into [an] open and direct clash with [the] U.S.A., U.S.S.R., and U.K. on any questions unless our own vital interests are affected . . . and try always to conciliate their differences with one another." [74]

Koo believed that the Sino-Soviet Treaty was the result of the allied perception of Chiang's government as weak, which in fact it was. He alluded to the misunderstanding between Washington and Chongqing over China's war policy, the British and Soviet inability to take China seriously as a great power, and Moscow's desire to get into the Pacific War, reaping spoils without the sacrifice. [75] Such thinking led to decisions at Teheran and Yalta to bring the Soviet Union into the war on the assumption that the Soviet contribution was vital to defeating Japan.

During World War II, Koo found himself in the difficult position of serving a genuinely patriotic leader whose nationalistic war aims and Pan-Asianism created tensions with his British and American allies. As middleman, Koo could only moderate Chiang Kai-shek's nationalistic tendencies, such as his insistence on recovering Tibet and the Hong Kong territories. As a young man, Koo took a hard-line position toward areas no longer controlled by China, but now he softened his stance. Koo wanted his government to give up its old "policy of coercion and manifesting superiority" and pursue a new policy "vis-à-vis the minorities in China esp[ecially] along the borders" that would secure the "goodwill and friendship" of those people and "make them feel their relation with the Chinese and China were beneficial to them in fact." [76] Koo never prevailed on Chiang Kai-shek to see his country as the allies did: weak, corrupt, and unwilling to take the war to Japan. In the end, Koo's diplomatic reasoning and propaganda could not whitewash the reality that China's weaknesses undermined any hope of it being a truly great power. Now as China entered the postwar era, Koo hoped that the United Nations, based on four or five powers, would permit China a voice while it dealt with its internal problems. The emerging international political power system, however, relegated China to minor power status because of that country's lack of power internally and internationally. And the Chinese civil war and great power rivalry soon chased away the peace that the Chinese longed for.

Chapter 8

COLLAPSE OF THE ROC, 1945–1949

DURING WORLD WAR II, KOO ASSURED FOREIGNERS that in the postwar period, there would be no more civil wars and that the communist problem would be easily resolved. He claimed as well that China would become "a fully-fledged democracy after the war."[1] But with Japan's surrender, both the CCP and Chiang's forces set out to retake territory held by the Japanese and to disarm Japanese forces. Chiang disregarded the advice of many that he launch a war against the CCP. He chose instead to negotiate. Civil war might cost Chiang U.S. aid, but negotiating avoided alienating the Americans and bought time for Chiang to move his forces into Japanese-occupied territory, especially Manchuria. Mao talked, but the CCP, elated by Soviet intervention into Manchuria, set out from Yan'an to link up with the 1.5 million Soviet troops. CCP membership now totaled 1.2 million, and the size of the army was 910,000 by April 1945. The CCP also controlled territory that held 90 million inhabitants. Manchuria's industries and agricultural surplus there would give the CCP a good base from which to operate, and its proximity to the Soviet Union facilitated receiving Soviet aid. As Chiang's forces moved slowly and cautiously into occupied territory, the CCP moved quickly toward Manchuria while warning the Americans that aid to Chiang would lead to civil war.

 Calls were made immediately to the United States for transport to move GMD troops into Manchuria. The Americans were not interested

Koo speaking before United Nations General Assembly, October 1946 (UN photo, courtesy of National Archives)

in communist expansion any more than Chiang, so Gen. Douglas MacArthur ordered Japanese forces to surrender only to Chiang's troops, not the CCP. And in early October, U.S. Marines landed in Hebei and Shandong Provinces. Concerned by the American landings on Chinese soil, the Soviet ambassador told Chiang that Soviet forces would withdraw from Manchuria by December 1. This gave Chiang an opening to ask for permission to put GMD troops in Dalian. The Soviets not only said no but declared that Japanese factories were deemed "war booty" and both sides could negotiate their disposition. Meanwhile, talks with Mao went nowhere and Chiang considered military action but backed away from that step, knowing it would anger the Soviets. Chiang knew, too, that the United States wanted to see his forces in Manchuria. To get American power behind him, Chiang pulled what forces he had in Manchuria back to Beijing. The Soviets, who had blocked GMD activities in Manchuria, now apologized and agreed to help Chiang occupy Manchuria, fearing further American intervention into the area. The Soviets agreed to stay in Manchuria until GMD forces arrived, so Chiang asked the Soviets to stay until February 1946.[2]

While the political situation grew tense in China, all was not going well for Chiang's government abroad. From September to October 1945, the powers gathered in London for the Foreign Ministers' Conference to deal with European questions. The whole notion of a council of the Foreign Ministers representing the Five Great Powers originated at the Potsdam Conference of July.[3] Although many of the issues discussed did not involve Asia and even though France was not one of the original four great powers, Secretary of State James Byrnes suggested that China and France participate on an equal basis in drawing up peace treaties, though neither had a final vote or say over the finished product. Although the Berlin Protocol written during the Potsdam Conference stated that neither France nor China could play a role in drafting treaties regarding defeated Germany, all of the delegates agreed with Byrnes' proposals.

Very quickly, the atmosphere of the meeting proved to be in Koo's words "discouraging, even depressing." The Chinese delegates could only sit on the side and watch as tempers flared between the American, British and Soviet delegations over Japan, Romania, and Greece. China did side with the other delegations against the Soviet Union in proposing collective trusteeship for Italy's colonies, but Koo and the delegates watched the Soviets and Americans battle it out over the Balkans. The United States refused to sign treaties with Bulgaria and Romania because their governments were not democratic. Infuriated, the Soviets reminded the Americans that they already dominated Japan and Italy, and, while the Soviets could tolerate democracy in Hungary and Finland, Moscow would not stand for unfriendly governments along its borders in the Balkans. When the Americans still would not recognize the East European countries as being under the Soviet sphere, V.M. Molotov, the Soviet Foreign Minister, pointed out that according to the procedures established at Potsdam, France and China could not participate in discussions of the East European treaties. Clearly, Molotov was not impressed with the Anglo-American effort to use France and China to build an anti-Soviet bloc. Molotov also called for creation of an Allied Control Council composed of representatives from all five powers to oversee the American occupation of Japan. Though the Soviets were correct in their interpretation of Potsdam, Byrnes opposed Molotov's proposal because he feared that neither would be treated as equals on the UN Security Council.

Unable to make headway, the conference broke up in October. The conference not only failed to usher in a new era of peace but expanded the cracks in the UN Alliance that had long existed. Koo wrote in his diary that it was preferable for China to have never been invited to the meeting than to participate and lose face by being told it could not participate in the signing of those treaties. If the Soviets got their way, "it would mean the break-up and destruction of the" United Nations, "leaving the guarding of the peace of the world . . . to three or even two [powers] in so far as questions arising [in regard to] the peace treaties are concerned."[4]

The growing rivalry between Moscow, London and Washington and the weakness of Chiang Kai-shek further diminished China's great power status. Despite Soviet promises to cooperate with Chiang in Manchuria, President Truman decided to send George C. Marshall, recently retired Army Chief of Staff, to China where reports from American officers there suggested that Chiang's forces were too weak to take over Manchuria if confronted with communist opposition. There was also concern that calling for unification of China under Chiang Kai-shek would not only heat up the Chinese civil war but bring the United States and the Soviet Union into direct conflict. Marshall's mission was to bring about a peaceful settlement of CCP-GMD political and military differences. Marshall was not going to China as an honest middleman, because his instructions ordered him to support Chiang Kai-shek, even if Chiang . proved more of an obstacle to peace than the CCP. Although Marshall had little respect for Chiang especially after the Stilwell affair, Marshall still wanted Manchuria to come under GMD control. On December 15, Truman issued his policy for China: U.S. Marines would remain in China where the United States would not only disarm the Japanese but also strive for the creation of a "unified, democratic and peaceful nation." Truman's speech scolded the GMD for its one party rule while blaming the CCP for insisting on retaining its army. "It was a very outspoken one and I could not but wish that we had succeeded in settling the communist question ourselves already," Koo lamented in his diary, "It was so unbecoming to our prestige as one of the big 5."[5]

Late in December, another Foreign Ministers' Conference was held in Moscow between Britain, the Soviet Union, and the United States. A major issue on the table was Korea. Although the United States had its sphere in Japan and in China, the Soviets extended their influence into not only Manchuria and Mongolia but northern Korea as well. A final communiqué from the conference stated that a Far Eastern Advisory Commission and Allied Control Council would be established in Japan, but the United States and Gen. Douglas MacArthur, Supreme Commander of the Allied Powers, really ran the occupation of Japan. Korea was divided in two, with the Soviets retaining influence in the north while United States oversaw the south. All three powers supported withdrawal of Soviet and American forces from China along with a unified, democratic China under Chiang's leadership, broad political participation in all branches of government, and the end of civil war. In a statement reminiscent of the Nine Power Treaty of 1922, all three powers promised to not interfere in China's internal affairs.[6]

For Koo, the communiqué was "painful," because China was treated as a question, similar to Romania or Korea. Despite fighting Japan for eight-years, "the question of control of Japan also was settled behind our back," and the Soviet Union's late entrance into the Asian conflict made it an equal partner with China, the United States, and Great Britain. "Now, not only Korea is taken out of [our] hands but even our own domestic situation has been made a subject of [an] international conference without our participation." Koo did not blame others, though. The onus lay with China for not reorganizing its army in 1942 and 1943 along lines suggested by Stilwell so that China would be prepared at the end of the war "to take over Manchuria and even Korea." Koo opposed the growing friction between the CCP and the GMD. He wanted unity first because in the postwar period, "the doctrine of power politics [was] in full-swing ... [and] China could not play her part without a unified government with a unified army and administration." Until this was done, China would have little voice as a power. "I do hope our people at home will see the anomalous and humiliating position of China in the international domain."[7]

Over the next few months, tensions between the Soviet Union and the United States increased in the Middle East over Turkey and Iran. Stalin gave a speech in February 1946 that declared that the Soviet Union lived in a hostile world, and communism and capitalism were incompatible. The next month, Winston Churchill visited the United States, and in Fulton, Missouri, the former Prime Minister called for cooperation of the English-speaking people to create a new world order, because from the Baltic to the Adriatic an iron curtain had descended across the Continent allowing the Soviet Union to rule Eastern Europe. As Soviet-U.S. hostility moved toward a Cold War, the fact that the United States was now a power to be reckoned with was not lost on Chiang Kai-shek. Britain was in decline as a power and in coming months, the British withdrew from Greece, Palestine and India, the Crown Jewel.

In March 1946, Koo returned to China. The previous September, T.V. Soong informed Koo that the latter would become the Chinese ambassador to Washington, because Sino-American relations were far more important than relations with Britain. But he wanted Koo to spend some time in China. According to Soong, Chiang Kai-shek liked Koo, and simply thought Koo to be "a little timid." The only people that Chiang supposedly did not like were those "with independent views" or who pointed out the generalissimo's "mistakes in judgement."[8]

It was not a propitious moment to be in China. On January 1, 1946, the CCP publicly rejected Chiang's one-party rule and called for the establishment of an executive committee composed of members from various parties to form a coalition government in Manchuria. Chiang refused especially as GMD forces continued to be transported to Manchuria by the United States. However, he agreed to talks with the CCP because he could not afford to lose American support. He also knew that antigovernment demonstrations in various cities in China made launching an attack against the CCP unfeasible. Marshall achieved his primary objective of bringing about a cessation of hostilities; by the end of February, he worked with both sides to lay down the basis for a coalition government and the integration of CCP units with GMD ones. But when February 1 arrived, Soviet forces were still in Manchuria, denying the GMD territory yet reclaimed. Stalin wanted Chiang to yield economic concessions in Manchuria. In particular, the Soviets demanded joint control of various industries with Chiang's government.

Koo arrived in China just in time to attend the meeting of the GMD Central Executive Committee. Those directly involved in negotiating the Sino-Soviet Treaty of the previous year came under fire for having "unnecessarily sacrificed China's sovereign rights" by making concessions to the Soviets in regard to Manchuria and Outer Mongolia. There was considerable consternation over Soviet refusal to withdraw their troops despite the February 1 deadline. And Moscow's dismantling of Japanese industries in Manchuria for transportation back to the war-ravaged Soviet Union led to a great deal of rancor. Complaints were made as well about the cease-fire agreement reached between the GMD and the CCP as a result of Marshall's mediation; many in the GMD saw this as interference in China's internal affairs. The Central Executive Committee wanted to send Moscow a strongly worded diplomatic note that raked the Soviets over the coals for their activities in Manchuria and faulted them for the communist problem. Koo tried to little avail to soften the language of the diplomatic note, fearing strong Soviet reaction.

Chiang Kai-shek was, however, able to nip such talk in the bud. Angered by the criticism directed at him over the Sino-Soviet Treaty and the January truce agreement with the communists, Chiang bluntly told the Central Executive Committee that if it was prepared to retake Manchuria by force, then the note would be sent to Moscow as written. Otherwise, it had better reconsider if it preferred to use "diplomacy and political means" to secure the return of Manchuria. Chiang also threw down the gauntlet: Any criticism leveled at those responsible for the Sino-Soviet Treaty was in fact criticism of his leadership since they were merely following **his** instructions. "Do you or do you not trust me?," Chiang Kai-shek asked, "Do you or do you not have confidence in me?" The critics, who reaffirmed their allegiance in Chiang's presence, were silenced at least for the moment. "It was an eye opening incident" for Koo who could see that Chiang's "firm attitude and suitable remarks enabled the awkward situation to be surmounted."[9]

Koo's stance on the Soviet-CCP problem differed from that of most people in the government. China made plenty of concessions "to buy the goodwill of Soviet Russia," and Koo felt that "it was not wise to quarrel over the 'war-booty,' thereby nullifying the good effect of our previous sacrifice." Better to split the booty down the middle and convince the Soviets to withdraw than to give them an excuse to remain in Manchuria. He feared that China's airing of its grievances would only serve to "further stiffen their [the Soviets'] attitude." China could recover Manchuria if the Chinese refrained from making provocative statements that would only further alienate the Soviets, making Manchuria "a possible cause of a third world war." "It was most important to get back the territory first and only of secondary importance to get back as many industrial plants as possible," Koo argued, because "U.S. promises could not be relied upon, because [the] U.S. did not know its own mind as to how far it should go. It could afford [to] sit backs [sic] and have nothing to fear." Koo disagreed with those who wanted to take a harder line with the Soviets because, in his mind, America was mercurial, "and is not always dependable as to its strength and final purpose."[10]

Although he believed that the United States was China's "primary friend really interested in helping us become strong and united" and agreed with T.V. Soong that "little could be expected from Russia," Koo thought that Nanjing's policy should be to "forestall any friction or animosity." The government could not assume American support should it take on the Soviet Union. He told Chiang Kai-shek that it was imperative that China engage in "quick negotiation with Soviet Russia on economic questions." "If we pursue a policy which would alleviate her suspicion and make her feel [that there is] nothing to worry about from us," Koo went on, "she would refrain from supporting [the] C.C.P. against the Gov't, as she is realistic and knows the Gov't is much stronger than [the] C.C.P." Chiang demurred because he was convinced that the Soviet

Union "would never drop the C.C.P.," and wanted to retain "the C.C.P. as a weapon." In any case, Koo felt that China could use American aid to build up its forces below the Great Wall and should not send troops to Manchuria in order to avoid exacerbating relations with Moscow.[11]

As for the CCP, Koo likewise refused to take a hard line. The diplomat promoted unity between the GMD and the CCP, which he believed would have a positive influence on China's foreign friends who expected to see democracy and prosperity develop in China. In late 1945, Koo advised the Chinese delegation to the International Youth Conference, which included a communist member, to maintain a united front. He later asserted his belief that political party quarrels were unnecessary since there was a common goal of every political party. "All wanted to make China strong and powerful so she could take her place in the family of nations." It was Koo's conviction, as he explained to one Chinese communist, that "No nation can be strong unless it is united; in the test of power politics of the modern postwar world, China could not play her part without a unified government and army." Japan was defeated; now was the time to unite in reconstruction.[12]

Although Koo wanted China to experience peaceful reconstruction, tensions continued to arise between Chiang and the Soviet Union. On March 6, Chiang's government protested the Soviet Union's refusal to withdraw and demanded an immediate pullout. Five days later, the Soviets announced their withdrawal from Manchuria. Stalin had already backed down in crises involving Iran and Turkey, and he could see that having troops in Manchuria was another political liability. Anti-Soviet demonstrations in China stiffened Chiang's resolve to not make economic concessions. Moreover, the presence of Soviet troops only increased support for Chiang's government, which claimed it was recovering national sovereignty, and the Soviets ran the risk of alienating Chiang, who could use force to grab Manchuria. By withdrawing from Manchuria, the Soviets removed any reason for American forces to remain in north China. With Soviet withdrawal, the CCP made plans to take control of Manchuria through military means while using the Marshall mission to limit GMD advance into the Northeast. Although both sides agreed to send truce teams into Manchuria to enforce the ceasefire, neither side, especially the CCP, wanted them to work effectively. The Soviets also refused to help the GMD extend its influence into Manchuria. With these developments, both sides thought of how to militarily eliminate the other. Chiang refused to reorganize the government in Manchuria, leading the CCP to accuse Chiang of breaking his promises. Marshall tried to convince both sides that a military solution was not feasible, but the GMD would not consider a truce as long as the CCP held Changchun, a city taken by the Chinese Red Army on April 18. The GMD later regained control of the city and forced the CCP to seek a truce, but Marshall warned Chiang Kai-shek that he could not win a military victory in Manchuria.[13]

By May, Koo saw the hope of a reorganized government based on the idea of national unity fade away quickly. The reorganization that did take place was superficial. Such a development may have disappointed Koo, who wanted to get on with the business of reconstruction. He rejected the opinion of those in the government that force was an option for dealing with the communists. He did not believe public opinion in China and abroad would support such a policy. Trying to solve the communist problem by force would be "suicidal" in Koo's opinion, because there was no certainty of success nor guarantee that force could solve the problem quickly. Koo preferred to cooperate with communists in creating a coalition government. This course would "at least ease the tension," and even if the attempt failed, no one could blame Nanjing for "refusing cooperation." "What China needs most is a period of tranquility," Koo argued, "to enable the work of reconstruction to start and go on." "If it [reconstruction] succeeds in this respect, the whole nation would support it and the C[ommunists] would lose their ground for agitation and opposition."

Making reconstruction problematic was the Soviet-U.S. rivalry in Asia. When asked if the Soviet Union would continue its policy of communizing the world, Koo replied in the affirmative. The pitting of communistic Soviet Union against the capitalistic, democratic, Anglo-American camp made the world unstable as both sides struggled for domination. This struggle, which could spill over into Manchuria and other fringe areas of China, would prove detrimental to China's desire for reconstruction. China could not become entangled in the Soviet-American rivalry in Manchuria nor could China take the firm stand that the United States was taking. Both countries could "speak out frankly or retaliate up to the point of war," but "we [are] not in a position to do so, and we would be the first to suffer." Nor did he think the Americans would go to war in order to oppose "Soviet expansion" because they did not acknowledge the "lesson of Pearl Harbor." The people of America and Britain were alike in this regard: They "like to see their Gov't adopt [a] firm policy but as soon as [the] danger of war appeared as a result, they would cry for peace. This is the weakness of democracy in conducting foreign relations." In this respect, Koo may have had in mind the Anglo-Saxon appeasement of the 1930s. Now that there was growing tension between the two emerging superpowers, the American people would not support going to war until the Soviets pulled a Pearl Harbor. Whereas the Soviet Union faced no domestic political constraints, the United States was not dependable because of American public opinion.[14]

When Chiang Kai-shek sought Koo's views on the Manchurian situation, both men agreed that the present tensions in Manchuria were the result of America's "mistaken policy . . . at Yalta." Both concluded that Marshall, who pushed for reorganization of the GMD government so that communists and liberals would be included, was desperate to find a solution because his and the Truman administration's reputations were on the line, particularly with presidential elections only two years away. With that in mind, Marshall had to "succeed in his effort to bring about peace, unity, and democracy in China. Otherwise, he would have nothing with which to defend his Yalta policy, which was really a stab in China's back." Both men agreed, too, that "U.S. foreign policy was often naive and impulsive, very generous when it was in the right mood but very brutal when displeased." One can only speculate that Koo was referring to how Washington's growing unhappiness with Chiang Kai-shek had led to agreements like Yalta and now the Marshall Mission.

The Marshall Mission proved to be a failure because Chiang Kai-shek did not trust the communists to the extent that Marshall did, and he pointed to incidents where the CCP showed its true colors by not cooperating or ignoring agreements. Chiang wanted the United States to take a firm stand against the Soviets, "and not be diffident in regard to Manchuria." "In 10 or 15 years," Chiang opined to Koo, "Soviet R[ussia] will not make war and she respects strength and firmness." Moreover,

Chiang wanted the United States to make it clear to the CCP that American aid would flow to him in order to strengthen the government. In Chiang's opinion, the GMD had to be strong because only then would the CCP "come to terms." Chiang admitted that he did not possess the power "to persuade the United States to adopt this policy unless it decided to do so itself," but the onus for the successful strengthening of his government lay with the United States as far as Chiang was concerned. Chiang also expected the communists to give up Changchun. If the CCP cooperated, then and only then would Chiang permit a coalition government. Otherwise, he "would leave them in Manchuria where they are, and not attempt to force them out. In China proper, Chiang would "clear them out altogether" and use that as a base, to "build up a strong China." Chiang complained that the Americans were giving him aid, "but only secretly and not in full measure." Nevertheless, he did not count upon U.S. aid as an "essential factor." Should the Soviets reintervene in Manchuria militarily, "there would be no danger of involving" the United States because all GMD troops would be withdrawn to China proper where they could await "a settlement of the Manchurian question by international means eventually."

When asked for his reaction, Koo again argued the need for reconstruction. Since Marshall and the Truman administration wanted their China policy to succeed, the GMD could exploit this American desire to avoid failure and reap benefits in the form of aid. Once the government implemented reconstruction and rebuilt China, this would make the communists more pliant, and Moscow would likewise be more willing to work with Chiang Kai-shek. Koo frowned on restarting the civil war because both the Chinese and American people would oppose it. Moscow would back the CCP, but Washington "could not and would not give full support" to Chiang should he wage his civil war. To maintain the status quo meant "drifting and continued uncertainty," and China's economic situation and international position would deteriorate further. Koo advised Chiang to establish a coalition government and not rely on force.

After presenting his own view, the two hour tête-à-tête with Chiang came to an end, but it was clear to Koo that Chiang was about to pursue a new policy and "not meekly and wholeheartedly follow U.S. bidding."

Chiang believed that Marshall was making too many concessions to the communists.[15] Koo would have acquiesced to American demands to reform and democratize the government in order to win support. He was willing to do whatever was necessary to acquire aid and assistance. This stance set him apart from Chiang, whose nationalism tolerated FDR's incessant demands but would not countenance Truman's and Marshall's.

Soon after this long conversation with Chiang, Koo sat down with Marshall to discuss the China issue. Almost immediately, Marshall described the political situation as not unlike that in the United States, and viewed the conflict between the GMD and CCP along lines similar to those that occurred between the Republicans and Democrats. Marshall remarked that the rivalry between the two was natural because "there was nothing but struggle, one to keep the power and the other to wrest it from their opponents. Obstruction was to be expected from political opponents." To prove his point, he cited two examples: Roosevelt's refusal to carry out Herbert Hoover's ideas to solve the banking crisis of 1932 until after the former was inaugurated and hence was in a position to get the glory; and Wilson's nomination of Louis Brandeis to the Supreme Court which was attacked by William Howard Taft as a "Leftist act." "But it was nothing of the kind," Marshall continued, "Political struggle bet[ween] parties always took the form of exploiting any advantage. The struggle between the GMD and the CCP was no different. "It was said [that] the [CCP's] method was unscrupulous," the general declared, "but that had nothing to do with Communism." Marshall praised the CCP's negotiating skills, which he deemed just as "clever" as those used by every Westerner he had ever dealt with, but added that this "had nothing to do with Communism either." Although he rejected assertions that he did not understand China, at least this conversation revealed that he did not and that he was imposing his understanding of American politics on the Chinese scene.

Marshall also observed that neither side was "lily-white." Both the CCP and the GMD engaged in deception, manufacturing canards, and not observing the truce agreement to the letter. Marshall thought Chiang Kai-shek "was sincere in his desire to reform," and acknowledged that "reforms could not all be done in a week." The general believed that if Chiang "succeeded in his reforms to 60 percent it would be a great credit

already. Any political party too long in power in any country would become corrupt and the thing to do would be to democratize the present
gov't." The only other alternative was force, and Marshall was convinced
"that war would mean the collapse of the [GMD] as a party and the fall
of the Gov't in the end." Marshall asked Koo "to try to work on the leaders of the [GMD] to make them see the folly of their present policy of
sabotaging cooperation with the Com[munists] because it would only
mean their own destruction in the end." The general ended the talk with
the warning that the GMD leaders "might think that the U.S. would be
bound in the end to help the Gov't side" and would put the Seventh Fleet
into action, but Marshall "said that was an illusion. He could in no circumstances allow the fleet to interfere on any side." Despite Marshall's
frowning on the utility of force, Koo learned that same day that the military "was for a showdown." And the civilian leaders, even though they
entertained their own misgivings about a military solution, so distrusted
the communists that they saw no other alternative but war.[16]

Around the time that Koo spoke with Marshall, the communist
forces at Changchun were defeated. Now the CCP asked for a truce, but
Chiang ordered his commanders to press the victory. Marshall insisted
that Chiang not seek a military solution, but Chiang's blood was up. He
accused Marshall of protecting the CCP with his mediation and would
have pursued his civil war. Instead, Marshall threw cold water on Chiang's
offensive by threatening to pack up his mediation mission and leaving.
Chiang could not afford to lose American aid, so on June 6 Chiang agreed
to a fifteen-day truce, but not before making it clear that if this attempt
to resolve his differences with the CCP failed, he would choose war.[17]

Several days later, Koo prepared to travel to Washington to take up
his new post. Before departing from China, Koo met with Chiang Kai-
shek twice to discuss publicity work in the United States. On both occasions, Chiang stressed the need to cultivate church organizations,
particularly Catholic ones, which he viewed as "influential in forming
[American] public opinion." Koo suggested that U.S. business and education leaders be targeted as well as radio and television broadcasters.
Following the British model, Koo advised that Chinese leaders cultivate
relations with their American counterparts. All could be done without
making people feel they were being used. "Americans had two traits,"

Koo told Chiang, "they were sentimental and yet at the same time very realistic and practical, afraid of being made suckers and dupes."

In the meantime, Koo put together a strategy for reaching American public opinion. In a memorandum, he focused on the political, cultural, and journalistic spheres. Beginning with the political, Koo stated the importance of developing close relations with American congressmen and senators, participating in voluntary organizations such as the Council for Foreign Relations, and of hiring "stooge writers." That is, American friends and sympathizers of China would write articles and letters, though in a manner that did not associate China with any particular political group. In the cultural sphere, Koo wanted to go into American schools with art exhibits and textbooks as a way of educating American young people about China. Finally, Koo sought closer ties with journalists and wanted to see a governmental agency with appropriately trained people distributing news releases about China.

What would be the message? Changing the stance that he took earlier with Chiang, Koo now agreed with Chiang's idea of "Unification before democracy and even peace" because otherwise reconstruction would founder. Koo assured Chiang that the Americans could accept this argument since Abraham Lincoln "had to resort to force in order to unify the rule of the Federal government. Without the struggle of 1861–65, [the] U.S.A. might be still divided and ineffective today as a country." Impressed by that example, Chiang laid out the points to be "stressed for publicity in America." The first was that Chiang wanted peace, not civil war, but the communists refused to respect the agreements that they had made with him. A second point to be emphasized was that unity "is absolutely necessary before [China] could be a strong and prosperous country," and Chiang cited the example of Lincoln that Koo provided. Finally, Chiang wanted Koo to refute Marshall's criticism that China was not democratic and was still under one party rule by informing Americans that nonparty men were holding important government positions and that the communists were to blame for the lack of democracy, since they "prevented the convocation of the National Assembly to draft a constitution."[18]

Koo arrived in Washington in July, but his publicity campaign got off to a bad start. To begin with, Koo nearly had a physical breakdown.

The diplomat suffered from insomnia and exhaustion and was prescribed daily Vitamin C shots to give him the necessary energy to carry out his duties. Then Koo had to use his first news conference not to emphasize the points outlined by Chiang but to deflect the effect of statements made by Chiang's sister-in-law, the widow of Sun Yat-sen. Madame Sun demanded that the U.S. government cease supporting Chiang Kai-shek, or otherwise there would be a war between the Soviet Union and the United States. Koo allowed Madame Sun the right to have her opinion but declared that her views did not represent that of most Chinese. He also used the occasion to lay the onus on the communists for their lack of cooperation.[19]

Coming on the heels of Madame Sun's statement were some American responses to the civil war. On June 30, the truce ended and Marshall proved unable to get both sides to agree to an extension after negotiations broke down. In July, after Chiang launched another offensive against the CCP, Marshall imposed an embargo on arms shipments to China; the embargo lasted through May 1947. A ceasefire was again proposed, but Chiang demanded the withdrawal of CCP forces from the areas where he pushed his troops. To this demand, the communists said no. On August 10, President Truman cabled Chiang Kai-shek his regret over Marshall's inability to make his mission a success because of "selfish aspirations" on the part of both the GMD and the CCP. Truman politely warned Chiang that his decision to use force instead of "democratic processes to settle major social issues" was leading some people in the United States to call for a new policy toward China.[20]

In undertaking publicity work to rehabilitate the image of the GMD government, Koo faced numerous obstacles. Koo traveled all over the United States answering questions, trying to dispel Americans of what he called communist myths. In an effort to "revise" American foreign policy, Koo turned to the owner of Time, Inc., Henry Luce. Born in China, this son of missionary parents was a longtime supporter of Chiang Kai-shek.[21] Either at Koo's prompting or on his own initiative, Luce met with Arthur Vandenberg, the Republican Senator from Michigan, and Secretary of State James Byrnes. Koo supplied the men with a memorandum that laid out the "efforts of our government to enlist communist cooperation to achieve national unity. It suggested that in view of [the] lack of sincerity on the part of Chinese communist party," Washington "should modify its policy . . . and support [the] Generalissimo in his effort to attain [the] largest measure of unification and democracy possible at [the] present moment."

Although Koo later denied the existence of a China Lobby, he exploited his connections with prominent Americans in order to both lobby Congress and influence the Truman administration's China policy. Such activity was necessary since people like Madame Sun were lobbying against Chiang Kai-shek.[22] Wherever possible, Koo painted a picture of GMD China as a country in transition, seeking to become "united, peaceful, democratic and prosperous." He described China as moving away from one-party rule under Chiang Kai-shek to that of a "genuine constitutional representative government." He acknowledged that there was opposition to the new constitution that his government was trying to promulgate, but he went on to remind his American audiences of the opposition to America's Constitution of 1789. He portrayed the GMD as taking liberal political and economic measures in order to industrialize and modernize China. On other occasions, Koo tried to discreetly and subtly explain to Americans that the onus of Yalta lay squarely at Washington's doorstep.[23] These were the types of arguments that Koo put forth to counter the bad press China received in the United States, but no amount of propaganda could veil events in China.

In October 1946, Marshall requested to be recalled. He deemed his mediation mission a failure as Chiang's forces scored successes against the CCP. Right-wingers in the GMD government were glad to see Marshall go, because they believed his mediation denied them the opportunity to destroy the CCP once and for all. There was also resentment of Washington's demands for internal reform, which smacked of foreign intrusion into China's internal affairs. On the other hand, the GMD could not complain too much. Despite Marshall's arms embargo, the United States still supplied to the GMD millions in reconstruction aid and military supplies, and sided with Chiang's government against the CCP. The war was Chiang's to win or lose.[24]

In January 1947, Marshall returned to the U.S. and was named secretary of state. Chiang viewed Marshall's new appointment as ominous. Relations between the two men were often strained after heated arguments during negotiations. And since Truman would see Marshall as a China expert, Koo expected Marshall to have complete control of the U.S.'s China policy. Members of the Republican party warned Koo that America's China policy would change. And people like Sen. Vandenberg hoped that the Chinese government would undergo thorough reform and that the corrupt, incompetent, feudalistic-thinking officials be purged and replaced by enlightened, incorruptible, capable individuals in order to change American public opinion. Although Koo believed Marshall to be a good, honest, open-minded man, he feared that Marshall would put all the blame for his failure on the GMD government after he returned to the United States. Marshall issued a statement blaming both sides for their inability to come to terms, but Koo soon learned just how bitter Marshall was with Chiang Kai-shek over his failure in China.[25]

On January 29, 1947, the State Department announced that all mediation efforts would cease and U.S. forces would be withdrawn from China. The announcement was followed by a renewed GMD offensive. Over the next several months, Koo met with Marshall to discuss a variety of issues: measures to improve China's economy; the need for a coalition government in Nanjing that represented other political parties; China's trade restrictions, which angered American businessmen; a loan for reconstruction in China; and military aid. But Koo found Marshall and the State Department resistant to granting further aid to Chiang Kai-shek. Marshall demanded internal reform before he would agree to loan Chiang more money.[26] He also found U.S. officials quite cold in personal relations. After one conversation with Marshall, the secretary of state refused to tell Koo how long he would be away from Washington during a conference in South America. "In the past 30 years I have conversed and done business with at least 30 to 40 foreign ministers of a dozen countries, including half a dozen United States Secretaries of State, but this is the first time I have found it difficult to have a cordial free exchange of views, not merely on questions of general interest, but even on special questions of particular interest to China and the U.S.A. There is almost always an atmosphere of formality and stiffness."[27]

Although Koo could explain away such attitudes to Marshall's military demeanor, he found it difficult to fathom the Truman administration's hostility toward Chiang Kai-shek, given America's commitment to fighting communism. In Greece, the government faced off against Greek communists who received military aid from Bulgaria and Yugoslavia. On March 12, 1947, Truman told Congress that the Soviet Union planned to take advantage of this civil war to expand communism and that the United States should pursue a policy of supporting free people throughout the world who are resisting armed subjugation and internal subversion. Truman asked for $400 million in military and economic aid for Greece and Turkey. Koo thought the Truman Doctrine to be a sound and welcomed replacement to what he deemed to be the ad hoc nature of U.S. policy toward the Soviet Union. Yet Washington avoided giving much support to Chiang even though the principles embodied in the Truman Doctrine were applicable to the Far East. Later Truman publicly stated that the Chinese situation was considered serious from an international point of view. If that was true, Koo thought China "was entitled to equal or even greater attention than the Greek situation." He hoped that "the U.S. would show greater interest in it in the form of moral and material support." He feared that U.S. withdrawal from China would lead to the communization of China.[28]

Despite Koo's pessimism, Washington had not entirely thrown Chiang to the wolves. Although Marshall hoped that withholding aid would deter further civil war, the reigning assumption within Marshall's State Department was that aid to Chiang would expand, especially since his troops were mostly armed with U.S. weapons requiring U.S.-made ammunition. By May, Marshall lifted the ban. Truman also ordered the navy to provide equipment and parts. Members of the cabinet, especially the secretaries of war and navy, increasingly sided with providing aid to Chiang and criticized Marshall's policy of withholding aid and withdrawing American forces. Pressure also came from Congress, where pro-Chiang politicians asked the same question Koo was asking: If the United States could lend Greece and Turkey a helping hand, why not Chiang Kai-shek?[29]

People in Washington had good reasons to worry about Chiang's fate. By May 1947, Chiang's offensive showed signs of weakening. Over the last several months, the CCP gave up a lot of territory as it retreated, but it was not routed or wiped out. Soon it switched to guerilla tactics. The People's Liberation Army took the initiative against Chiang's forces, who were now overextended. In the early months of 1947, PLA forces in Manchuria launched a series of hit-and-run attacks on GMD troops that inflicted heavy casualties and supplied the communists with ammunition and weapons. And they never lost the initiative for the rest of the civil war and soon surrounded GMD forces, who only held the cities in Manchuria. There was much popular resentment in Manchuria against Chiang Kai-shek. Wherever GMD troops went, be it Manchuria, Taiwan or other Japanese-occupied territory, they engaged in carpetbagging that only further alienated the local people.[30]

There was no evidence that Chiang's defeat was inevitable, but these setbacks for Chiang were cause for concern in Washington. The Joint Chiefs of Staff suggested further American intervention to prevent the expansion of Soviet power into South and Southeast Asia, but Marshall's State Department argued that the United States could do nothing to save the situation in China. Chiang only had himself to blame for not taking American advice to reform. Besides, increased American intervention might provoke the same of the Soviet Union. Such attitudes, though, did not prevent Marshall from providing as much military equipment to Chiang as possible. And Marshall decided in July to send an American mission under Gen. Albert Wedemeyer, who replaced Stilwell in 1944, to China. There, Wedemeyer found morale low, and when he left in August, he suggested that Chiang could still win if he would only institute economic and political reform. Wedemeyer's comments infuriated Chiang Kai-shek, whose ardor for U.S. aid cooled for a time. In a message to Chiang, Koo blamed Marshall for supposedly not providing any aid or assistance because of "grudges which he does not seem to forget against" Chiang. Koo also faulted the State Department for "much unfavorable propaganda" that put Chiang in a bad light by making charges of "corruption and inefficiency" against the government. Koo said such notions originated with communists but were picked up by Washington "to justify lack of help to her [China]."[31]

Again, Koo could see the difference in Washington's attitude toward Europe from that toward China. After being appointed secretary of state, Marshall went to Moscow for long negotiations over Germany which remained divided into zones of occupation by the British, French, Soviets, and Americans. Marshall wanted to make a joint effort to relieve

Europe of its economic distress, but Stalin refused. Marshall feared the expansion of communism in Europe if nothing was done to resolve the economic plight. When he returned from Europe, Marshall called for a plan to reconstruct Europe. The European Recovery Plan, or what became known as the Marshall Plan, asked Congress for $13 billion in economic aid; eventually, Congress approved a package giving Europe $17 billion over four years.

There was no such plan for China, even though the United States was in 1947 reconsidering its occupation policy in Japan. When the Americans took over Japan, demilitarization and democratization drove U.S. occupation policy. But with the onset of Soviet-U.S. rivalry, the United States backed off democratization and liberalization of Japan and focused more on rehabilitating Japan's economic power. A reconstructed Japan could renew old trade ties with Southeast Asia, thus improving Asia's economy and preventing the spread of communism. Germany and Japan played a prominent role in the containment of communism, but not China.

Although the Truman administration's attitude toward Chiang Kai-shek in 1947 was hardly an amicable one, there were Americans who sympathized with China's plight. Koo later referred to November 1947 as the turning point in which pressure within the United States began to build on the Truman administration to do something for China. It was that month that Koo became aware of the views of various American Congressmen, cabinet leaders, and other friends of China that a new China bill was needed. In the fall of 1947, some Congressional leaders pressured the Truman administration to give Chiang more aid, and Henry Luce ran articles and newspaper advertisements that proposed providing Chiang with $1.35 billion over three years. In November when Truman asked Congress to provide assistance for Western Europe, members of both Houses demanded to know why money for China was not included. Arthur Vandenberg worked with the State Department to provide $18 million to Chiang, but the pro-Chiang congressmen sent a clear message to Truman that aid to Europe could be held up should money not be forthcoming to Chiang. Although Koo complained that the $18 million was a "mere gesture to appease China's friends," at least his government had friends in Washington.[32]

Without doubt, Chiang Kai-shek needed friends at the end of 1947. The CCP not only made gains in northern China, but the PLA captured cities in Manchuria. U.S. advisers on the ground suggested that Chiang pull his forces out of Manchuria while he could, but he rejected the advice. As the situation in China deteriorated day-by-day, Koo could see that the GMD could not win the civil war without American help.[33]

While Chiang was in retreat in China, pro-Chiang forces in Washington launched an offensive on his behalf. Chiang suffered defeat on the battlefield, the economy worsened in China, and Marshall's State Department did what it could to avoid being dragged deeper into a China quagmire. But the pressure for aid to China intensified, and Marshall worried that the European Recovery Plan would be held up unless something was done for China. On February 18, 1948, Truman sent the China Aid bill to Congress asking for $70 million in assistance to Chiang Kai-shek. Koo "could detect between the lines that there was no enthusiasm behind it" as there was for the Marshall Plan. Newspapers noted that the "heart of Gen. Marshall was not in it." Indeed, Marshall had already begun to ask various Chinese intellectuals if there was a political alternative to Chiang Kai-shek.[34]

Although Koo was pleased that a China Aid bill had been sent to Congress, the delay in implementing the aid package and Marshall's opposition was not encouraging. Marshall told Congressional leaders that he was not interested in providing long-term aid to Chiang Kai-shek and that a great deal of military supplies had already been given to China, a statement that Koo described in his diary as false. Marshall believed Chiang's government to be doomed, making China an ineffective ally. Koo argued that his government needed four things: "commodity credit, silver loan for preliminary stabilization, program reconstruction projects, and military aid." In trying to build up support among Americans, Koo argued that the China Aid package should be a part of the European Recovery Program, because "China and Europe formed 2 parts of one picture and U.S. policy to contain Communism should not discriminate in favour of Europe and against China." Koo described the present defense of China as more important to the United States than the defense of Pearl Harbor against Japanese attack in 1941.[35]

To Koo's relief, the China Aid Act passed on April 2. China would be given $463 million in military and economic aid, with $125 million in military assistance being made immediately available. However, the United States was under no obligation to become involved in the civil war. Still, Koo believed China's economy would stabilize and "slow down inflation." He thought the GMD army could defeat the communists if only Nanjing could get its hands on more military aid. "China in 5000 years of her history had had many crises, some worse than the present one, but had always managed to surmount them," Koo wrote in his diary. China might not have peace in his time, but the next generation could enjoy that peace because the "Chinese people were sound and sensible and hard working." He thought 1948 was no worse than 1938, because no one thought the GMD could defeat the Japanese then. He claimed to have had faith in 1938 "that the world would come to China's aid in the end, and it did." Hence, it was important for everyone to "have faith." Koo later commented that Chinese like him, from the educated class, "always believed in the eternity of China, perhaps on account of their training in the Confucian classics and in Chinese culture."[36]

Yet 1948 was worse than 1938. From September 1948 through January 1949, the PLA launched three campaigns that saw GMD defeat in Manchuria, the loss of north China and the collapse of the last GMD obstacle to communist advance toward the Yangzi River. In September, Koo received a confidential cable from Chiang Kai-shek that appealed to Truman "to do everything in his power to facilitate and expedite military aid" under the China Aid Act. The letter's "language [was] very pressing, almost alarming in its tone." Koo learned from visiting Chinese officials that Chiang "was losing his grip on the situation." GMD progressives and younger members of the party were telling Chiang to his face that he needed to surrender some of his power to the cabinet and replace the deadwood in the party with some fresh, young blood. In one instance when Chiang was confronted, he simply put on his cap and walked out the door in anger, refusing to answer.[37]

As the GMD lost ground to the communists, there was one last remaining hope: that a Republican be elected president of the United States. Since it was mostly Republicans who spearheaded the drive to provide aid to China, GMD leaders felt certain that the election of Thomas Dewey, former governor of New York, would bring about a dra-

matic change in U.S. policy toward China. All the polls taken weeks before the election suggested that Dewey would be a sure winner, but to
the shock of the GMD, Dewey was defeated. Worse, the Democrats controlled both houses of Congress. Koo told Chiang Kai-shek that now
there would be less friction between the White House and Congress over
issues of foreign policy. Koo did not believe that Truman would be a real
detriment to China's cause. Truman possessed no ill-will or prejudice
toward Chiang, but because of his lack of experience in foreign affairs,
the president had in his first years deferred to Marshall who was, in Koo's
opinion, the real force behind America's China policy. With his election
by the people, Truman was in a position to assert his own views. Where
Koo expected trouble was in Congress, particularly the left-wing of the
Democratic Party. Koo was also disturbed with the reaction to the American election at home. American newspapers printed numerous reports
of GMD disappointment and dissatisfaction with the Democratic victory, and Koo warned his government against expressing such views, saying that the American people had made their choice. It was not China's
place to quarrel with it.[38]

   While Truman savored victory, Chiang Kai-shek tasted the bitter
gall of defeat. The loss of Manchuria was imminent, and in desperation,
Chiang begged Truman to speed up military aid. It was during these
moments of crisis that Madame Chiang went on another mission to the
United States to speak with Truman and Marshall. She begged Marshall
to send an "outstanding American officer" to China to be "the 'spark
plug' of the Chinese military effort." Marshall refused, saying that such
an officer would need to take over the entire Chinese government to
accomplish his mission.[39] In the end, the Madame's mission was a failure. The Americans were not interested in making a commitment to
Chiang Kai-shek.

   Although George Marshall stepped down as secretary of state, the
State Department still retained its animosity for Chiang Kai-shek. When
Koo met with Robert Lovett, the acting secretary of state, and W. Walton
Butterworth, the director of the Office of Far Eastern Affairs, he learned
that Chiang again requested the United States to send a high-ranking
military officer to take command of Chinese forces. The answer to the
latter question was a flat no. The Chinese diplomat was told in "cold and

very unsympathetic" terms that it was unreasonable for Americans to take command of Chinese forces that had just suffered defeat in the field and to take responsibility for a civil war. When Koo asked for more aid, he received the retort that supplies were not the problem, it was the lack of will to fight. When Koo asked about the situation in Manchuria, Butterworth "gleefully" replied that all was calm, giving Koo "the impression that the communists were not bad people after all and that one could do business with them." Koo, feeling depressed and rather surprised that Chiang Kai-shek wanted Americans to command his troops, left the two Americans. "How long had it been that the Generalissimo had been emphasizing no infringement on China's sovereignty?"[40]

As Manchuria slipped away from GMD grasp, Koo "felt depressed by reports from China" and by the "defeatist attitude" emanating from the Truman administration. Looking back on China's historical past, Koo could not believe that China would be lost to the communists. Although he declared Marshall's analogy of the CCP as being too simple, just like that of the Republicans or Democrats, Koo admitted later that he thought they only wanted political control. He did not expect the Chinese communists to implement measures in the 1950s that would lead to the deaths of thousands of landlords and other individuals who were deemed a threat to the communist revolution. "I always thought that while they may have embraced the communist ideology, that was for their political purpose of assuring themselves of the support of Moscow, and therefore the eventual success of their political struggle. I didn't expect that they would go to the extreme of acting in a manner so alien to Chinese tradition and Chinese political philosophy. That was probably naiveté on my part." Koo was not alone. In his opinion, not only did Washington fail to see the true nature of the communists, but neither did Chinese liberals who believed China needed a change of government.[41]

On January 14, 1949, Mao Zedong issued his eight-point peace proposals that, among other things, demanded the abolition of the GMD government and branded Chiang Kai-shek, T.V. Soong, and Wellington Koo as war criminals. Chiang turned down the peace offer but announced his retirement. In the last months of the GMD government's nominal control of China, Koo believed the only way to salvage the situation was an "Asiatic Security and Mutual Aid Pact" much like that of the North

Atlantic Treaty Organization for Europe. In 1949, NATO was created to defend various nations from Soviet expansion. Koo wanted an Asian NATO, but his security scheme got nowhere because the Americans were not interested. Their attitudes toward China and Koo reflected the Truman administration's animosity toward Chiang Kai-shek. In January, when Koo met again with Lovett and Butterworth, the Chinese diplomat felt that Butterworth "looked upon me as if I was the Soviet Amb[assador], judging [from] the caution and reserve he assumed. Unusual for an Am[erican] diplomat toward a Chinese representative; [I have] never experienced same in my 36 years of dealing with Americans."[42]

If not a pact, American aid remained essential. But China could not expect others to help until it helped itself. If Chiang returned to Nanjing from retirement, there was hope that reform measures could be implemented. Koo felt that several steps had to be taken. Chiang, who still wielded much power despite his retirement, first, needed "a new set of selfless, courageous, experienced advisers to assist him." Then he had to "reorganize the army and put it on a really modern basis" replacing the deadwood with younger, "honest, capable and experienced officers." Another step would be to appoint civilians as provincial governors "in order to regain [the] confidence and cooperation of people," and find positions for college and university graduates. Finally, Koo believed that the government should pursue laissez faire trade and economic policies so as to give people a chance "to make their living more easily and to [allow] foreign merchants to do business in China" so there would be no disgruntlement.[43]

In February, Koo tried to speak with Dean Acheson, who replaced Marshall as secretary of state the previous month, about the China situation, but Acheson gave Koo the "impression [that] he did not attach great importance to it." In fact, Acheson was quite blunt. He told Koo that the United States had given the Chinese much advice, but "the Chinese Government had been ingenious in making so many mistakes to a point where its armed forces had refused to fight the communists." Running down a list of American assistance to China, Acheson said he "did not know what the United States could further do to help her." Being forthright himself, Koo retorted that while there had been mistakes on the Chinese side, he pointed to the "decisions taken at Yalta" which "had adversely affected the situation, especially in Manchuria where the communist success had really started." Yalta illustrated how another government's policies and actions might affect another. But when Koo asked for an American statement of support for what remained of the GMD government, Acheson refused to answer.[44] Such conversations convinced Koo that Marshall wielded considerable influence in the State Department, and he believed that Butterworth "was trying to carry out even more loyally" Marshall's "policy of abandonment of China." Marshall aside, the GMD was losing the war, and for months to come, the Americans watched Koo strain to make the case that the GMD forces were putting up effective resistance.[45]

As the situation grew hopeless for the GMD, the State Department decided that this was an opportune time to state its position on past Sino-American relations by publishing what became known as the China White Paper. This document absolved Washington of any responsibility for the GMD government's imminent demise, but instead blamed corruption and incompetence on the part of the GMD and Chiang Kai-shek for its defeat. Nanjing's Foreign Ministry instructed Koo to remind Americans of China's eight-year war effort against Japan and the Yalta Agreement. Expecting the White Paper to have a detrimental effect on Sino-American relations, Koo did his best to limit the damage.[46]

In the meantime, Koo continued to look to drastic reform to save the day. He dispatched telegrams to what remained of the government in China to pursue a three-point plan of unifying the anticommunist elements, resisting the communists with a unified military command, and winning popular support. Such reform would not only shore up the government's position in China, but would convince the United States that a liberal government existed.[47] All such efforts on Koo's part proved in vain. Chiang Kai-shek was in Taiwan, and President Li Zongren, who replaced Chiang, remained in China. Neither was willing to cooperate. In the months to come, the Chinese communists would announce the creation of their own government in Beijing. GMD China, the so-called great power, had nearly disappeared.

In reflecting on its defeat, Koo believed that the GMD debacle showed "something had been wrong" internally. Koo's government was not 100 percent at fault because he believed that U.S. policy had been wrong; not in the entire period running from 1945 to 1949, but at certain moments, particularly Yalta and during the Marshall Mission. Still, Koo could see that "something had been wrong for years past in our political, military and economic policies. The principle of observing the will of the people in governing a country had been neglected to the detriment of China. . . . They are the stockholders of the country and the government is only the board of directors. The latter cannot run the company against the interests of the stockholders without arousing their suspicion, losing their support, and making them rise in protest and opposition." The imminent fall of the GMD government in 1949 also led Koo to reflect "that personal government, no matter how well meant, is never so desirable as government by law. The latter is [the] only solid foundation on which to build a nation."[48] Koo thus returned to the notion that constitutional government was preferable to dictatorship. It was this "personal government" in the form of Chiang Kai-shek that rejected Koo's solutions to the myriad problems facing China after 1945. Early on Koo saw the futility of civil war. He wanted China to unite and rebuild so that it could truly be a great power. He wanted to see the creation of a liberal government that would permit the participation of the Chinese communists if they were willing to shed their military and act like a true political party.

Yet his leader was a man who was far more conservative and less willing to accommodate either the Chinese communists or the Americans. In 1948, Koo criticized Chinese political parties who were "composed mostly of politicians and scholars who attach too much academic importance to theories and doctrines and are not solidly grounded in the support of practical interests in the country like labour, farmers, business groups, etc."[49] By contrast, Mao Zedong understood mass politics and, partly for that reason, defeated Chiang Kai-shek. Koo's reform solutions were also flawed by his lack of understanding of the situation on the ground. Koo did not comprehend the extent to which the Sino-Japanese War had weakened the government. Nor did he fully appreciate the extent to which the government had lost popular support or the fact that consequently his reform measures would have met with popular resistance.[50] Chiang's government was beyond salvation.

This explains why years later, Koo still could not comprehend the defeat of Chiang Kai-shek. He still could not answer the question: "How could things have come to such a pass so soon after the great success of our war of resistance, how could the situation have deteriorated so fast, as to make it a real grave danger to the continuing existence of the government, and how to explain the popularity of the communists." Koo knew from Chinese history that dynasties changed every few hundred years or so, but he could not believe that anticommunist Chinese masses welcomed Chinese communist forces into their cities and villages. Koo never dreamed that the people would reject Chiang Kai-shek despite all his faults because communism was unpopular: "It was something quite unintelligible to me."[51]

Chapter 9

THE ROC ON TAIWAN
AND THE EARLY COLD WAR

ON OCTOBER 1, 1949, THE PRC WAS PROCLAIMED in Beijing. Mao Zedong told the Chinese people that China had finally stood up. Once again, Koo stood on the opposite side of revolution. As ambassador, he represented a government whose diplomatic recognition would soon be endangered. Despite efforts by the United States, Britain and India immediately recognized the new PRC government followed by nine other noncommunist regimes. Even the status of Taiwan as a base remained in question. Taiwan was a colony of Japan's from 1895 until 1945, and Koo knew that "juridically" Taiwan's status was "open to challenge" being based upon the Cairo and Potsdam agreements. There were reports that the United States considered proposing a UN trusteeship for Taiwan, an idea that Chiang Kai-shek opposed. Koo preferred that the Americans jointly occupy Taiwan with the GMD in order to deny the PRC any claim to the territory.[1]

In Washington, Truman and Acheson did not lean toward recognition of the PRC. Instead, they initially pursued a policy of Titoism in China. In 1948, Josef Tito's Yugoslavia split from Stalin, and for the first time there was a communist nation independent of the Soviet Union. Truman and Acheson likewise hoped to prevent closer ties between the PRC and the Soviet Union. Such a policy meant that the Truman administration was unwilling to throw complete support behind Chiang Kai-shek and might even sacrifice Chiang to bring about Chinese Titoism. Truman and Acheson (neither of whom knew very much about Asia or

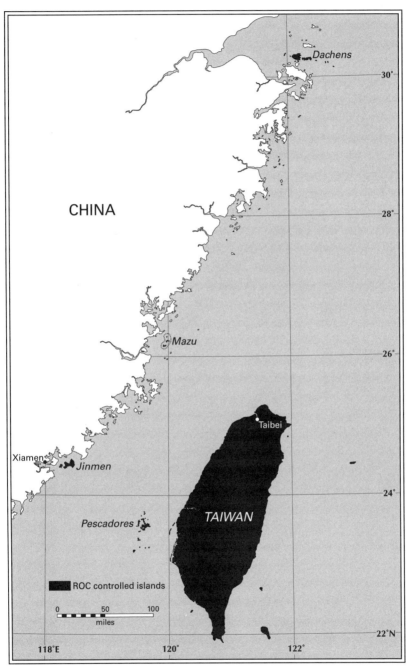

Map 5: ROC-controlled Taiwan and neighboring islands.

bothered to learn) rejected calls from within Congress and the military
to take Taiwan by force or turn it over to the UN. The U.S. Navy especially saw Taiwan as valuable because if the Soviet Union acquired a sub-
marine base on a PRC-controlled Taiwan, the Soviets could threaten U.S.
security in the Pacific. In January 1950, Truman, however, announced
that the United States had no intention of putting military bases on Taiwan, and that the United States would not prevent the PRC from attacking
Taiwan. That same month, Acheson gave his famous National Press Club
speech in which he reiterated the point that intervention by the United
States into the Chinese civil war would only anger the Chinese people,
who were glad to see Chiang Kai-shek out of power. Acheson's speech was
a response to critics in the United States who pressed Washington save
Chiang Kai-shek, but Acheson refused to take any action that would drive
the PRC closer to Moscow. Hence, in laying out his "defensive perimeter"
strategy for East Asia, it was no coincidence that Taiwan was excluded.[2]

While Taiwan's fate hung in the balance, Koo spent the last years of
his career trying to obtain the necessary political, economic, and military assistance to defend Taiwan. Chiang Kai-shek complicated this effort because he, so it was said, was the central obstacle to bringing the
United States fully behind Taiwan. Over the next several years, Americans reiterated time and again to Koo and his compatriots that a "Third
Force" was needed in China. By a Third Force, it was meant a liberal,
democratic alternative to both the conservative, authoritarian generalissimo and the CCP. Those opposing the generalissimo pointed to the large
amount of aid given in previous years that brought few returns. And
there was the perception, one not off the mark, that Chiang was willing
to sit on his military funding and supplies and wait for World War III to
save him, just as World War II did nearly ten years before. Chiang also
carried with him political baggage that stretched back to World War II.
He represented all that had gone wrong in China since 1944 if not before. U.S. government officials, Congressmen from both political parties
and military officers (some of whom preferred that the U.S.-educated
Gen. Sun Liren "take charge and that would make it easy for China-U.S.
cooperation in the military field"[3]), as well as many friends of China,
made it clear to various Chinese officials that Chiang Kai-shek had to go
before Taiwan could save itself or be saved.[4]

Koo tried to fix everything that had damaged the prestige of Chiang Kai-shek, particularly the charges of corruption. Rehabilitating the image of Chiang Kai-shek was a daunting responsibility. Koo needed the facts: "We cannot hope to pull the wool over peoples' eyes by ignoring such questions as: Why did our 4 million troops not fight the Com[munists] with favorable odds of 10-1 in number and with added advantages of an air force and navy? Why did we not manage our finances better to forestall the collapse of our currency? Why did the people refuse to support the Gov't?" Fortunately for Koo, the political atmosphere of the early 1950s was ripe for using public opinion against the Truman administration. The communist takeover of China came as a shock to the American public as did the announcement that the Soviet Union exploded its first atomic weapon in September 1949. Increasingly, Republicans, especially Senator Joseph McCarthy, accused the Truman administration of being a hotbed of communist spies. Republicans, conservative Democrats, and members of the China Lobby denounced Truman's refusal to support Chiang Kai-shek. Some members of Truman's administration and the Joint Chiefs of Staff held clandestine meetings with GMD officials and surreptitiously supplied military aid to Chiang Kai-shek.[5]

In an effort to change U.S. foreign policy, Koo launched a propaganda campaign that portrayed Taiwan as the last bastion of noncommunist Chinese who were essential for containing communism in Asia. In an article for *Reader's Digest*, Koo declared that the *"Chinese Communists are tools of the Soviet Union."* (Italicized in original). He called for an end to the appeasement of communism and for assistance in defending Free China. Finally, he made the plea that the United States not recognize the new regime in Beijing. All of these steps were necessary to prevent the enslavement of the Asian people and ultimately the enslavement of the free world. In another speech, he declared that Chiang Kai-shek's army was the "largest single unit in whole Asia bent upon fighting Communist imperialism," and used the analogy of Churchill "offering aid unsolicited to [the] U.S.S.R" in 1941 in arguing for providing Taiwan with military assistance.[6] Such rhetoric not only had the purpose of garnering support from the U.S. government, but Koo's pleas for help were also a way of using public opinion against the Truman administration. He had faith in Americans in general to assist the Chiang's government, and Koo assumed that he could do an end run around an administration that held Chiang Kai-shek in contempt.

Koo also tried to prevent Chiang's accusers from having any ammunition to use against Chiang's regime. "I found the most difficult accusation to answer," Koo explained to a Chinese general, "was the corruption of the high Chinese officials" of the GMD government, especially Chiang's relatives. "Americans did not know much about the military incompetence or economic mishandling, but they all understood what was meant by corruption." He implored various Chinese officials that had grudges against Chiang Kai-shek to settle their grievances quietly. He pointed out to one such disgruntled individual that "our only hope was to work for [a] U.S. change of policy in our favour, without its aid and support, we would not hope to fight back to our mainland." One favorite target for Free China's accusers was Lend-Lease. Every six months, President Truman made it a point to remind Congress that the Soviet Union and GMD China were the only two countries that had failed to settle their debts. Intensely annoyed, Koo wanted to take away the Truman administration's stick. He told Chiang Kai-shek that if the $500 million credit could be repaid, it would "put an end to talk of corruption . . . and forestall any backfire on [the] part of [the] U.S. against us in future proposals of financial aid from us."[7]

Another measure taken by Koo was to maintain unity among the Chinese in general and support the generalissimo in particular. For a brief time, Koo was interested (a fact that Chiang Kai-shek was well aware of) in sponsoring a liberal party that possessed a draft constitution in order to provide a political alternative that would appease the American desire for a Third Force.[8] The idea originated with Jiang Tingfu, Koo's old acquaintance from the 1920s who was now the ROC's ambassador to the UN, who wanted to form what he called a Chinese Liberal Party with the goal of replacing Chiang Kai-shek. Initially, Koo wanted a cabinet made up of a "group of well-known, clean, liberal" U.S.-educated students that had Chiang's support. The GMD would stand aside and let the liberal cabinet "have the full power to run the gov't and deal with the situation in a democratic way." He argued that this would show the Chinese and American people that the government was resolved to get its act together. "The psychology of looking to U.S. aid to raise the morale of our soldiers and people is wrong," Koo wrote in his diary, "We must show self-help in order to win help from [the] U.S." If Chiang Kai-shek dealt only with military affairs, leaving "politics and government to the civilians, we still could pull China out of her present plight." Koo and Jiang Tingfu wanted Hu Shi, another old friend that was also one of the most famous Chinese liberals inside or outside of China, to head this party, but Hu refused, not wanting to reenter politics.[9]

Over time, a Third Force alternative seemed impossible. Jiang Menglin, former chancellor of Beijing University, explained to Koo that "Americans think Chinese liberals should and could take charge of the situation, but . . . there were no such 'animals' in China. The trouble is . . . China cannot get along with Chiang and also cannot get along without him because of [the] lack of new leaders, and because Chiang is self-centered and likes to dictate and [is] unwilling and unable to surround himself with other than 'yes' men." Koo and his friends likewise reached the same conclusion that their party scheme did not hold water. Although they faulted the United States for the "loss of China," they also blamed Chiang for not implementing the reforms that Koo and others had urged. Since they could not get rid of Chiang, Koo and his compatriots had no choice but to support the man. When the Americans argued that an alternative was necessary, Koo continually replied, "No other leadership could be created overnight." Koo deemed Chiang to be "a patriot and, in spite of the mistakes he had made while ruling the mainland, is still respected there as the outstanding leader to liberate them from Communist oppression."[10]

To support the propaganda and publicity effort, Koo traveled to Taiwan in the summer of 1950 to obtain facts for himself. Relations between the mainlanders and the Taiwanese were strained. When GMD forces took over Taiwan after 1945, they engaged in a large-scale carpetbagging operation. When the Taiwanese revolted in 1946 and asked for a new governor, Chiang Kai-shek sent thousands of troops that killed hundreds if not thousands of Taiwanese. By now though, Chiang Kai-shek was entrenched on Taiwan with little hope of being toppled by an independence movement. Under martial law, the GMD's authority could not be legally challenged. The forming of new political parties and newspapers were prohibited. Besides creating a GMD bastion on Taiwan, Chiang's government had to deal with economic problems. In 1950, Taiwan's inflation rate was 300 percent, and the island needed to undergo land reform in order to increase agricultural yields.[11]

During Koo's short visit, he heard the "complaints and aspirations and hopes" of the "so-called" Taiwanese people. And he found their attitude toward Chiang and the government on the whole "loyal and trusting and their grievances were being taken care of." Not everything was rosy though. Koo observed several areas in which GMD control had a negative effect, "such as [the] harsh manner of collecting special defense tax; occupation of school buildings by troops, thus preventing children from getting their education regularly; indiscriminate arrests by special police to root out Communist spies and break up spy-rings; denial of full opportunity to [Taiwanese] in lower echelons of employment [but] rather [a] preference for mainlanders in filling such posts in railway, postal, police and school teaching service."[12]

These problems aside, Koo was encouraged to see partial success in running the government "in accordance with the Constitution." Seemingly, Chiang dictated less and less and permitted more debate in the cabinet. Such changes were necessary, since the United States had lost confidence in Chiang and "were desirous of finding a new face." Indeed, strong supporters of Chiang Kai-shek, including Republican Representative Walter Judd, former missionary to China and longtime backer of Chiang Kai-shek, suggested to Koo and others that Chiang Kai-shek "become a Constitutional President with the task of governing to be performed by the others—constitutional organs without his interference or control."[13]

And there were Chinese supporters of Chiang Kai-shek who wanted him to distance himself from the GMD. Some liberal intellectuals, such as Hu Shi, wanted the generalissimo to "divest himself of the presidency of the [GMD]—a party of rotters or a rat hole" in order to get U.S. backing. Koo agreed and allegedly spoke frankly with Chiang on this issue, because Koo knew that people rarely spoke their minds to the generalissimo: "Too many people told him only agreeable things—things which he would like to hear and withheld unpleasant comments or opinions." Koo told Chiang and the GMD Central Reform Committee that American friends deemed three steps as necessary in order to improve the GMD's image in America. One was to, "Change the name of the party." Another was to put the "Principle of the People's Livelihood" before the

"Principle of Nationalism" and the "Principle of Democracy." Finally, "Democratize the structure and system of control of the party" by throwing out those aspects of the government that Americans considered as "characteristic of the Communist or Fascist Party." Koo argued that the "Principle of Nationalism" was the underlying cause for India's and Burma's anti-GMD policy. Sun Yat-sen's Pan-Asianism under Chiang struck many as hegemony. Koo also impressed on Chiang the fact that the GMD "had become an international target and was looked upon as a symbol . . . of reaction in politics." By 1952, a number of reforms brought new blood into the GMD and a number of members were purged for corruption or incompetence.[14] Nevertheless, Chiang remained firmly in power and the GMD maintained a one-party dictatorship.

Koo's overall attempt to reform the generalissimo's image met with only limited success. President Li Zongren went to the United States where his subordinates accused Koo of being uncooperative and publicly criticized Chiang Kai-shek for being a dictator and an unconstitutional president. "It is a typical case of washing dirty linen in public," Koo wrote in his diary, "and much to be deplored."[15] Charges of corruption continued as well by Chinese officials and Americans alike. Drew Pearson of the *Washington Post* accused Koo of doing under-the-table favors for various Chinese, and claimed that Koo's wife did not pay her income taxes. Koo responded quickly to these charges, showing them to be unfounded, but he could not do the same with those made against GMD officials, including the accusation that Chiang Kai-shek received millions of dollars from the "China Lobby." The continued attacks took their toll on the Chinese ambassador. "I and many private Chinese feel much hurt," Koo told a friend, "by the persistent talk of corruption of our Gov[ernment], as if every Ch[inese] official could not be trusted but was a corrupt man."[16]

The change in U.S. policy that Koo anxiously awaited in response to his efforts to make Chiang Kai-shek worthy in American eyes did not materialize. However, international events worked in Chiang's favor. In February 1950, Mao and Stalin signed the Treaty of Friendship, a thirty-year alliance that committed both communist countries to assist one another militarily if either were attacked by Japan and/or its allies, meaning the United States. This treaty undermined the U.S. policy of Titoism and the potential for Soviet aircraft and naval vessels operating out of Taiwan would likewise undermine the defensive perimeter strategy.[17]

Then came the Korean War. On June 25, North Korea invaded South Korea. The reaction to the attack, according to Koo, was reminiscent of Pearl Harbor. Truman ordered Gen. Douglas MacArthur, top U.S. commander in Occupied Japan, to send U.S. forces there to Korea to stop the communist onslaught. The Truman White House also sent units of the Seventh Fleet into the Taiwan Straits to prevent both a PRC-invasion of Taiwan and Chiang Kai-shek from launching attacks against the mainland. A communist victory in Taiwan or a broader war would threaten Japan, the vital key to the U.S.'s containment policy for Southeast Asia. The Korean War further moved Truman to approve a military assistance package for Taiwan that included the dispatch of a military advisory mission.[18]

Although Koo thought that the war forced the United States "to be more realistic in dealing with" Taiwan, he quickly saw that June 25 did not signal a change in attitude toward Chiang Kai-shek. When Chiang proposed to send troops to Korea (an idea that appealed to MacArthur who visited Chiang in Taiwan), Koo found the U.S. State Department rather cynical and sarcastic in its response to Chiang's proposal. The Americans were probably correct in their estimate of the GMD Chinese fighting man at the time, but their appraisal more than annoyed Koo. He thought the real reason why the Americans refused Chiang's request was because of the White Paper. "Acceptance [of Chiang's request] would mean acknowledgement of the error of judgment on the part of the United States Government in the past." In fact, Koo's reading of the Truman administration was not too far off the mark. Initially, Truman and Acheson did not want to reestablish close political ties with Chiang nor make U.S. aid readily available to the ROC government. Still, even if the American attitude toward China remained the same, Koo welcomed the change in policy toward Taiwan because "it served to open the door a little more for us to work for improvement of our relations with them."[19]

If the Korean War saved Chiang Kai-shek from communist takeover, for many, it seemed to be the next step to World War III, which could lead to GMD victory over the communists on the mainland. The notion of world war breaking out in the near future had been prevalent in Chinese military circles since 1949. Koo knew that this was a view that

U.S. "officials laugh at and even resent." The Chinese were not laughing. Many were convinced that world war was imminent and saw this as the true salvation of Chiang Kai-shek because the United States might back Chiang in launching an attack against the mainland. Koo demurred. The Soviet Union was still recovering from the ravages of the last war, and there was no evidence that the United States wanted war either. And even if World War III broke out and the United States won, this would not guarantee that the United States would support the generalissimo in recovering the mainland. The former was, in Koo's opinion, more likely to "look for some group, noncommunist and liberal minded, on the mainland, or even a mixed group."[20]

As the Korean War grew in intensity and expanded, Taiwan's position became increasingly secure. In September 1950, Douglas MacArthur made his brilliant landing at Inchon, thirty miles from Seoul and miles behind North Korean lines farther south. In October, MacArthur's forces moved across the 38th Parallel into North Korea. In response, Mao ordered PLA forces to Manchuria, including many units previously poised to attack Taiwan, and across the Yalu River into North Korea. The next month, MacArthur assured the American people that their boys would be home by Christmas, but on November 28, PLA troops hit MacArthur's armies, inflicting a humiliating defeat on U.S. troops who now scrambled pall-mall for the 38th Parallel. PLA and North Korean troops captured Seoul, but by the end of 1950, UN forces retook Seoul. A seesaw of offensives continued before the lines stabilized in 1951.

The PRC's entry into the war indeed convinced the United States to provide military assistance to Taiwan. In 1951, the U.S. established the Military Assistance and Advisory Group-Taiwan. For the next fourteen years, MAAG-Taiwan provided Chiang with $100 million per year in nonmilitary aid and twice that amount in military assistance.[21] PRC intervention in Korea also helped the ROC's representation in the UN. At the UN, the Soviets initially attempted to get the PRC a seat there. Indeed, the Soviets boycotted the UN for several months in 1950 because of the refusal to oust the ROC and were not present when the UN passed U.S.-sponsored resolutions demanding an end to hostilities and the withdrawal of North Korean forces back across the 38th Parallel. Wanting to ensure that the PRC remained dependent on the Soviet Union, the Soviet delegation to the UN stopped raising the issue of giving the PRC a seat and ousting the ROC. Another irony was that at a time when the Soviets were silent on the ROC's place in the UN, noncommunist states supported the PRC's entry at the ROC's expense. After the PRC intervened in Korea, the British suggested to Washington that the PRC be permitted entry into the UN and that China's claim to Taiwan be recognized in order to conciliate Beijing. Acheson rejected the idea, saying that he could not see how sacrificing Taiwan would make China more peaceful. And the ROC's support of U.S. resolutions proved vital. Without ROC support, U.S. resolutions regarding Korea would have been defeated. Not wanting to alienate its U.S. ally and frustrated with the PRC for not ending the Korean War on Western terms, Britain in 1951 supported a U.S. resolution that called for a moratorium on discussion of the question of which China deserved to be in the UN.[22]

Although the moratorium lasted ten years and even though the ROC's seat in the UN seemed fairly secure, Chiang Kai-shek's penchant to withdraw from any international organization once the PRC became a member deeply disturbed Koo. He thought it "inadvisable" to withdraw "on our own initiative" because "withdrawal would only be a sign of weakness and facilitate admission" of the PRC. "Better to face expulsion and protest against it," argued Koo, "than voluntarily withdraw for fear of sure expulsion in [the] end."[23] Koo's advice went unheeded. Chiang Kai-shek's narrow-minded ideology that dominated his foreign policy did not permit compromise and contributed to Taiwan's gradual isolation from the world.

Despite the confidence inspired by America's change of policy toward Taiwan in which the United States now protected Taiwan from the PRC, Koo had evidence that there were enemies of GMD Taiwan in Washington, especially in the State Department and Congress, who sought to "besmirch" Chiang and to advocate Titoism in China. It was true that while the Korean War changed U.S. policy toward Taiwan, some in the Truman Administration still clung to the idea of Titoism in China.[24]

Much to Koo's annoyance, the Truman administration was not always willing to use its leverage to protect Chiang Kai-shek's prestige. A clear example was the signing of the San Francisco Treaty in 1951. Since the end of World War II, a treaty officially ending the Pacific War had yet to be signed with Japan. In the months after Chiang Kai-shek's retreat to Taiwan, the issue received a great deal of attention from the Pacific allies, particularly the United States and Britain. John Foster Dulles, an old acquaintance of Koo's who was a respected lawyer, assisted the State Department in drawing up the treaty. Two aspects of the proposed treaty that troubled Chiang and Koo were the U.S. insistence that Japan not pay reparations to the ROC and the provision that Taiwan's status be settled by the United Nations. Worse, neither Britain nor the U.S. could agree on which China should be permitted to sign the treaty, so a compromise was reached: Neither China would be invited to San Francisco to sign the treaty and Japan was free to determine what attitude to take toward the PRC. (In reality, Britain wanted Japan to renew ties with the PRC while Dulles wanted Japan to follow a pro-Taiwan policy.) Not only was the PRC furious, but so was the ROC. Koo told Dulles that the Anglo-American compromise was "not only a blow to its [the ROC's] prestige" but likewise would be a blow to U.S. prestige in Asia, because people there would conclude "that the friendship of the United States was never dependable because at a critical moment the United States might let its friends down." Koo blamed the British for trying to counterbalance the power of the United States in the Pacific by opposing the ROC.[25]

Dulles' formula was to have Japan grant diplomatic recognition and trade agreements so that the ROC would not lose prestige. The ROC would benefit from the treaty without having to sign the treaty. Koo expected that formula to be rejected by Taibei, so he suggested that all the countries sign, but at different times, with the ROC signing near the end in order to give face to the countries who recognized the PRC.[26] Dulles went to London where a formula was worked out that permitted the ROC to sign a bilateral treaty with Japan separately from the multilateral treaty. Dulles thought this was a 90 percent success for the ROC. Koo disagreed, saying that the ROC stood not "on an equal footing with the other Powers and . . . was really a discriminatory treatment." Dulles reminded Koo that the ROC could get the blame for blocking the treaty, but Koo remarked that it seemed more important to not have the ROC sign than to have a peace treaty and that the blame should go to the U.K. and others, not the ROC. The Chinese diplomat went on to say that the ROC signed the Yalta Agreement "against its better judgment . . . in order to shows its spirit of cooperation with the United States." In his opinion, Koo felt that the Chinese people would not look upon the separate signing of the treaty as a "diplomatic success" either for Taiwan or the U.S.[27]

Naturally, Chiang Kai-shek insisted that either the ROC sign the multilateral treaty or sign a bilateral treaty at the same time that the other countries signed a *multilateral* treaty. Dean Rusk, a member of the State Department, rejected both scenarios and reminded Koo that the ROC was in various international organizations "due solely to the support of the United States" and that rejection of the ROC's participation was not unrealistic since the ROC had no power over the mainland. Koo retorted that that during World War II, the numerous governments-in-exile in London received diplomatic recognition from the allies and participated in all important proclamations "for the sake of upholding the moral principle as well as the principle of allied solidarity in common defense of the cause of freedom." Koo's government was simply asking "to be treated on a footing of equality with other Allied Powers, a principle of equality for which China had been struggling and fighting for the last fifty years beginning with the struggle for the abolition of unequal treaties."[28] Despite providing Dulles with different formulas, the Americans stuck to the one agreed on by the British.

This "loss of face" infuriated Chiang Kai-shek who wanted some face saving formula. In July, Koo suggested to Dulles that the United States invite the ROC to the San Francisco Conference, and pressure Japan into negotiating a ROC-Japan bilateral treaty at the San Francisco Conference. Chiang wanted a treaty with Japan as soon as possible, because he wanted Japan's military strength to be rebuilt so that both sides could cooperate in containing communist expansion. Japanese military experts, veterans of the Sino-Japanese War, were already assisting in the training of GMD troops.[29] Washington eventually forced Tokyo to sign a Peace Treaty and to recognize Chiang's government. The price Taiwan paid was that the treaty signed with Japan only recognized Chiang's authority as encompassing Taiwan and the Pescadores, and the ROC never received an invitation to San Francisco. Still bitter with the Americans, Chiang said that exclusion of his government from the San Francisco Peace Conference "would stand as one of the darkest pages in U.S. history."[30]

The exclusion of the ROC from San Francisco angered Koo. He

deemed it a humiliation. His conclusion was that "Power politics dominated even U.S. policy with expediency overriding considerations of moral principles and international justice." Koo could see too that "international law has lost much of its prestige and authority in the Post-War rivalry bet[ween] the Free World and [the] Communist group." A decade had not passed since millions died as a result of Japan's attempt at Pacific hegemony, but the treaty with Japan treated the Japanese not only as equals, but as friends. When a Filipino diplomat remarked that the Americans did not understand the Japanese mentality, Koo replied "the American people were young and emotional. It seemed that they must have some country to pet upon at a given time and now it was Japan." And although they liked to picture the Cold War as an ideological conflict, the Americans had no qualms about humiliating their anticommunist allies in Taiwan or elsewhere in the name of expediency.[31]

Given the Truman administration's persistent antagonism toward Chiang, Koo and others looked to the 1952 election to bring in a new Congress and president to effect a positive change in the status quo. There was much for the Chinese to like in Dwight D. Eisenhower. His party ran on a platform that called for ending the Korean War and for taking on communism and corruption in the U.S. government. The man who would become Eisenhower's secretary of state, John Foster Dulles, also called for the liberation of those peoples in Europe and Asia living under communist rule. The election of Eisenhower to the presidency in 1952 made the Chinese community in the U.S. "more cheerful and optimistic." Indeed, when Eisenhower gave his first State of the Union address, he declared he was unleashing Chiang Kai-shek, meaning that the generalissimo, in theory, had a free hand to attack the PRC. Nevertheless, Koo warned his close friends "against expecting too much too soon." He knew that Eisenhower was a "Europe-firster, and, if elected, unlikely to change his stand much in favour of Asia." In his opinion, Eisenhower "knew little about the Far East" and doubted that Eisenhower would show much interest in Asia.[32]

Koo's understanding of Eisenhower's foreign policy views was more accurate than that of his compatriots. When Eisenhower decided to run for the presidency, he generally agreed with Truman's foreign policy initiatives and opposed the unilateralism of conservative Republicans like Robert Taft of Ohio who wanted to withdraw the United States from international affairs. Although he had reservations about Truman's China policy and although Eisenhower spoke of "liberation" and unleashing Chiang during the presidential campaign, Eisenhower had no intention of mounting a military campaign to "liberate" mainland China.[33]

Despite Dulles' and Eisenhower's public rhetoric of liberation, Koo (and eventually Chiang Kai-shek) understood that no one in the administration thought a GMD recovery of the mainland realistically possible. In the U.S. military establishment, opinion toward Taiwan remained divided, as Marshall's supporters were "still influential," or so Koo claimed. The State Department was not as antagonistic as before, but individuals opposed to Chiang remained. Hence, Koo knew that he had to work "more cautiously." Whether Koo understood or not, neither Dulles nor Eisenhower liked Chiang Kai-shek. And the Chinese recognized in no time that having the party of their choice in the White House was a two-edged sword. Madame H.H. Kung told Koo that when the "Democrats were in power, we could say to Republicans what we thought of the U.S.'s policy toward Free China. Now with Rep[ublicans] in power and they have been friendly on the whole, we could not always complain or ask for more and more aid."[34]

Over the next several years, Koo and his government would have much to complain about. Time and again, Koo pressed the Americans to take direct actions against the communists. Eisenhower bluntly rebuffed a proposal to support Chiang in retaking the mainland. On one occasion when Koo made a similar proposal, Dulles retorted that the "danger in vigorous application of a policy of pressures was that a totalitarian regime when near the point of break-up may lash out recklessly in order to avoid or postpone an internal crisis." Koo disagreed. In Koo's mind, the only way to deal with the communist threat was through a long-range policy that "would take in the whole free world as a unit and which would help the weak nations to build up their military strength for resisting Communist aggression and at the same time develop their respective economies and raise their standards of living." The latter was important because as "long as the under-developed and unfortunate countries were weak and poor, they could not but become happy hunting grounds for Communist imperialism which would seize every opportunity to push forward its objectives."[35]

Koo's feelings about the whole issue of the United States actively rolling back communism revolved around his sense of history and the present relationship between Chiang Kai-shek and the United States. Throughout Koo's life, he watched Japan slowly encroach on Chinese territory before expanding throughout the Pacific, and he was in Europe when Hitler nearly conquered that continent. Those personal historical experiences led Koo to view past Japanese and German expansionism and the present threat of communism as similar, if not the same, in means and methods.

Koo's stance against power politics did not mean that he was unsympathetic to Western Europe's defense needs, but rather that he thought the United States too Eurocentric for its own good. Koo told American audiences that Asia was the prime target of the Kremlin in its plan for world domination. He rejected what he called the "Churchillian view of Europe being the center of gravity" because the Soviet Union was a "bicontinental Eurasian mass" making it just as much a threat to Asia than Europe. Koo and other Asians wanted the United States to provide the Asian equivalent of NATO to ensure Asia's security and protect the Free World everywhere.[36] And he called on the Europeans to follow the U.S.'s lead and "not hamper the efforts of the U.S. in defending its own vital interests, which in the long run, is also of importance to the Allies." Both Western Europe and Asia were "faced with a common danger and they should not discriminate against or underestimate or disregard the danger in Asia." "[M]utual coexistence" was an impossibility.[37]

Even more disturbing to Koo was the premium that the Eisenhower administration placed on political expediency. Seeing that the Korean War was hurting the U.S. economy, Eisenhower determined to end the conflict. The issue that prevented all sides from ending the fighting was the question of what to do about Chinese prisoners who wanted to go to Taiwan. Initially, the PRC demanded that all Chinese prisoners be repatriated to China. There was a possibility that the political problems creating that conflict would not be solved, and that a dishonorable peace would be the result. With more enemies than friends in the UN, the anti-ROC countries were, in Koo's words, "bent upon admitting Red China into [the] U.N." More importantly, Koo blamed the White House for being "overanxious to get an armistice at any cost for domestic political reasons and because of the pressure of the Allies." Koo wanted the Americans to ignore the communist-appeasing allies, and "stand firm on principles and not yield to the argument of expediency."[38] In 1953, though, the deadlock in negotiations over the fate of the Chinese POWs was broken. Stalin's death in March, the war's toll on the communist powers' economies, and fear that the U.S. would expand the war were among several factors that led the communists to agree that Chinese prisoners could choose whether or not to return to the PRC. Meanwhile, Korea remained divided.[39]

The stalemate in Korea was not to Koo's liking. The unwillingness to roll back communism in Korea gave the ROC government little hope of U.S. support against the PRC. In Koo's opinion, the U.S. ended the war in the name of political expedience, which he viewed as dangerous to collective security. For example, it undermined the UN. In 1950, Koo warned John Foster Dulles that "If this world organization should fail by sacrificing principle to expediency which, in this case, would mean putting a premium on aggression, then . . . the whole free world would lose its hope for the future. The United Nations would then go the way of the League of Nations." By 1954, Koo believed the UN to be ineffective because of political expediency. "But the peace and security of the world must be built," Koo argued, "upon the more solid foundation of moral principles as well as military strength."[40]

Koo had other reasons to worry about ROC-U.S. relations in the mid-1950s. In the United States, he heard descriptions of Taiwan as a "police state," lacking in democracy, and Chiang Kai-shek was accused of trying to build his own dynasty. Koo regarded those criticisms as too harsh. Taiwan was "threatened with invasion by the Communists from the mainland, and the question of security must be regarded as [a] top priority matter." The ROC was in a state of war and could not make all the reforms being demanded of it. Koo saw no difference between the actions of Taiwan and that of the Western democracies during World War II. He remembered that democracy was suspended in Britain "in the interest of national security," and believed the GMD government was correct in its actions.[41]

Of particular concern was Taiwan's economy. Since 1950, the economy had improved considerably. Inflation dropped to 8.8 percent a year, and higher agricultural yields meant that Taiwan's agricultural exports amounted to $114 million in 1952. The United States pumped money into Taiwan, but there were limits to the Taiwanese "consumption of commodities." Farmers were not exporting much rice for fear of war, and people were buying more land because the GMD was about to implement a program to buy land from the landlords and resell it to the peasants.[42] And "American capitalists" refused to invest money in Taiwan because of the instability in Asia and because, Koo wrote, "our laws governing foreign investment are too restrictive." In 1953, the government sent several representatives to "explore the possibility of the U.S. market for Taiwan products." Improving Taiwan's economy was critical, particularly since despite high taxes to eliminate the deficit, Taibei could never balance its budget without U.S. aid.[43] Failure to do so limited the amount of money that the foreign ministry could spare to Koo to use for propaganda purposes. People continually complained to Koo that the American people did not know the truth about Taiwan, but Koo was too limited financially to do the kind of publicity work necessary. He reached the conclusion that Taiwan was spending far less money on propaganda than states like India, Pakistan, the Philippines, and South Korea.[44]

In 1954, Koo visited Taiwan again. By this time, the GMD implemented land reform and spent most of its nonmilitary U.S. aid building communication, transportation, and electrical infrastructure that enabled Taiwan to undergo agricultural and industrial development. The government also instituted Economic Development Plans that targeted the development of electricity, fertilizers, and textiles. After many days of inspection, Koo was impressed by "the spirit of solidarity of the officers and men, the modernization of our military prisons, the progress and achievements in raising the living standard of our farmers." And he was confident that the GMD's reforms made it a "more compact body and a more effective instrument to help implement the Government's basic policies." He ignored the fact that Taiwan was undergoing a "white terror" in which thousands were arrested and executed on charges of being communist spies. Opposition forces and criticisms from liberals, such as Hu Shi, were not tolerated by the regime. In any case, Koo made a trip to the outer islands from where he could see the mainland only a mile away. The high mountain ranges and "feeling the continental smell of the air" made him long "to go back to the mainland." The experience gave him more confidence "that one day I, in my life time, would be able to see the recovery of the mainland and the liberation of the people under the leadership" of the generalissimo.[45]

Back in the United States, Koo put his propaganda skills to work by portraying Taiwan as representing the "real China." He told Americans that the PRC was a totalitarian regime that did not have the full support of the Chinese people, that it implemented anti-Chinese policies (such as banning Confucian texts), and pursued "a policy of flagrant aggression and constitutes a menace to peace in Asia." In Taiwan, however, Chiang Kai-shek's government was the legitimate government of China because he had been elected by delegates representing all the provinces of China. On the local level, mayors were elected by the people. Taiwan was far more democratic and protected the constitutional rights of its citizens. Naturally, Koo did not explain that Chiang and GMD were a one-party dictatorship like that of the CCP. At any rate, Koo claimed that Taiwan sought peaceful cooperation with other countries, was a believer in the principle of collective security, and was a supporter of the UN. In an effort to make Taiwan even more appealing to Americans, Koo laid out examples of the PRC's anti-Americanism which contrasted with the alleged pro-Americanism that could be found in Taiwan. He declared that "While every major power in the world in the past century committed aggression or waged war against China, the United States, like China herself . . . has always pursued a policy of peace and friendship toward her." Now, the "real China" and the United States cooperated in their anticommunist policies. Even more important, once the ROC government returned to mainland China, there would a "true and new China" because it would be based on Chinese tradition and "the pattern of the United States."[46]

The hope of returning to the mainland died for the most part the next year. In September 1954, the PRC commenced shelling Jinmen and Mazu, two GMD-controlled islands located in the Taiwan Strait. Koo believed that Taiwan was safe as long as the Seventh Fleet was in the area and as long as the United States gave Taiwan the logistical support necessary for its defense. But with November Congressional elections coming up, he did not think that the United States would do "much in the way of actual participation in our defense against actual invasion" of those islands. Previously, Koo had proposed to the State Department that Taiwan and the United States sign a mutual defense pact, much like those signed between the United States and other countries in Asia. Dulles frowned on the idea, not wanting to commit the United States to recovery of the mainland, and he believed such a pact would make the Chinese communists think "that they are immune from attack so long as they do not start an invasion" of Taiwan. The Americans also wanted to avoid being dragged into a general war over Taiwan .[47]

Now with the PRC shelling the islands in the Strait, there was an opportunity for such a pact to become reality. The United States, using New Zealand as a proxy, had already submitted a cease-fire resolution to the UN. Since 1950, the U.S. tinkered with the idea of using the UN to neutralize Taiwan and eventually lay the basis for two Chinas. Chiang angrily rejected the idea of turning to the UN because he did not want to see two Chinas, like two Koreas, two Vietnams, and two Germanies. Besides, neutralizing Taiwan prevented Chiang from attacking the PRC. The generalissimo did agree to a mutual defense pact on the condition that the offshore islands were included and that the treaty be signed before the New Zealand proposal was taken up by the UN.[48]

When Koo learned that the U.S. proposed to enter into a security pact with Chiang, he was surprised and wanted time to better ascertain the "origin, the motivation, and object" behind this U.S. conversion to a treaty that Koo had previously sought to no avail. Did Washington want to create two Chinas through the UN, "in whose lap, the U.S. had been anxious to throw the delicate and difficult [Taiwan] question?" Was the United States afraid of a general war being sparked by the Jinmen-Mazu crisis? In meetings with Assistant Secretary of State Walter Robertson, Koo and George Yeh, the foreign minister, Koo explained that while the ROC did not intend to drag America into a war, it did not want to limit its sovereignty to Taiwan and the Pescadores.[49]

When Dulles presented a draft of the treaty to Koo and Yeh, the offshore islands were excluded. Dulles restated his support for the New Zealand resolution, which he believed "promised to pay big dividends." Dulles did not elaborate on what those "big dividends" were, but apparently they far outweighed the alternative, which was a resolution being presented by a "less friendly delegation." The U.S. also introduced a protocol that said that Chiang Kai-shek would not undertake offensive operations against the PRC without the consent of Washington. Koo could see that the Americans were trying to "tackle the problem of [the] offshore islands and our policy of fighting back one day to recover the mainland." The Chinese could not accept such a protocol, because it was tantamount to declaring that the GMD had given up all hope of returning to China. Koo thought the protocol was "embarrassing for the Chinese Government." He argued that "it would raise a wave of protest and despondence among the Chinese" on Taiwan and overseas. He added: "At present, so far [as] the public was aware Free China had at least the nominal right to reclaim the Mainland. The U.S., so far as the Chinese public knew, could not exercise a veto of this right." Recovering the mainland was a hope. "Whether the hope was well founded or not, the prospect was a sustaining and motivating force." But Koo warned, "If you publicly take this away and let all the world see a U.S. leash around the neck of Free China, you have lost something very important."[50]

Upon hearing the Chinese objections, Dulles decided that instead of inserting the protocol into the treaty, there would be an exchange of notes in addition to the treaty. Koo said that the Taiwan government would accept this if the exchange of notes were signed "on a different day from the signature of the Treaty so that they would not seem to be directly connected." In fact, Koo wanted at least a ten-day span between the signing of both, and he thought it preferable for the notes to be kept confidential to prevent Taibei from losing face. Robertson rejected these proposals, saying that one could not keep notes secret from the Senate Foreign Relations Committee, and he thought a seven- to ten-day delay too long.

Then, Koo submitted the ROC's counterproposal, which Robertson complained essentially suggested "that the Chinese Government be given joint control over use of American forces stationed on the U.S. islands in the West Pacific." Koo defended the proposal based on the need for reciprocity. Chiang Kai-shek did not want an actual voice over U.S. operations in the Pacific, but he would accept the leash only if the Americans put it down on paper so that they, too, were leashed by Taiwan. Otherwise, the treaty looked too "one-sided."[51] The Americans, though, were not about to accept the Chinese counterproposal.

Despite displeasure with continued American insistence on restraining Taiwan's military, the Chinese agreed to accept the leash as long as the United States committed itself to protecting the offshore islands. But the Eisenhower administration refused to make that concession, though it did agree to ambiguous language in the treaty that permitted the U.S. to defend those islands should it choose to do so. Thus, the U.S.-ROC Mutual Defense Treaty was signed on December 2. Koo had his treaty, but it was not what he had expected, and there seemed no hope of changing it. Koo tried to put a positive spin on the notes by saying that they were "reciprocal" and "[did] not mean we have given up [the] right of recovering [the] main-land."[52] Nearly three weeks later, Yeh and Koo delivered to Eisenhower a message from Chiang Kai-shek asking the president "to nip in the bud" the "promotion of a 'two-China' theory" and to give Taiwan more "assurance" as to the safety of the offshore islands. Eisenhower explained why it was impossible to extend the treaty to the islands, and in Koo's opinion, "did not give a satisfactory answer to any of the proposals put to him."[53]

The situation in the Taiwan Strait, meanwhile, turned for the worse. On January 10, 1955, the PRC air force launched raids against the Dachens, a group of islands north of Jinmen and Mazu, followed on January 18 with an assault. Reports arrived as well of massive PRC troop movements toward that area. The next day, Eisenhower made the decision to aid the evacuation of GMD troops from the Dachens and to defend Jinmen. Koo explained to the State Department that his government was desirous of "strong moral and logistic support" from the United States because the loss of the Dachens would be a "grave [psychological] blow to the Chinese Government." On January 21, Dulles revealed to Koo part of the message that Eisenhower would present to Congress in asking for a resolution that would give the president broad power in protecting the GMD-held islands. The message mentioned not only Jinmen, but Mazu. It was only a draft that had not yet been seen by Eisenhower and was subject to revision. Yet, the message was encouraging. Chiang Kai-shek, on the other hand, was highly suspicious of the U.S. desire to evacuate the Dachens and of Eisenhower's insistence on getting a Congressional resolution. He feared that there was a secret arrangement between Dag Hammarskjöld, the UN secretary general, and Zhou Enlai, the PRC's foreign minister, to call a cease-fire, evacuate the Dachens, release eleven American airmen, and push for two Chinas. And

he thought Eisenhower's resolution would be used to "pigeon-hole ratification of the Mutual Defense Treaty." Despite his reservations, Chiang
agreed to the American proposals.[54]

As Eisenhower sent the Formosa Resolution to Capitol Hill, which
if passed by Congress, gave the president full authority to take whatever
actions he thought necessary to defend Taiwan, the Pescadores, and "such
other territories as may be determined." Eisenhower decided not to mention any islands by name when presenting his message before Congress
because Britain opposed the defense of Jinmen. Eisenhower did use diplomatic channels to convey to Chiang the American commitment to protect Jinmen and Mazu. Koo implored Dulles to publicly state that
commitment, but Dulles refused given the opposition to the treaty by
some senators. Chiang Kai-shek was furious with this omission. He had
been led to believe that Eisenhower would mention the islands by name,
and now he was adamant in his refusal to evacuate the Dachens. Eventually, Washington applied pressure that brought him around to the American point of view, but Chiang remained sore for months over
Washington's "vacillating policy."[55]

The U.S. handling of the Jinmen-Mazu crisis led Koo to reflect on
Americans and their approach to foreign affairs. Koo described them as
"sentimental" and agreed with the statement made by other foreign diplomats that one never knew for certain what the Americans would do
next. He could see the contradictions inherent in American opinion. On
the one hand, Americans "were predominately anti-Communist" and
"like their government to stand firm against [the] Communist menace
and aggression." On the other hand, they were "peace-loving and opposed to war."[56] Such attitudes undermined the notion of rolling back
communism in China, and the Chinese ambassador knew that the United
States would not support an invasion of the mainland. In March 1955,
Koo reported to Chiang Kai-shek on the trends in American public opinion. He found Americans favoring easing of tensions in Taiwan and opposed to the U.S. defending Jinmen and Mazu, although the "grass root
opinion, while strong for peace, did not like the Government here to
appease the Chinese Communists either." Over the following months,
the State Department likewise made the point that the American people
opposed going to war to unite Germany and Korea, and the same was true

for China. And it complained about Chiang Kai-shek's statements to recover the mainland, which only "alienated support here and created anxiety generally" as well as weakened Taiwan's "international position." Koo defended Chiang as a peacelover that "wanted a real, honorable and lasting peace." And the generalissimo "felt he must do everything possible to preserve the legitimate aspirations of his people and to keep up morale."[57]

From Koo's point of view, the Americans took a contradictory attitude toward communism that spelled doom for hopes of returning home. Many Chinese like Koo knew that without U.S. help, the invasion of China was impossible. Time was running out on their chances of returning to China. A Chinese general observed that if Taiwan did not invade the mainland by 1957, the window of opportunity would be lost because Taiwan's military strength would peak at that point. Some intellectuals told Koo that they "did not think we would see our recovery of the mainland in our life time."[58]

There were also signs that the ROC would lose its place in the UN. The episode that made this fact painfully clear was the controversy over the admission of Outer Mongolia into the UN. In the summer of 1955, the United States made a political deal with the Soviet Union in which the latter agreed to permit thirteen U.S. allies to have membership in the UN in return for the acceptance of five Soviet satellites including Mongolia. The United States knew that Taibei would veto such a deal because of Outer Mongolia, but Washington believed that an ROC veto would anger many in the UN, leading to calls for admission of the PRC to the detriment of Anglo-U.S. relations and American public opinion. Eisenhower asked Chiang to not exercise the veto, saying that the admission of thirteen free nations was "worth . . . the price" of five Soviet satellites. Besides, the Vandenberg Resolution of 1948 prohibited the United States from exercising a veto on membership questions. Chiang's reply to Eisenhower was a firm no. He blamed the United States for the independence of Outer Mongolia that resulted from Chiang's 1945 treaty with Stalin "which we entered into on the well-intentioned advice of the United States Government."[59]

After the ROC exercised its veto, Koo faulted the United States and other members of the free world for failing to recognize a spade as a spade. He was firm in his conviction that one could not give any ground to the enemy, and remarked that "the real difficulty of the free world . . . was the lack of a firm stand on the part of the free world in dealing with the Communist countries." Earlier in 1955 when the U.S. welcomed Soviet farmers to their country, Koo "thought the Americans were rather naive, which was perhaps due to their lack of experience in tackling world problems." In his opinion, the communists held the initiative while the Western powers simply reacted to crises. Koo could understand the Western people's abhorrence of war, but "that did not mean that they should not pursue a positive and long-range policy . . . to check further Communist expansion and gradually push it back."[60]

In any case, Koo and his government grew more sensitive to any perceived moves by the United States to secure the admission of the PRC into the UN. During the Geneva Conference of 1956, the United States and the PRC tried to reach an agreement that renounced the use of force in resolving the Chinese civil war. The proposals gave Chiang Kai-shek the impression that the United States accorded Beijing de facto recognition, put Beijing on an equal footing with the United States, and was working "toward a one China—a Red China—concept." Chiang viewed the U.S. statements coming out of Geneva as the "worst possible blow to the Chinese Government." When a State Department official denied all the above, Koo asked, "Suppose the Communists accept your no force proposal. Would the United States then consider the Chinese Communists as peace loving?" Koo, who was referring to Eisenhower's recent statements that the "UN Charter required members to be 'peace loving,'" felt that Washington was merely giving opponents to the ROC an open door by which to pressure the UN to accept the PRC as a member. Although Koo later expressed gratification for the president's remarks in favor of ROC representation in the UN, he knew that the ROC was living on borrowed time as far as the UN was concerned.[61]

Koo's views of the Americans were generally correct, and he was right to argue that power and influence were based on things other than military power. Yet he, too, was naive. He completely discounted the possibility that World War III could have involved nuclear weapons and he ignored the extent to which the world was war-weary and tired of constant confrontation. And, more importantly, Koo simply did not understand the thinking of the Chinese people, much less that of the Chinese communists. He described China as a place of disillusioned youth and of increasing "popular discontent." Reiterating the old special relationship argument, he described the Chinese people as having "always been most friendly toward the American people," and he labeled the anti-American propaganda emanating from the PRC as "unChinese."[62] He wanted to believe that the people there would welcome Chiang Kai-shek back even though he knew that it was disillusionment with the generalissimo that led to his downfall in the first place. Even if the United States had attempted to recover the mainland there was no guarantee of success, because the people in China simply would not welcome their former leader.

The Jinmen-Mazu crisis of 1954 and 1955 proved to be Koo's last as a diplomat. Like international law, he felt old and in need of replacement as ambassador. Besides being tired by forty-four years of service, he lacked an estate to sustain him in his retirement years. Some of his homes in China had been destroyed and his land turned into an airfield by the Japanese during the war. His salary as ambassador was quite low, so he wanted to find new work in order to earn money for his retirement. Koo seriously considered retiring in 1952, but Chiang insisted that he remain at his post. In March 1956, Koo finally had his way and resigned as a diplomat for the ROC government. Someone once told Koo that military work was a "thankless job and an endless job." Koo felt that diplomacy was the same: "One could not see the results of one's effort, whereas in other fields one could feel one was building something and in [the] course of time could see it function." Another drawback of diplomacy was that "one had to face one crisis [after] another not only calling for unremitting effort but causing continued anxiety and worry." At his age, he found it "uphill work all the time turning from one crisis to another." And the last several years had had its share of crises and disappointments, particularly since the government's defeat on the mainland had "so radically altered other nations' opinion of our position." "Having lived and experienced the glory of the heyday during the 2nd world war as representative of one of the 4 great powers of the world," Koo keenly felt the "difference in other's regard" for the ROC and its representatives.[63] No one treated him as ambassador from a great power any longer, but as a representative of a tiny island in the Pacific. Though doyen of the GMD government's diplomatic corps, his career as diplomat lost its allure.

CONCLUSION

FOR SEVERAL MONTHS FOLLOWING RETIREMENT, Koo served as one of Chiang Kai-shek's foreign policy advisors. Then in 1957, he filled a vacancy on the International Court at the Hague where he served as a justice for the next ten years. After stepping down from the Court, he became an American citizen and lived in New York City. He never returned to China, even though Mao Zedong issued an invitation in 1972. The year before, the ROC walked out of the United Nations once it was clear that it would be replaced on the Security Council by the PRC. Mao asserted to one of his diplomats that he respected Koo's diplomatic talents, and that the reunification of Taiwan with China was the common goal of all Chinese patriots. Koo rejected the invitation, and remained in the United States until his death in 1985.[1] He lived long enough to see Richard Nixon's visit to China and Jimmy Carter's decision to cut off diplomatic recognition to Taiwan in 1979.

Nearly twenty years after his death, V.K. Wellington Koo might have been surprised at the attention that his life and career received in both Taiwan and the PRC at the turn of a new century. Numerous articles appeared in scholarly and popular magazines on both sides of the Taiwan Strait. In 1999, PRC moviegoers watched a film entitled "1919" that looked, in part, at Koo's heroic stand at Paris. The next year, a three-day conference on Koo and Chinese foreign policy was held in China, bringing together a group composed of scholars from China, Taiwan, Japan, the United Kingdom, and the United States.[2] These conference papers, as do most studies of Koo's diplomacy between 1912 and 1956, tend to be uncritical and portray Koo as a hero. Ultimately, Koo's diplomacy must be scrutinized. Where did he succeed and where did he fail? What part did Koo play in the emergence of modern China? These questions can be answered by assessing separately his efforts to revise the unequal treaty system and his handling of crises created by Japanese expansion and the tensions with foreign allies.

Wellington Koo chose a career as diplomat with the intent of saving a country perceived by its people as standing on the verge of breakup and removing the "humiliations" imposed on China by foreign powers. He wanted to adjust China's relations with the foreign powers by revising the unequal treaties and recovering territory lost either to the imperialists or independence movements. Koo's diplomatic objectives were very similar to those pursued by the People's Republic of China after 1949: regain a freedom of initiative in foreign relations; make China the center of the Asian system of states; attain cooperative relations with other states in order to enhance security and develop the economy; tie economic development to foreign policy; and involve China in international organizations.[3] In Koo's mind, his measures constituted reform designed to put China on the road to modernization and eventually great power status. His tools were international law, alliances, propaganda, and economic coercion and enticements. Unlike agricultural or educational reform, Koo's diplomatic reform was a top-down approach to China's problems. The fact that he served his country all those many years as diplomat, foreign minister, and prime minister was somewhat unique. Chinese nationalists bemoaned China's condition as a semicolony, but at least China, and Japan before it, had the advantage of possessing a diplomatic corps that could fight to improve China's international standing. The same could not be said of other Asian countries colonized by Westerners and Japan.

In assessing Koo's contribution to the emergence of a modern China, one can point to some successes. The China of 1912 was very different from that of 1949, at least in terms of the imperialist presence in China. When Koo entered government service, the foreign powers had imposed unequal treaties, leased Chinese territory, and stationed military forces in China. In the fight to make China free, Koo succeeded in representing China's interests before the world. The greatest moment in Koo's diplo-

matic career was, of course, the Paris Peace Conference. Not because he
secured any concrete changes, such as revising the unequal treaties or
recovering the German leasehold in Shandong, but because he took the
initiative and presented China's case before the world. Koo stood up to
the powers by not signing the Versailles treaty and sealed his place in
Chinese history as a defender of China's rights.[4] Public opinion abroad,
the rise of Chinese nationalism, and World War I's weakening of the
European powers ultimately forced the powers to talk about revising the
unequal treaty system at the Washington Conference. In the 1920s, Koo's
patriotic diplomacy chipped away at the imperialist system using international law and the notion of *rebus sic stantibus*. In the end, he laid a
foundation for the more unified GMD government that appeared in
1928.[5] During World War II, Koo's efforts proved crucial in the negotiations behind the Sino-British treaty of 1943 that eliminated what remained of the unequal treaty system. By 1949, Koo played a major role
in the collective effort that abolished the unequal treaties, recovered some
of the territory lost to the imperialists, laid the groundwork for eventual
recovery of parts of the empire, and enabled China to enter the international system.[6] Mao proclaimed in 1949 that China had finally stood up.
The statement was not entirely true because much work remained to be
done. Nevertheless, much had already been accomplished and, the PRC
came to power on a foundation built by Koo and others.

   Despite Koo's successes and contributions, there is no denying that
he ended up on the wrong side of revolution twice in his career. He represented the best that China could produce to play the game of international politics according to the powers' rules. Nevertheless, Koo paid a
price in that his Americanization opened him to charges of being a col-
laborationist if not a traitor. Warren Cohen once observed that Koo's
"nationalism was political, not cultural. He loved the nation, but not its
culture."[7] There is some truth to this statement. He was not antiforeign,
and proved willing to compromise in negotiations if he could avoid domestic pressure to do otherwise. However, Koo's gradualist approach to
treaty revision did not sit well with the Chinese in the 1920s who grew
impatient in demanding change, and he became tainted by his attempts
to cooperate with the powers and by his association with the warlords.
Worse, Koo's top-down approach to China's ills offered no solution for,

say, improving the lot of the peasant other than to support education initiatives.

Several years after the communist revolution of 1949, Koo told Chiang Kai-shek that one reason for failure on the mainland was "attributable, in essence, to the love of ease and mutual comforts and the lack of a guiding philosophy of life based upon devotion to principle and loyal service and personal integrity."[8] Koo's career generally reflected loyalty and integrity, but even that was not enough. He never had an ideology, such as that of Sun Yat-sen's or Mao's, that appealed to a broad mass of people. After the PRC came to power in 1949, Koo found himself lumped in a group known as reactionaries. Such labels proved meaningless in the end. Chiang Kai-shek praised Koo for his treaty revision in the late 1920s and Mao Zedong admitted that Koo was a patriot. Today, scholars consistently judge him to be a nationalist and not a puppet of any foreign country. Even his wife, who had plenty of grievances against her ex-husband, acknowledged that Koo "had fought all his life to keep China from being partitioned."[9] Still, Koo did not lead China in a glorious revolution that enabled the Chinese people to stand up, and he had to live with the bitter irony that his patriotic aspiration to make China a "free and independent country" was fulfilled by others.

One other aspect of Koo's diplomacy that must be assessed regards his handling of various crises between 1914 and 1956. Somewhere in the middle or on the periphery of those crises stood V. K. Wellington Koo. As he explained to an acquaintance years later, it was his "fate to be mixed up with every major crisis in China's international relations ever since 1912."[10] During that time, China stood on the verge of complete domination by a foreign power, primarily Japan. Koo's diplomacy, in part, played a role in preventing the colonization of China. The Chinese dealt with the crisis of Japanese expansion during World War I by using various tactics, such as declaring neutrality, creating and canceling the war zone in Shandong, stalling in negotiations, leaking information to the powers, declaring war on Germany and becoming an ally, and then taking their case to the Paris Peace Conference. For the most part, these tactics failed, but leaking the existence of the demands did bring enough outside pressure on Japan to drop the worst of the Twenty-One Demands that would have made China a protectorate of Japan. Koo played a direct role in both, suggesting such a tactic and implementing it. However, Koo's advice that China resort to military force was wrong. Yuan Shikai's policy of appeasing Japan and avoiding war proved the correct one, given Japan's military superiority.

In the 1930s, Chinese diplomacy shifted again from rolling back imperialism in general to focusing on preventing Japanese expansion. Koo proved active on the international scene, especially at the League of Nations, but again his advice to Chiang was unrealistic. Although he condemned Yuan Shikai publicly for appeasing Japan during World War I, Chiang Kai-shek recognized that his government was in no position to wage war with Japan. Chiang tried to use the Western powers to pressure Japan. Failing this, he appeased Japan and correctly rejected the advice of Koo and others who wanted to take a stronger stand against Japan. Koo preferred that China engage in self-help, but that option did not exist because preparations for war with Japan would have been interpreted by Japan as a threat. Instead, Chiang bided his time, looking for a favorable international environment that would help him to build a coalition against Japan.

In the late 1930s to early 1940s, Koo's record as a diplomat was mixed. Koo never succeeded in bringing about an anti-Japan coalition. This was too heavy a burden for just one individual. Convincing the foreign powers to provide concrete assistance was nearly as heavy a burden. Koo did secure various forms of assistance particularly during the Sino-Japanese War, but more often than not he failed to win aid. The obstacles that prevented such assistance were not of Koo's making, and his rhetorical skills could not always overcome those obstacles. From 1941 to 1945, Koo tried to use diplomacy not only to destroy the imperialist system but to ensure the victory of China and the creation of a better security system for China in the postwar world. More than Chiang Kai-shek, he was willing to moderate his patriotism in order to maintain China's position within the United Nations' alliance. Koo exerted much energy in trying to maintain good relations with both Britain and the United States. To a certain degree, China's weakness from both civil war and war with Japan, the impression that China was not carrying out the fight, and the conflict in war aims between the powers and Chiang Kai-shek undercut to a certain extent Koo's more cooperative approach. Still,

China proved to be a member of a winning coalition, became a member of the major international organizations of the time, and emerged from years of war bloodied but unfettered and free.

In dealing with the crisis of civil war, Koo faced numerous obstacles and experienced little success. His greatest difficulty and failure was the inability to convince the United States to throw its lot entirely behind Chiang's government. He tried but could not exert enough influence on Americans that convinced them of the need to fight the CCP to defend Chiang's forces. International events such as Pearl Harbor or the Korean War did more to save Koo's government than years of effort on his part. His attempts to circumvent Washington by appealing to U.S. public opinion likewise failed. In fact, Koo's diplomacy betrayed the weakness of overreliance on the United States in both assisting China in revising the imperialist system and protecting China from other powers. Like his nineteenth century predecessors,[11] Koo assumed that the United States could be enticed into the balance of power game by waving the China market and other concessions in the faces of U.S. officials. Despite being disappointed by Wilson at Paris or U.S. officials at the Washington Conference or the Brussels Conference, only Yalta finally awakened Koo to the reality that United States would not resort to military force to support China and would do whatever was necessary to avoid conflict with other powers over China. Even if the United States proved willing to play the role of aiding and democratizing China as envisioned by Koo in the late 1940s, most Chinese, many of whom were antiforeign, would have opposed U.S. expansion into China. Indeed, people like Hu Shi came under increasing attack not only from the Chinese Communists, but even noncommunist Chinese who were angered by the U.S. presence in China at the time and by Washington's China policy.[12] In this respect, Koo was also out of touch with his own people.

The story of Koo's role in Chinese foreign relations from 1912 to 1956 is a bittersweet one. He established his place in the history of his own people as well as that of world history, but heroism in the face of insurmountable odds usually did not translate into success. The fact that he survived numerous domestic and foreign crises was no small feat, but that in itself was no consolation for a man whose patriotic aspirations were fulfilled by others. The modern China that the CCP established was nothing like he dreamed. No liberal or democratic China emerged to forestall the campaigns of the early 1950s that eliminated thousands who were deemed enemies of the revolution; Mao's Great Leap Forward of the late 1950s combined with famine to kill millions, or the Cultural Revolution of the 1960s and 1970s. The China that Koo wanted to create was a benign great power that somehow held the balance of power without threatening its neighbors. Instead, post-1949 China earned respect for the manner in which it fought the Korean War, but the PRC also became feared, especially when it possessed its own nuclear weapons. No matter how Koo reflected on his career later in life, there must have been a tinge of pain and disappointment mixed in with the few pleasant memories of the distant past. Maybe after all those years, Koo took consolation in the words that John Bassett Moore quoted in a letter to Koo after the Paris Peace Conference: "It is a cause, not the fate of a cause, which is a glory."[13]

NOTES

Chapter 1. The Making of a Chinese Patriot

1. Koo Oral History, vol. 1: 1–5; Chu, *V.K. Wellington Koo*, p. 4; Koo, *An Autobiography*, p. 125; Idem., *No Feast Lasts Forever*, p. 125.

2. Eastman, "The May Fourth Movement as a Historical Turning Point," pp. 124–129.

3. Feurwerker, "The Foreign Presence in China," pp. 129–132, 141–142.

4. Osterhammel, "Semi-Colonialism and Informal Empire in Twentieth-Century China," pp. 290–309; Iriye, "Imperialism in East Asia," pp. 139–140; For the origins of the Consortium, see Edwards, *British Diplomacy and Finance in China*, chs. 6–8.

5. Cohen, "The New Coastal Reformers," pp. 256–257; Saari, *Legacies of Childhood*, p. 215.

6. Hao, *The Comprador in Nineteenth Century China*; Bastid-Bruguiere, "Currents of Social Change," pp. 556–558; Bergere, *The Golden Age of the Chinese Bourgeoisie*, pp. 37–48; See also, Cohen, "The New Coastal Reformers," p. 257; Eastman, *Family, Fields, and Ancestors*, p. 197; John King Fairbank, "Introduction: Maritime and Continental in China's History," pp. 6, 25.

7. Hunt, "Chinese National Identity and the Strong State," p. 63; Cohen, "The New Coastal Reformers," pp. 257–258; The life of one reformer who was influenced by his littoral life is described in, Cohen, *Between Tradition and Modernity*; For a discussion of British-settler attitudes toward the Chinese, see, Bickers, *Britain in China*, ch. 3.

8. Johnson, *Shanghai*, chs. 9 & 12; Clifford, *Spoilt Children of Empire*, pp. 21–26; Koo, *The Status of Aliens in China*, pp. 233–235.

9. Koo Oral History, vol. 5C: 494–495.

10. Sigel, "Foreign Policy Interests," pp. 272–274.

11. John Schrecker, "The Reform Movement," p. 44; For an in-depth look at this approach, see, Hao and Wang, "Changing Chinese Views of Western Relations," pp. 172–188; Eastman, "Ch'ing-i and Chinese Policy Formation," pp. 595–611.

12. Leonard, *Wei Yuan*, pp. 184–199; Hunt, *The Genesis of Chinese Communist Foreign Policy*, ch. 1; Also, Hao and Wang, "Changing Chinese Views of Western Relations," pp. 188–199; Tang Xiujian is an example of a Chinese patriot who opposed imperialism but was not a xenophobe. See, Chi, "Shanghai-Hangchow-Ningpo Railway Loan," pp. 92–93, 99, 101, 104–106; For Li Hongzhang, see essays by Kwang-ching Liu in Chu and Liu, eds., *Li Hung-chang and China's Early Modernization*; Bergere, *The Golden Age*, pp. 48–49.

13. Saari, *Legacies of Childhood*, pp. 26, 215–216; For the full story of those regula-

tions, see, Bickers and Wasserstrom, "Shanghai's 'Dogs and Chinese Not Admitted' Sign," pp. 444–466; Chu, "V.K. Wellington Koo: The Diplomacy of Nationalism," p. 129.

14. Koo Diary, December 28, 1936, V.K. Wellington Koo Papers.

15. Morrison Diary, April 7 and 8, 1919, Morrison Papers, item 112.

16. Saari, *Legacies of Childhood*, pp. 217–218.

17. Koo Oral History, vol. 1: 6, 20–22, 46; Koo Diary, January 21, 1945.

18. Lamberton, *St. John's University*, p. 51.

19. Koo, *No Feast Lasts Forever*, p. 125.

20. Quoted in Lutz, *China and the Christian Colleges*, p. 21.

21. Spurr, *The Rhetoric of Empire*, p. 105; Yeh, *The Alienated Academy*, pp. 62, 64; Xu, "Religion and Education," pp. 11–16; Lutz, *China and the Christian Colleges*, p. 32; Koo Oral History, vol. 1: 31; *St. John's University*, p. 4; Koo, *An Autobiography*, p. 126; Chu, *V.K. Wellington Koo*, p. 6.

22. Koo to Mott, January 28, 1911, Mott Papers, Series No. B519, box 64, folder 524.

23. *St. John's University*, p. 7. Quote from p. 9; Also, Yeh, *The Alienated Academy*, p. 62; For a description of those campus publications and others, see, Xu, "Shanghai shi dangan guan."

24. Xu, "Religion and Education," p. 25; KOH, vol. 1: 36–37.

25. Y.S. Zau, "The Importance of Studying Chinese History," *St. John's Echo*, 12 (August 20, 1901): 13–15.

26. *The St. John's Echo*, 12 (April 20, 1901): 8; Xu, "Religion and Education," p. 29.

27. *St. John's University*, p. 8; Yeh, *The Alienated Academy*, p. 67; Clifford, *Spoilt Children of Empire*, p. 57.

28. W.W. Yen, "The Educating of the Chinese," *St. John's Echo* 11 (December 20, 1900): 3–6; N.L. Nien, "Absolute Monarchy a Better Form of Government for China than Republic," *Ibid.*, 12 (February 20, 1901): 11–13; idem, "Self-Reform or Partition," *Ibid* (August 20, 1901): 15–20; Z.Z. Zee, "Is the Chinese Government Sincere in Reformation?" *Ibid.*, 13 (October 20, 1902): 17–19; "The Reform Party in China," *Ibid.*, 14 (February 20, 1903): 9–11; T. C. Dzung, "The First Step of China's Independence," *Ibid.*, 15 (June 20, 1904): 19–21; Nathan, *Chinese Democracy*, pp. 47–48.

29. KOH, vol. 1: 30–35; see also, Wang, "A Patriotic Christian Leader;" pp. 34–35; Hunt, *Ideology and U.S. Foreign Policy*, ch. 4.

30. Xu, "Religion and Education," pp. 87–94.

31. *The Dragon Flag: 1904*, p. 99.

32. Wang, *Chinese Intellectuals and the West*, ch. 3; Chen, *China and the West*, pp. 153–154.

33. Reynolds, *China, 1898–1912*, pp. 42, 44–45.

34. K.F. Chang, "The Alliance of the Yellow Race," *St. John's Echo*, 13 (April 20, 1902): 11–14; Z.T. Yui, "Japanese Influence," *Ibid.*, 15 (June 20, 1904): 15–19; F.K. Woo, "Chinese Students in Japan," *Ibid.*, 13 (June 20, 1902): 6–8.

35. Grieder, *Intellectuals and the State in Modern China*, pp. 210–211; Liu, *Americans and Chinese*, pp. 30–31.

36. Koo Diary, December 25, 1950.

37. Koo, *No Feast Lasts Forever*, p. 124; "History of the Chinese Educational Mission," *Chinese Students' Monthly*, 11 (December 1915): 92.

38. Koo Oral History, vol. 1: 37–39, 41–42, 45–49.

39. Chen, *China and the West*, p. 161; Said, *Culture and Imperialism*, p. 9; Nandy, *The Intimate Enemy*, p. 7.

40. For an example of either a contemptuous or paternalistic attitude, see, Mudge,

China; Ross, *The Changing Chinese*; Works that either reject or modify such views are, Parker, *China: Her History, Diplomacy and Commerce*; Johnston, *China and Its Future*; Giles, *The Civilization of China*; Idem., *China and the Chinese*; and essays in, Singleton, ed., *China as Described by Great Writers*.

41. Mosher, *China Misperceived*, pp. 41–42.
42. Koo Oral History, vol. 1: 83–84.
43. Koo to Mott, January 28, 1911, Mott Papers.
44. Koo Diary, April 3, 1942.
45. Koo Oral History, vol. 1: 38–39; Chen, *China and the West*, p. 156; Koo, "The Task Before China's Students Today," pp. 322–323.
46. Koo Oral History, vol. 1: 83, 85.
47. Hyne Sun, "The Returned Students and the Coolie," *Chinese Students' Monthly*, 8 (May 10, 1913): 456; Koo, "The Task Before China's Students Today," pp. 321, 322.
48. Koo Oral History, vol. 1: 149–150; See also, Franke, "Sung Embassies: Some General Observations," pp. 116–141; Folsom, *Friends, Guests, and Colleagues*, p. 5; Wright, *The Last Stand of Chinese Conservatism*, pp. 224–226; Hsu, *China's Entrance into the Family of Nations*, ch. 12.
49. Koo Oral History, vol. 1: 45–46, 54–56; Robinson and Beard, eds., *Readings in Modern European History*, vol. 2, p. 118; Jiang Tingfu, who received a Ph.D. from Columbia, commented "I became an admirer of Bismarck, and I worshipped the three great leaders of Italy, Cavour, Mazzini and Garibaldi." The Reminiscences of Tsiang T'ing-fu, p. 65.
50. Koo, "Problems and Difficulties of Returned Students," p. 26; Koo Diary, April 2, 1943.
51. Koo Oral History, vol. 3: 282, 286–287.
52. "Koo: Suave Spokesman for 'Quarter of Human Race,'" *Newsweek*, 1 (March 4, 1933): 18; Paul Windels Interview, Columbia Oral History Project, p. 14.
53. "Minister Koo tells why China is in War," *New York Times* (October 2, 1918): 17; Moore to Wunsz King, August 16, 1922, Moore Papers, box 48.
54. Wright, *The Last Stand*, pp. 237–248; Hsu, *China's Entrance into the Family of Nations*, ch. 8; Schrecker, "The Reform Movement," pp. 43–53; Gong, *The Standard of 'Civilization,'* pp. 54–64, 146–147.
55. Somit and Tanenhaus, *The Development of American Political Science*, pp. 8, 18–19; Herman, *Eleven Against War*, pp. 22–54; Marchand, *The American Peace Movement*, pp. 39–73; Wiebe, *The Search for Order*, pp. 260–261, 262; Hepp, "James Brown Scott," pp. 17, 22–23.
56. Hoxie et al., *A History of the Faculty*, pp. 88, 263–4; Moore, *A Digest of International Law*; On American foreign policy, see, idem., *Four Phases of American Development*; Idem., *American Diplomacy*; Coon, *Columbia*, p. 228; *Columbia University in the City of New York Catalogue and General Announcement, 1906–1907*, pp. 100–101.
57. Herman, *Eleven Against War*, p. 43; Hepp, "James Scott Brown," p. 19.
58. "Mr. Hay's Work in Diplomacy," *The Collected Papers of John Bassett Moore*, vol. 3: 202–212; "Franklin as a Diplomatist," *Ibid.*, pp. 245–251; "McKinley as a Diplomatist," *Ibid.*, pp. 452–457; KOH, vol. 3: 282.
59. "The Advantages of a Permanent System of Arbitration," *The Collected Papers of John Bassett Moore*, vol. 2, pp. 24–26; "International Arbitration," *Ibid.*, pp. 71–83 *passim*; "Progress of International Law in the Century," *Ibid.*, p. 439; "Progress of International Law in the Century," *Ibid.*, pp. 440–449; "The Old Diplomacy and the New," *Ibid.*, p. 200;

"The Federal Tendency," *Ibid.*, vol. 3, p. 312; "The Advantages of a Permanent System of Arbitration," *Ibid.*, vol. 2, pp. 24–26; "International Arbitration," *Ibid.*, pp. 71–83 *passim*.

60. "Progress of International Law in the Century," *Ibid.*, vol. 2: 448–449; Koo Diary, April 2, 1943.

61. Koo Oral History, vol. 2: 68–69, 71–72.

62. Grieder, *Hu Shih*, pp. 57–58; Geyer and Bright, "World History in a Global Age," p. 1049; Robinson, "Non-European Foundations of European Imperialism," pp. 120–121.

63. A.S. Devin to Koo, September 29, 1937, Koo Papers, box 28, folder 7a.

64. Robinson and Beard, *Outlines of European History*, vol. 2, p. 313.

65. Moore, *American Diplomacy*, pp. 123–125, 251; Megargee, "The Diplomacy of John Bassett Moore," pp. 81, 129–130; See also the essays in, George H Blakeslee, ed., *China and the Far East*; Smith, *China and America Today*.

66. See review of Howard Richard's "The Awakening of China," *Chinese Students' Monthly*, 4 (January 1909): 189; In Young, "China and the United States," *Ibid.* (May 1909): 446–447.

67. Editorial, *Ibid,*, (November 1908): 5; Editorial, *Ibid.*, 5 (November 1909): 2; *Ibid.*, (January 1910); *Ibid.*, (February 1910).

68. Y.S. Tsao, "America and the Far East," *Ibid.*, (March 1910): 296–299; Chengting T. Wang, "China and America," *Ibid.*, 6 (March 10, 1911): 460–465.

69. Koo Diary, April 2, 1943.

70. Koo, *The Status of Aliens in China*, pp. 7–8.

71. *Ibid.*, pp. 18, 21–23, 26–27.

72. *Ibid.*, pp. 32, 47–48, 60, 63–79.

73. *Ibid.*, pp. 80, 138, 146, 153–154, 156–165.

74. *Ibid.*, pp. 293–309, 336–342, 350.

75. *Ibid.*, pp.351–352.

76. For just a smattering of a vast literature on this subject, see, Boulger, *China*, pp. 522–523, 529–530; Colquhuon, *China in Transformation*, ch. 6; Parker, *China: Her History, Diplomacy and Commerce*, ch. 7; Gascoyne-Cecil, *Changing China*, pp. 22–23, 28–30, 31–32.

77. Koo, *The Status of Aliens in China*, pp. 354–355.

78. Hull, *The New Peace Movement*, pp. 120–121. Quote from p. 121; Angell, *The Great Illusion*, pp. 46–47, 50–51, 153–154, 220–221.

79. Koo, *The Status of Aliens in China*, p. 356.

80. Isaacs, *Images of Asia*, pp. 104–105; Hunt, *Ideology and U.S. Foreign Policy*, pp. 69–70.

81. Koo, *The Status of Aliens in China*, p. 356.

82. Koo Oral History, vol. 1: 122–123, vol. 2: 146.

83. E.T. Williams Diary, July 10, 1912, vol. 6, C-B 977, ctn. 3, E.T. Williams Papers; Yen, *East-West Kaleidoscope*, p. 54; I borrow the terms from Nathan, *Peking Politics*, pp. 51, 53.

84. Yen, *East-West Kaleidoscope*, p. 46.

85. Koo, *An Autobiography*, p. 114; Koo Oral History, vol. 1: 84, 86–106; For suggestion that Koo did not secure a divorce until 1913 because he was threatened with arrest and a lawsuit from the woman's family, see, Nelson T. Johnson Reminiscences, Columbia Oral History Project, pp. 386–389; Koo, "American Commercial Opportunities in China," *Chinese Students' Monthly*, 11 (April 1916): 431.

86. *The North-China Herald* (June 7, 1913): 701; Hinners, *Tong Shao-yi and his Fam-*

ily, p. 26; Johnson Reminiscences, pp. 386–389; Koo Oral History, vol. 2: 34–35; Nathan, *Peking Politics*, p. 54.

87. Koo to Taft, February 12, 1912, Records of the Department of State Relating to the Internal Affairs of China, 1910–29, (National Archives Microfilm Publications Microcopy No. 329), 893.00/634.

88. Koo to Moore, March 25, 1912, Moore Papers, box 18; Koo later claimed that he did not jump at the offer. See, Koo Oral History, vol. 1: 133–135.

Chapter 2. China and World War I

1. Hinners, *Tong Shao-yi and his Family*, p. 41; Young, *The Presidency of Yuan Shikai*, pp. 86, 117–118.

2. "Waijiaobu tiaoyue Yanjiu hui guanyu zhengqu geguo chengren zhonghua minguo de baogao" (The Foreign Ministry's Treaty Study Commission's report on the attempt to gain recognition of the Republic of China), in *Beiyang zhengfu shiqi waijiao*, pp. 28–30.

3. Harrison, *The Making of the Republican Citizen*, pp. 17–18; Koo Oral History, vol. 2: 68–69, 71–72.

4. McKinnon, *Power and Politics in Late Imperial China*, pp. 182–186; Hunt, *Frontier Defense and the Open Door*; idem., *The Making of a Special Relationship*.

5. Young, *The Presidency of Yuan Shih-k'ai*, pp. 70, 71; Iriye, *Pacific Estrangement*, p. 200; Gong, "China's Entry into International Society," p. 181; Yen, *East-West Kaleidoscope*, p. 114; Hunt, *Making of a Special Relationship*, pp. 219–220.

6. Yen, *East-West Kaleidoscope*, pp. 72, 74, 78; Koo Oral History, vol. 2: 2–5, 17; vol. 3: 230, 274.

7. Wang, *Chinese Intellectuals and the West*, p. 93; Koo Oral History, vol. 3: 246; vol. 2:36–40; "Waijiaobu yangai jilue" (Outline of the Foreign Ministry's successive changes), in *Zhonghua minguo shi dangan ciliao jibian*, vol. 3, *Beiyang zhengfu shiqi waijiao*, pp. 1–20; Chang, "The Organisation of the Waichiaopu," pp. 36–39; Pong, "The Ministry of Foreign Affairs During the Republican Period 1912 to 1949," pp. 136–140; Uhalley, "The Wai-Wu Pu, The Chinese Foreign Office from 1901 to 1911," pp. 9–27; Yen, *East-West Kaleidoscope*, p. 77.

8. Koo to Morrison, December 19, 1913, MP, vol. 77; Morrison to Koo, December 16, 1913, *Ibid.*; Morrison to Koo, January 27, 1914, *The Correspondence of G.E. Morrison*, pp. 284–285.

9. Cen, *Sanshui Liang Yensun xiansheng nienbiao*, vol. 1, pp. 193–196; Administrative Council to Foreign Ministry, August 6, 1914, *Zhong ri guanxi shiliao: ou zhan yu shandong wenti*, no. 29, pp. 11–12; Foreign Ministry to all embassies, August 6, 1914, *Ibid.*, no. 34, p. 13; Morrison diary, October 22, 1914, MP, item 103.

10. Nish, *Japanese Foreign Policy 1869–1942*, pp. 93–96; Lowe, *Great Britain and Japan*, pp. 177–182; Barnhart, *Japan and the World since 1868*, p. 50; Dickinson, *War and National Reinvention*, pp. 87–88.

11. Iriye, *Pacific Estrangement*, ch. 7; Also, idem., "Japan as a Competitor, 1895–1917," *Mutual Images*, pp. 73–99; Huang, "Zhongguo dui ou zhan de qubu fanying," p. 262; Foreign Ministry to Lu, August 6, 1914, in *World War I*, no. 23, p. 6; Koo-MacMurray conversation, *Ibid.*, no. 26, p. 9; Bryan to Wilson, August 8, 1914, *Wilson Papers*, vol. 30: 363.

12. MacMurray to Bryan, August 20, 1914, *FRUS: 1914*, Supplement, pp. 173–174; Bryan to MacMurray, August 20, 1914, *Ibid.*, p. 174; Sun-MacMurray conversation, September 29, 1914, in *Zhong ri guanxi shiliao: Lukuang jiaoshe*, p. 190.

13. Koo Oral History, vol. 2: 77–79; Chi, *China Diplomacy*, pp. 3, 20; Foreign Ministry

to Yan, September 3, 1914, *World War I*, no. 286, pp. 129–30; Sun-German minister conversation, September 3, 1914, *Ibid.*, no. 281, pp. 127–128; Foreign Ministry to all Chinese ministers abroad, *Ibid.*, no. 285, p. 129.

14. Dickinson, *War and National Reinvention*, pp. 55–56; Morrison Diary, October 5, 1915, MP, item 103.

15. Morrison Diary, November 3, 1914, *Ibid.*; Koo Oral History, vol. 2: 99; Pugach, *Paul S. Reinsch*, pp. 68, 137; Macmurray to Mother, February 19, 1914, John V.A. MacMurray Papers, Box 17, Mudd Library, Princeton University; Reinsch to Wilson, October 5, 1914, *Wilson Papers*, vol. 31, pp. 285–288; Reinsch to Wilson, November 28, 1914, *Ibid.*, p. 367; Reinsch to Wilson, December 22, 1914, *Ibid.*, p. 512.

16. Sun-Reinsch conversation, October 7, 1914, *Zhong ri guanxi shiliao: Lukuang jiaoshe*, p. 213; Pugach, *Paul S. Reinsch*, p. 145; "Qingdao zhanhou wenti yanjiu hui huiyi lu" (Minutes of a meeting of the Qingdao rehabilitation study commission), January 22, 1915, in *Beiyang zhengfu shiqi waijiao*, pp. 152–157; "Wu Chaochu, Wellington Koo, deng suo ni 'Shandong wenti zhi fenxi' gao," *Ibid.*, pp. 161–164.

17. Dickinson, *War and National Reinvention*, pp. 84–116; Chi, *China Diplomacy*, p. 31.

18. Secretariat to Foreign Ministry, February 1, 1915, *Zhong ri guanxi shiliao: ershiyi tiao jiaoshe*, no. 24, pp. 16–19; *Ibid.*, no. 22, pp. 7–9; Administrative Council to Wang, March 10, 1915, *Ibid.*, no. 1122, pp. 777–778; Chi, *China Diplomacy*, p. 34; Koo Oral History, vol. 3: 272–273.

19. Morrison Diary, April 29, 1915, MP, item 104; Koo Oral History, vol. 2: 82–83, 84–85; vol. 3: 272–273; Chi, *China Diplomacy*, pp. 34, 38, 41; Pugach, *Paul S. Reinsch*, pp. 148–149; Second meeting between Lu and Hioki, February 5, 1915, *Zhong ri guanxi shiliao: ershiyi tiao jiaoshe*, no. 31, p. 22.

20. Chi, *China Diplomacy*, pp. 36–40, 43–48; Israel, *Progressivism and the Open Door*, p. 131; Gowen, "Great Britain and the Twenty-One Demands of 1915," pp. 87–91, 97.

21. Chi, *China Diplomacy*, pp. 50–51, 55–58; House to Wilson, May 7, 1915, *Wilson Papers*, vol. 33, p. 121; Shi to the Foreign Ministry, May 8, 1915, *Zhong ri guanxi shiliao: ershiyi tiao jiaoshe*, no. 387, p. 289; Foreign Ministry to all consuls in Russia and Europe and Shah Kai Fu, May 9, 1915, *Ibid.*, no. 396, pp. 291–292; For the text of the agreement and the ultimatum, see MacMurray, *Treaties*, pp. 1231–1235.

22. Morrison Diary, May 12 and May 19, 1915; Cao, *Yisheng*, p.100; MacMurray, *Treaties*, p. 1236.

23. Morrison Diary, May 28, 1915, MP, item 104; Chi, *China Diplomacy*, pp. 59–60; Eto, "China's International Relations," pp. 99–100; Gowan, "Great Britain and the Twenty-One Demands," pp. 105–106; MacMurray, *Treaties*, p. 1236; Kawamura, *Turbulence in the Pacific*, pp. 35–58.

24. Williams Diary, August 8, 1912, C-B 977, ctn. 3, vol. 5; Cao, *Yisheng*, p. 102; Young, *The Presidency of Yuan Shih-k'ai*, p. 221; Morrison Diary, August 2, 1915, item 104.

25. Morrison Diary, August 17, 1915, item 104; Extract from Pall Mall Gazette, 1920, FO 371, 5344, F3323, 2090, 10; V.K.W. Koo to Editor, *New York Sun* (January 4, 1912), reprinted under original newspaper heading, "Confusing Counsel From America to the Revolutionists," *Chinese Students' Monthly*, pp. 352–353; Harrison, *The Making of a Republican Citizen*, pp. 20–21; Cao, *Yisheng*, pp. 114–115.

26. Cao, *Yisheng*, pp. 114–115; Morrison Diary, January 28, 1919, item 112; Young, *The Presidency of Yuan Shih-k'ai*, pp. 172–176, 221–222; Pugach, "Embarrassed Monarchist;" Chih, "Goodnow's Mission to China, 1913–1915," pp. 197–217; Jordan to Grey,

August 25, 1915, *British Documents on Foreign Affairs: Part II, Series E, Asia, 1914–1939*, vol. 22, p. 74; Reinsch, *An American Diplomat in China*, p. 171; Koo Oral History, vol. 3: 243–244.

27. Wilson to Lansing, October 31, 1915, *Wilson Papers*, vol. 35: 143, 144; Reinsch to Lansing, November 19, 1915, *FRUS: 1915*, p. 78; Nish, "Dr. Morrison and China's Entry into the World War," p. 328; Chi, *China Diplomacy*, pp. 71–75.

28. Lu to Koo, January 6, 1916, Waijiao dangan, RG 03–12, box 17:5; "China's Envoy No Pacifist," *New York Times* (January 30, 1916): 12; Young, *The Presidency of Yuan Shih-k'ai*, p. 215; Koo, "The Building of a Nation as Illustrated by the History of the United States and China," pp. 5–13.

29. McCord, *The Power of the Gun*; Sheridan, "The Warlord Era," pp. 284–295; Leong, *Sino-Soviet Diplomatic Relations*, p. xx; Nathan, "A Constitutional Republic," p. 266.

30. Nish, *Japanese Foreign Policy*, pp. 106–107, 110; Iklé, "Japanese-German Peace Negotiations during World War I," pp. 62–76; Lowe, *Britain in the Far East*, p. 110.

31. Pugach, *Paul S. Reinsch*, pp. 189–190; Chi, *China Diplomacy*, p. 115; Lowe, *British Strategy in the Far East*, p. 108; Sheridan, "The Warlord Era," p. 304; Koo Oral History, vol. 2B: 132–136; *New York Times* (November 17, 1916): 17.

32. Ferrell, *Woodrow Wilson and World War I*, pp. 8–11; Li, *Woodrow Wilson's China Policy*, p. 208; Chi, *China Diplomacy*, pp. 116–117, 121–122; Gardner, *Safe for Democracy*, p. 92; Kawamura, *Turbulence in the Pacific*, pp. 61–72; Li, *Zuijin sanshi nian zhongguo zhengzhi shi*, p. 400.

33. Cao, *Yisheng zhi huiyi*, pp. 160–161; Chi, *China* Diplomacy, pp. 122–123; Morrison Diary, February 20 & 22, March 1 & 10, 1917.

34. Knock, *To End All Wars*, pp. 116–117, 121–122.

35. Koo Oral History, vol. 2B: 140; Koo to Lu, April 12, 1917, Waijiao dangan, RG 03–36, box 13:2; Koo to Lu, April 21, 1917, (in English), *Ibid.*, RG 03–12, box 8:1; Koo to Lu, April 18, 1917, *Ibid.*, RG 03–36, box 13:2.

36. Chi, *China Diplomacy*, pp.123–125; Li, *Zuijin sanshi nian*, pp. 401–403; Jin, *Gu Weijun zhuan*, p. 43.

37. Nish, *Japanese Foreign Policy*, p. 112; Chi, *China Diplomacy*, pp. 104–114; Kawamura, *Turbulence in the Pacific*, pp. 77–82, 102–103; Koo-Long conversation, October 18, 1917, Long Papers, China file, box 179; Koo to Foreign Ministry, November 6, 1917, Waijiao dangan, 03–33, box 77:2; Koo Oral History, vol. 2B: 157; Gardner, *Safe For Democracy*, p. 222; MacMurray, *Treaties*, p. 1397.

38. Koo to Moore, August 3, 1917, Moore Papers, box 36; Moore to Koo, October 11, 1918, *Ibid.*, box 38; Koo to Moore, October 17, 1918, Moore Papers, box 94.

39. Millard to Morrison, November 11, 1918, *Correspondence of G.E. Morrison*, p. 713.

40. Koo Oral History, vol. 2B: 163; Memorandum of Koo-Long conversation, November 27, 1918, Peace Conference file, box 186, Long Papers.

41. Koo Oral History, vol. 6A: 20–21.

42. Crunden, *Ministers of Reform*, pp. 232–235; Levin, *Woodrow Wilson and World Politics*, pp. 2–3; Koo Oral History, vol. 3: 127; Hu Shi admired Wilson for his ideals and his humanitarian foreign policy. See, Grieder, *Hu Shih*, p. 52; Jiang Tingfu later remarked, "Every word uttered by President Wilson seemed true and noble to me." Reminiscences of Tsiang T'ing-fu, p. 68.

43. Knock, *To End All Wars*, pp. 142–145; Mayer, *Wilson vs. Lenin*, pp. 17–22, 268, 342–343.

44. Morrison Diary, January 27, 1919, item 112; Koo, "The Administration of Inter-

national Law," pp. 1–25; See also, "Koo Favors Peace Courts," *New York Times* (February 18, 1916): 9; *Ibid.,* (December 16, 1916): 14.

45. Koo Oral History, vol. 2B: 161, 169; Wilson-Koo conversation, November 26, 1918, *Wilson Papers,* vol. 57, pp. 632–634; Zhang, *China in the International System,* pp. 42–43, 51; Morrison Diary, February 28, 1919, MP, item 112.

46. Knock, *To End All Wars,* pp. 189–192; Morrison Diary, January 28 & 29, February 28, 1919, MP, item 112; On the other hand, several American supporters, such as Paul Reinsch, did not support the complete abrogation of the unequal treaties. See, Chi, "China and Unequal Treaties," p. 57.

47. Zhang, *China in the International System,* p. 52; Morrison Diary, February 27, 1919, MP, item 112; Koo Oral History, vol. 3G: 176–177.

48. Knock, *To End All Wars,* pp. 197–201; Leffler, *The Specter of Communism,* pp. 6–12.

49. Zhang, *China in the International System,* pp. 44–47; Chi, "China and Unequal Treaties," p. 52; MacMurray, *Treaties,* vol. 2, p. 1445; Chi, "Bureaucratic Capitalists in Operation," pp. 678–685; Morrison Diary, January 29, 1919, item 112.

50. Elleman, *Wilson and China,* pp. 41, 43; See, [in English] Wu to Koo, March 29, 1918, Waijiao dangan, 03–12, box 8:2; Koo to Wu, n.d., *Ibid.;* Minutes of the Chinese delegation's meetings, January 21 and January 22, 1919, *Ibid.,* RG 03–37, box 11:3; Lu to Foreign Ministry, January 23, 1919, *Ibid.,* RG 03–33, box 150:1.

51. Dockrill and Goold, *Peace Without Promise,* pp. 64–68; Morrison Diary, January 27, 1919, item 112; Hankey's Notes of Two Meetings of the Council of Ten, January 27, 1919, *Wilson Papers,* vol. 54, pp. 291–293; see telegrams, Lu to the Foreign Ministry, January 27, 1919, Koo Papers, box 2; Zhang, *China in the International System,* p. 54.

52. Morrison diary, March 9, 1919, MP, item 112; Lu to the Foreign Ministry, January 30, 1919, Koo Papers, box 2; Hankey's Notes of Two Meetings of the Council of Ten, January 28, 1919, in *Wilson Papers,* vol. 54, pp. 315, 316–318; Lu to Foreign Ministry, January 29, 1919, Waijiao dangan, RG 03–33, box 150:1; Lu to Foreign Ministry, February 2, 1919, *Ibid.*

53. E.T. Williams to Long, February 21, 1919, Long Papers, box 186; See also, Chi, "China and Unequal Treaties," p. 53; Knock, *To End All Wars,* pp. 210–213; From the Diary of Dr. Grayson, January 28, 1919, *Wilson Papers,* vol. 54, pp. 308–309; Wilson to Xu (Hsu Shih-ch'ang), January 28, 1919, *Ibid.,* p. 331; Koo Oral History, vol. 2C: 205.

54. Lu to Foreign Ministry, January 30, 1919, Waijiao dangan, RG 03–33, box 150:1; Koo to House, E. M. House Papers, box 67, folder 2213, Yale University; Lansing to Wilson, February 4, 1919, *Wilson Papers,* vol. 54, p. 474 and fn. 2; Long Diary, January 31, 1919, Long Papers, box 2; See also, Lu-Obata conversation, February 5, 1919, Waijiao dangan, RG 03–33, box 124:3; Lu Ben-Obata conversation, February 6, 1919, *Ibid.*; Williams Diary, February 12, 1919, C-B 977, ctn. 3, diary vol. 7; Lansing to Long, February 14, 1919, Long Papers, box 186.

55. Morrison Diary, January 28 & 29, February 27 & 28, 1919, MP, item 112; Jin, *Gu Weizhun zhuan,* pp. 63–64; Liao, "Gu Weijun yu bali hehui zhongguo daibiao tuan," pp. 59–60, 78n.44.

56. Foreign Ministry to Lu, January 31, 1919, Koo Papers, box 2; Zhang, *China in the International System,* pp. 55–56; Elleman, *Wilson and China,* p. 49.

57. T'ang, *Beijing zhengfu yu guoji lianmeng,* pp. 13–14; Miller, *The Drafting of the Covenant,* vol. 1, pp. 125, 140, 147, 151, 152; Knock, *To End All Wars,* pp. 214–218; Koo to

Wilson, April 25, 1919, Wilson Papers, Library of Congress; Koo-Wilson conversation, March 24, 1919, Koo Papers, box 1, folder 3.

58. Knock, *To End All Wars*, pp. 223–224, 249; Koo to Foreign Ministry, February 13, 1919, Koo Papers, box 2; Williams Diary, March 26, 1919; Miller, *Drafting of the Covenant*, vol. 1, p. 336; Minutes of a Meeting of the League of Nations Commission, April 11, 1919, *Wilson Papers*, vol. 57, p. 263; Williams Diary, March 26, 1919.

59. Morrison Diary, April 29 & May 2, 1919.

60. Knock, *To End All Wars*, pp. 246–249.

61. Lu to Foreign Ministry, March 29, 1919, Waijiao dangan, RG 03–33, 150:1; Wilson-Koo conversation, March 24, 1919, Koo Papers, box 1, folder 3; Williams Diary, March 26, 1919.

62. Williams to Long, March 28, 1919, Long Papers, box 186; Lansing to Wilson, April 12, 1919, *Wilson Papers*, vol. 57, pp. 298–301.

63. Morrison dairy, April 8 & 17, 1919, MP, item 112; Koo to Wilson, April 17,1919, *Wilson Papers*, vol. 57, p. 431.

64. Dockrill and Goold, *Peace Without Promise*, p. 68; Levin, *Woodrow Wilson and World Politics*, pp. 239–244; Zhang, *China in the International System*, pp. 68–70; Dreifort, *Myopic Grandeur*, pp. 26–27.

65. Carr, *The Twenty Years' Crisis*, pp. 182–183; Dower, *Empire and Aftermath*, pp. 49–50.

66. Morrison Diary, April 7, 27, 30, and May 2, 1919; Bonsal, *Suitors and Supplicants*, p. 239; Pearl, *Morrison of Peking*, p. 385; Zhang, *China in the International System*, pp. 70–71; Lu to Foreign Ministry, May 6, 1919, Koo Papers, box 2.

67. Koo-House conversation, April 21, 1919, *Ibid.*, box 1, folder 3.

68. Koo-Williams conversation, April 21, 1919, *Ibid.*

69. Lu to Wilson, April 24, 1919, *Wilson Papers* , vol. 58, pp, 68–70; *FRUS: The Paris Peace Conference*, vol. 5, p. 607.

70. Williams Diary, May 1, 1919; Cabinet to Lu, May 6, 1919, Koo Papers, box 2; Foreign Ministry to Lu, May 8, 1919, *Ibid.*; Cabinet to Lu, May 8, 1919, *Ibid.*; Strand, *Rickshaw Beijing*, pp. 105, 108, 173–177; Bonsal, *Suitors and Supplicants*, pp. 241–244.

71. Lu to Foreign Ministry, May 1, 1919, Koo Papers, box 2; Lu to Foreign Ministry, May 3, 1919, *Ibid.*; Koo to Foreign Ministry, May 15, 1919, *Ibid.*; Zhang, *China in the International System*, pp. 78–82.

72. Koo to Foreign Ministry, May 27, 1919, Koo Papers, box 2; *FRUS: The Paris Peace Conference*, vol. 6, p. 710; Koo-House conversation, May 22, 1919, Koo Papers, box 1, folder 3.

73. Morrison Diary, July 14, 1919, Morrison Papers, item 112; Walworth, *Wilson and his Peacemakers*, p. 374; Koo Oral History, vol. 2C: 236; Zhang, *China in the International System*, pp. 91, 217, fn. 280; Koo memorandum to Lansing, June 25, 1919, Waijiao dangan, RG 03–37, box 22:4; Hankey's Notes of a Meeting of the Council of Four, June 26, 1919, *Wilson Papers*, vol. 61, pp. 209; Koo to Foreign Ministry, June 27, 1919, Koo Papers, box 3.

74. For a more detailed treatment on the torturous path taken to finally reach a decision on whether to sign or not, see, Zhang, *China in the International System*, pp. 82–88; Chi, "China and Unequal Treaties," p. 60; Koo Oral History, vol. 2C: 245.

75. Saari, *Legacies of Childhood*, p. 225; Editorial, *Chinese Students Monthly*, vol. 15 (January 1920): 6; Schoppa, *Blood Road*, p. 65; Niu, "The Origins of Mao Zedong's Thinking on International Affairs," p. 4; Hunt, *The Genesis of Chinese Communist Foreign Policy*, pp. 60–74; Bergere, *Sun Yat-sen*, p. 278; Clifford, *Spoilt Children of Empire*, pp. 13–14.

76. Koo Oral History, vol. 2C: 251.

Chapter 3. Chinese Nationalism and Treaty Revision, 1921–1928

1. Schlerath to MacMurray; Lansing Diary, November 12, 1921; Morrison Diary, October 24, 1919; January 4 & 9, 1920; Koo Oral History, vol. 2C: 260; Geddes to Earl Curzon, January 14, 1921, FO 371, A903/903/45; Lampson to Curzon and the King, February 17, 1921, FO 371, 6641/F589/589/10; Memorandum on "Principal Delegates to the Washington Conference," November 3, 1921, FO 371, 6660/F4052/2635/10.

2. James Sheridan, "The Warlord Era," p. 311.

3. Morrison Diary, March 6, 1919, MP, item 112; For a full discussion of these proposals, see, Zhang, *China in the International System*, pp. 61–65; Kirby, *Germany and Republican China* p. 24.

4. Yen, *East-West Kaleidoscope*, pp. 298, 299.

5. Dirlik, *The Origins of Chinese Communism*, pp. 23–41, 193, 194; Leong, *Sino-Soviet*, pp. 130–135, 139–140, 147–161; Zhang, *China in the International System*, pp. 165–167, 178–196; Elleman, *Diplomacy and Deception*, pp. 23–27.

6. Koo to Foreign Ministry, October 22, 1920, *Shandong Wenti*, no. 262, pp. 275–276; "Waijiao fangzhen yijian shu" (A proposal of China's foreign policy principle), in *Beiyang zhengfu shiqi waijiao*, pp. 21–25.

7. Cohen, *Empire Without Tears*, pp. 46–50; Fifield, "Secretary Hughes and the Shantung Question," p. 374; Zhang, *China in the International System*, pp. 124–127.

8. Curzon to Alston, July 8, 1921, *Documents on British Foreign Policy*, First Series, vol. 14, pp. 329–330; Curzon Memorandum, July 14, 1921, *Ibid.* pp. 345–351; Crowe-Hayashi conversation, July 25, 1921, *Ibid.*, p. 352; Eliot to Curzon, August 1, 1921, *Ibid.*, p. 365; Alston to Curzon, July 14, 1921, *Ibid.*, p. 341; See also, Gardner, *Safe For Democracy*, pp. 308–309.

9. Koo Oral History, vol. 2D: 269, 270; An example of how the British perceived American antipathy toward Britain and Japan over China is found in, Alston to Curzon, August 13, 1921, *Documents on British Foreign Policy*, First Series, vol. 14, pp. 373–377.

10. Fifield, "Secretary Hughes," p. 375; Koo to Yen, October 26, 1921, *Shandong Wenti*, p. 331;Yen-Schurman conversation, September 24, 1921, Waijiao dangan, RG 03–11, box 1:4.

11. Koo to Yen, October 26, 1921, *Shandong Wenti*, no. 377, pp. 332–333; Curzon to Alston, October 24, 1921, *Documents on British Foreign Policy*, First Series, vol. 14, pp. 451–452.

12. "Memorandum of the Attitude of China in the Washington Conference," n.d., Private Memoranda, Lansing Papers, (microfilm), Library of Congress; Williams Diary, July 26 & October 24, 1921; Pugach, "American Friendship for China," p. 75.

13. Geddes to Curzon, September 21, 1921, *Documents on British Foreign Policy*, First Series, vol. 14, pp. 400–401.

14. The Reminiscences of Tsiang T'ing-fu, p. 85; Koo Hui-lan, *Autobiography*, p. 158.

15. Pollard, *China's Foreign Relations*, pp. 205–209; Dreifort, *Myopic Grandeur*, pp. 36–37; Dayer, *Bankers and Diplomats in China*, p. 98; Balfour to Foreign Office, November 19, 1921, FO 371, 6660/F4252/2635/10.

16. Koo Oral History, vol. 2D: 275.

17. Balfour to Foreign Office, November 19, 1921, *Documents on British Foreign Policy*, First Series, vol. 14, p. 488; Lansing Diary, February 10, 1922, Lansing Papers, Princeton; December 10, 1921; Castle Diary, February 8, 1922, Castle Papers; Sullivan, *The Great Adventure at Washington*, pp. 254–256.

18. Alston to Curzon, November 28, 1921, *Documents on British Foreign Policy*, First Series, vol. 14, p. 518; Newton to Alston, November 22, 1921, Tel. 349, FO 371.

19. Lansing Diary, December 4, 1921.

20. MacMurray to Hughes, November 23, 1921, Hughes Papers, box 161; For an overview of these meetings, see, Pollard, *China's Foreign Relations*, pp. 210–219; Borg, *American Policy and the Chinese Revolution*, pp. 9–11; MacNair, *Modern Far Eastern International Relations*, p. 191.

21. Balfour to Curzon, November 25, 1921, *Documents on British Foreign Policy*, First Series, vol. 14, p. 511; Hughes to Schurman, November 25, 1921, *FRUS: 1922*, vol. 2, p. 934; Schurman to Hughes, November 27, 1921, *Ibid.*, p. 936.

22. MacMurray to Hughes, November 25, 1921, Hughes Papers; Hughes to Schurman, December 7, 1921, *FRUS: 1922*, vol. 2, pp. 274–275; Lansing Diary, December 1, 1921.

23. Lansing Diary, January 25, 1922; For a fuller account of Koo's work, see, Chu, *V.K. Wellington Koo*, pp. 37–66; Koo Oral History, vol. 2D: 283–293; *Ibid.*, vol. 3I: 283.

24. Hughes to Schurman, January 22, 1922, *FRUS: 1922*, vol. 2, p. 943; Hughes to Schurman, January 25, 1922, *Ibid.*, p. 945; Lansing Diary, January 23 and 26, 1922; Williams Diary, January 19 and 25, 1922.

25. Borg, *American Policy and the Chinese* Revolution, p. 12; For the argument that a "new order" was created, see, Iriye, *After Imperialism*, pp. 15–21; An alternative view is found in Fung, *The Diplomacy of Imperial Retreat*, pp. 18–21; Elleman, *Diplomacy and Deception*, p. 119.

26. Borg, *American Policy and the Chinese Revolution*, pp. 12–13; The Reminiscences of Tsiang T'ing-fu, p. 87.

27. Sheridan, "The Warlord Era," p. 308; Zhang, *Beiyang zhengfu guowu cengli liezhuan*, pp. 251–269; Dreyer, *China at War*, pp. 83–88, 97–102; King to Moore, June 7, 1922, Moore Papers, box 48.

28. Fung, *The Diplomacy of Imperial Retreat*, pp. 27–29; Sun, *Cai Yuanpei xiansheng nianpu zhuanji*, pp. 605–606; Allitto, *The Last Confucian*, pp. 135–136.

29. "Peking's Search for a Premier," *North-China Herald* (August 26, 1922): 582; "China's Financial Independence," *Ibid.* (September 16, 1922): 792.

30. Grieder, *Hu Shih*, p. 204, fn. 58; Zhang, *Liang Qichao yu minguo zhengzhi*, pp. 235–236; Hu Shi, *Hu Shi de riji*, p. 388; Quote in Waldron, "Warlordism Versus Federalism," p. 117; See also, Grieder, *Hu Shih*, pp. 194–195.

31. Waldron, "The Warlord," pp. 1094–1095; Bergere, *The Golden Age*, p. 249; Li, *Zuijin sanshi nian*, pp. 463–471; Waldron, "Warlordism Versus Federalism," pp. 124–125; Nathan, *Peking Politics*, p. 201.

32. Kagen, "From Revolutionary Iconoclasm to National Revolution," p. 68; Koo, "Some Aspects of China's Permanent Constitution," pp. 182–185; Koo, "China and Great Britain," *North-China Herald* (May 27, 1922): 625; *Ibid.*, (May 20, 1922): 538; Koo Oral History, vol. 3: 143–144.

33. Charlotte Furth, "Intellectual Change," p. 403; Jerome Chen, "The Chinese Communist Movement to 1927," in *Ibid.*, pp. 509–510, 517; Kagen, "From Revolutionary Iconoclasm to National Revolution," pp. 67–69.

34. Koo, *Autobiography*, p. 197; Wou, *Militarism in Modern China*, pp. 151–197; Koo Oral History, vol. 3: 65; Koo Oral History, vol. 3:17; Leong, *Sino-Soviet*, p. 218; Nathan, *Peking Politics*, pp. 189–193.

35. Li, *Zuijin sanshi nian*, p. 519; Sheridan, *Chinese Warlord*, p. 119, fn.

36. *North-China Herald* (August 26, 1922): 582; *Ibid.* (September 16, 1922): 792; *Ibid.* (June 24, 1922): 871; Nathan, *Peking Politics*, p. 193.

37. Wou, *Militarism in Modern China*, pp. 168–173; Cohen, *The Chinese Connection*,

pp. 108–118; Stremski, "Britain and Warlordism in China," pp. 92–93; Dayer, *Bankers and Diplomats*, ch. 4.

38. Leong, *Sino-Soviet*, pp. 217–218; *North-China Herald* (December 2, 1922): 569; *Ibid.* (December 9, 1922): 642; Nathan, *Peking Politics*, pp. 197–200; Koo Oral History, vol. 3: 63.

39. Koo Oral History, 3H: 227–230, 234–238, 240; Wang, "Patriotic Christian Leader," pp. 37–40.

40. Iriye, *After Imperialism*, pp. 25–28; Yen, *East-West Kaleidoscope*, p. 131.

41. For an account of the incident, see Nonzinski, *Outrage at Lincheng;* Macleay to MacDonald, April 22, 1924, in *British Documents on Foreign Affairs*, vol. 19, pp. 189–191.

42. "Dr. Koo's Appeal for Patience," *North-China Herald* (July 28, 1923): 226; Koo Oral History, vol. 3G: 162; Macleay to MacDonald, April 22, 1924, in *British Documents on Foreign Affairs*, vol. 19, pp. 175, 190.

43. Koo Oral History, vol. 3G: 162–164; Schurman to Hughes, September 28, 1923, *FRUS: 1923*, vol. 1, p. 694.

44. *North-China Herald* (September 29, 1923): 890; Also, Rodney Gilbert, "Dr. Wellington Koo's Rejection of the Lincheng Note," *Ibid.* (October 6, 1923): 16–17; For Koo's note, see, *Ibid.* (September 29, 1923): 894–896.

45. Macleay to MacDonald, April 22, 1924, in *British Documents on Foreign Affairs*, vol. 19, pp. 175, 191.

46. See, Iriye, *After Imperialism*, p. 29; Chan, "The Lincheng Incident," pp. 172–173,186; Bergere, *The Golden Age*, pp. 267–268; Hughes to Schurman, October 4, 1923, *FRUS: 1923*, vol. 1, p. 703; DeAngelis, "Resisting Intervention," pp. 401–416.

47. Schurman to Hughes, February 16, 1924, *FRUS: 1924*, vol. 1, pp. 521–522. Quotes from p. 522.

48. Aide-Memoire (in English), Waijiao dangan, RG 03–34, box 3:1; Shi to Foreign Ministry, March 11, 1924, (in English), *Ibid.*, box 3:2; Memorandum, March 27, 1924, *Ibid.;* Macleay to MacDonald, April 22, 1924, in *British Documents on Foreign Affairs*, vol. 19, pp. 191–192; Iriye, *After Imperialism*, p. 29.

49. Fitzgerald, *Awakening China*, pp. 143–144.

50. Leong, *Sino-Soviet*, pp. 213–214; Iriye, *After Imperialism*, pp. 37–41; Chan, "Sun Yat-sen and the Origins of the Kuomintang Reorganization," p. 27.

51. Fitzgerald, "The Misconceived Revolution," pp. 326, 329; For an overview of the revolution, see, Wilbur, "The Nationalist Revolution," pp. 527–720; For more on the warlords, see, Sheridan, "The Warlord Era," pp. 284–321.

52. Hunt, "The May Fourth Era: China's Place in the World," pp. 182–188; Sun, *China and the Origins*, pp. 2–5; Sharman, *Sun Yat-sen*, p. 302; Fung, *The Diplomacy of Imperial Retreat*, pp. 30–32.

53. Macleay to MacDonald, April 22, 1924, in *British Documents on Foreign Affairs*, vol. 19, pp. 176–178; Palairet to Chamberlain, May 7, 1925, *Ibid.*, p. 249; Atwell, *British Mandarins and Chinese Reformers*, pp. 124–133; Koo Oral History, vol. 3G: 201–203.

54. Whiting, *Soviet Policies in China*, pp. 212–218.

55. Palairet to Chamberlain, May 7, 1925, *British Documents on Foreign Affairs*, vol. 19, p. 259; Schurman to Hughes, March 11, 1924, *FRUS: 1924*, vol. 1, p. 478; Schurman to Hughes, March 21, 1924, *Ibid.*, p. 483; Koo Oral History, vol. 3G: 176–177; Leong, *Sino-Soviet*, pp. 252–253, 259, 263, 266, 267–268; Jin, *Gu Weijun zhuan*, p. 110.

56. Koo Oral History, vol. 3G: 182, 184; *Jiaoyun zazhi* (Education Magazine), vol. 16, no. 5, pp. 1–2. Reprinted in *Zhonghua minguo shishi jiyao, 1925*, part 1, p. 700; Li, *Cong ronggong dao qingdang*, pp. 89–91.

57. Leong, *Sino-Soviet*, pp. 269–270; See also, Bell to Hughes, May 15, 1924, *FRUS: 1924*, vol. 1, pp. 490–491.
58. Koo Oral History, vol. 3G: 187–190, 192; Koo to Moore, July 24, 1924, Moore Papers, box 52; Basil Newton minute, May 21, 1924, FO 371/10243/F1749/19/10.
59. Koo to Moore, July 24, 1924; Leong, *Sino-Soviet*, pp. 271–272, 275, 276–290; Whiting, *Soviet Policies*, p. 224; Waldron, *From War to Nationalism*, pp. 178–179; Elleman, *Diplomacy and Deception*, pp. 120–127, 180–181; Chu, *V.K. Wellington Koo*, p. 117.
60. Koo Diary, July 23, 1944.
61. Mayer to MacMurray, July 10, 1924, MacMurray Papers, box 24; Blakeslee to MacMurray, September 25, 1924, box 25; *Dongfang zazhi* (The Eastern Miscellany) vol. 21, no. 14, p. 30.
62. "Notes on David Yui's Remarks at Dinner Given to Foreign Secretaries at Bankers' Club, January 11, 1926," Young Men's Christian Association Archives, University of Minnesota, Minneapolis. (The author is grateful to Peter Chen-main Wang for pointing out this source.)
63. See, Cai Hesen, "Qing kan ying mei diguo zhuyi zeyang zai beijing gonggu tamen guyong di waijiao xi zhengfu" (Look how the British and American imperialists foster the "Diplomatic Clique" government in Beijing, which is in their employ!), *Xiangdao zhoubao* (The Guide Weekly), no. 5 (October 11, 1922): 44; idem., "Beijing zhengbian yu ying mei" (Britain, America and the new Beijing government), *Ibid.*, nos. 31, 32 (July 11, 1923): 230; Chunmu, "Gu Weijun jiu waizhang zhi he zhongguo guojie diwei" (Foreign Minister Wellington Koo and China's international position), *Ibid.*, no. 34 (August 1, 1923): 256; Zhenyu, "Guomindang benbu buying zhaodan meiguo zhanluo jia," (American aggression specialists should not be welcomed into the Guomindang), *Ibid.*, no. 41 (September 23, 1923): 311.
64. Renzheng, "Meiguo qiaoshang tuanti zhi dui hua zhuzhang" (American business groups and their view of China), *Ibid.*, no. 33 (July 18, 1923): 247–248; Cai Hesen, "Meiguo jiguan bao bianhu chengren Beijing zhengfu de liyo" (The reason why America defended its recognition of the Beijing government), *Ibid.*, no. 45 (November 7, 1923): 341–342; Mianhui, "Shuerman yu meiguo dui hua de waijiao," (Schurmann and America's policy toward China), *Ibid.*, no. 97 (December 31, 1924): 811–813; Qu Qiubai, "Taiping yang wenti yu meiguo qiandan li de zhongguo" (The Pacific Question and the China in America's moneybag) *Qianfeng* (The Vanguard), no. 2 (1923): 9–16; Chen Duxiu, "1923 nian lieqiang dui hua zhi huigu" (Looking back on the great powers and China in 1923), *Ibid.*, no. 3 (1924): 1–8.
65. Waldron, "The Warlord," p. 1088.
66. Strand, *Rickshaw Beijing*, pp. 182–192; Ding Wenjiang et al, *Liang rengong xiansheng nianpu changbian chugao*, vol. 3: 672–673; Chen, *China and the West*, p. 420.
67. Strand, *Rickshaw Beijing*, pp. 192–195; MacMurray to Kellogg, May 14, 1926, *FRUS: 1926*, vol. 1: 616; Iriye, *After Imperialism*, pp. 63–86 passim; Waldron, *From War to Nationalism*, ch. 8.
68. Lampson to Chamberlain, January 18, 1927, *British Documents on Foreign Affairs*, vol. 19, pp. 378–379; See also, FO minute on "Who's Who in China," February 10, 1927, FO 371/12473/F1398/10; Strand, *Rickshaw Beijing*, pp. 8, 286.
69. *Zongtong*, vol. 1, p. 242; Fung, *Diplomacy of Imperial Retreat*, pp. 83–85, 157; Idem., "Nationalist Foreign Policy," p. 190; Wilbur, "The Nationalist Revolution," pp. 527–721.
70. Strand, *Rickshaw Beijing*, pp. 222, 223–224; McCormack, *Chang Tso-lin in Northeast China*, p. 210.

71. T'ang, "Britain and Warlordism in China," pp. 207–229; Fung, *The Diplomacy of Imperial Retreat*, pp. 101–104, 105–107; Lampson Diary, December 28 & December 30, 1926, vol. 1, Sir Miles Lampson Papers; Lampson to FO, December 29, 1926, FO 371/ 11664/F5807/10/10.

72. Byrne, "The Dismissal of Sir Francis Aglen," pp. 8, 27–28, 31–33.

73. Koo Oral History, 3F: 121.

74. MacMurray to Kellogg, February 5, 1927, *FRUS: 1927*, vol. 2, pp. 458–460.

75. Byrne, "The Dismissal of Sir Francis Aglen," p. 36; MacMurray to Kellogg, February 8, 1927, *FRUS: 1927*, pp. 461–462; Koo Oral History, vol. 3F: 127; T'ang, "Britain and Warlordism," pp. 213–215; Yen, *East-West Kaleidoscope*, p. 166.

76. Lampson Diary, February 25, 1927; The extent of Lampson's anger is captured in Atkins, *Informal Empire in Crisis*, p. 36.

77. Koo Oral History, vol. 3F: 129–131, 136; Bickers, *Britain in China*, pp. 121–122.

78. Lampson to FO, February 23, 1927, FO 371/12402/F1777/2/10; Koo Oral History, vol. 3G: 211, 212.

79. *Ibid.*, pp. 213–214; Fishel, *The End of Extraterritoriality in China*, pp. 127–129; "Foreigners Fear for Rights in China," *New York Times* (November 9, 1926): 4; "Peking Coup Seen on Belgian Treaty," *Ibid.* (December 19, 1926), sect. 2, p. 3.

80. Wang, "Beijing zhengfu xiuyue yuandong jianlun," pp. 140–143; Yue, "Gaiyue waijiao," pp. 160–164; Lampson to Chamberlain, p. 379.

81. *New York Times* (March 15, 1927): 5.

82. Lampson to FO, February 23, 1927, FO 371/12402/F1777/2/10; Iriye, *After Imperialism*, pp. 115–117.

83. Fourth meeting of Sino-French negotiations, February 9, 1927, (in English), Waijiao dangan, RG 03–23, box 8:1; Seventh meeting of Sino-French negotiations, April 5, 1927, *Ibid.*

84. Cohen, *Empire Without Tears*, pp. 80–81; The resolution is printed in *FRUS: 1927*, vol. 2, pp. 341–343; Shi-Kellogg conversation, January 24, 1927, *Ibid.*, p. 54; Kellogg to Mayer, January 25, 1927, *Ibid.*, p. 350; Shi-Kellogg conversation, January 27, 1927, *Ibid.*, pp. 353–354. Quote from p. 354; MacMurray to Kellogg, February 10, 1927, *FRUS: 1927*, pp. 360–361; MacMurray to Kellogg, October 21, 1927, *Ibid.*, p. 363; Iriye, *After Imperialism*, pp. 106–107.

85. Strand, *Rickshaw Beijing*, p. 11.

86. Lampson to Tientsin, July 13, 1928, and Frank Ashton-Gwatkin minute, July 13, 1928, FO 371/13236/F3707/3707/10; Also, Lampson Diary, July 13, 1928.

87. Lampson to FO, no. 886 (6/91 A) August 2, 1928, FO 371/13236/F5437/3707/10; Lampson to Foreign Office, July 24, 1928, FO 371/13236/F5437/3707/10; "Comments on Current Events, September 24–October 7, 1929," October 9, 1929, *U.S. Military Intelligence*, reel 1.

88. Fung, "Nationalist Foreign Policy," pp. 190–194; Iriye, *After Imperialism*, pp. 228–229.

89. Clifford, *Spoilt Children of Empire*, pp. 13–14; Bergere, *The Golden Age*, pp. 248–258.

Chapter 4. China, Japanese Imperialism, and Collective Security, 1931–1937

1. See, Jenkins to Johnson, February 2, 1931, *Internal Affairs of China, 1930–1939* reel 3; Perkins to Stimson, March 18, 1931, *Ibid.*; Koo Oral History, vol. 3J: 308–309.

2. Iriye, *After Imperialism*, pp. 214, 284–285, 290–293; Coble, *Facing Japan*, pp. 11–27; Jordan, *Chinese Boycotts versus Japanese Bombs*, pp. 7–15.

3. Diary Entry, July 15, 1929, *Zongtong*, vol. 2: 25; Chiang to Zhang, July 27, 1929, *Ibid.*, p. 29.

4. Eastman, "Nationalist China during the Nanking Decade, 1927–1937," pp. 1–14; Chen, "The Communist Movement, 1927–1937," pp. 53–90; Koo Oral History, vol. 3J: 305–306; Ingram to FO, tel. 70, February 17, 1931, FO 371/15447/F1101/10; Lampson to FO, June 6, 1931, FO 371/15474/F5373/69/10.

5. Jordan, "The Place of Chinese Disunity in Japanese Army Strategy," pp. 44–54.

6. Meeting chaired by Chiang Kai-shek, September 21, 1931, *Dui ri kangzhan shiqi*, vol. 1, part 1, p. 281; Sun, *China and the Origins*, p. 21; Wu, "Contending Political Forces," pp. 57–58.

7. Foreign Ministry to Shi, September 21, 1931, in vol. 6, *Kuilei zuzhi*, vol. 6, part 1, no. 2, p. 264; Nish, *Japan's Struggle with Internationalism*, pp. 4–6, 16–17, 38; Yen, *East-West Kaleidoscope*, p. 179; Koo Oral History, vol. 3J: 317–318; Lampson to the FO, October 7, 1931, *Documents on British Foreign Policy*, Second Series, vol. 8: 716; Lampson to FO, tel. 445, October 1, 1931, FO 371/15490/F5362/1391/10.

8. Nish, *Japan's Struggle with Internationalism*, pp. 44–45, 49–54; Lampson to Simon, November 22, 1931, *Documents on British Foreign Policy*, Second Series, vol. 8, pp. 941–942; Lampson to Simon, November 24, 1931, *Ibid.*, p. 950; Koo-Wilden conversation, November 25, 1931, Koo Papers, box 4; Koo-Lampson conversation, November 26, 1931, *Ibid.*; Koo-Trautmann conversation, November 28, 1931, *Ibid.*; Koo-Peck conversation, December 13, 1931, *Internal Affairs of China, 1930–39*, reel. 4.

9. Reading to Lampson, October 9, 1931, *Documents on British Foreign Policy*, Second Series, vol. 8, p. 733; Lampson to Reading, October 10, 1931, *Ibid.*, pp. 745–746; Lampson to Ingram, October 11, 1931, *Ibid.*, pp. 750–751; Thorne, *The Limits of Foreign Policy*, pp. 137–140, 146–147, 155–162; Dreifort, *Myopic Grandeur*, pp. 47–52.

10. Chiang to Zhang, October 6, 1931, *Dui ri kangzhan shiqi*, part 1, p. 291; Haslam, *The Soviet Union and the Threat from the East*, pp. 5–8; Ulam, *Expansion and Coexistence*, pp. 200–201.

11. Jordan, *Chinese Boycotts versus Japanese Bombs*, pp. 240–241; Koo Oral History, vol. 3J: 323, 332–333; Lampson to Sir John Simon, December 1, 1931, FO 371/15474/F7832/69/10.

12. Comments on Current Events, December 8, 1931, *U.S. Military Intelligence Reports*, reel 1; Koo Oral History, vol. 3J: 331; Lampson to Simon, November 25, 1931, *Documents on British Foreign Policy*, Second Series, vol. 8, pp. 954–955; Tyrell to Simon, December 6, 1931, *Ibid.*, pp. 989–990; Forbes to Stimson, December 9, 1931, Castle Papers, box 2, folder 157; Shaw to Stimson, December 10, 1931, *Ibid.*; Stimson to Grew, December 11, 1931, *Ibid.*; Tyrrell to Simon, December 8, 1931, *Documents on British Foreign Policy*, Second Series, vol. 8, p. 998.

13. Jordan, *Chinese Boycotts versus Japanese Bombs*, pp. 242–245; Johnson to Stimson, December 15, 1931, *FRUS: 1931*, vol. 3, p. 684; Reminiscences of Tsiang T'ing-fu, p. 143; Lampson to Simon, January 19, 1932, *Documents on British Foreign Policy*, Second Series, vol. 9, p. 165.

14. Jordan, *Chinese Boycotts versus Japanese Bombs*, pp. 250–254; Coble, *Facing Japan*, pp. 37–38.

15. Jordan, *Chinese Boycotts versus Japanese Bombs*, pp. 277–285, 301–310, 315–322, 325–326; Coble, *Facing Japan*, pp. 39–50; Nish, *Japan's Struggle with Internationalism*, pp. 90–101.

16. Koo-McCoy conversation, September 22, 1932, Koo Papers, box 4; Koo-Peck conversation, December 13, 1931, *Ibid.*; Nish, *Japan's Struggle with Internationalism*, p. 252,

fn. 30; Johnson to Stimson, January 11, 1932, *FRUS: 1932*, vol. 3: 21; Johnson to Stimson, January 20, 1932, *Ibid.*, pp. 38, 39; Johnson to Stimson, February 14, 1932, *Ibid.*, p. 328; Johnson to Stimson, February 24, 1932, *Ibid.*, pp. 438–439.

17. Jordan, *Chinese Boycotts versus Japanese Bombs*, pp. 264–265, 322; Thorne, *The Limits of Foreign Policy*, pp. 210–211, 233–235 238, 248–269; Borg, *The United States and the Far Eastern Crisis*, pp. 8–15; LaFeber, *The Clash*, pp. 171–172; Dreifort, *Myopic Grandeur*, pp. 62–69.

18. Nish, *Japan's Struggle with Internationalism*, pp. 123–125; Ingram to FO, November 15, 1932, FO 371/17060/F94/94/10. See also, Confidential Police Report enclosed in No. 394, November 8, 1932, FO 371/17060.

19. Koo Diary, May 19, May 22, May 20, 1932, June 1; Koo Oral History, vol. 3J: 343–344, 349; Nish, *Japan's Struggle with Internationalism*, pp. 129–132.

20. Chu, *V.K. Wellington Koo*, p. 131; Koo-Pignatti conversation, January 26, 1933, Koo Papers, box 44, folder 12; Koo Diary, May 21, 1932; Koo to Foreign Ministry, August 5, 1932, *Kuilei zuzhi*, vol. 6, part 1, no. 25, pp. 592–609.

21. Wang, "Wang Jingwei and the Policy Origins of the 'Peace Movement,'" pp. 23–26; Coble, *Facing Japan*, pp. 56–69.

22. Koo-Wilden conversation, June 7, 1932, Koo Papers, box 4; Koo-Wilden conversation, August 12, 1932, *Ibid.*; Koo-Johnson conversation, August 5, 1932, *Ibid.*; Koo-Johnson conversation, August 12, 1932, *Ibid.*

23. Koo Oral History, vol. 4A: 15–16, 36; Koo-McCoy conversation, September 22, 1932, Koo Papers, box 4.

24. Nish, *Japan's Struggle with Internationalism*, pp. 166–167, 175–177; Sun, *China and the Origins*, pp. 34–35; see also, Ingram to Simon, October 31, 1932, *Documents on British Foreign Policy*, vol. 11: 42–44.

25. Koo Oral History, vol. 4A: 45; Koo to Chinese Embassy, Washington, November 5, 1933, Koo Papers, box 39; Koo-Lytton conversation, March 30, 1932, *Ibid.*, box 4, folder 2; Koo to Nanjing, November, 1932, *Ibid.*, box 8. No date mentioned in dispatch; Koo-Lester conversation, January 2, 1933, *Ibid.*, box 44, folder 13.

26. Nish, *Japan's Struggle with Internationalism*, pp. 184, 190–197; Koo to Foreign Ministry, November 6, 1932, Koo Papers, box 39.

27. Thorne, *The Limits of Foreign Policy*, pp. 293–296; Memorandum by Sir J. Pratt respecting the Sino-Japanese Dispute, December 5, 1932, *Documents on British Foreign Policy*, vol. 11: 111.

28. Nish, *Japan's Struggle with Internationalism*, pp. 197–200.

29. Coble, *Facing Japan*, pp. 90–95; Thorne, *The Limits of Foreign Policy*, pp. 328–329.

30. Koo Oral History, vol. 4B: 218–219, 223, 224–225; Koo-Osusky conversation, January 4, 1933, Koo Papers, box 44, folder 12; Koo-Cot conversation, January 5, 1933, *Ibid.*; Memorandum by Lord Cecil, October 8, 1932, FO; Koo-Edge conversation, January 3, 1933, Koo Papers, box 44, folder 12.

31. Nish, *Japan's Struggle with Internationalism*, pp. 202–203, 207–214; Thorne, *The Limits of Foreign Policy*, pp. 330, 335–336, 345–368; Dreifort, *Myopic Grandeur*, pp. 82–83; Koo-Eden conversation, February 8, 1933, Koo Papers, Box 44, folder 12.

32. Nish, *Japan's Struggle with Internationalism*, pp. 221–222; Haslam, *The Soviet Union and the Threat from the East*, p. 19.

33. Koo-Painleve conversation, January 26, 1933, *Ibid.*; Koo-Simon conversation, March 17, 1933, Koo Papers, box 44, folder 13; Koo-Simon conversation, March 17, 1933, *Ibid.*; See also, Koo-Davis conversation, April 22, 1933, *Ibid.*, folder 12.

34. Koo Oral History, vol. 4A: 168–169; B:208–209; Koo and Quo to Foreign Ministry, April 5, 1933, Koo Papers, box 9; Koo-Yen-Quo Memorandum, "The International
Situation and the Sino-Japanese Conflict," April 24, 1933, Koo Papers, box 4.
35. Koo Oral History, vol. 4B: 263, 271, 278; Dreifort, *Myopic Grandeur*, pp. 90–91.
36. Coble, *Facing Japan*, pp. 98–119; Sun, *China and the Origins*, pp. 41–43; Wang,
"Wang Jingwei and the Policy Origins of the 'Peace Movement,'" pp. 26–28.
37. Koo Oral History, vol. 4B: 287, 290, 294; Soong, Yen, Quo and Koo memorandum, "Summary of a Discussion Relative to the Formulation of a Foreign Policy for the
Immediate Future," June 30, 1933, Koo Papers, box 23, folder 1.
38. Wang, "Wang Jingwei and the Policy Origins of the 'Peace Movement,'" pp. 28–29;
Kirby, *Germany and Republican China*, pp. 217–223; Fox, *Germany and the Far Eastern
Crisis*, pp. 52–63.
39. Endicott, *Diplomacy and Enterprise*, pp. 45–50; Dreifort, *Myopic Grandeur*, p. 97;
Borg, *The United States and the Far Eastern Crisis*, pp. 55–88; Sun, *China and the Origins*,
pp. 49–50; Coble, *Facing Japan*, pp. 149–162, 180–181.
40. Koo to Hussey, September 15, 1933, Koo Papers, box 28, folder 2; Paul K. Whang,
"Will W.W. Yen and Wellington Koo Return to Their Posts?," *China Weekly Review*, 67
(July 28, 1934): 350; Koo Oral History, vol. 4C: 390, 392, 393, 399.
41. Koo was possibly referring to the Tanaka Memorial that is now considered a forg-
ery. See Stephan, "The Tanaka Memorial," pp. 733–745; Cadogan Diaries, January 16,
1936, Churchill Archives Center; Cadogan to Eden, January 17, 1936, FO 371/20242/
F1216/96/10; S. Harcourt-Smith minute, March 5, 1936, *Ibid.*
42. Cohen, *America's Response*, pp. 113–116; Endicott, *Diplomacy and Enterprise*, pp.
59–78; Parker, *Chamberlain and Appeasement*, pp. 43–44.
43. Koo Diary, June 11, 1936; November 2, 1936; Haslam, *The Soviet Union and the
Threat from the East*, pp. 32–34; Marks, *Wind over Sand*, pp. 21–27, 64.
44. Carley, *1939*, pp. 14–18; Haslam, *The Soviet Union and the Threat from the East*, p.
61; Dreifort, *Myopic Grandeur*, pp. 98–99.
45. Koo Diary, July 5, 1936.
46. Coble, *Facing Japan*, pp. 297–303; Duus, *Rise of Modern Japan*, pp. 213–214; Iriye,
Origins of the Second World War in Asia, pp. 23, 32–33; Nester, *Power Across the Pacific*, p.
116; Haslam, *The Soviet Union and the Threat from the East*, p. 80.
47. Haggie, *Brittania at Bay*, ch. 4; Endicott, *Diplomacy and Enterprise*, pp. 52–59; Weber, *The Hollow Years*, ch. 9; Young, *France and the Origins of the Second World War*, p. 60.
48. Koo Oral History, vol. 4D: 453; Sun, *China and the Origins*, pp. 70–74; Haslam,
The Soviet Union and the Threat from the East, pp. 54–64.
49. *Ibid.*, pp. 66–79; Coble, *Facing Japan*, pp. 309–335, 342–343, 352–354; Sun, *China
and the Origins*, pp. 70, 74–83; Koo Oral History, vol. 4D: 458–460; Koo Diary, December
21 & 22, 1936; Eastman, *Abortive Revolution*, pp. 269–270; Idem., "Nationalist China
During the Sino-Japanese War," p. 126.
50. Koo-Leger conversation, May 21, 1937, Koo Papers, box 45; Koo Diary, June 4 &
11, 1936; November 2, 1936; Koo Oral History, vol. 4D: 447, 456, 461–462.
51. Koo-Sourits conversation, July 2, 1937, Koo Papers, box 45; Koo-Delbos conversation, July 13, 1937, *Ibid.*; Koo Oral History, vol. 4E: 496–513 *passim*.
52. Harrison, "A Neutralization Plan for the Pacific," pp. 47–72; Endicott, *Diplomacy
and Enterprise*, pp. 163–165; Trotter, *Britain and East Asia*, pp. 199–201, 202–203; Dreifort,
Myopic Grandeur, p. 103; Haslam, *The Soviet Union and the Threat from the East*, pp. 88–89.
53. Koo Diary, March 8 & 18, 1937; Koo Oral History, vol. 4E: n.p.

Chapter 5. Sino-Japanese War and the Specter of Sellout, 1937–1941

1. Coble, *Facing Japan*, pp. 370–374; Koo Diary, July 12 & 13, 1937.

2. *Ibid.*, July 25, 29, 30 and 31, 1937; Koo Oral History, vol. 4E: 525, 530, 536, 537–538, 553–554, 574; Sun, *China and the Origins*, p. 90.

3. Koo Diary, July 25, 1937; Koo-Sourits conversation, July 30, 1937, Koo Papers, box 45; Koo Oral History, vol. 4E: 542, 554–555.

4. Koo Diary, July 27, 1937; Bullitt to Hull, July 28, 1937, *FRUS: 1937*, vol. 3, pp. 288–289; Koo Oral History, vol. 4E: 544–545.

5. Haslam, *The Soviet Union and the Threat From the East*, pp. 90, 92–94; Garver, *Chinese-Soviet Relations*, pp. 18–23; Sun, *China and the Origins*, pp. 109–113; Lee, *Britain and the Sino-Japanese War*, pp. 32, 38–39; Clifford, *Retreat From China*, p. 28.

6. *Ibid.*, p. 93; Eden to Knatchbull-Hugessen, July 30, 1937, *BDFA*, vol. 45, p. 54; Bullitt to Hull, August 26, 1937, *FRUS: 1937*, vol. 3, p. 477; Koo Oral History, vol. 4E: 607.

7. Koo Diary, September 10 & 11, 1937; See note of Koo-Bullitt conversation attached to Koo-Delbos conversation, July 13, 1937, Koo Papers, box 45; Koo-Delbos, July 16, 1937, *Ibid.*; Koo Oral History, vol. 4E: 529, 531; Bucknell to Hull, September 15, 1937, *Ibid.*, vol. 4: 19; Koo Oral History, vol. 4E: 608–610, 613–614, 626; Shai, *Origins of the War in the East*, pp. 67–70; Dreifort, *Myopic Grandeur*, pp. 105–106; Delbos quote found on p. 106; Laffey, "French Far Eastern Policy in the 1930s," p. 133; Clifford, *Retreat From China*, pp. 36–37; Lee, *Britain and the Sino-Japanese War*, pp. 51–52; Haslam, *The Soviet Union and the Threat from the East*, pp. 95–96.

8. Koo Diary, September 11 & 12, 1937; Koo Oral History, vol. 4E: 627; Koo-Delbos conversation, September 10, 1937, Koo Papers, box 45.

9. Koo Diary, September 13 & 14, 1937; Koo Oral History, vol. 4E: 633–634; Also, Sun, *China and the Origins*, p. 93.

10. Edmond to the Foreign Office, September 17, 1937, *Documents on British Foreign Policy*, Second Series, vol. 21, p. 327; Also, Bucknell to Hull, September 16, 1937, *FRUS: 1937*, vol. 4, pp. 20, 21; Edmond to the Foreign Office, September 18, 1937, *Documents on British Foreign Policy*, Second Series, vol. 21, p. 330.

11. Koo Oral History, vol. 4E: 650, 655, 659–660, 664, 665–666; Harrison to Hull, September 28, 1937, *FRUS: 1937*, vol. 4, p. 45; Harrison to Hull, September 29, 1937, *Ibid.*, p. 47; Edmond to the Foreign Office, September 30, 1937, *Documents on British Foreign Policy*, Second Series, vol. 21, pp. 356–357; Shai, *Origins of the War in the East*, pp. 70–71, 74, 76.

12. Harrison to Hull, October 1, 1937, *FRUS: 1937*, vol. 4, p. 49; Koo Oral History, vol. 4E: 667–668; Clifford, *Retreat from China*, pp. 37–38; Shai, *Origins of the War*, pp. 79–82; Lee, *Britain and the Sino-Japanese War*, pp. 53–54.

13. Harrison to Hull, October 5, 1937, *FRUS: 1937*, vol. 4, pp. 55–57. Quotes from pp. 56, 57; Edmond to Eden, October 5, 1937, *Documents on British Foreign Policy*, Second Series, vol. 21, p. 367.

14. Koo-Delbos conversation, July 28, 1937, Koo Papers, box 45; Koo-Wilson conversation, October 19, 1937, *Ibid.*; Koo-Delbos conversation, August 2, 1937, *Ibid.*; Koo-Lukasiewicz conversation, September 3, 1937, *Ibid.*; Koo Oral History, vol. 4E: 772–776, 786, 789.

15. Foreign Ministry to Koo and Guo, October 24, 1937, in *Zuozhan jingguo*, vol. 2, part 2, pp. 206–207.

16. Bullitt to Hull, October 23, 1937, *FRUS: 1937*, vol. 3, p. 639; Koo-Litvinoff conversation, October 9, 1937, Koo Papers, box 45.

17. Davis-Hornbeck-Koo conversation, October 28, 1937, *Ibid.*; Koo-Davis conversation, November 15, 1937, *Ibid.*; Koo Oral History, vol. 4E: 792–802.

18. *Ibid.*, pp. 754, 808–809, 813–815.

19. *Ibid.*, pp. 815, 819–821; Davis to Hull, November 3, 1937, *FRUS: 1937*, vol. 4, p. 156.

20. Roosevelt memorandum, n.d., *Ibid.*, p. 85; Davis to Hull, November 2, 1937, *Ibid.*, vol. 4, p. 146; Davis to Hull, November 6, 1937, *Ibid.*, pp. 157–158; Davis to Hull, November 7, 1937, *Ibid.*, pp. 162–164; Davis to Hull, November 14, 1937, *Ibid.*, p. 184; MacDonald-Davis-Delbos conversation, November 3, 1937, *Documents on British Foreign Policy*, Second Series, vol. 21, p. 429; Koo-Davis conversation, November 15, 1937, Koo Papers, box 45; MacDonald-Davis-Delbos conversation, November 3, 1937, *Documents on British Foreign Policy*, Second Series, vol. 21, pp. 428–430.

21. Extract from Cabinet Conclusions, October 13, 1937, *Ibid.*, p. 392; Eden to Howe, November 19, 1937, *Ibid.*, p. 511.

22. Koo-Hornbeck conversation, November 17, 1937, Koo Papers, box 45; Chu, *V.K. Wellington Koo*, pp. 150–154; Sun, *China and the Origins*, p. 95; Clifford, *Retreat From China*, pp. 42–43; Dallek, *Franklin D. Roosevelt and American Foreign Policy*, p. 152.

23. Koo-Davis conversation, November 20, 1937, Koo Papers, box 45; See also, Davis to Hull, November 17, 1937, *FRUS: 1937*, vol. 4, pp. 204–205; Davis to Hull, November 19, 1937, *Ibid.*, p. 215; Davis to Hull, November 17, 1937, *Ibid.*, p. 200.

24. Koo Oral History, vol. 4E: 833–834; Haslam, *The Soviet Union and the Threat from the East*, pp. 96–100; Borg, *The United States and the Far Eastern Crisis*, pp. 415–417.

25. Clive to Eden, November 22, 1937, *Documents on British Foreign Policy*, Second Series, vol. 21, pp. 521–522; Clive to Eden, November 24, 1937, *Ibid.*, p. 528; Minute by Lord Cranborne, November 25, 1937, *Ibid.*, Second Series, vol. 21, p. 532; See also, Davis to Hull, November 21, 1937, *FRUS: 1937*, vol. 4, p. 221; Koo Oral History, vol. 4E: 916, 926, 927, 929; Borg, *The United States and the Far Eastern Crisis*, p. 438.

26. Koo-Davis conversation, December 2, 1937, *FRUS: 1937*, vol. 4, pp. 231–232; Koo-Blum conversation, November 30, 1937, Koo Papers, box 45.

27. Fox, *Germany and the Far Eastern Crisis*, pp. 229–259, 261, 265; Dreifort, *Myopic Grandeur*, pp. 132–133; Lee, *Britain and the Sino-Japanese War*, p. 75; Koo-Davis conversation, December 2, 1937, *FRUS: 1937*, vol. 4: 231–232; Garver, *Chinese-Soviet Relations*, pp. 23–27; Sun, *China and the Origins*, pp. 113–114, 187, fn. 48; Haslam, *The Soviet Union and the Threat from the East*, p. 100; Garver, "China's Wartime Diplomacy," p. 11.

28. Sun, *China and the Origins*, p. 97; Fox, *Germany and the Far Eastern Crisis*, pp. 277–290.

29. Barnhart, *Japan Prepares for Total War*, pp. 126–127; Parker, *Chamberlain and Appeasement*, pp. 105–107; Koo Oral History, vol. 4E: 906–907, 910, 912, 934–935; Koo Diary, Memoranda 1937.

30. Koo to Chiang, August 6, 1937, *Zhanshi waijiao*, vol. 3, part 2, p. 731; Koo to Chiang Kai-shek, October 18, 1937, *Ibid.*, p. 733; Koo to Chiang, October 18, 1937, *Ibid.*, pp. 735–736; Koo to Kung, June 3, 1938, *Ibid.*, pp. 741–742; Koo to Foreign Ministry, June 22, 1938, *Ibid.*, pp. 743–744; Koo to Foreign Ministry, June 28, 1938, *Ibid.*, pp. 744–745; Laffey, "French Far Eastern Policy in the 1930s," pp. 133–137, 149; Lee, *Britain and the Sino-Japanese War*, pp. 85–88; Best, *Britain, Japan and Pearl Harbor*, p. 55; Dreifort, *Myopic Grandeur*, pp. 120–121, 134–138, 144; Fox, *Germany and the Far Eastern Crisis*, pp. 315–317; Garver, *Chinese-Soviet Relations*, p. 38; Haslam, *The Soviet Union and the Threat from the East*, pp. 92–94. 103–107; Koo Diary, January 31, 1938.

31. Foreign Office to Lindsay, January 3, 1938, *Documents on British Foreign Policy*,

Second Series, vol. 21, pp. 632–633; Lindsay to Foreign Office, January 5, 1938, *Ibid.*, pp. 636–637; United Kingdom Delegation to Foreign Office, January 29, 1938, *Ibid.*, pp. 672–675; Koo Oral History, vol. 4–1: 60.

32. Koo Diary, February 1, 1938; Bucknell to Hull, January 29, 1938, *FRUS: 1938*,vol. 3, p. 496; Bucknell to Hull, January 31, 1938, *Ibid.*, pp. 498–499; Bucknell to Hull, February 2, 1938, *FRUS: 1938*, vol. 3, p. 503; Koo Oral History, vol. 4–1: 66, 73–75, 92.

33. Parker, *Chamberlain and Appeasement*, pp. 132–133, 139–140; Weber, *The Hollow Years*, p. 175; Young, *France and the Origins of the Second World War*, p. 29; Iriye, *The Origins of the Second World War in Asia*, pp. 50–52.

34. Zhang, "Chinese Policies toward the United States," p. 15; Sun, *China and the Origins*, pp. 101–104; Boyle, *China and Japan at War*, p. 191; Wang, "Wang Jingwei and the Policy Origins," p. 36.

35. Watt, *How War Came*, pp. 27–29; Parker, *Chamberlain and Appeasement*, ch. 8; Young, *France and the Origins of the Second World War*, pp. 29–31; Weber, *The Hollow Years*, pp. 176–177; Marks, *Wind Over Sand*, p. 146; Haslam, *The Soviet Union and the Search for Collective Security*, p. 167; Carley, *1939*, p. 72.

36. Koo-Litvinoff conversation, September 12, 1938, Koo Papers, box 46; Koo to Foreign Ministry, September 2, 1938, *Ibid.*, box 39; Bucknell to Hull, September 13, 1938, *FRUS: 1938*, vol. 3, p. 508; Bucknell to Hull, September 17, 1938, *Ibid.*, p. 509.

37. Koo, Butler, Paul-Bancour, Avenol conversation, September 26, 1938, Koo Papers, box 46; Also, Koo-Sandler conversation, September 13, 1938, *Ibid.*

38. Koo to Kung, October 4, 1938, *Ibid.*, box 39.

39. Speech by H.E. Dr. V.K. Wellington Koo at the Banquet of Peace at Paris, May 5, 1938, *Ibid.*, box 27, folder 63; Koo to Hu Shi, October 3, 1938, *Ibid.*, box 39; Koo Diary, October 10, 1938; August 31, 1939.

40. Sun, *China and the Origins*, pp. 105–106; Iriye, *Origins of the Second World War*, pp. 67–68; Bunker, *The Peace Conspiracy*, p. 89.

41. Huang and Yang, "Nationalist China's Negotiating Position During the Stalemate, 1938–1945," pp. 58, 60; Sun, *China and the Origins*, pp. 106–107; Koo Diary, 1938 Memoranda; Garver, "China's Wartime Diplomacy," pp. 8–9.

42. Garver, *Chinese-Soviet Relations*, pp. 78, 80–81.

43. Koo-Bonnet conversation, January 12, 1939, Koo Papers, box 46; Clifford, *Retreat From China*, pp. 94–95; Lee, *Britain and the Sino-Japanese War*, pp. 158–162; Iriye, *Origins of the Second World War*, pp. 70–71; Laffey, "French Far Eastern Policy in the 1930s," p. 141; Dallek, *Franklin D. Roosevelt*, p. 193; Schaller, *The U.S. Crusade in China*, pp. 17, 27–29, 35.

44. Dallek, *Franklin D. Roosevelt*, p. 179; Laffey, "French Far Eastern Policy in the 1930s," p. 142; Clifford, *Retreat From China*, pp. 100–101.

45. Diary Entry, April 15, 1939, *Zongtong*, vol. 4: 340; Diary Entry, April 25, 1939, *Ibid.*, pp. 346–347; Bucknell to Hull, January 17, 1939, *FRUS vol. 3: 1939*, pp. 330, 331; Memorandum, March 1939, Koo Papers, box 21, folder 27; Koo, *The Open Door Policy and World Peace*, p. 8; Garver, "China's Wartime Diplomacy," pp. 5, 12; Sun, *China and the Origins*, pp. 120–121; Clifford, *Retreat from China*, p. 133; Dreifort, *Myopic Grandeur*, p. 152.

46. Parker, *Chamberlain and Appeasement*, pp. 200–245; Carley, *1939*, pp. 116–117, 120, 133, 135, 256; Brendon, *The Dark Valley*, p. 680; Weber, *The Hollow Years*, pp. 260–261.

47. Dreifort, *Myopic Grandeur*, pp. 150, 168; Utley, *Going to War With Japan*, p. 56;

Lee, *Britain and the Sino-Japanese War,* pp. 177–178; Haslam, *The Soviet Union and the Threat from the East,* pp. 112–132.

48. Diary Entry, June 17, 1939, *Zongtong,* vol. 4: 371; Diary Entry, June 20, 1939, *Ibid.,* p. 373; Chiang to Roosevelt, July 20, 1939, *Zhanshi waijiao* part 1, pp. 82–86; Chiang to Roosevelt, July 20, 1939, *FRUS: 1939,* vol. 3, pp. 687–691; See, Clifford, *Retreat From China,* pp. 112–120; Shai, *Origins of the War in the Far East,* ch. 6; Lee, *Britain and the Sino-Japanese War,* pp. 190–191, 193; Parker, *Chamberlain and Appeasement,* pp. 253, 254; Koo Oral History, vol. 4–9: 673, 678; Laffey, "French Far Eastern Policy in the 1930s," pp. 144–145.

49. Lee, *Britain and the Sino-Japanese War,* pp. 195–196; Phipps to FO, tel 468, July 26, 1939, FO 371/23528/F7948/6457/10.

50. Lee, *Britain and the Sino-Japanese War,* pp. 196–197; Langer and Gleason, *The Challenge to Isolation,* p. 158; Dallek, *Franklin D. Roosevelt,* p. 195.

51. Koo-Leger conversation, July 27, 1939, Koo Papers, box 46; see also, Koo Oral History, vol. 4–9: 679, 682–683; Diary entries, July 25, 27 & 29, 1939, *Zongtong,* vol. 4: 390, 391; Chiang to Hu, January 24, 1940, *Zhanshi waijiao,* p. 91; Schaller, *The U.S. Crusade in China,* p. 30.

52. Carley, *1939,* pp. 206–212; Haslam, *The Soviet Union and the Threat from the East,* pp. 128–137; Barnhart, *Japan Prepares for Total War,* pp. 136–141, 142–143; Sun, *China and the Origins,* pp. 122–123; Iriye, *Origins of the Second World War,* pp. 80–81.

53. Koo to Kung, August 25, 1939, Koo Papers, box 40; Koo to Chiang, August 26, 1939, *Ibid.*

54. Lee, *Britain and the Sino-Japanese War,* pp. 203–204; Clifford, *Retreat From China,* pp. 128–130 Dreifort, *Myopic Grandeur,* pp. 168, 170; Koo Oral History, vol. 4–10: 715–716; Koo to Foreign Ministry, August 26, 1939, *Zhanshi Waijiao,* part 2, pp. 755–756; Laffey, "French Far Eastern Policy in the 1930s," pp. 146–147.

55. Koo Diary, September 1, 1939; Koo to the Foreign Ministry, September 7, 1939, Koo Papers, box 40.

56. Koo Diary, October 26 & 27, 1939; September 29, 1939; Koo Oral History, vol. 4–10: 729; vol. 4–11: 802, 807–808, 810–811; Haslam, *The Soviet Union and the Threat from the East,* pp. 135–136; Garver, "China's Wartime Diplomacy," p. 15.

57. Koo Oral History, vol. 4–12: 893, 895–896, 898–899; Garver, *Chinese-Soviet Relations,* pp. 99–104; Idem., "China's Wartime Diplomacy," p. 16.

58. Koo Diary, September 29, 1939; Koo Oral History, vol. 4–11: 848–849; Northedge, *The League of Nations,* p. 277.

59. Diary Entry, September 3, 1939, *Zongtong,* vol. 4, p. 406; Diary Entry, September 6, 1939, *Ibid.,* p. 407; Diary Entry, September 9, 1939, *Ibid.,* p. 409; Diary Entry, September 30, 1939, *Ibid.,* p. 416; Iriye, *Origins of the Second World War,* pp. 89–94; Dreifort, *Myopic Grandeur,* pp. 184–185; Clifford, *Retreat From China,* p. 139; Schaller, *The U.S. Crusade in China,* p. 32.

60. Diary Entry, August 29, 1939, *Zongtong,* vol. 4, p. 404; Chiang to Hu, August 29, 1939, *Zhanshi waijiao,* pp. 86–87; Hu to Chiang, September 2, 1939, *Ibid.,* pp. 87–88; Chiang to Hu, September 3, 1939, *Ibid.,* p. 88; Chiang to Hu, September 18, 1939, *Ibid.,* p. 89.

61. Dreifort, *Myopic Grandeur,* pp. 196–197, 202–212; Utley, *Going to War With Japan,* pp. 106–107; Dallek, *Franklin D. Roosevelt,* pp. 238–239; Best, *Britain, Japan and Pearl Harbor,* pp. 118–119; Koo to Chinese Embassy, Washington, August 5, 1940, Koo Papers, box 41; Koo to Chinese Embassy, Washington, August 22, 1940, *Ibid.*

62. Roosevelt to Chiang, November 10, 1939, *FRUS: 1939,* vol. 3: 715; Roosevelt to Chiang, November 9, 1939, *Zhanshi waijiao,* part 1, p. 90; Soong to Chiang, July 2, 1940, *Ibid.,* p. 94; Diary Entry, February 14, 1940, *Zongtong,* vol. 4: 493; Utley, *Going to War With Japan,* pp. 97–101.

63. Diary Entry, July 18, 1940, *Zongtong,* vol. 4: 560; Diary Entry, October 18, 1940, *Ibid.,* p. 588; October 31, 1940, *Ibid.,* p. 592; Diary Entry, November 9, 1940, *Ibid.,* pp. 594–595; Soong to Chiang, October 14, 1940, *Zhanshi waijiao,* part 1, p. 99; Chiang to Soong, November 1, 1940, *Ibid.,* pp. 107–108; Chiang to Soong, November 1, 1940, *Ibid.,* pp. 108–110; Chiang to Soong, November 9, 1940, *Ibid.,* pp. 111–112; Chiang to Soong, November 21, 1940, *Ibid.,* no. 40, pp. 119–120; Soong and Hu to Chiang, November 27, 1941, *Ibid.,* no. 41, pp. 120–121; Utley, *Going to War With Japan,* pp. 103–104; Garver, "China's Wartime Diplomacy," p. 18.

64. Koo to Foreign Ministry, October 28, 1940, Koo Papers, box 41.

65. Iriye, *The Origins of the Second World War,* pp. 114–115; Sun, *China and the Origins,* pp. 143–145, 148–150; LaFeber, *The Clash,* p. 194; Koo to Hu, October 18, 1940, Koo Papers, box 41; Koo to Hu, October 24, 1940, *Ibid.*

66. Elleman, *Modern Chinese Warfare,* p. 210; Clifford, *Retreat From China,* p. 147; Best, *Britain, Japan and Pearl Harbor,* pp. 126, 129, 131, 136–138.

67. Garver, *Chinese-Soviet Relations,* pp. 38, 82, 99–104, 129–130, 142–143; Schaller, *The U.S. Crusade in China,* pp. 43, 46–51; Haslam, *The Soviet Union and the Threat from the East,* pp. 150–156; Sun, *China and the Origins,* pp. 126–128.

68. Haslam, *The Soviet Union,* p. 150; Diary Entry, April 13, 1941, *Zongtong,* vol. 4: 671; Garver, *Chinese-Soviet Relations,* p. 116.

69. Best, *Britain, Japan and Pearl Harbor,* pp. 165, 167; Iriye, *The Origins of the Second World War,* pp. 136–137; Lattimore to Currie, August 2, 1941, *FRUS: 1941,* vol. 4: 362; Diary Entry, October 18, 1940, *Zongtong,* vol. 4: 588; October 31, 1940, *Ibid.,* p. 592; Diary Entry, November 9, 1940, *Ibid.,* pp. 594–595; Diary Entry, November 21, 1940, *Ibid.,* p. 597.

70. Koo Diary, April 20, 1941; Garver, *Chinese-Soviet Relations,* p. 17; FO371/27615 F2406/60/10; F3607/2509/10; FO371/27710, F3022/2509/10; FO371/27710 F3607/2509/10; Koo Diary, April 20, 1941; Koo Oral History, vol. 4–19, 20: 1450; vol. 5A: 3, 56.

71. FO371/27615 F3572/60/10; Thorne, *Allies of a Kind,* pp. 66–68.

72. Koo-Cadogan conversation, July 17, 1941, FO371/27616 F6438/60/10; Eden to Kerr, July 19, 1941, FO371/27616 F6303/60/10.

73. Eden to Kerr, July 25, 1941, FO 371/27609 F6815/26/10; See also Ashley Clark memo.

74. Eden to Kerr, August 1, 1941, FO371/27609 F6855/26/10; Eden to Kerr, August 13, 1941, FO371/27641 F7768/145/10; Eden to Kerr, August 22, 1941, FO371/27642 F7718/145/10.

75. FO371/27609 F7236.

76. Eden to Clark Kerr, August 22, 1941, FO371/27616 F8281/5412/10.

77. Gauss to Hull, August 27, 1941, *FRUS: 1941,* vol. 4, pp. 395, 396; Currie to Welles, August 3, 1941, *Ibid.,* p. 361; Currie to Welles, August 3, 1941, *Ibid.,* p. 361.

78. Eden to Kerr, September 19, 1941, FO 371/27609/F9716/60/10; Koo Diary, January 8, 1943; Diary Entry, September 1, 1941, *Zongtong,* vol. 4: 718; Richard Law minute, August 28, 1941, FO 371/27616/F8496/60/10; Koo Oral History, vol. 5A: 66–69.

79. FO371/27616 F9516/60/10.

80. Koo to Foreign Ministry, November 9, 1941, Koo Papers, box 41; Currie to Hull,

November 25, 1941, *FRUS: 1941,* vol. 4, p. 652; Lattimore to Currie, November 25, 1941, *Ibid.;* Currie to Roosevelt, July 11, 1941, *Ibid.,* pp. 1005–1006; Soong to Chiang, July 12, 1941, *Zhanshi waijiao,* part 1, pp. 144–145; Lattimore to Currie, August 2, 1941, annex to *FRUS: 1941,* vol. 4, p. 362.

   81. Heinrichs, *The Threshold of War,* pp. 178, 185, 187, 192–193, 208–211, 213–214; Currie to Hull, November 25, 1941, *FRUS: 1941,* vol. 4: 652; Best, *Britain, Japan and Pearl Harbor,* pp. 183–184; Sun, *China and the Origins of the Pacific War,* pp. 153–154.

   82. Koo Diary, November 26, 1941; December 1 & 7, 1941; Koo Oral History, vol. 5A: 70.

   83. Jin, *Gu Weizhun zhuan,* p. 198.

Chapter 6. Sino-British Tensions, 1941–1944

   1. Koo, "China and the War Against Aggression," p. 20; Grenville, *The Major International Treaties,* pp. 205, 212; Kirby, "Traditions of Centrality, Authority, and Management in Modern China's Foreign Relations," p. 17.

   2. Divine, *Roosevelt and World War II,* pp. 50–58; Dallek, *Franklin D. Roosevelt,* pp. 389–391; Schaller, *The U.S. Crusade in China,* pp. 98–100; Thorne, *Allies of a Kind,* pp. 308–309.

   3. For a brief look at post-1919 Chinese Pan-Asianism including that of Sun's, see, Hunt, "The May Fourth Era," pp. 191–195; Kindermann, "Sun Yat-sen's Views on Foreign Policy and Imperialism"; Koo Diary, October 31, November 2, and December 13, 1942.

   4. Chiang, *China's Destiny,* pp. 231–234.

   5. Ch'i, *Nationalist China at War,* pp. 91–92; Eastman, *Seeds of Destruction,* pp. 135–138.

   6. Garver, *Chinese-Soviet Relations,* pp. 182–191.

   7. Diary Entry, December 24, 1941, *Zongtong,* vol. 4: 787; Spector, *Eagle Against the Sun,* pp. 326–327; Garver, "China's Wartime Diplomacy," p. 21.

   8. Thorne, *Allies of a Kind,* pp. 77–80, 175–176, 184–186; Spector, *Eagle Against the Sun,* p. 327; Garver, *Chinese-Soviet Relations,* pp. 192–195.

   9. Koo Oral History, vol. 5A: 50–52, 91–94; Koo to Soong, January 20, 1942, Soong Papers, box 5, Hoover Institute; Koo Diary, January 20 and March 25, 1942; Diary Entry, January 17, 1942, *Zongtong,* vol. 5: 10; Thorne, *Allies of a Kind,* pp. 186–187.

   10. FO371/31632 F1012/74/10; Koo Diary, May 5, 1942; Thorne, *Allies of a Kind,* pp. 187; Spector, *Eagle Against the Sun,* pp. 327–328; Garver, "China's Wartime Diplomacy," p. 21.

   11. Kerr to Foreign Office, January 28, 1942, FO371/31632 F1030/74/10; FO371/31626 F1448/54/10; Seymour to Foreign Office, March 28, 1942, FO371/31626 F2543/54/10; FO371/31626 F3133/54/10.

   12. FO371/31626 F3191/54/10; Eden to Seymour, May 30, 1942, FO371/31626 F4096/54/10;Eden to Kerr, January 5, 1942, FO 371/31618 F196/7/10; Koo to Soong, February 13, 1942, Soong Papers.

   13. Eden to Seymour, April 20, 1942, FO 371/31619 F3043/7/10; See also, Eden note to Koo, May 13, 1942, FO 371/31619 F3468/7/10; Eden to Seymour, July 9, 1942, FO 371/31619 F4940/7/10.

   14. Jin, *Gu Weijun zhuan,* pp. 200–201.

   15. Diary Entry, August 30, 1941, *Zongtong,* vol. 4: 717–718; Thorne, *Allies of a Kind,* p. 237.

   16. Koo Diary, October 31 & November 3, 1942; Chiang-Linlithgow conversation, February 10, 1942, *Zhanshi waijiao,* part 3, p. 358; Churchill to Eden, February 13, 1942, FO371/31633.

   17. Chiang-Kerr conversation, February 15, 1942, *Zhanshi waijiao,* pp. 392–393; Chiang-Gandhi conversation, February 18, 1942, *Ibid.,* pp. 411–423; Chiang-Nehru con-

versation, February 20, 1942, *Ibid.*, pp. 425–431; Chiang speech, February 21, 1942, *Ibid.*, pp. 431–433; Spector, *Eagle Against the Sun*, p. 335.

18. Chiang to Koo, February 23, 1942, *Zhanshi waijiao*, pp. 434–435.

19. Koo to Chiang, February 24, 1942, *Ibid.*, pp. 435–436; Koo to Chiang, February 25, 1942, *Ibid.*, pp. 436–437; Koo to Chiang, February 26, 1942, *Ibid.*, pp. 438–439; Koo to Chiang, February 28, 1942, *Ibid.*, pp. 440–441; Koo to Chiang, February 28, 1942, *Ibid.*, pp. 441–442; Koo to Chiang, March 3, 1942, *Ibid.*, p. 444.

20. Koo to Chiang, March 4, 1942, *Ibid.*, p. 445; Koo Oral History, vol. 5A: 38, 120; Koo Diary, June 3 & September 3, 1942; Churchill-Koo conversation, June 3, 1942, Premier 4/45/4, PRO.

21. Spector, *Eagle Against the Sun*, pp. 335–339; Chiang-Seymour conversation, June 25, 1942, *Zhanshi waijiao*, part 3, pp. 462–463; Chiang to Koo, June 28, 1942, *Ibid.*, p. 466; Chiang-British diplomat conversation, August 12, 1942, *Ibid.*, pp. 478–479.

22. Chiang to Roosevelt, July 24, 1942, *Zhanshi waijiao*, part 3, pp. 471–473; Churchill to Chiang, August 31, 1942, *Ibid.*, pp. 485–487; Chiang to Koo, August 12, 1942, *Ibid.*, p. 482; Koo Oral History, vol. 5A: 41, 42, 44–45, 121, 122.

23. Jin, *Gu Weijun zhuan*, p. 202; Koo Diary, November 22, 1942.

24. Koo Oral History, vol. 5B: 152–153, 174; Koo Diary, October 15, 28, & 31, 1942; November 22 & 28, 1942.

25. Diary Entry, July 4, 1942, *Zongtong*, vol. 5: 132; Koo Oral History, vol. 5B: 175; Notes for the Secretary's Meeting with the Chinese Ambassador, November 3, 1942, FO371/31627; FO371/31657 F3190/828/10.

26. FO371/35776 F1520/73/10; Koo Diary, October 31, November 2 & 5, December 13, 1942; Koo Oral History, vol. 5B: 262; For British views, see, Thorne, *Allies of a Kind*, pp. 189–190, 310–311.

27. Koo Diary, June 16, 1942 & December 13, 1942; Koo Oral History, vol. 5B: 249

28. FO371/31633 F2775/74/10.

29. Koo Diary, June 23, December 25, 27, & 30, 1942; Koo Oral History, vol. 5A: 28–29, 31; vol. 5B: 276–279, 282; Thorne, *Allies of a Kind*, p. 179.

30. *Ibid.*, p. 287; Chan, "Hong Kong in Sino-British Diplomacy, 1926–1945," p. 81; For a look at mostly the British side of these relations, see, Idem., "The Abrogation of British Extraterritoriality in China 1942–43," pp. 257–291; Koo Diary, December 31, 1942; Thorne, *Allies of a* Kind, p. 311; Chiang, *China's Destiny*, pp. 151–153.

31. Koo Diary, January 2, 1943; January 6, 1944; Koo Oral History, vol. 5B: 294.

32. Chu, *V.K. Wellington Koo*, p. 163; Liao, *Antiforeignism and Modernization in China*, pp. 102–103; Chiang, *China's Destiny*, p. 154; FO371/31659 F7137/828/10.

33. Koo Oral History, vol. 5B: 328, 349, 357–358, 376–377.

34. Chiang-Currie conversation, August 3, 1942, *Zhanshi waijiao*, part 1, pp. 680–681; Chiang-Currie conversation, August 4, 1942, *Ibid.*, p. 703; Koo Diary, April 7, 1943; Koo Oral History, vol. 6F: 78; FO371/31633 F5964/74/10.

35. Koo Diary, April 7, 1943; Koo Oral History, vol. 5A: 122–127.

36. Koo Diary, June 16, 1942.

37. *Ibid.*, December 13, 1942; Koo Oral History, vol. 5A: 364–366, 369–370, 382.

38. Koo Diary, March 23, 1943; Koo Oral History, vol. 5B: 330, 372, 374; vol. 5C: 408.

39. *Ibid.*, vol. 5B: 318; 5C: 416–418.

40. *Ibid.*, pp. 494–495.

41. Koo Diary, May 4, 1943; Koo believed that China had to ensure that "Indochina should not again become a nuisance to her." *Ibid.*, October 6, 1943.

42. *Ibid.*, June 20, 1943.

43. Diary Entry, November 18, 1943, *Zongtong*, vol. 5: 432; Koo Diary, December 1 & 3, 1943; Garver, *Chinese-Soviet* Relations, pp. 196–199; Schaller, *The U.S. Crusade in China*, pp. 150–156; Sainsbury, *The Turning Point*, pp. 177, 184–185.

44. "What is a Great Power?," *Economist* (March 11, 1944): 331; Koo Diary, March 13, 1944.

45. *Ibid.*, May 14, 1944; May 15, 1944; June 4, 1944; Jespersen, *American Images of China*, pp. 108–117; On the other hand, there is evidence that London newspapers wrote glowing articles about China and Chiang Kai-shek. See, Thorne, *Allies of a Kind*, p. 443.

46. Koo Diary, June 18, 1943; *Ibid.*, September 12, 1943; *Ibid.*, April 21, 1944; June 4, 1944; June 8, 1944.

47. *Ibid.*, September 9, 1942; April 5, 1945.

48. *Ibid.*, March 16, 1945; March 31, 1944.

49. *Ibid.*, January 21, 1945.

50. *Ibid.*, December 9, 1941; January 12, 1937.

51. *Ibid.*, January 26, 1945.

52. *Ibid.*, August 5, 1944.

53. *Ibid.*, January 6, 1944; FO371/46180 F1732/57/10.

Chapter 7. Sino-American Tensions, 1944–1945

1. Ch'i, *Nationalist China at War*, pp. 63, 67–68; Eastman, *Seeds of Destruction*, pp. 143, 146–147; Idem., "Nationalist China during the Sino-Japanese War 1937–1945," in *The Nationalist Era in China*, pp. 137–139; Spector, *Eagle Against the Sun*, pp. 328–332, 338, 341–342; Thorne, *Allies of a Kind*, pp. 322–327; Garver, "China's Wartime Diplomacy," pp. 21–22.

2. Schaller, *The U.S. Crusade in China*, pp. 150–152; Garver, *Chinese-Soviet Relations*, p. 199; Idem., "China's Wartime Diplomacy," p. 22; Diary Entry, January 11, 1944, *Zongtong*, vol. 5: 471; Diary Entry, February 26, 1944, *Ibid.*, p. 488.

3. Eastman, *Seeds of Destruction*, pp. 28–29; Idem., "Nationalist China during the Sino-Japanese War 1937–1945," pp. 148–149; Ch'i, *Nationalist China at War*, pp. 79–82.

4. Koo Diary, October 6, 1944; Chiang to Kung, August 10, 1944, *Zhanshi waijiao*, part 3, p. 837.

5. Koo, "China and the Problem of World Order," p. 184.

6. Koo Diary, October 6, 1943; Koo, "China and the Problem," pp. 189–190.

7. Koo Diary, May 4, 1943; May 16, 1944; and Gardner, *Spheres of Influence*, p. 150.

8. Chiang to Kung, August 16, 1944, *Zhanshi waijiao*, part 3, p. 865; Chiang to Kung, August 17, 1944, *Ibid.*; Koo Diary, August 25, 1944; Liu, *A Partnership for Disorder*, p. 26.

9. Chiang, *China's Destiny*, p. 234.

10. Chiang to Kung, August 18, 1944, *Zhanshi waijiao*, part 3, p. 868; Koo Diary, August 28, 1944.

11. Hilderbrand, *Dumbarton Oaks*, pp. 60–62.

12. Koo Diary, August 25, 1944; Koo to the Foreign Ministry, August 31, 1944, *Zhanshi waijiao*, part 3, p. 888; Koo, Wei, Hu, and Shang to Foreign Ministry, September 9, 1944, *Ibid.*, p. 889.

13. Hilderbrand, *Dumbarton Oaks*, pp. 75–76, 79; Koo Diary, August 5, 29 & September 9, 1944; Jin, *Gu Weijun zhuan*, p. 217.

14. Koo Diary, September 13, 1944; Halifax to Foreign Office, August 20, 1944, FO371/38547 AN3268/20/45.

15. Koo Diary, September 14, 1944.
16. *Ibid.*, September 21, 1944.
17. *Ibid.*, September 12, 1944; Koo-Hornbeck conversation, September 5, 1944, Koo Papers, box 77.
18. Koo-Reston conversation, September 11, 1944, *Ibid.*; Koo Diary, September 11, 1944; Koo-Cadogan conversation, September 29, 1944, Koo Papers, box 77.
19. Koo-Roosevelt conversation, October 3, 1944, *Ibid.*; Koo Oral History, vol. 5E: 652, 653.
20. Koo Diary, August 12 & 28; September 27, 1944; Meeting at Kung's Apartment, August 28, 1944, Koo Papers, box 75, folder 1; Koo Oral History, vol. vol. 5B: 303; vol. 5E: 624.
21. Hilderbrand, *Dumbarton Oaks*, pp. 229–231.
22. *United States Relations with China*, p. 66; Chiang to Kung, July 8, 1944, *Zhanshi waijiao*, part 3, p. 636; Chiang to Kung, July 8, 1944, *Ibid.*, p. 637; Chiang to Roosevelt, July 8, 1944, *FRUS: 1944*, vol. 6, pp. 120–121; Chiang to Kung, July 10, 1944, *Zhanshi waijiao*, part 3, pp. 637–638; Chiang to Kung, July 11, 1944, *Ibid.*, p. 639.
23. Roosevelt to Chiang, August 21, 1944, *FRUS: 1944*, vol. 6, pp. 148–149; Kung to Chiang, August 25, 1944, *Zhanshi waijiao*, part 3, p. 656.
24. Roosevelt to Chiang, September 16, 1944, *FRUS: 1944*, vol. 6, pp. 157, 158; Chiang to Kung, September 28, 1944, *Zhanshi waijiao*, part 3, p. 675; Garver, "China's Wartime Diplomacy," p. 23; Koo Diary, September 22, 1944.
25. *Ibid.*, September 12 & 27, 1944; The gist of Koo's cable is found in, Diary Entry, October 5, 1944, *Zongtong*, vol. 5: 619; Koo Oral History, vol. 5E: 689.
26. *Ibid.*, pp. 673, 690.
27. Koo Diary, September 28 & 30, 1944; *Zongtong*, vol. 5, p. 639; Garver, "China's Wartime Diplomacy," p. 24.
28. Koo Diary, September 8, 9, & 20, 1944.
29. *Ibid.*, September 30, 1944; Jin, *Gu Weijun zhuan*, p. 219.
30. Informal Minutes of Meeting No. 2 of the Joint Steering Committee, October 5, 1944, *FRUS: 1944*, vol. 1, p. 856; See also, Hilderbrand, *Dumbarton Oaks*, pp. 231–232, 234.
31. Koo Diary, October 5, 1944; Koo Oral History, vol. 5E: 655–657, 663.
32. Hilderbrand, *Dumbarton Oaks*, p. 236; Jin, *Gu Weijun zhuan*, pp. 220–221.
33. Koo Diary, September 18, 1944.
34. Stettinius to Hull, October 3, 1944, *FRUS: 1944*, vol. 1, pp. 864–5; Hilderbrand, *Dumbarton Oaks*, pp. 237–240; Koo Diary, July 27, 1944.
35. Stettinius to Hull, October 4, 1944, *FRUS: 1944*, vol. 1, p. 867; Hilderbrand, *Dumbarton Oaks*, pp. 240–241.
36. "Notes for Speech at Twin Oaks, October 9, 1944," Koo Diary, loose material, diary 15; Koo Oral History, vol. 5E: 663–665, 666.
37. For the different reactions, see, Divine, *Second Chance*, pp. 228–233; Koo Diary, October 7, 1944.
38. Roosevelt to Chiang, October 5, 1944, *FRUS: 1944*, vol. 6, p. 165; Koo Diary, October 5 & 7, 1944.
39. *Ibid.*, October 10, 1944. Koo mentions Marshall as sending the cable, but in fact, it was Roosevelt.
40. Chiang to Kung, October 10, 1944, *Zhanshi waijiao*, part 3, pp. 687–688; see also Aide-memoire from Chiang to Hurley, October 9, 1944, *FRUS: 1944*, vol. 6, pp. 167–169; Koo Oral History, vol. 5E: 694; Chiang to Roosevelt, October 9, 1944, *Outbreak of War*, part 3, p. 529; Schaller, *The U.S. Crusade in China*, pp. 169–175.

41. *Ibid.*, pp. 180–188; Thorne, *Allies of a Kind*, pp. 434–439; Garver, *Chinese-Soviet Relations*, pp. 237–241, 247–251; Hunt, *Genesis of Chinese Communist Foreign Policy*, pp. 147, 149–154.
42. Koo-Hopkins conversation, October 10, 1944, Koo Papers, box 77.
43. Draft Memo, October 1944, *Ibid.*, folder 12A; Koo Diary, October 15 & 25, 1944.
44. Koo-Hopkins conversation, October 10, 1944, Koo Papers, box 77.
45. Koo to Chiang, October 14, 1944, *Zhanshi waijiao*, part 2, p. 539; Koo to Chiang, November 9, 1944, *Ibid.*, p. 540.
46. Spector, *Eagle Against the Sun*, pp. 370–372.
47. Schaller, *The U.S. Crusade in China*, pp. 195–200; Hunt, *The Genesis of Chinese Communist Foreign Policy*, pp. 154–155; Westad, *Cold War and Revolution*, p. 27.
48. Schaller, *The U.S. Crusade in China*, pp. 209–212; Garver, *Chinese-Soviet Relations*, pp. 105–107, 236, fn. 221; Westad, *Cold War and Revolution*, pp. 1–13, 29–30.
49. Koo Diary, March 2, 1945.
50. *Ibid.*, March 7, 1945.
51. Stettinius to Hurley, March 15, 1945, *FRUS: 1945*, vol. 7, p. 284; Koo Diary, March 23, 1945; Wei to Hull, March 27, 1945, *FRUS: 1945*, vol. 1, p. 160.
52. Koo Diary, March 19, 1945; Koo Oral History, vol. 5E: 762–763, 768, 771.
53. Koo Diary, March 31 & April 8, 1945.
54. *Ibid.*, April 12 & 16, 1945.
55. Wei to Chiang, March 12, 1945, *Zhanshi waijiao*, part 3, p. 542; Soong to Chiang, April 15, 1945, *Ibid.*, part 3, p. 545.
56. Koo Diary, April 16, 1945.
57. Koo-Leahy conversation, April 11, 1945, Koo Papers, box 77; Koo to Chiang, April 13, 1945, *Zhanshi waijiao*, part 3, pp. 543–544.
58. Chiang to Soong, May 23, 1945, *Zhanshi waijiao*, part 3, p. 547; Soong to Chiang, May 26, 1945, *Ibid.*, p. 548; Koo Oral History, vol. 5E: 921.
59. Westad, *Cold War and Revolution*, pp. 33, 34.
60. Koo Diary, May 30 & June 4 & 9, 1945.
61. *Ibid.*, March 22, 1945; Koo Oral History, vol. 5E: 775, 776.
62. Koo Diary, March 31 & June 13, 1945; Koo-Officer conversation, March 6, 1945, Koo Papers, box 77.
63. Minutes of the First Four-Power Consultative Meeting on the Charter Proposal, May 2, 1945, *FRUS: 1945*, vol. 1, p. 564.
64. Koo-Evatt conversation, June 22, 1945, Koo Papers, box 77; Koo Diary, May 4, 1943; May 6, 1945.
65. *Ibid.*, April 18, 1945; Koo Oral History, vol. 5E: 832–834; Minutes of the Twelfth Four-Power Consultative Meeting on the Charter Proposal, June 2, 1945, *FRUS: 1945*, vol. 1, p. 1102; Chu, *V.K. Wellington Koo*, p. 167.
66. Stettinius to Acting Secretary of State, September 28, 1945, *FRUS: 1945*, vol. 1, p. 1453
67. Koo-Evatt conversation, June 22, 1945, Koo Papers, box 77; Summary of the Chinese Position in the Security Council, National Archives, Ringwalt File, box 8.
68. Koo Diary, December 28, 1945; Koo, "Basic Problems of the United Nations," pp. 78–83. Quote from p. 82.
69. Koo Diary, July 9, 1945; Koo Oral History, vol. 5E: 850.
70. Garver, *Chinese-Soviet Relations*, pp. 210–214; Gallicchio, *The Cold War Begins in Asia*, pp. 20–21; Westad, *Cold War and Revolution*, pp. 34–36.
71. Koo Diary, May 24, 1945; June 4, 1945.

72. Westad, *Cold War and Revolution*, pp. 48, 56; Garver, *Chinese-Soviet Relations*, pp. 224–228.

73. Koo Oral History, vol. 5E: 874–875.

74. Koo Diary, August 23, September 3 & November 22, 1945; Koo Oral History, vol. 5E: 885–887; Gallicchio, *The Cold War Begins in Asia*, pp. 27, 89–92.

75. Koo Oral History, vol. 5E: 882.

76. Koo Diary, March 7, 1945.

Chapter 8. Collapse of the ROC, 1945–1949

1. Koo Diary, April 3, 1944; Ballantine to Stettinius, January 17, 1944, *FRUS: 1944*, vol. 6, p. 309; Koo Diary, April 19, 1944.

2. Westad, *Cold War and Revolution*, pp. 78–85, 92–97; Levine, *Anvil of Victory*, pp. 24–26, 41–42, 46–51; Van Slyke, "The Chinese Communist Movement during the Sino-Japanese War, 1937–1945," pp. 708–709.

3. Gormly, *The Collapse of the Grand Alliance*, ch. 3.

4. Yergin, *Shattered Peace*, pp. 122–127; Gaddis, *The United States and the Origins of the Cold War*, pp. 263–266; Gormly, *The Collapse of the Grand Alliance*, ch. 4; Koo Diary, September 30 & October 1, 1945.

5. *Ibid.*, December 16, 1945.

6. Gormly, *The Collapse of the Grand Alliance*, pp. 98, 99, 176, 177; Levine, *Anvil of Victory*, pp. 51–54, 56–57; Westad, *Cold War and Revolution*, pp. 131–135.

7. Koo Diary, November 22, 1945; December 16 & 28, 1945; In fact, Chiang Kai-shek did take note of the Moscow communiqué. See, *Zongtong*, vol. 5, part 2, p. 910.

8. Koo Diary, May 24, September 18 & 19, 1945.

9. Levine, *Anvil of* Victory, pp. 58–76; Westad, *Cold War and* Revolution, pp. 144–145, 152–153; Koo Diary, March 15 &16, 1946; Koo Oral History, vol. 5E: 993–996.

10. Koo Diary, February 17 & March 10, 1946; Koo Oral History, vol. 5E: 978, 991–992.

11. Koo Diary, April 19, 1946.

12. Koo Oral History, vol. 5E: 884, 928–929, 930.

13. Levine, *Anvil of* Victory, pp. 77–83; Westad, *Cold War and Revolution*, pp. 151–152.

14. Koo Oral History, vol. 5E: 1031–1033; Koo Diary, May 14, 1946.

15. Koo Oral History, vol. 5E: 1037–1040; Koo Diary, May 17, 1946.

16. *Ibid.*, May 20, 1946; Marshall described for Frank Price, an American missionary and close friend of Chiang Kai-shek, the GMD and the CCP in the same terms. Price wrote in his diary, "Seems too simple." Frank Price Papers, box 12, folder "Wartime China."

17. Levine, *Anvil of Victory*, pp. 83–84.

18. Koo Diary, June 14, 1946; Memorandum, found in *Ibid.*, June 13, 1946; Koo Oral History, vol. 5E: 1062, 1069–1070.

19. *Ibid.*, 6A: 2–3; "Dr. Koo Discounts View of Mme. Sun," *New York Times* (July 25, 1946), in Koo Diary, July 25, 1946.

20. Pepper, "The KMT-CCP Conflict, 1945–1949," pp. 733–734; Truman to Chiang, August 10, 1946, in *United States Relations with China*, p. 652.

21. Luce is described in hostile terms in, Swanberg, *Luce and His Empire*; For a favorable view of Luce, see, Patricia Neils, *China Images in the Life and Times of Henry Luce*; A recent critical work is Jespersen, *American Images of China*.

22. Koo to Soong, December 4, 1946, Soong Papers; Koo to Soong, July 30, 1946, *Ibid.*

23. Koo, "China in Transition: Political, Economic, Social and Cultural Changes," pp. 313–320; Quote from p. 313; Koo Oral History, vol. 6B: 1.

24. Pepper, "The KMT-CCP Conflict," pp. 734–737; Eastman, *Seeds of Destruction*, pp. 159–160.

25. Koo to Song, January 7, 1947, *Zhanhou zhongguo*, part 3, p. 268; Koo to Chiang, January 13, 1947, *Ibid.*, p. 269; Koo Diary, September 4, 1946, May 16, 1947, August 9, 1947; Wang-Marshall Conversation, September 14, 1947, Koo Papers, box 124; Koo Oral History, vol. 6B: 4–5.

26. Koo-Marshall Conversation, February 17, 1947, Koo Collection, box 124; Koo-Marshall Conversation, March 3, 1947, *Ibid.*; Koo-Marshall Conversation, June 25, 1947, *Ibid.*; Koo-Marshall Conversation, November 13, 1947, *Ibid.*; Koo Oral History, vol. 6B: 26; Jin, *Gu Weijun zhuan*, p. 239.

27. Koo Oral History, vol. 6F:64.

28. Koo-Acheson conversation, March 11, 1947, Koo Papers, box 77; Koo Oral History, vol. 6C: 19–20, 23, 24, 36; Koo Diary, August 13, 1946; Koo to Chiang, August 12, 1946, *Zhanhou zhongguo*, part 3, pp. 209–210.

29. Stueck, *The Road to Confrontation*, pp. 36–44.

30. Pepper, "The KMT-CCP Conflict," pp. 759–768; Idem., *Civil War in China*, pp. 167–168.

31. Stueck, *The Road to Confrontation*, pp. 44–48; Koo Diary, December 17, 1947.

32. Stueck, *The Road to Confrontation*, pp. 52–54; Koo Oral History, vol. 6E: 121, 122, 139; vol. 6F: 4.

33. Pepper, "The KMT-CCP Conflict," pp. 770–774; Koo Oral History, vol. 6C: 25.

34. Stueck, *The Road to Confrontation*, pp. 58–59; Koo Diary, January 5, February 18 & 19, 1948.

35. Koo Oral History, vol. 6F: 33, 44, 48, 50; Koo Diary, February 25 & March 12, 1948.

36. Stueck, *The Road to Confrontation*, p. 59; Koo Diary, May 5 & August 6, 1948; Koo Oral History, vol. 6F: 174.

37. Pepper, "The KMT-CCP Conflict," p. 775; Koo Diary, September 30 & November 9, 1948.

38. Koen, *The China Lobby*, p. 79; Koo Oral History, vol. 6G: 72–73, 76–77, 80–81.

39. Marshall-Madame Chiang conversation, December 3, 1948, Harry S. Truman Library; Memorandum, "Madame Chiang Kai-shek," December 15, 1948, Central Intelligence Agency, *Ibid.*

40. Koo Oral History, vol. 6H: 28, 36; Koo Diary, November 11, 1948.

41. Koo Oral History, vol. 6H: 55–56, 68.

42. MacNair and Lach, *Modern Far Eastern International Relations*," p. 546; Pepper, "The KMT-CCP Conflict," pp. 782–783; Koo Diary, January 8 & 13, 1949.

43. *Ibid.*, January 28, 1949; Koo Oral History, vol. 6I: 36.

44. Koo Diary, February 15, 1949; Koo-Acheson conversation, February 15, 1949, Koo Papers, box 130; Koo-Acheson Conversation, February 15, 1949, HSTL; Koo Oral History, vol. 6I: 55.

45. Koo Diary, May 4, 1949; See also, Koo-Dulles conversation, April 18, 1949, Koo Papers, box 130; Koo-Butterworth conversation, May 11, 1949, HSTL.

46. Stueck, *The Road to Confrontation*, pp. 130–131; Cohen, "Acheson, His Advisers, and China," pp. 24–25; Koo Diary, September 22 & 23, 1949; Foreign Ministry to Koo, July 27, 1949, *Zhanhou zhongguo*, part 3, pp. 398–399; Koo to Chiang, August 4, 1949, *Ibid.*, p. 399.

47. Koo Diary, May 27, 1949; June 4, 5, & 16, 1949.
48. *Ibid.*, March 19 & 20, 1949; Koo Oral History, vol. 6I: 119
49. Koo Diary, November 25, 1948.
50. Eastman, *Seeds of Destruction*, pp. 218, 223.
51. Koo Oral History, vol. 6I: 25–26.

Chapter 9. The ROC on Taiwan and the Early Cold War

1. Koo Diary, August 10 & September 12, 1949.
2. Chang, *Friends and Enemies*, pp. 9–12, 20–23; Stueck, *The Road to Confrontation*, pp. 137–143; Cohen, "Acheson and China," pp. 25–30; Gaddis, "The Strategic Perspective," pp. 61–118; John W. Garver, *The Sino-American Alliance*, pp. 14–21; Stueck, *The Korean War*, p. 30.
3. Koo Diary, September 13, 1949; December 29, 1950; February 1, 1951; Tucker, "Nationalist China's Decline and Its Impact on Sino-American Relations," pp. 153–154.
4. Koo Diary, March 16, 1950; May 9 & 11, 1950; July 7 & 24, 1950; September 25, 1950; January 31, 1951.
5. Koo Diary, December 22 & 29, 1949; January 24 & March 9, 1950; February 3, 1951; Gaddis, *Russia, the Soviet Union and the United States*, pp. 195–196, 202; Tucker, *Taiwan, Hong Kong, and the United States*, pp. 30–32.
6. Koo Diary, December 12, 1950; Koo, "China is Worth Saving," pp. 39–44.
7. Koo Diary, November 15, 1950; February 3, 1951; March 20, 1951; May 7, 1951.
8. Dispatches from Nationalist Chinese Representatives in the United States to their Government, 1949–1950, Herbert Hoover Presidential Library, Post-Presidential Subject File-China.
9. Lilley, "A Mid-Level Bureaucrat's Dream to Save China," pp. 41–49; Koo Diary, July 25, 1949; August 9, 1949; September 14 & 15, 1949.
10. *Ibid.*, July 7 & December 29, 1950; January 10, April 2 & September 19, 1951.
11. Wang, "Bastion Created, Regime Reformed, Economy Reengineered," pp. 323–324.
12. Koo Diary, August 31, 1950.
13. *Ibid.*, September 1, 1950; April 22, 1951.
14. *Ibid.*, July 24, 1950; April 22, 1951; Wang, "Bastion Created, Regime Reformed, Economy Reengineered," pp. 321–322; Riggs, *Formosa Under Chinese Nationalist Rule*, pp. 37–39.
15. Koo Diary, September 21, 1949; December 28, 1949; March 1, 1950; Quote from February 27, 1950; For fuller discussion, see, Tucker, "Nationalist China's Decline," pp. 149–152.
16. Koo Diary, June 8 & 12, 1951; October 8 & November 10, 1951; February 18, 1952.
17. Garver, *Sino-American Alliance*, pp. 21–26; Gaddis, *Russia, the Soviet Union and the United States*, pp. 203–205.
18. Koo Diary, June 24, 1950; Stueck, *The Road to Confrontation*, pp. 196–198; Tucker, *Taiwan Hong Kong, and the United States*, pp. 32–33.
19. Koo Diary, June 29, 1950; Koo Diary, July 7, 1950; September 5, 1951; Koo-Zuleta-Angel conversation, January 20, 1951, Koo Papers, box 180; Accinelli, *Crisis and Commitment*, p. 32.
20. Koo Diary, November 15, 1949; July 24 & October 2, 1950; July 2, 1951; July 29, 1951; August 2, 1951; September 11, 1951; November 24, 1951; July 26, 1952.

21. Stueck, *The Korean War*, p. 364; Accinelli, *Crisis and Commitment*, pp. 67–68; Wang, "Bastion Created, Regime Reformed, Economy Reengineered," p. 325; Mendel, *The Politics of Formosan Nationalism*, p.125.

22. Tucker, *Taiwan Hong Kong, and the United States*, pp. 33–34; Garver, *Sino-American Relations*, p. 27; Foot, *The Practice of Power*, p. 30; Zhai, *The Dragon, the Lion, and the Eagle*, pp. 98–104.

23. Koo Diary, May 21, 1950.

24. *Ibid.*, October 10, 1951; Garver, *Sino-American Relations*, pp. 35–48, 61.

25. Koo-Dulles conversation, May 31, 1951, Koo Papers, box 180; Koo-Dulles conversation, June 2, 1951, *Ibid.*; See also, Koo-Dulles conversation, May 29, 1951, *FRUS: 1951*, vol. 6, pp. 1052–1053; Zhai, *The Dragon, the Lion and the Eagle*, pp. 109–111; Accinelli, *Crisis and Commitment*, pp. 78–89.

26. Koo-Dulles conversation, May 31, 1951, Koo Papers, box 180; Koo-Dulles conversation, June 2, 1951, *Ibid.*; See also, Koo-Dulles conversation, May 29, 1951, *FRUS: 1951*, vol. 6, pp. 1052–1053.

27. Koo-Dulles-Rusk conversation, June 16, 1951, Koo Papers, box 180.

28. Koo-Dulles-Rusk conversation, June 19, 1951, *Ibid.*

29. Koo Diary, June 20, 21, & 23, 1951; August 3, 1951; Koo-Dulles conversation, August 2, 1951, Koo Papers, box 180; Koo-Rusk conversation, August 9, 1951, *Ibid.*; Dulles to U.S. Embassy in Taiwan, July 10, 1951, *FRUS: 1951*, vol. 6, p. 1188.

30. Koo Diary, August 29, 1951; Garver, *Sino-American Relations*, pp. 55–56.

31. Koo Diary, September 8, 1951; April 24, 1952; Koo-Romulo conversation, April 8, 1952, Koo Papers, box 187; Koo-Al-Shabandar conversation, January 26, 1954, *Ibid.*, box 191.

32. Tucker, *Taiwan Hong Kong, and the United States*, p. 36; Koo Diary, August 23, 1950; April 12, 1952; January 1, 1953; Koo-Romulo conversation, April 8, 1952, Koo Papers, box 187.

33. Gaddis, *Strategies of Containment*, pp. 127–136; Accinelli, *Crisis and Commitment*, pp. 111–112.

34. Koo Diary, March 4 & 17, 1953; August 25, 1954; An observation similar to Madame Kung's was also made by Karl L. Rankin, the U.S. ambassador to Taiwan. See, Memorandum of conversation by Rankin, July 1, 1953, *FRUS: 1952–54*, vol. 14, p. 224.

35. Koo-Yeh-Dulles conversation, February 10, 1955, *FRUS: 1955–1957*, vol. 2, pp. 258–259; Koo-Rockefeller conversation, December 16, 1955, Koo Papers, box 195; Chang, *Friends and Enemies*, pp. 81–84.

36. Koo-Spender conversation, September 13, 1950, *Ibid.*, box 180; Koo Diary, January 16 & February 3, 1953.

37. *Ibid.*, June 1, 1953; April 20, 1954.

38. *Ibid.*, April 9, May 23, & June 20, 1953.

39. Stueck, *The Korean War*, pp. 306–347.

40. Koo-Dulles conversation, December 19, 1950, Koo Papers, box 180; See also, Koo-Rusk conversation, January 18, 1951, *FRUS: 1951*, vol. 8, pp. 1518–1519; Koo-Al-Shabandar conversation, January 26, 1954, Koo Papers, box 191.

41. Koo Diary, March 24, 1954.

42. Wang, "Bastion Created, Regime Reformed, Economy Reengineered," p. 325; Koo Diary, May 11, 1953.

43. *Ibid.*, July 7, 1953; September 2, 1953; October 8, 1953; December 1, 1953; January 6, 1954.

44. *Ibid.*, December 1, 1953; January 6, 1954.

45. Wang, "Bastion Created, Regime Reformed, Economy Reengineered," pp. 326–331; Koo Diary, August 15 & 25, 1954.

46. Koo, "The Real China," pp. 72–75, 78, 82.

47. Koo Diary, September 14, 1954; Koo-Dulles conversation, March 19, 1953, *FRUS: 1952–54*, vol. 14, p. 158; Koo-Dulles conversation, May 19, 1954, *Ibid.*, pp. 423–424; Koo-Dulles conversation, May 19, 1954, *Ibid.*, pp. 422–425; Koo-Drumright conversation, July 16, 1954, *Ibid.*, pp. 493.

48. Brands, "Testing Massive Retaliation," pp. 130–134.

49. Koo Diary, October 16 & 18, 1954; Koo-Yeh-Dulles conversation, October 27, 1954, *FRUS: 1952–54*, vol. 14, pp. 797–801.

50. Koo-Yeh-Dulles conversation, November 2, 1954, *FRUS: 1952–54*, vol. 14, pp. 842–850; Koo-Yeh-Robertson conversation, November 6, 1954, *Ibid.*, pp. 871, 872, 874, 878; Koo Diary, November 6, 1954.

51. Koo-Robertson conversation, November 9, 1954, *FRUS: 1952–54*, vol. 14, pp. 881–882; Koo-Robertson conversation, November 12, 1954, *Ibid.*, pp. 887–892.

52. Koo-Yeh-Robertson conversation, November 16, 1954, *FRUS: 1952–54*, vol. 14: 896–903; Koo-Yeh-Robertson conversation, November 19, 1954, *Ibid.*, pp. 904–911.

53. Koo-Yeh-Robertson conversation, December 20, 1954, *Ibid.*, pp. 1040–1041; For Dulles and the idea of two Chinas, see, Tucker, "John Foster Dulles and the Taiwan Roots of the 'Two Chinas' Policy," pp. 235–262; Koo Diary, December 20, 1954; January 3, 1955; Accinelli, *Crisis and Commitment*, pp. 174–175.

54. Chang, *Friends and Enemies*, pp. 121–122; Koo-Robertson conversation, January 12, 1955, *FRUS: 1955–1957*, vol. 2: 13, 14; Koo Diary, January 21 & 22, 1955; Koo-Yeh-Robertson conversation, January 22, 1955, *FRUS: 1955–1957*, vol. 2, pp. 106–107.

55. Chang, *Friends and Enemies*, pp. 122–124; Accenelli, *Crisis and Commitment*, pp. 190–191; Koo-Yeh-Dulles conversation, January 28, 1955, *FRUS: 1955–1957*, vol. 2, pp. 152–157; Koo Diary, January 28 & 31, 1955; May 2, 1955.

56. *Ibid.*, January 29 & February 18, 1955.

57. Koo Diary, March 29, 1955; Koo-Robertson conversation, July 28, 1955, *FRUS: 1955–1957*, vol. 2: 684; Koo-Robertson conversation, February 1, 1956, *Ibid.*, vol. 3, p. 301.

58. *Ibid.*, December 9, 1955; September 29, 1955.

59. Lodge to Dulles, November 16, 1955, *FRUS: 1955–1957*, vol. 11, p. 368; Lodge to Dulles, November 18, 1955, *Ibid.*, pp. 374–378; Dulles to Rankin, November 22, 1955, *Ibid.*, p. 388; Dulles to Rankin, November 22, 1955, *Ibid.*, pp. 389, 390; Dulles to Lodge, November 16, 1955, *Ibid.*, p. 401.

60. Koo-Gork conversation, December 22, 1955, Koo Papers, box 195.

61. Eisenhower-Eden conversation, January 31, 1956, *FRUS: 1955–1957*, vol. 11, p. 468; Koo-Robertson conversation, February 1, 1956, *Ibid.*, vol. 3, pp. 295–302. Quotes from pp. 296, 297, 298, 301; Koo-Robertson conversation, March 1, 1955, *Ibid.*, vol. 11, p. 470.

62. Koo Diary, July 8, 1954.

63. *Ibid.*, December 25, 1950; March 18 & November 30, 1951; October 14, 1952; April 9 & August 18, 1953.

Conclusion

1. Jin, *Gu Weijun zhuan*, p. 302.

2. Jin, "Gu Weijun yu zhongguo waijiao."

3. Robinson and Shambaugh, eds., *Chinese Foreign Policy*.

4. Zhang Chunlan, "Gu Weizhun de hehui waijiao," pp. 31–52.

5. Tang, "Beijing zhengfu yu guomin zhengfu," pp. 1–44; Strauss, *Strong Institutions in Weak Polities*, pp. 153–156.

6. Kirby, "The Internationalization of China," pp. 437–451; Zhang, *China in the International System*, pp. 193–194.

7. Cohen, "The Americanization of Ku Wei-chun," p. 11.

8. Koo Diary, August 15, 1954.

9. Koo, *No Feast Lasts Forever*, p. 7.

10. Koo Diary, December 25, 1950.

11. Hunt, *The Making of a Special Relationship*, pp. 303–304.

12. Grieder, *Hu Shih*, pp. 304–305.

13. Moore to Koo, August 22, 1919, Moore Papers, box 94.

BIBLIOGRAPHY

Archives and Manuscript Collections

Australia

George E. Morrison Papers, Mitchell Library, Sydney

Taiwan

Waijiao dangan (Diplomatic Archives), 1861–1928, Academia Sinica, Nangang

Guomindang Historical Archives, Yangmingshan

United Kingdom

Public Records Office, Kew

Diaries of Sir Miles Wedderburn Lampson, Lord Killearn, St. Antony's College, Oxford

United States

William R. Castle Papers, Herbert Hoover Presidential Library, West Branch, Iowa

Herbert Hoover Papers, Herbert Hoover Presidential Library, West Branch, Iowa

Charles Evans Hughes Papers, Library of Congress, Washington, D.C.

Nelson T. Johnson Papers, Library of Congress, Washington, D.C.

V.K. Wellington Koo Papers, Columbia University, New York

Robert Lansing Papers, Library of Congress, Washington, D.C.

Robert Lansing Papers, Princeton University, Firestone Library

Breckinridge Long Papers, Library of Congress, Washington, D.C.

John V.A. MacMurray Papers, Princeton University, Firestone Library

John Bassett Moore Papers, Library of Congress, Washington, D.C.

John R. Mott Papers, Yale Divinity Library

Frank Price Papers, George C. Marshall Research Foundation, Lexington, Virginia

T.V. Soong Papers, Hoover Institute of War and Peace, Stanford
Truman Presidential Library, Independence, Missouri
Edward T. Williams Papers, University of California—Berkeley
Woodrow Wilson Papers, Library of Congress, Washington, D.C.

Primary Sources

Documents on British Foreign Policy, 1919–1939. London: Her Majesty's Statio-
nery Office, 1966, First Series, vol. 14.

Documents on British Foreign Policy, 1919–1939. London: Her Majesty's Statio-
nery Office, 1960, Second Series, vol. 8.

Documents on British Foreign Policy, 1919–1939. London: Her Majesty's Statio-
nery Office, 1965, Second Series, vol. 9.

Documents on British Foreign Policy, 1919–1939. London: Her Majesty's Statio-
nery Office, 1970, Second Series, vol. 11.

Documents on British Foreign Policy, 1919–1939. London: Her Majesty's Statio-
nery Office, 1984, Second Series, vol. 20.

Documents on British Foreign Policy, 1919–1939. London: Her Majesty's Statio-
nery Office, 1984, Second Series, vol. 21.

*British Documents on Foreign Affairs: Reports and Papers from the Foreign Office
Confidential Print, Part II, Series E, Asia, 1914–1939.* University Publications of America, 1996, 45 vols.

Department of State. *United States Relations with China: With Special Reference
to the Period 1944–1949.* Washington: U.S. Government Printing Office,
1949.

———. *Foreign Relations of the United States, 1914.* Supplement, Washington:
U.S. Government Printing Office, 1928.

———. *Foreign Relations of the United States: The Paris Peace Conference.* Vols. 5
and 6. Washington: U.S. Government Printing Office, 1944.

———. *Foreign Relations of the United States, 1922.* Vol. 2. Washington: U.S.
Government Printing Office, 1938.

———. *Foreign Relations of the United States, 1923.* Vol. 1. Washington: U.S.
Government Printing Office, 1938.

———. *Foreign Relations of the United States, 1924.* Vol. 1. Washington: U.S.
Government Printing Office, 1939.

———. *Foreign Relations of the United States, 1927.* Vol. 2. Washington: U.S.
Government Printing Office, 1942.

———. *Foreign Relations of the United States, 1937.* Vols. 3 and 4. Washington:
U.S. Government Printing Office, 1954.

———. *Foreign Relations of the United States, 1938.* Vol. 3. Washington: U.S.
Government Printing Office, 1954.

————. *Foreign Relations of the United States, 1939*. Vol. 3. Washington: U.S. Government Printing Office, 1955.

————. *Foreign Relations of the United States, 1941*. Vol. 4. Washington: U.S. Government Printing Office, 1956.

————. *Foreign Relations of the United States, 1944*. Vols. 1 and 6. Washington: U.S. Government Printing Office, 1966, 1967.

————. *Foreign Relations of the United States, 1945*. Vols. 1 and 7. Washington: U.S. Government Printing Office, 1967, 1968.

————. *Foreign Relations of the United States, 1950*. Vol. 6. Washington: U.S. Government Printing Office, 1976.

————. *Foreign Relations of the United States, 1951*. Vols. 6 and 8. Washington: U.S. Government Printing Office, 1977, 1983.

————. *Foreign Relations of the United States, 1952–1954*. Vol. 14. Washington: U.S. Government Printing Office, 1985.

————. *Foreign Relations of the United States, 1955–1957*. Vol. 2. Washington: U.S. Government Printing Office, 1986.

Records of the Department of State Relating to the Internal Affairs of China, 1910–29. Washington.

Records of the Department of State Relating to the Internal Affairs of China, 1930–49. Bethesda: University Publications of America, 1985.

U.S. Military Intelligence Reports: China, 1911–1941. Frederick, MD: University Publications of America, 1983.

Secondary Sources

Accinelli, Robert. *Crisis and Commitment: United States Policy Toward Taiwan, 1950–1955*. Chapel Hill: University of North Carolina Press, 1996.

Adams, Randolph Greenfield. *A History of the Foreign Policy of the United States*. New York: The Macmillan Company, 1939.

Allitto, Guy S. *The Last Confucian: Liang Shu-ming and the Chinese Dilemma of Modernity*. Berkeley: University of California Press, 1979.

Angell, Norman. *The Great Illusion: A Study of the Relation of Military Power in Nations to their Economic and Social Advantage*. London: William Heinemann, 1911.

Atkins, Martyn. *Informal Empire in Crisis: British Diplomacy and the Chinese Customs Succession, 1927–1929*. Ithaca: Cornell East Asian Program, 1995.

Atwell, Pamela. *British Mandarins and Chinese Reformers: The British Administration of Weihaiwei (1898–1930) and the Territory's Return to Chinese Rule*. Hong Kong: Oxford University Press, 1985.

Barnhart, Michael A. *Japan Prepares for Total War: The Search for Economic Security, 1919–1941*. Ithaca: Cornell University Press, 1987.

Bastid-Bruguiere, Marianne. "Currents of Social Change." In *The Cambridge*

History of China: Late Ch'ing, 1800–1911. Edited by John K. Fairbank and Albert Feuerwerker. Cambridge: Cambridge University Press, 1980, vol. 11, pp. 535–602.

Bergere, Marie-Claire. *The Golden Age of the Chinese Bourgeoisie, 1911-1937.* Translated by Janet Lloyd. Cambridge: Cambridge University Press, 1986.

———. *Sun Yat-sen.* Translated by Janet Lloyd. Stanford: Stanford University Press, 1998.

Best, Anthony. *Britain, Japan and Pearl Harbor: Avoiding War in East Asia, 1936-41.* London: Routledge Kegan & Paul, 1995.

Bickers, Robert A. and Wasserstrom, Jeffrey N. "Shanghai's 'Dogs and Chinese Not Admitted' Sign: Legend, History and Contemporary Symbol." *China Quarterly.* Vol. 142, (June 1995), pp. 444–466.

———. *Britain in China: Community, Culture and Colonialism 1900–1949.* New York: Manchester University Press, 1999.

Blakeslee, George H., ed. *China and the Far East.* New York: Thomas Y. Crowell, 1910.

Bonsal, Stephen. *Suitors and Supplicants: The Little Nations at Versailles.* New York: Prentice-Hall, Inc., 1946.

Borg, Dorothy. *American Policy and the Chinese Revolution, 1925–1928.* New York: American Institute of Pacific Relations, 1947.

———. *The United States and the Far Eastern Crisis of 1933–1938: From the Manchurian Incident through the Initial Stage of the Undeclared Sino-Japanese War.* Cambridge: Harvard University Press, 1964.

———., and Heinrichs, Waldo. *Uncertain Years: Chinese-American Relations, 1947–50.* New York: Columbia University Press, 1980.

Boulger, Demetrius Charles. *China.* New York: Peter Fenelon Collier, 1898.

Boyle, John Hunter. *China and Japan at War, 1937–1945: The Politics of Collaboration.* Stanford: Stanford University Press, 1972.

Brands, Jr., H.W. "Testing Massive Retaliation: Credibility and Crisis Management in the Taiwan Strait." *International Security.* Vol. 12 (Spring 1988), pp. 124–151.

Brendon, Piers. *The Dark Valley: A Panorama of the 1930s.* New York: Vintage Books, 2002.

Bunker, Gerald E. *The Peace Conspiracy: Wang Ching-wei and the China War, 1937–1941.* Cambridge: Harvard University Press, 1972.

Burns, Richard Dean and Edward M. Bennett, eds. *Diplomats in Crisis: United States-Chinese-Japanese Relations, 1919–1941.* Santa Barbara: Clio Books, 1974.

Byrne, Eugene. "The Dismissal of Sir Francis Aglen as Inspector of the Chinese Maritime Customs Service, 1927." *Leeds East Asia Paper.* Leeds: University of Leeds, 1995.

Cao, Rulin. *Yisheng zhi huiyi* (Reminiscences of my life). Taibei: Biographical Literature, 1980.

Carley, Michael Jabara. *1939: The Alliance That Never Was and the Coming of World War II*. Chicago: Ivan R. Dee, 1999.

Carr, Edward Hallett. *The Twenty Years' Crisis, 1919–1939: An Introduction to the Study of International Relations*. New York: Harper & Row, 1964, 2nd ed.

Cavendish, Patrick. "The 'New China' of the Kuomintang." In *Modern China's Search for Political Form*. Edited by Jack Gray. London: Oxford University Press, 1969, pp. 138–186.

Cen, Xuelu. *Sanshui Liang Yensun xiansheng nienbiao* (Chronological biography of Liang Shiyi). Taibei: reprint; 1962, 2 vols.

Chan, F. Gilbert. "Sun Yat-sen and the Origins of the Kuomintang Reorganization." In *China in the 1920s: Nationalism and Revolution*. Edited by F. Gilbert Chan and Thomas H. Etzold. New York: New Viewpoints, 1976, pp. 15–37.

Chan, K.C. "The Abrogation of British Extraterritoriality in China 1942–43: A Study of Anglo-American-Chinese Relations." *Modern Asian Studies*. Vol. 11 (April 1977), pp. 257–291.

Chan Lau Kit-Ching. "The Lincheng Incident—A Case Study of British Policy in China Between the Washington Conference (1921–22) and the First Nationalist Revolution (1925–28)." *Journal of Oriental Studies*. Vol. 10 (July 1972), pp. 172–186.

———. "Hong Kong in Sino-British Diplomacy, 1926–1945." In *Precarious Balance: Hong Kong Between China and Britain 1842–1992*. Edited by Ming K. Chan. Armonk, NY: M.E. Sharpe, 1994.

Chang, Gordon H. *Friends and Enemies: The United States, China, and the Soviet Union, 1948–1972*. Stanford: Stanford University Press, 1990.

Chang, Yu Chuan. "The Organisation of the Waichiaopu." *Chinese Social and Political Science Review*. Vol. 1 (1916), pp. 36–39.

Chen, Fengxiang. *Jindai riben de dalu zhengce* (Japan's recent China policy). Taibei: Jinhe chuben she, 1992.

Chen, Jerome. *China and the West: Society and Culture, 1815–1937*. Bloomington: Indiana University Press, 1979.

———. "The Chinese Communist Movement to 1927." In *Cambridge History of China: Republican China, 1912–1949*. Edited by John K. Fairbank and Albert Feuerwerker. Cambridge: Cambridge University Press, 1986, vol. 12, pp. 505–720.

Chen, Liwen. *Song Ziwen yu zhanshi waijiao* (T.V. Soong and China's wartime diplomacy). Taibei: Academia Historica, 1991.

Cheng, Sih-gung. *Modern China: A Political Study*. Oxford: Clarendon Press, 1919.

Chi, Madeliene. *China Diplomacy, 1914–1918*. Cambridge: Harvard University Press, 1970.

———. "China and Unequal Treaties at the Paris Peace Conference of 1919." *Asian Profile*. Vol. 1 (August 1973), pp. 49–61.

———. "Shanghai-Hangchow-Ningpo Railway Loan: A Case Study of the Rights Recovery Movement." *Modern Asian Studies*. Vol. 7 (January 1973), pp. 85–106.

———. "Bureaucratic Capitalists in Operation: Tso Ju-lin and His New Communications Clique." *Journal of Asian Studies*. Vol. 34 (May 1975), pp. 675–688.

Ch'i, Hsi-sheng. *Warlord Politics in China 1916–1928*. Stanford: Stanford University Press, 1976.

———. "Chiang Kai-shek and Franklin D. Roosevelt." In *FDR and His Contemporaries: Foreign Perceptions of an American President*. Edited by Cornelis A. van Minnen and John F. Sears. New York: St. Martin's Press, 1992, pp. 127–142.

Chiang, Kai-shek. *China's Destiny and Chinese Economic Theory*. New York: Roy Publishers, 1947.

Chih, Yü-ju. "Goodnow's Mission to China, 1913–1915." *Tsing-hua Journal of Chinese Studies*. Vol. 13 (December 1981), pp. 197–217.

Chu, Pao-chin. "V.K. Wellington Koo: The Diplomacy of Nationalism." In *Diplomats in Crisis: United States-Chinese-Japanese Relations, 1919–1941*. Edited by Richard Dean Burns and Edward M. Bennett. Santa Barbara: Clio Books, 1974, pp. 125–152.

———. "From the Paris Peace Conference to the Manchurian Incident: The Beginnings of China's Diplomacy of Resistance Against Japan." In *China and Japan: A Search for Balance Since WWI*. Edited by Alvin D. Coox and Hilary Conroy. Santa Barbara: Clio Books, 1978, pp. 62–82.

———. *V.K. Wellington Koo: A Case Study of China's Diplomat and Diplomacy of Nationalism, 1912–1966*. Hong Kong: The Chinese University Press, 1981.

Chu, Samuel C. and Liu, Kwang-ching, eds. *Li Hung-chang and China's Early Modernization*. Armonk, New York: M.E. Sharpe, 1994.

Clements, Kendrick A. *The Presidency of Woodrow Wilson*. Lawrence: University Press of Kansas, 1992.

Clifford, Nicholas R. *Retreat From China: British Policy in the Far East, 1937–1941*. Seattle: University of Washington Press, 1967.

———. *Spoilt Children of Empire: Westerners in Shanghai and the Chinese Revolution of the 1920s*. Hanover: Middlebury College Press, 1991.

Coble, Parks M. *Facing Japan: Chinese Politics and Japanese Imperialism, 1931–1937*. Cambridge: Harvard University Press, 1991.

Cohen, Paul. *Between Tradition and Modernity: Wang T'ao and Reform in Late Ch'ing China*. Cambridge: Harvard University Press, 1974.

————. "The New Coastal Reformers." In *Reform in Nineteenth-Century China*. Edited by Paul A. Cohen and John E. Schrecker. Cambridge: Harvard University Press, 1976, pp. 255–264.

Cohen, Paul and John E. Schrecker, eds. *Reform in Nineteenth-Century China*. Cambridge: Harvard University Press, 1976.

Cohen, Warren I. *The Chinese Connection: Roger S. Greene, Thomas W. Lamont, George E. Sokolsky and American-East Asian Relations*. New York: Columbia University Press, 1978.

————. *Empire Without Tears: America's Foreign Relations 1921–1933*. New York: McGraw-Hill, 1987.

————. "Acheson, His Advisers, and China, 1949–1950." In *Uncertain Years: Chinese-American Relations, 1947–50*. Edited by Dorothy Borg and Waldo Heinrichs. New York: Columbia University Press, 1980, pp. 13–52.

Coon, Horace. *Columbia: Colossus on the Hudson*. New York: E.P. Dutton, 1947.

Coox, Alvin D. and Hilary Conroy, eds. *China and Japan: A Search for Balance Since WWI*. Santa Barbara: Clio Books, 1978.

Colquhuon, Archibald R. *China in Transformation*. New York: Harper Brothers, 1899).

Crowley, James B. *Japan's Quest for Autonomy: National Security and Foreign Policy 1930–1938*. Princeton: Princeton University Press, 1966.

Crunden, Robert M. *Ministers of Reform: The Progressives' Achievement in American Civilization, 1889–1920*. Urbana: University of Illinois Press, 1984.

Current Biography 1941. New York: The H.W. Wilson Co., 1941.

Dallek, Robert. *Franklin D. Roosevelt and American Foreign Policy, 1932–1945*. New York: Oxford University Press, 1979.

Dayer, Roberta Allbert. *Bankers and Diplomats in China, 1917–1925: The Anglo-American Relationship*. London: Frank Cass, 1981.

DeAngelis, Richard C. "Resisting Intervention: American Policy and the Lin Ch'eng Incident." *Jindai shi yanjiu so jikan* (Bulletin of the Institute of Modern History). Vol. 10 (1981), pp. 401–416.

Dickinson, Frederick R. *War and National Reinvention: Japan in the Great War, 1914–1919*. Cambridge: Harvard University Press, 1999.

Ding, Wenjiang et al. *Liang rengong xiansheng nienpu changbian qugao* (First draft of an extended chronology of the life of Mr. Liang Qichao). Taibei: Shijie shuju, 1958, 3 vols.

Dirlik, Arif. *The Origins of Chinese Communism*. New York: Oxford University Press, 1989.

Dittmer, Lowell and Kim, Samuel S., eds. *China's Quest for National Identity*. Ithaca: Cornell University Press, 1993.

Divine, Robert A. *Second Chance: The Triumph of Internationalism in America During World War II*. New York: Atheneum, 1967.

Dockrill, Michael L. and J. Douglas Goold. *Peace Without Promise: Britain and the Peace Conferences, 1919–1923.* Hamden, Conn.: Archon Books, 1980.

Dower, John. *Empire and Aftermath: Yoshida Shigeru and the Japanese Experience, 1878–1954.* Cambridge: Harvard University Press, 1979.

Dreifort, John E. *Myopic Grandeur: The Ambivalence of French Foreign Policy toward the Far East, 1919–1945.* Kent: Kent State University Press, 1991.

Dreyer, Edward L. *China at War, 1901–1949.* New York: Longman, 1995.

Duus, Peter. *The Rise of Modern Japan.* Boston: Houghton Mifflin Company, 1976.

Eastman, Lloyd E. *The Abortive Revolution: China Under Nationalist Rule, 1927–1937.* Cambridge: Harvard University Press, 1974.

———. *Seeds of Destruction: Nationalist China in War and Revolution, 1937–1949.* Stanford: Stanford University Press, 1984.

———. *Family, Fields, and Ancestors: Constancy and Change in China's Social and Economic History, 1550–1949.* New York: Oxford University Press, 1988.

———. "Ch'ing-i and Chinese Policy Formation During the Nineteenth Century." *Journal of Asian Studies.* Vol. 24 (August 1965), pp. 595–611.

———. "Nationalist China during the Nanking Decade, 1927–1937." In *Cambridge History of China: Republican China, 1912-1949.* Edited by John K. Fairbank and Albert Feuerwerker. Cambridge: Cambridge University Press, 1986, vol. 13, pp. 116–167.

———. "The May Fourth Movement as a Historical Turning Point: Ecological Exhaustion, Militarization, and Other Causes of China's Modern Crisis." In *Perspectives on Modern China: Four Anniversaries.* Edited by Kenneth Lieberthal et al. Armonk, New York: M.E. Sharpe, Inc., 1991, pp. 123–138.

Edwards, E.W. *British Diplomacy and Finance in China, 1895–1914.* Oxford: Clarendon Press, 1987.

Elleman, Bruce A. *Diplomacy and Deception: The Secret History of Sino-Soviet Diplomatic Relations, 1917–1927.* Armonk, NY: M.E. Sharpe, 1997.

———. *Modern Chinese Warfare, 1795–1989.* New York: Routledge, 2001.

———. *Wilson and China : A Revised History of the Shandong Question.* Armonk, NY: M.E. Sharpe, 2002.

———. "The Soviet Union's Secret Diplomacy Concerning the Chinese Eastern Railway, 1924–1925." *Journal of Asian Studies.* Vol. 53 (May 1994), pp. 459–486.

Endicott, Stephen Lyon. *Diplomacy and Enterprise: British China Policy, 1933–1937.* Vancouver: University of British Columbia Press, 1975.

Eto, Shinkichi. "China's International Relations 1911–1931." *Cambridge History of China: Republican China, 1912–1949.* Edited by John King Fairbank and Albert Feuerwerker. Cambridge: Cambridge University Press, 1980, vol. 13, pp. 74–115

Fairbank, John King and Liu, Kwang-Ching eds. *The Cambridge History of China: Late Ch'ing, 1800–1911.* Cambridge: Cambridge University Press, 1980, 2 vols.

———., ed. *Cambridge History of China: Republican China, 1912–1949.* Cambridge: Cambridge University Press, 1983, vol. 12.

———. "Introduction: Maritime and Continental in China's History." In *Cambridge History of China: Republican China, 1912–1949.* Edited by John K. Fairbank. Cambridge: Cambridge University Press, 1983, vol. 12, pp. 1–27.

Ferrell, Robert. *Woodrow Wilson and World War I, 1917–1921.* New York: Harper & Row, 1985.

Feuerwerker, Albert. "The Foreign Presence in China." In *Cambridge History of China: Republican China, 1912–1949.* Edited by John K. Fairbank. Cambridge: Cambridge University Press, 1983, vol. 12, pp. 128–207.

Fifield, Russell H. "Secretary Hughes and the Shantung Question," *Pacific Historical Review.* Vol. 23 (November 1954), pp. 373–385.

Fishel, Wesley R. *The End of Extraterritoriality in China.* Berkeley: University of California Press, 1952.

Fitzgerald, John. *Awakening China: Politics, Culture, and Class in Nationalist Revolution.* Stanford: Stanford University Press, 1996.

———. "The Misconceived Revolution: State and Society in China's Nationalist Revolution, 1923–26." *Journal of Asian Studies.* Vol. 49 (May 1990), pp. 323–343.

Folsom, Kenneth E. *Friends, Guests, and Colleagues: The Mu-Fu System in the Late Ch'ing Period.* Berkeley: University of California Press, 1968.

Foot, Rosemary. *The Practice of Power: US Relations With China Since 1949.* New York: Oxford University Press, 1997.

Fox, John P. *Germany and the Far Eastern Crisis 1931–1938: A Study in Diplomacy and Ideology.* Oxford: Clarendon Press, 1982.

Franke, Herbert. "Sung Embassies: Some General Observations." In *China Among Equals: The Middle Kingdom and its Neighbors, 10th–14th Centuries.* Edited by Morris Rossabi. Berkeley: University of California Press, 1983.

Fung, Edmund S.K. *The Diplomacy of Imperial Retreat: Britain's South China Policy, 1924–1931.* Hong Kong: Oxford University Press, 1991.

———. "The Chinese Nationalists and the Unequal Treaties, 1924–1931." *Modern Asian Studies.* Vol. 21 (October 1987), pp. 793–819.

———. "Nationalist Foreign Policy, 1928–1937." In *Ideal and Reality: Social and Political Change in Modern China, 1860–1949.* Edited by David Pong and Edmund S.K. Fung. Lanham: University Press of America, 1985, pp.185–217.

Furth, Charlotte. "Intellectual Change: From the Reform Movement to the May Fourth Movement, 1895–1920." In *Cambridge History of China: Republi-*

can China, 1912–1949. Edited by John K. Fairbank. Cambridge: Cambridge University Press, 1983, vol. 12, pp. 322–405.

Gaddis, John Lewis. The United States and the Origins of the Cold War, 1941–1947. New York: Columbia University Press, 1972.

———. Strategies of Containment: A Critical Appraisal of Postwar American National Security Policy. New York: Oxford University Press, 1982.

———. Russia, the Soviet Union and the United States: An Interpretative History. New York: McGraw-Hill, 1990, 2nd ed.

———. "The Strategic Perspective: The Rise and Fall of the 'Defensive Perimeter' Concept, 1947–1951." In Uncertain Years: Chinese-American Relations, 1947–50. Edited by Dorothy Borg and Waldo Heinrichs. New York: Columbia University Press, 1980, pp. 61–118.

Gallicchio, Marc. The Cold War Begins in Asia: American East Asian Policy and the Fall of the Japanese Empire. New York: Columbia University Press, 1988.

Gao, Ke. Waijiao yu zhanzheng: Gu Weijun waijiao guan shengzu pianduan (Diplomats and War: A Segment of V.K. Wellington Koo's diplomatic career). Shanghai: Renming chuben she, 1995.

Gardner, Lloyd C. Safe For Democracy: The Anglo-American Response to Revolution, 1913–1923. New York: Oxford University Press, 1984.

———. Spheres of Influence: The Great Powers Partition Europe, from Munich to Yalta. Chicago: Ivan R. Dee, 1993.

Garver, John W. Chinese-Soviet Relations, 1937–1945: The Diplomacy of Chinese Nationalism. New York: Oxford University Press, 1988.

———. The Sino-American Alliance: Nationalist China and American Cold War Strategy in Asia. New York: M.E. Sharpe, 1997.

———. "China's Wartime Diplomacy." In China's Bitter Victory: The War With Japan, 1937–1945. Edited by James C. Hsiung and Steven I. Levine. Armonk: M.E. Sharpe, 1997, pp. 3–32.

Gascoyne-Cecil, William. Changing China. New York: D. Appleton, 1913.

Giles, Herbert Allen. The Civilization of China. London: Williams and Norgate, 1911.

———. China and the Chinese. New York: Columbia University Press, 1912.

Gong, Gerrit W. The Standard of 'Civilization' in International Society. Oxford: Clarendon Press, 1984.

———. "China's Entry into International Society." In The Expansion of International Society. Edited by Hedley Bull and Adam Watson. Oxford: Clarendon Press, 1984, pp. 143–184.

Gormly, James L. The Collapse of the Grand Alliance, 1945–1948. Baton Rouge: Louisiana State University Press, 1987.

Gowen, Robert Joseph. "Great Britain and the Twenty-One Demands of 1915:

Cooperation versus Effacement." *Journal of Modern History.* Vol. 43 (March 1971), pp. 76–106.

Grenville, J.A.S. *The Major International Treaties 1914–1973: A History and Guide with Texts.* New York: Stein & Day, 1974.

Grieder, Jerome. *Hu Shih and the Chinese Renaissance: Liberalism in the Chinese Revolution, 1917–1937.* Cambridge: Harvard University Press, 1970.

Guo, Zheyin. *Guomindang paixi douzheng shi* (A history of Guomindang factional struggles). Taibei: Zhuguan dushu gufen yoxian gongsi, 1993.

Haggie, Paul. *Brittania at Bay: The Defence of the British Empire against Japan, 1931–1941.* Oxford: Clarendon Press, 1981.

Hao, Yen-ping. *The Comprador in Nineteenth Century China: Bridge Between East and West.* Cambridge: Harvard University Press, 1970.

Hao, Yen-ping and Wang, Erh-Min. "Changing Chinese Views of Western Relations, 1840–1895." In *The Cambridge History of China: Late Ch'ing, 1800–1911.* Edited by John K. Fairbank and Kwang-Ching Liu. Cambridge: Cambridge University Press, 1980, vol. 11 pp. 142–201.

Harrison, Henrietta. *The Making of the Republican Citizen: Political Ceremonies and Symbols in China, 1911–1929.* New York: Oxford University Press, 2000.

Harrison, Richard A. "A Neutralization Plan for the Pacific: Roosevelt and Anglo-American Cooperation, 1934–1937." *Pacific Historical Review.* Vol. 50 (1988), pp. 47–72.

Haslam, Jonathan. *The Soviet Union and the Search for Collective Security in Europe, 1933–39.* New York: St. Martin's Press, 1984.

———. *The Soviet Union and the Threat from the East, 1933–41: Moscow, Tokyo and the Prelude to the Pacific War.* Pittsburgh: University of Pittsburgh Press, 1992.

He, Lie. "Minqu zhong ying xicang jiaoshe" (Anglo-Chinese negotiations over Tibet during the early Republican period). In *Zhongguo jindai xiandai shi lunji* (Essays on recent modern Chinese history): *Minqu waijiao* (Early Republican foreign policy). (Taibei: Commercial Press, 1986), vol. 23, part 1, pp. 155–200.

Heinrichs, Waldo. *Threshold of War: Franklin D. Roosevelt and American Entry into World War II.* New York: Oxford University Press, 1988.

Herman, Sondra. *Eleven Against War: Studies in American Internationalist Thought, 1898–1921.* Stanford: Stanford University Press, 1969.

Hilderbrand, Robert C. *Dumbarton Oaks: The Origins of the United Nations and the Search for Postwar Security.* Chapel Hill: University of North Carolina Press, 1990.

Hinners, David. *Tong Shao-yi and his Family: A Saga of Two Countries and Three Generations.* Lanham, University Press of America, 1999.

Hoxie, R. Gordon, et al. *A History of the Faculty of Political Science, Columbia University.* New York: Columbia University Press, 1955.

Hsu, Immanuel C.Y. *China's Entrance into the Family of Nations: The Diplomatic Phase, 1858–1880.* Cambridge: Harvard University Press, 1968.

Hu, Shi. *Hu Shi de riji: liuluo zaiwai de Hu Shi riji* (Hu Shi's diary while wandering abroad). Taibei: Hanjing wenhua shiye youxian gongsi,1987.

Huang, Meizhen and Yang Hanqing, "Nationalist China's Negotiating Position During the Stalemate, 1938–1945." In *Chinese Collaboration with Japan, 1932–1945: The Limits of Accommodation.* Edited by David P. Barrett and Larry N. Shyu. Stanford: Stanford University Press, 2001, pp. 56–76.

Huang, Jiamo. "Zhongguo dui ou zhan de qubu fanying" (China's initial policy toward World War I). In *Zhongguo jindai xiandai shi lunji* (Essays on recent modern Chinese history): *Minqu waijiao* (Early Republican foreign policy). Taibei: Commercial Press, 1986, vol. 23, pp. 261–278.

Hull, William I. *The New Peace Movement.* Boston: World Peace Foundation, 1912.

Hunt, Michael H. *Frontier Defense and the Open Door: Manchuria in Chinese-American Relations, 1895–1911.* New Haven: Yale University Press, 1973.

———. *The Making of a Special Relationship: The United States and China to 1914.* New York: Columbia University Press, 1983.

———. *Ideology and U.S. Foreign Policy.* New Haven: Yale University Press, 1987.

———. *The Genesis of Chinese Communist Foreign Policy.* New York: Columbia University Press, 1996.

———. "The May Fourth Era: China's Place in the World." In *Perspectives on Modern China: Four Anniversaries.* Edited by Kenneth Lieberthal et al. Armonk, New York: M.E. Sharpe, Inc., 1991, pp. 178–200.

———. "Chinese National Identity and the Strong State: The Late Qing-Republican Crisis." In *China's Quest for National Identity.* Edited by Lowell Dittmer and Samuel S. Kim. Ithaca: Cornell University Press, 1993, pp. 62–79.

Hunt, Michael H. and Jun, Niu, eds. *Toward a History of Chinese Communist Foreign Relations, 1920s–1960s: Personalities and Interpretive Approaches.* Washington: Asia Program Occasional Paper Woodrow Wilson International Center, 1995.

Iklé, Frank W. "Japanese-German Peace Negotiations during World War I." *American Historical Review.* Vol. 71 (October 1965), pp. 62–76.

Iriye, Akira. *After Imperialism: The Search for a New Order in the Far East, 1921–1931.* Cambridge: Harvard University Press, 1965.

———. *Pacific Estrangement: Japanese-American Expansion, 1897–1911.* Cambridge: Harvard University Press, 1972.

———. *The Origins of the Second World War in Asia and the Pacific.* London: Longman, 1987.

———. "Imperialism in East Asia." In *Modern East Asia: Essays in Interpreta-*

tion. Edited by James B. Crowley. New York: Harcourt, Brace & World, 1970, pp. 122–150.

———. "Japan as a Competitor, 1895-1917." *Mutual Images: Essays in American-Japanese Relations*. Edited by Akira Iriye. Cambridge: Harvard University Press, 1975, pp. 73–99.

———. "Japanese Aggression and China's International Position 1931–1949." In *Cambridge History of China: Republican China 1912–1949*. Edited by John K. Fairbank and Albert Feuerwerker. Cambridge: Cambridge University Press, 1986, vol. 13, pp. 492–546.

Isaacs, Harold R. *Images of Asia: American Views of China and India*. New York: Capricorn Books, 1962.

Israel, Jerry. *Progressivism and the Open Door: America and China, 1905–1921*. Pittsburgh: University of Pittsburgh Press, 1971.

Jespersen, T. Christopher. *American Images of China, 1931–1949*. Stanford: Stanford University Press, 1996.

Jiang, Yongjing. "Gu Weijun yu jiuyiba shibian," (V.K. Wellington Koo and the September 18 Incident). In *Guomin zhengfu chuli jiuyiba shibian zhi zhongyao wenxian* (Important Nationalist government documents on the Manchurian Incident). Edited by Li Yunhan. Taibei: Guomindang Historical Commission, 1992, pp. 669–694.

Jin, Guangyao. *Gu Weijun zhuan* (A Biography of V.K. Wellington Koo). Hebei: Hebei renming chuben she, 1999.

———. "Gu Weijun yu zhongguo waijiao guoji xueshu taolun hui zongshu (Summarizing the international conference on V.K. Wellington Koo and Chinese foreign policy). In *Lishi yanjiu* (Historical Studies) 6 (2000): pp. 185–187.

Johnson, Linda Cooke. *Shanghai: From Market Town to Treaty Port, 1074–1858*. Stanford: Stanford University Press, 1995.

Johnston, James. *China and Its Future: In the Light of the Antecedents of the Empire, Its People and Their Institutions*. London: Elliot Stock, 1899.

Jordan, Donald A. *Chinese Boycotts versus Japanese Bombs: The Failure of China's "Revolutionary Diplomacy," 1931–1932*. Ann Arbor: University of Michigan, 1991.

———. "The Place of Chinese Disunity in Japanese Army Strategy During 1931." *China Quarterly*. No. 109 (March 1987), pp. 42–63.

Kagen, Richard C. "From Revolutionary Iconoclasm to National Revolution: Ch'en Tu-hsiu and the Chinese Communist Movement." In *China in the 1920s: Nationalism and Revolution*. Edited by F. Gilbert Chan and Thomas H. Etzold. New York: New Viewpoints, 1976, pp. 55–72.

Kawamura, Noriko. *Turbulence in the Pacific: Japanese-U.S. Relations During World War I*. Westport: Praeger, 1999.

Kennedy, Malcolm D. *The Estrangement of Great Britain and Japan, 1917–1935.* Berkeley: University of California Press, 1969.

Kirby, William C. *Germany and Republican China.* Stanford: Stanford University Press, 1984.

———. "Traditions of Centrality, Authority, and Management in Modern China's Foreign Relations." In *Chinese Foreign Policy: Theory and Practice.* Edited by Thomas W. Robinson and David Shambaugh. Oxford: Clarendon Press, 1994, pp. 13–29.

———. "Chinese-American Relations in Comparative Perspective, 1900–1949." In *Pacific Passage: The Study of American-East Asian Relations on the Eve of the Twenty-First Century.* Edited by Warren I. Cohen. New York: Columbia University Press, 1996, pp. 163–189.

———. "The Internationalization of China: Foreign Relations at Home and Abroad in the Republican Era." *The China Quarterly.* Vol. 152 (June 1997), pp. 433–451.

Knock, Thomas J. *To End All Wars: Woodrow Wilson and the Quest for a New World Order.* Princeton: Princeton University Press, 1992.

Koen, Ross Y. *The China Lobby in American Politics.* New York: Harper & Row, 1974.

Koo Hui-Lan. *Hui-Lan Koo [Madame Wellington Koo]: An Autobiography as Told to Mary Van Rensselaer Thayer.* New York: Dial Press, 1943.

Koo, Madame Wellington. *No Feast Lasts Forever.* New York: Quadrangle Books, 1975.

Koo, Vi Kyuin Wellington. *The Status of Aliens in China.* New York: Columbia University, 1912.

———. *China and the League of Nations.* London: Unwin Press, 1920.

———. *The Open Door Policy and World Peace.* London: Oxford University Press, 1939.

———. V.K. Wellington Koo Oral History Collection. Chinese Oral History Project, East Asian Institute, Columbia University.

———. "The Task Before China's Students Today." *Chinese Students' Monthly.* Vol. 4 (March 1909), pp. 321–324.

———. "American Commercial Opportunities in China." *Chinese Students' Monthly.* Vol. 11 (April 1916), pp. 425–435.

———. "The Building of a Nation as Illustrated by the History of the United States and China." *Johns Hopkins University Circular.* (1916), pp. 5–13.

———. "Speech on the Occasion of the Dedication of the Flag of the Chinese Republic to the Cause of the War on China Day, October 1, 1918." *Chinese Students' Monthly.* Vol. 14 (November 1918), pp. 21–24.

———. "Problems and Difficulties of Returned Students: Address Made at the Platform Meeting of the Chinese Students' Conference at Brown University, Providence, R.I., on September 6, 1917." *Chinese Students' Monthly.* Vol. 13 (November 1917), pp. 20–28.

———. "The Administration of International Law." *Chinese Social and Political Science Review.* Vol. 2 (September 1917), pp. 1–25.

———. "China, Great Britain and the United States." *Chinese Students' Monthly.* Vol. 16 (June 1921), pp. 547–549.

———. "Duiyu jiuyiba shibian zhi kanxiang," (Thoughts on the Mukden Incident). *Waijiao yuebao* (Foreign affairs monthly). Vol. 1, no. 3 (September 18, 1932), p. 2.

———. "China and the War Against Aggression." *Asiatic Review.* Vol. 37 (October 1941), pp. 16–21.

———. "China and the Problem of World Order." *New Commonwealth Quarterly.* Vol. 7 (January 1942), pp. 183–190.

———. "China's Intellectual and Social Revolution." *Great Britain and the East.* Vol. 59 (November 28, 1942), pp. 13–14.

———. "Life and Outlook of the Chinese People." *Great Britain and the East.* Vol. 59 (December 5, 1942), pp. 23, 25.

———. "Basic Problems of the United Nations." *The Annals of the American Academy of Political and Social Science.* Vol. 252 (July 1947), pp. 78–83.

———. "China in Transition: Political, Economic, Social and Cultural Changes." *Vital Speeches of the Day.* Vol. 14 (March 1, 1948), pp. 313–320.

———. "China is Worth Saving." *Reader's Digest.* Vol. 55 (November 1949), pp. 39–44.

———. "The Crisis in Asia: National Independence vs. Communistic Imperialism." *Vital Speeches of the Day.* Vol. 16 (August 1, 1950), pp. 620–623.

———. "The Real China." *The Annals of the American Academy of Political and Social Science.* Vol. 294 (July 1954), pp. 71–82.

Laffey, John F. "Lyonnais Imperialism in the Far East, 1900–1938." *Modern Asian Studies.* Vol. 10 (April 1976), pp. 225–248.

———. "French Far Eastern Policy in the 1930s." *Modern Asian Studies.* Vol. 23 (January 1989), pp. 117–149.

Lamberton, Mary. *St. John's University, Shanghai, 1879–1951.* New York: United Board for Christian Colleges in China, 1955.

Langer, William L. and S. Everett Gleason. *The Challenge to Isolation 1937–1940.* New York: Harper Brothers, 1952.

Lee, Bradford. *Britain and the Sino-Japanese War, 1937–1939: A Study in the Dilemmas of British Decline.* Stanford: Stanford University Press, 1973.

Lee, En-han. *Beifa qianhou de "geming waijiao" 1925–1931* (Nationalist China's "Revolutionary Diplomacy." Taibei: Academia Sinica, 1993.

LaFeber, Walter. *The Clash: U.S.-Japanese Relations Throughout History.* New York: W.W. Norton, 1998.

Leffler, Melvyn P. *The Specter of Communism: The United States and the Origins of the Cold War, 1917–1953.* New York: Hill & Wang, 1994.

Leonard, Jane Kate. *Wei Yuan and China's Rediscovery of the Maritime World.* Cambridge: Harvard University Press, 1984.

Leong, Sow-theng. *Sino-Soviet Diplomatic Relations, 1917–1926.* Honolulu: The University Press of Hawaii, 1976.

Levin, N. Gordon. *Woodrow Wilson and World Politics: America's Response to War and Revolution.* New York: Oxford University Press, 1967.

Levine, Steven I. *Anvil of Victory: The Communist Revolution in Manchuria, 1945–1948.* New York: Columbia University Press, 1987.

Li, Guopei. "Deguo dangan zhong yuguan zhongguo zhanjia diyici shijie dazhan de jixiang jizai" (The German archives and a record of China's entrance into the First World War). *Zhongguo jindai xiandai shi lunji* (Essays on recent modern Chinese history). *Minqu waijiao,* (Early Republican foreign policy), vol. 33, pp. 279–294.

Li, Jianneng. *Zuijin sanshi nian zhongguo zhengzhi shi* (China's political history in the past thirty years). Shanghai: Pacific Bookstore, 1933.

Li, Nianxuan et al, eds. *Zhong e guanxi shiliao: qubing xibailiya* (Historical documents related to Sino-Russian relations: Sending troops to Siberia). Nangang: Academia Sinica, 1984.

Li, Tien-yi. *Woodrow Wilson's China Policy, 1913–1917.* New York: University of Kansas Press, 1952.

Li, Yunhan. *Cong ronggong dao qingdang* (From admission of the Communists to the purification of the Guomindang). Taibei: Chinese Academic Scholarship Association, 1966.

———. "Kangzhan qian zhongguo zhishi fenzi de jiuguo yuandong" (Chinese intellectuals and the national salvation movement preceding the Sino-Japanese War). In *Zhongguo xiandai shi lunji* (Essays on Modern Chinese History). Edited by Zhang Yufa. *Shinian jianguo* (Ten Years of National Reconstruction). Taibei: Lianqing quban shiye kongsi, 1982, vol. 8, pp. 337–363.

———. "Gu Weijun yu jiuyiba shibian zhi zhongri jiaoshe," (V.K. Wellington Koo and Sino-Japanese negotiations after the September 18 Incident). In *Guomin zhengfu chuli jiuyiba shibian zhi zhongyao wenxian* (Important Nationalist government documents on the Manchurian Incident). Edited by Li Yunhan. Taibei: Guomindang Historical Commission, 1992, pp. 647–668.

Li, Yushu et al eds. *Zhong ri guanxi shiliao: ou zhan yu shandong wenti, sannian zhi wunian* (Historical documents related to Sino-Japanese Relations: The First World War and the Shandong Problem, 1914–16). Taibei: Academia Sinica, 1974.

Li, Yushu et al eds. *Zhong ri guanxi shiliao: Lukuang jiaoshe* (Historical documents related to Sino-Japanese Relations: Negotiations over Roads & Mines, 1911–16). Taibei: Academia Sinica, 1976.

―――. *Zhong ri guanxi shiliao: tongshang yu shuiwu (jinyun fu)* (Historical documents related to Sino-Japanese Relations: Commercial trade and customs (embargo), 1911–16). Taibei: Academia Sinica, 1976.

Li, Yushu, Lin Mingde et al, eds. *Zhong ri guanxi shiliao: ershiyi tiao jiaoshe, sinian zhi wunian,* (Historical documents related to Sino-Japanese Relations: The Twenty-One Demands negotiations, 1915–1916). Nangang: Academia Sinica, 1985.

―――. eds. *Zhong ri guanxi shiliao: yiben jiaoshe, 1911–16* (Historical documents related to Sino-Japanese Relations: General relations). Nangang: Academia Sinica, 1986.

―――. eds. *Zhong ri guanxi shiliao: shandong wenti, 1920–1926* (Historical documents related to Sino-Japanese Relations: The Shandong Question). Nangang: Academia Sinica, 1987.

Liang, Chin-tung. *General Stilwell in China, 1942–1944: The Full Story.* New York: St. John's University Press, 1972.

Liao, Kuang-sheng. *Antiforeignism and Modernization in China, 1860–1980: Linkage between Domestic Politics and Foreign Policy.* Hong Kong: The Chinese University Press, 1984.

Liao, Minshu. "Gu Weijun yu bali hehui zhongguo daibiao tuan," (V.K. Wellington Koo and the Chinese delegation at the Paris Peace Conference). In *Gu Weijun yu zhongguo waijiao* (Wellington Koo and Chinese Diplomacy). Edited by Jin Guangyao. Shanghai: Shanghai guji chuban she 2001, pp. 52–85.

Lieberthal, Kenneth et al, eds. *Perspectives on Modern China: Four Anniversaries.* Armonk, New York: M.E. Sharpe, Inc., 1991.

Lilley, Charles R. "A Mid-Level Bureaucrat's Dream to Save China." *SHAFR Newsletter.* Vol. 33 (June 2002), pp. 41–49.

Link, Arthur S., ed. *The Papers of Woodrow Wilson.* Princeton: Princeton University Press, 1966–94, 69 vols.

Liu, Kwang-ching. *Americans and Chinese: A Historical Essay and a Bibliography.* Cambridge: Harvard University Press, 1963.

Liu, Xiaoyuan. *A Partnership for Disorder: China, the United States, and their Policies for the Postwar Disposition of the Japanese Empire, 1941–1945.* Cambridge: Cambridge University Press, 1996.

Lo, Hui-min, ed. *The Correspondence of G.E. Morrison.* Cambridge: Cambridge University Press, 1978, 2 vols.

Louis, William Roger. *British Strategy in the Far East, 1919–1939.* Oxford: Clarendon Press, 1971.

Lowe, Peter. *Great Britain and Japan, 1911–15: A Study of British Far Eastern Policy.* London: St. Martin's Press, 1969.

―――. *British Strategy in the Far East.* London: Longman, 1981.

Lutz, Jessie Gregory. *China and the Christian Colleges, 1850–1950.* Ithaca: Cornell University Press, 1971.

MacMurray, John V.A., ed. *Treaties and Agreements With and Concerning China, 1894–1919*. New York: Oxford University Press, 1921, 2 vols.

MacNair, Harley F. and Lach, Donald F. *Modern Far Eastern International Relations*. New York: Norstrand Company, 1955.

Marchand, C. Roland. *The American Peace Movement and Social Reform, 1898–1918*. Trenton: Princeton University Press, 1972.

Marks, Frederick W. *Wind over Sand: The Diplomacy of Franklin Roosevelt*. Athens: University of Georgia Press, 1988.

May, Ernest R. and Fairbank, John K., eds. *America's China Trade in Historical Perspective: The Chinese and American Performance*. Cambridge: Harvard University Press, 1986.

Mayer, Arno J. *Wilson vs. Lenin: Political Origins of the New Diplomacy, 1917–1918*. Cleveland: First Meridian, 1964.

McCord, Edward A. *The Power of the Gun: The Emergence of Modern Chinese Warlordism*. Berkeley: University of California Press, 1993.

McCormack, Gaven. *Chang Tso-lin in Northeast China, 1911–1928: China, Japan and the Manchurian Idea*. Kent: William Dawson and Sons, 1977.

McKinnon, Stephen R. *Power and Politics in Late Imperial China: Yuan Shi-kai in Beijing and Tianjin, 1901–1908*. Berkeley: University of California Press, 1980.

Mendel, Douglas. *The Politics of Formosan Nationalism*. Berkeley: University of California Press, 1970.

Miller, David Hunter. *The Drafting of the Covenant*. New York: G.P. Putnam's Sons, 1928.

Moore, John Bassett. *A Digest of International Law*. Washington: U.S. Government Printing Office, 1906, 8 vols.

———. *Four Phases of American Development: Federalism—Democracy—Imperialism—Expansion*. Baltimore: The Johns Hopkins Press, 1912.

———. *American Diplomacy: Its Spirit and Achievement*. New York: Harper & Brothers, 1905.

———. *The Collected Papers of John Bassett Moore*. New Haven: Yale University Press, 1944, 7 vols.

Mosher, Steven W. *China Misperceived: American Illusions and Chinese Reality*. New York: Basic Books, 1990.

Mudge, James. *China: Her History, Productions, Customs, Government, Laws, Religions, Superstitions, Missions and Martyrs*. Chicago: Thomas Craven, 1900.

Nathan, Andrew. *Peking Politics, 1918–1923: Factionalism and the Failure of Constitutionalism*. Berkeley: University of California Press, 1976.

———. *Chinese Democracy*. Berkeley: University of California Press, 1985.

————. "A Constitutional Republic: The Peking Government, 1916–1928." In *Cambridge History of China: Republican China, 1912–1949*. Edited by John Fairbank and Albert Feurerwerker. Cambridge: Cambridge University Press, 1983, vol. 12, pp. 256–283.

Neils, Patricia. *China Images in the Life and Times of Henry Luce*. Savage, MD: Rowman & Littlefield, 1990.

Nester, William R. *Power Across the Pacific: A Diplomatic History of American Relations with Japan*. New York: New York University Press, 1996.

Nish, Ian. *Japanese Foreign Policy 1869–1942: Kasumigaseki to Miyakezaka*. London: Routledge and Kegan Paul, 1977.

————. *Japan's Struggle with Internationalism: Japan, China, and the League of Nations, 1931-1933*. London: Kegan Paul International, 1993.

————. "Dr. Morrison and China's Entry into the World War, 1915–1917." In *Studies in Diplomatic History: Essays in Memory of David Bayne Horn*. Edited by R. Hatton and M.S. Anderson. London: Archon Books, 1970, pp. 322–338.

Niu, Jun. "The Origins of Mao Zedong's Thinking on International Affairs (1916–1949)." In *Toward a History of Chinese Communist Foreign Relations, 1920s–1960s: Personalities and Interpretive Approaches*. Edited by Michael H. Hunt and Niu Jun. Washington: Asia Program Occasional Paper Woodrow Wilson International Center, 1995, pp. 3–26.

Nonzinski, Michael J. *Outrage at Lincheng: China Enters the Twentieth Century*. Scarborough, Ont.: Glenbridge Publishing, 1991.

Northedge, F.S. *The League of Nations: Its Life and Times, 1920–1946*. New York: Holmes & Meier, 1986.

Osterhammel, Jurgen. "Semi-Colonialism and Informal Empire in Twentieth-Century China: Towards a Framework of Analysis." In *Imperialism and After: Continuities and Discontinuities*. Edited by Wolfgang J. Mommsen and Jurgen Osterhammel. London: Allen & Unwin, 1986, pp. 290–309.

Parker, Edward H. *China: Her History, Diplomacy and Commerce: From the Earliest Times to the Present Day*. London: John Murray, 1901.

Parker, R.A.C. *Chamberlain and Appeasement: British Policy and the Coming of the Second World War*. New York: St. Martin's Press, 1993.

Pearl, Cyril. *Morrison of Peking*. Angu and Robertson, 1967.

Pepper, Suzanne. *Civil War in China: The Political Struggle, 1945–1949*. Berkeley: University of California Pres, 1978.

————. "The KMT-CCP Conflict, 1945–1949." In *Cambridge History of China: Republican China, 1912–1949*. Edited by John K. Fairbank and Albert Feuerwerker. Cambridge: Cambridge University Press, 1986, vol. 13, pp. 723–788.

Pollard, Robert T. *China's Foreign Relations, 1917–1931.* New York: The MacMillan Company, 1933.

Pong, David. "The Ministry of Foreign Affairs During the Republican Period 1912 to 1949." In *The Times Survey of the Foreign Ministries of the World.* Edited by Zara Steiner. London: Times Books, 1982, pp. 135–153.

Pugach, Noel. *Paul S. Reinsch: Open Door Diplomat in Action.* Millwood, N.J.: KTO Press, 1979.

———. "Embarrassed Monarchist: Frank J. Goodnow and Constitutional Development in China, 1913–1915." *Pacific Historical Review.* Vol. 42 (November 1973), pp. 499–517.

———. "American Friendship for China and the Shantung Question at the Washington Conference." *Journal of American History.* Vol. 64 (June 1977), pp. 67–86.

Reardon-Anderson, James. *Yenan and the Great Powers: The Origins of Chinese Communist Foreign Policy, 1944–46.* New York: Columbia University Press, 1980.

Reinsch, Paul S. *World Politics At The End of the Nineteenth Century as Influenced by the Oriental Situation.* New York: The MacMillan Company, 1900.

———. *An American Diplomat in China.* Garden City: Doubleday, Page & Co., 1922; Reprint, Taibei: Chengwen Publishing Co., 1967.

Reynolds, Douglas R. *China, 1898–1912: The Xinzheng Revolution and Japan.* Cambridge: Harvard University Press, 1993.

Riggs, Fred W. *Formosa Under Chinese Nationalist Rule.* New York: MacMillan, 1952.

Robinson, James Harvey and Beard, Charles A., eds. *Readings in Modern European History.* Boston: Ginn & Co., 1909, 2 vols.

———. *Outlines of European History.* Boston: Ginn and Company, 1912, 2 vols.

Robinson, Ronald. "Non-European Foundations of European Imperialism: Sketch for a Theory of Collaboration," *Studies in the Theory of Imperialism.* Edited by Roger Owen and Bob Sutcliffe. London: Longman, 1972, pp. 117–142.

Robinson, Thomas W. and Shambaugh, David, eds. *Chinese Foreign Policy: Theory and Practice.* Oxford: Clarendon Press, 1994.

Ross, Edward Alsworth. *The Changing Chinese: The Conflict of Oriental and Western Cultures in China.* New York: The Century Co., 1912.

Saari, Jon L. *Legacies of Childhood: Growing Up Chinese in a Time of Crisis, 1890–1920.* Cambridge: Harvard University Press, 1990.

Sainsbury, Keith. *The Turning Point: Roosevelt, Stalin, Churchill, and Chiang Kai-shek, 1943: The Moscow, Cairo, and Teheran Conferences.* London: Oxford University Press, 1985.

Schaller, Michael. *The U.S. Crusade in China, 1938-1945.* New York: Columbia University Press, 1979.

Schoppa, R. Keith. *Blood Road: The Mystery of Shen Dingyi in Revolutionary China.* Berkeley: University of California Press, 1995.

Schran, Peter. "The Minor Significance of Commercial Relations Between the United States and China, 1850–1931." In *America's China Trade in Historical Perspective: The Chinese and American Performance.* Edited by Ernest R. May and John K. Fairbank. Cambridge: Harvard University Press, 1986, pp. 237–258.

Schrecker, John. "The Reform Movement, Nationalism, and China's Foreign Policy." *Journal of Asian Studies.* Vol. 29 (November 1969), pp. 43–53.

Schroeder, Paul W. *The Axis Alliance and Japanese-American Relations, 1941.* Ithaca: Cornell University Press, 1958.

Shai, Aron. *Origins of the War in the East: Britain, China and Japan, 1937–1939.* London: Croom Helm, 1976.

———. *Britain and China, 1941–1947: Imperial Momentum.* Oxford: St. Antony's College, 1984.

Sharman, Lyon. *Sun Yat-sen: His Life and its Meaning: A Critical Biography.* Stanford: Stanford University Press, 1968, rep.

Sheridan, James E. *Chinese Warlord: The Career of Feng Yü-hsiang.* Stanford: Stanford University Press, 1966.

———. "The Warlord Era: Politics and Militarism under the Peking Government, 1916–28." In *Cambridge History of China: Republican China, 1912–1949.* Edited by John Fairbank. Cambridge: Cambridge University Press, 1983, vol. 12, pp. 284–321.

Sigel, Louis T. "Foreign Policy Interests and Activities of the Treaty-Port Chinese Community." In *Reform in Nineteenth-Century China.* Edited by Paul A. Cohen and John Schrecker. Cambridge: Harvard University Press, 1976, pp. 272–285.

Singleton, Esther, ed. *China as Described by Great Writers.* New York: Dodd, Mead & Company, 1912.

Smith, Arthur H. *China and America Today: A Study of Conditions and Relations.* New York: Fleming H. Revell, 1907.

Somit, Albert and Tanenhaus, Joseph, eds. *The Development of American Political Science: From Burgess to Behavioralism.* Boston: Allyn and Bacon, Inc., 1967.

Spector, Ronald H. *Eagle Against the Sun: The American War with Japan.* New York: Vintage Books, 1985.

Spurr, David. *The Rhetoric of Empire: Colonial Discourse in Journalism, Travel Writing, and Imperial Administration.* Durham: Duke University Press, 1993.

St. John's University, 1879–1929. Reprint, Taibei: St. John's University Alumni Association, 1972.

Steiner, Zara, ed. *The Times Survey of the Foreign Ministries of the World.* London: Times Books, 1982.

Stephan, John J. "The Tanaka Memorial (1927): Authentic or Spurious?" *Modern Asian Studies.* Vol. 7 (1973), pp. 733–745.

Strand, David. *Rickshaw Beijing: City People and Politics in the 1920s.* Berkeley: University of California Press, 1989.

Stremski, Richard. "Britain and Warlordism in China: Relations with Feng Yü-Hsiang, 1921–1928." *Journal of Oriental Studies.* Vol. 11 (January 1973), pp. 91–106.

Strauss, Julia C. *Strong Institutions in Weak Polities: State Building in Republican China, 1927–1940.* Oxford: Clarendon Press, 1998.

Stueck, Jr., William Whitney. *The Road to Confrontation: American Policy Toward China and Korea, 1947–1950.* Chapel Hill: University of North Carolina Press, 1981.

———. *The Korean War: An International History.* Princeton: Princeton University Press, 1995.

Sullivan, Mark. *The Great Adventure at Washington: The Story of the Conference.* London: William Heinemann, 1922.

Sun, Changwei. *Cai Yuanpei xiansheng nienpu zhuanji* (A chronological biography of Cai Yuanpei). Taibei: Academia Historica, 1985, 2 vols.

Sun, Youli. *China and the Origins of the Pacific War, 1931–1941.* New York: St. Martin's Press, 1993.

Swanberg, W.A. *Luce and His Empire.* New York: Charles Scribner's Sons, 1972.

Sze, Alfred Sao-ke. *Sao-ke Alfred Sze: Reminiscences of his Early Years as Told to Anming Fu.* Translated by Amy C. Wu. Washington, D.C.: privately published, 1962.

T'ang Ch'i-hua. *Beijing zhengfu yu guoji lianmeng* (China and the League of Nations, 1919–1928). Taibei: Dongda dushu gongsi, 1998.

———. [In English] "Britain and Warlordism in China: Relations with Chang Tso-lin, 1926–1928." *Xing da lishi xuebao* (Zhongxing University's journal of history). No. 2 (March 1992), pp. 207–229.

———. [In English] "Britain and the Raid on the Soviet Embassy by Chang Tso-lin, 1927." *Zhongxing taxue wenxue yuan shixue bao* (Journal of the College of Liberal Arts of Zhongxing University). Vol. 22 (March 1992), pp. 185–197.

———. "Beijing zhengfu yu guomin zhengfu de waijiao she de huodong guanxi, 1925–1928," (The parallel diplomatic goals of the Beijing and Nationalist governments). *Hsingda lishi bao,* (Zhongxing University's journal of history). No. 4 (May 1994), pp. 1–44.

Thorne, Christopher. *The Limits of Foreign Policy: The West, the League and the Far Eastern Crisis of 1931–1933*. New York: G.P. Putnam's Sons, 1973.

————. *Allies of a Kind: The United States, Britain, and the War Against Japan, 1941–1945*. New York: Oxford University Press, 1978.

Ting, Lee-hsia Hsu. *Government Control of the Press in Modern China, 1900–1949*. Cambridge: Harvard University Press, 1974.

Tsiang, T'ing-fu. The Reminiscences of Tsiang T'ing-fu. Chinese Oral History Project, East Asian Institute, Columbia University, 1975.

Tung, William. *V.K. Wellington Koo and China's Wartime Diplomacy*. New York: St. John's University Press, 1977.

Tucker, Nancy Bernkopf. *Taiwan, Hong Kong, and the United States, 1945–1992: Uncertain Friendships*. New York: Twayne Publishers, 1994.

————. "Nationalist China's Decline and Its Impact on Sino-American Relations, 1949–1950." In *Uncertain Years: Chinese-American Relations, 1947–50*. Edited by Dorothy Borg and Waldo Heinrichs. New York: Columbia University Press, 1980, pp. 131–171.

————. "John Foster Dulles and the Taiwan Roots of the 'Two Chinas' Policy." In *John Foster Dulles and the Diplomacy of the Cold War*. Edited by Richard H. Immerman. Princeton: Princeton University Press, 1990, pp. 235–262.

Uhalley, Jr., Stephen. "The Wai-Wu Pu, The Chinese Foreign Office from 1901 to 1911." *Journal of the China Society*. Vol. 5 (1967), pp. 9–27.

Ulam, Adam B. *Expansion and Coexistence: Soviet Foreign Policy 1917–73*. New York: Praeger, 1974, 2nd ed.

Utley, Jonathan. *Going to War with Japan, 1937–1941*. Knoxville: University of Tennessee Press, 1985.

van Minnen, Cornelis A. and John F. Sears, eds. *FDR and His Contemporaries: Foreign Perceptions of an American President*. New York: St. Martin's Press, 1992.

Van Slyke Lyman P. "The Chinese Communist Movement during the Sino-Japanese War, 1937–1945." In *Cambridge History of China: Republican China, 1912–1949*. Edited by John K. Fairbank and Albert Feuerwerker. Cambridge: Cambridge University Press, 1986, vol. 13, pp. 609–722.

Waldron, Arthur N. *From War to Nationalism: China's Turning Point, 1924–1925*. Cambridge: Cambridge University Press, 1995.

————. "Warlordism Versus Federalism: The Revival of a Debate?" *China Quarterly*. Vol. 121 (March 1990), pp. 116–128.

————. "The Warlord: Twentieth-Century Chinese Understandings of Violence, Militarism, and Imperialism." *American Historical Review*. Vol. 96 (October 1991), pp. 1073–1100.

Walworth, Arthur. *Wilson and his Peacemakers: American Diplomacy at the Paris Peace Conference, 1919*. New York: W.W. Norton, 1986.

Wang, Jianlang. "Beijing zhengfu xiuyue yuandong jianlun: Jiansu Gu Weijun dengxin yidai waijiao jiade jueqi" (V.K. Wellington Koo and abolishing the unequal treaties in the 1920s). In *Gu Weijun yu zhongguo waijiao* (Wellington Koo and Chinese Diplomacy). Edited by Jin Guangyao. Shanghai: Shanghai guji chuban she 2001, pp. 132–149.

Wang Ke-wen. "Wang Jingwei and the Policy Origins of the 'Peace Movement,' 1932–1937." In *Chinese Collaboration with Japan, 1932–1945: The Limits of Accommodation*. Edited by David P. Barrett and Larry N. Shyu. Stanford: Stanford University Press, 2001, pp. 21–37.

Wang, Peter Chen-main. "A Bastion Created, A Regime Reformed, An Economy Reengineered, 1949–1970." In *Taiwan: A New History*. Edited by Murray A. Rubenstein. Armonk: M.E. Sharpe, 1999, pp. 320–338.

———. "A Patriotic Christian Leader in Changing China—Yu Rizhang in the Turbulent 1920s." In *Chinese Nationalism in Perspective: Historical and Recent Cases*. Edited by C. X. George Wei and Xiaoyuan Liu. Westport, CT: Greenwood, 2001, pp. 33–51.

Wang, Y.C. *Chinese Intellectuals and the West, 1872–1949*. Chapel Hill: University of North Carolina Press, 1965.

Wang, Yunsheng. *Liushi nian lai Zhongguo yu riben* (Sixty years of Sino-Japanese Relations). Tianjin: L'Impartial, 1934, 7 vols.

Wang, Yuzhun, ed. *Zhong e guanxi shiliao: e zhengbian yu yiben jiaoshe* (Historical documents related to Sino-Russian relations: The Russian revolution and general negotiations). Nangang: Academia Sinica, 1984.

Watt, Donald Cameron. *How War Came: The Immediate Origins of the Second World War, 1938–1939*. New York: Pantheon, 1989.

Weber, Eugene. *The Hollow Years: France in the 1930s*. New York: W.W. Norton, 1995.

Westad, Odd Arne. *Cold War and Revolution: Soviet-American Rivalry and the Origins of the Chinese Civil War*. New York: Columbia University Press, 1993.

Whiting, Allen S. *Soviet Policies in China 1917–1924*. Stanford: Stanford University Press, 1968, pap. ed.

Wiebe, Robert W. *The Search for Order, 1877–1920*. New York: Hill and Wang, 1967.

Wilbur, C. Martin. *Sun Yat-sen: Frustrated Patriot*. New York: Columbia University Press, 1976.

———. "The Nationalist Revolution: from Canton to Nanking, 1923–28." In *Cambridge History of China: Republican China, 1912–1949*. Edited by John Fairbank and Albert Feuerwerker. Cambridge: Cambridge University Press, 1983, vol. 12, pp. 527–721.

Wou, Oderic Y.K. *Militarism in Modern China: The Career of Wu P'ei-fu, 1916–1939*. Dawson: Australian National University Press, 1978.

Wright, Mary Clabaugh. *The Last Stand of Chinese Conservatism: The T'ung-Chih Restoration, 1862–1874.* Stanford: Stanford University Press, 1962.

Wu, T'ien-wei. "Contending Political Forces during the War of Resistance." In *China's Bitter Victory: The War With Japan, 1937–1945.* Edited by James C. Hsiung and Steven I. Levine. Armonk: M.E. Sharpe, 1997, pp. 51–78.

Xie, Bendi, *Yuan Shikai yu beiyang zhunfa* (Yuan Shikai and the Warlords). Shanghai: Renming chuben she, 1984.

Xie Junmei and Shen Qian. "Gu Weijun de Jingshi pinge jiqi cheng yuan," (The Formation of Gu Weijun's Jingshi Thought." In *Gu Weijun yu zhongguo waijiao* (Wellington Koo and Chinese Diplomacy). Edited by Jin Guangyao. Shanghai: Shanghai guji chuban she 2001, pp. 474–489.

Yan, Qianhou. *Gu Weijun yu kangri waijiao.* Shijiazhuang: Hebei renmin chuban she, 1998

Yeh, Wen-hsin. *The Alienated Academy: Culture and Politics in Republican China, 1919–1937.* Cambridge: Harvard University Press, 1990.

Yen, W.W. *East-West Kaleidoscope 1877–1944: An Autobiography.* New York: St. John's University Press, 1974.

Yergin, Daniel. *Shattered Peace: The Origins of the Cold War.* New York: Penguin Books, 1990.

Young, Ernest P. *The Presidency of Yuan Shih-k'ai: Liberalism and Dictatorship in Early Republican China.* Ann Arbor: University of Michigan Press, 1977.

Young, Robert J. *France and the Origins of the Second World War.* New York: St. Martin's Press, 1996.

Yuan, Daofeng. *Gu Weijun qiren qishi* (V.K. Wellington Koo: The man and his deeds). Taibei: Commercial Press, 1988.

Yue, Qianhou. "Gaiyue waijiao: Gu Weijun minzu zhuyi jichi yunzuo gean," (V.K. Wellington Koo's nationalistic foreign policy). In *Gu Weijun yu zhongguo waijiao* (Wellington Koo and Chinese Diplomacy). Edited by Jin Guangyao. Shanghai: Shanghai guji chuban she 2001, pp. 150–167.

Zhai Qiang. *The Dragon, the Lion, and the Eagle: Chinese-British-American Relations, 1949–1958.* Kent, Ohio: Kent State University Press, 1994.

Zhang, Baijia. "Chinese Policies toward the United States, 1937–1945." In *Sino-American Relations, 1945–1955: A Joint Reassessment of a Critical Decade.* Edited by Harry Harding and Yuan Ming. Wilmington: Scholarly Resources, 1989, pp. 14–28.

Zhang, Chunlan. "Gu Weijun de hehui waijiao: yi xiuhui shandong zhuzhuan wenti wei zhongxin (V.K. Wellington Koo's diplomacy at the Paris Peace Conference: A study of his role in the Shandong question). *Jindai shi yanjiu so jikan* (Bulletin of the Institute of Modern History, Academia Sinica). Vol. 23 (June 1994), pp. 31–52.

Zhang, Pengyuan. *Liang Qichao yu minguo zhengzhi* (Liang Qichao and Republican government). Taibei: Shihua shixue yeshu, 1981.

Zhang, Pumin. *Beiyang zhengfu guowu zongli liezhuan* (Premiers from the Beiyang period). Taibei: Commercial Press, 1984.

Zhang, Yongjin. *China in the International System, 1918–20: The Middle Kingdom at the Periphery.* New York: St. Martin's Press, 1991.

Zhang, Zhongfu. "Minsan shandong wenti zhi jiaoshe" (Negotiation of the Shantung problem). In *Zhongguo jindai xiandai shi lunji* (Essays on recent modern Chinese history): *Minqu waijiao* (Early Republican foreign policy). Taibei: Commercial Press, 1986, vol. 23, pp. 249–260.

Zheng Tianfang. *Shi de huiyilu* (Recollections of my Ambassadorship to Germany). Taibei: National Political University, 1967.

Zhonghua minguo shi dangan ciliao jibian (A collection of archival materials from the Republican era). Vol. 3, *Beiyang zhengfu shiqi waijiao* (The diplomacy of the warlord period). Jiangsu: Jiangsu gujie chuben she, 1991.

Zhonghua minguo shishi jiyao, 1925 (Important historical facts from the Republic of China). Taibei: Zhonghua minguo shiliao yenjiu zhongxin, 1975.

Zhonghua minguo zhongyao shiliao qubian: Dui ri kangzhan shiqi (Compilation of Important Republican China Historical Documents: Period of the War of Resistance against Japan). Vol. 1, Taibei: Guomindang Historical Commission, 1981, 3 parts.

Zhonghua minguo zhongyao shiliao qubian: dui ri kangzhan shiqi (Compilation of Important Republican China Historical Documents: Period of the War of Resistance against Japan). Vol. 2, *Zuozhan jingguo* (Outbreak of war). Taibei: Guomindang Historical Commission, 1981, 4 parts.

Zhonghua minguo zhongyao shiliao qubian: dui ri kangzhan shiqi (Compilation of Important Republican China Historical Documents: Period of the War of Resistance against Japan). Vol. 3, *Zhanshi waijiao* (Wartime Diplomacy). Taibei: Guomindang Historical Commission, 1981, 3 parts.

Zhonghua minguo zhongyao shiliao qubian: dui ri kangzhan shiqi (Important Historical Documents on the Republic of China during the Sino-Japanese War). Vol. 4, *Zhanshi jianshe* (Wartime Construction). Taibei: Guomindang Historical Commission 1988, 4 parts.

Zhonghua minguo zhongyao shiliao qubian: dui ri kangzhan shiqi (Compilation of Important Republican China Historical Documents: Period of the War of Resistance against Japan). Vol. 5, *Zhonggong huodong zhenxiang* (The Truth About the Communist Movement). Taibei: Guomindang Historical Commission, 1985, 4 parts.

Zhonghua minguo zhongyao shiliao qubian: dui ri kangzhan shiqi (Compilation of Important Republican China Historical Documents: Period of the War of Resistance against Japan). Vol. 6, *Kuilei zuzhi* (The Puppet Governments). Taibei: Guomindang Historical Commission, 1981, 4 parts.

Zhonghua minguo zhongyao shiliao qubien: dui ri kangzhan shiqi, (Compilation of Important Republican China Historical Documents: Period of the War of Resistance against Japan). Vol. 7, *Zhanhou zhongguo*, (Postwar China). Taibei: Guomindang Historical Commission, 1981, 4 parts.

Zongtong Jiang gong dashi changbian qugao (Preliminary extensive chronology of President Chiang). Taibei: Guomindang History Commission, 1978, 8 vols.

Unpublished Sources

Cohen, Warren I. "The Americanization of Ku Wei-chün." (Unpublished manuscript in author's possession).

Hepp IV, John Henry. "James Brown Scott and the Rise of the Science of Public International Law in the United States." M.A. Thesis, University of North Carolina-Chapel Hill, 1993.

Kindermann, Gottfried-Karl. "Sun Yat-sen's Views on Foreign Policy and Imperialism: Their National and Global Significance." Paper presented at the Centennial Symposium on Sun Yat-sen's Founding of the Guomindang for Revolution, Taibei, Taiwan, November 1994.

Megargee, Richard. "The Diplomacy of John Bassett Moore: Realism in American Foreign Policy." Ph.D. dissertation, Northwestern University, 1963.

Xu, Edward Yihua. "Religion and Education: St. John's University as an Evangelizing Agency." Ph.D. dissertation, Princeton University Doctoral Dissertation, October 1994.

———. "Shanghai shi dangan guan guancang shengyue kan daxue dangan jieshao." (An introduction to the archives of St. John's University held in the Shanghai Municipal Archives." Paper presented at the International Symposium on Historical Archives of Pre-1949 Christian Higher Education in China, Hong Kong, December 1993.

INDEX